W9-BQV-452

# VOCABULARY EXPANSION

# HCC WRITING LAB

# VOCABULARY EXPANSION

## Second Edition

## Dorothy Rubin
Trenton State College

Macmillan Publishing Company

New York

Editor:   Barbara A. Heinssen
Production Supervisor:   Peggy M. Gordon
Text Designer:   Eileen Burke
Cover Designer:   Eileen Burke
Cover Art: Slide Graphics

This book was set in Aster by V & M Graphics and
printed and bound by Semline, Inc.

Copyright © 1991 by Macmillan Publishing Company,
a division of Macmillan, Inc.

Printed in the United States of America

All rights reserved. No part of this book may be reproduced or
transmitted in any form or by any means, electronic or mechanical,
including photocopying, recording, or any information storage and
retrieval system, without permission in writing from the Publisher.

Earlier edition copyright © 1982 by Dorothy Rubin.

Macmillan Publishing Company
866 Third Avenue, New York, New York 10022

Collier Macmillan Canada, Inc.
1200 Eglinton Avenue East, Suite 200
Don Mills, Ontario, M3C 3N1

*Library of Congress Cataloging-in-Publication Data*

Rubin, Dorothy.
    Vocabulary expansion / Dorothy Rubin.
      p.   cm.
    Derived from: Gaining word power / Dorothy Rubin. 1986.
    ISBN 0-02-404245-5
    1. Vocabulary.  I. Rubin, Dorothy. Gaining word power.
  II. Title.
  PE 1449.R83 1991          89-14563
    428.1—dc20                    CIP


Printing:  1 2 3 4 5 6 7      Year:  1 2 3 4 5 6

*With love to my understanding and supportive husband, Artie,*
*my precious daughters, Carol and Sharon,*
*my delightful grandchildren, Jennifer, Andrew, and Melissa,*
*my charming sons-in-law, John and Seth,*
*and my dear brothers and sister.*

# TO THE INSTRUCTOR

Vocabulary development is an essential factor in reading comprehension. It is an important element in the successful completion of any academic curriculum and forms a standard component of academic achievement and aptitude tests. *Vocabulary Expansion*, Second Edition, can be used in two- and four-year colleges to provide a systematic, participatory approach to building and retaining a functional college-level vocabulary.

## Pedagogical Features of the Text

*Vocabulary Expansion*, Second Edition, applies a number of sound psychological learning principles and pedagogical techniques to vocabulary building.

- Overlearning, the continuation of practice beyond the point at which students think they know the material, shapes the instruction given in the text because overlearning is essential to the retention of information. Once introduced, a word will usually recur in many subsequent exercises. Later exercises build on what has been presented earlier, thus helping the student use newly learned vocabulary.

- Words are presented in graduated levels of difficulty.

- The learning process in each lesson is stimulated by a variety of practices.

- Students have immediate knowledge of results.

- Scoring scales allow students to evaluate their own progress; this provides a non-threatening learning environment for the student.

- Students' individual differences are accommodated not only in the self-contained chapters that permit each reader to work at his or her own pace, but also in the extra practice for those who need it and in the extension into more difficult words for those who are ready to absorb them.

Although this text has a pedagogical structure, the structure is diffused among a variety of practices and drills, analogy activities, and cartoons. To heighten interest, the words for each exercise are presented in context in a story. In addition, the more difficult words are presented with a more challenging approach. In each chapter extra practices are given in a separate section called "Additional Practice Sets." In this section a variety of alternative practices cover words introduced in the chapter. Tests and scoring scales permit users of the book to determine their rate of achievement. Also, this book encourages students to use the words in writing as well as in reading and speaking by presenting practices that require students to write sentences and paragraphs using the chapter vocabulary.

*Vocabulary Expansion* emphasizes combining forms and words derived from them. Combining forms are defined as word parts that join with a word or another word part to form a word or a new word. A knowledge of combining forms is fundamental to the accurate use and construction of words as well as to the understanding of their meanings.

## Features New to This Edition

The new edition retains all the features of the earlier edition that have made it such a popular book among professors and students while broadening its scope and coverage. The new features include the following:

- There is a greater emphasis on interrelating vocabulary with writing.
  Exercises require students to put vocabulary words into sentences.
  Exercises require students to put vocabulary words into paragraphs.

- Words are presented in the context of a story to stimulate interest.

- True/false tests at the end of chapters require students to change all answers that are false so that they become true; this requires higher-order thinking.

- Additional combining forms have been included.

- A "To the Student" section provides students with an outline of the organization of the book as well as guidance on using the pedagogical structure of the book to the students' best advantage.

- A Glossary/Index gives the main entry page for each combining form or vocabulary word.

*Vocabulary Expansion* is derived in large part from its precursor, *Gaining Word Power* (Macmillan, 1986). It can be used in a comprehensive vocabulary building program, in a conventional class, or in a tutorial or self-instructional program.

## Acknowledgments

I would like to thank my editor Barbara Heinssen for her insightful comments and suggestions on the revision of this book, my production editor Peggy Gordon for overseeing the production of my book, and especially Carol Smith for her very thorough proofreading. I'd also like to express my gratitude to the following professors for their scholarly suggestions and helpful reviews of my manuscript:

Naomi Barnett, Lorain County Community College
Carolyn Smith Brown, L.D.S. Business College
Sarah S. Ducksworth, Kean College of New Jersey
Eric P. Hibbison, J. Sargeant Reynolds Community College
Fred S. Kai, El Camino College
Deborah A. Madden, University of Cincinnati
John T. McAlear, Lansing Community College
Barbara G. Pogue, Essex County College
Richard Strugala, Middlesex County College
Sebastian J. Vasta, Camden County College
Paulette Vrett, McHenry County College

In addition, I would like to express my appreciation to Dr. Phillip Ollio, Dean of the School of Education, Trenton State College, and Dr. Eileen Burke, Chairperson, Department of Reading and Language Arts, for their continued support.

# TO THE STUDENT
# A Key to the Organization of This Book

*Vocabulary Expansion*, Second Edition, deals with vocabulary building through combining forms. Combining forms in this book are defined as word parts that join with a word or another word part to form a word or a new word. (More will be said about combining forms in Chapter One.) The emphasis is on the overlearning of the combining forms so that they can help you unlock the meanings of many words. Overlearning is the continuation of practice beyond the point at which you think you know the material, so that you will retain the information. (More will be said about overlearning in Chapter One.) Many words made up from combining forms are presented.

## How Words Are Presented

The combining forms and words presented are a base from which you can increase your vocabulary quickly and easily. Combining forms and words have been selected on the basis of how often they appear in novels, stories, poems, textbooks and other non-fiction books, newspapers, and magazines. Words that are commonly used in college lectures are also included.

Words are presented with the following information to help your understanding of the word:

1.  Correct spelling and plural (abbreviated *pl.*). Only irregular plurals are shown.
2.  Division into syllables. For example: bi·ol·o·gy.
3.  Pronunciation. The phonetic (pronunciation) spelling of the word may differ from the regular spelling to describe the pronunciation of the word. For example: **biology** (bī·ol′·o·jē) The syllabication and pronunciation aids are combined in one entry if the phonetic spelling of the word is similar to the regular spelling of the word. Otherwise, an extra entry is given following the syllabication entry for the word. If a word is a one-syllable word, there is obviously no syllabication entry for the word.
4.  Kind of word it is: *v.* for verb, *n.* for noun, *adj.* for adjective, *adv.* for adverb, and *prep.* for preposition.
5.  Meaning of the word.[1]

[1]The meanings of the words are based on *Webster's Third New International Dictionary*, Unabridged; Funk & Wagnalls *Standard College Dictionary; Random House Dictionary of the English Language; The American Heritage Dictionary of the English Language; The World Book Dictionary;* and *Webster's New Twentieth Century Dictionary*, 2nd ed.

6. Use of the word in a sentence. Only one sentence is given for each word even though the word may have more than one meaning.

Here is an example of the presentation of a word with an extra entry:

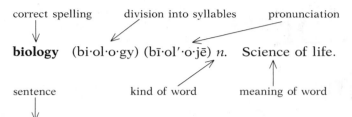

*Because I intend to be a doctor, I am taking a course in* **biology** *to learn about living things.*


## How Exercises Are Presented

The exercises are presented in four steps. The steps are the same for all exercises:

Step I.  *Presentation of new combining forms and their meanings.*
  A. Learn new combining forms with their meanings.
  B. Cover the meanings of the combining forms, read the combining forms, and try to recall their meanings. Check the answers immediately.
  C. Cover the combining forms, read the meanings, and try to recall the combining forms. Check the answers immediately.
  D. Cover the meanings of the combining forms again, read the combining forms, and write their meanings in the space provided.

Step II.  *Presentation of vocabulary derived[2] from combining forms.*
  Learn words with their meanings and other information as you see the words used in sentences. The words are based on the combining forms learned in Step I.

Step III.  *Presentation of words in context.*
  Learn words from seeing them in the context of a paragraph. Try to figure out the meaning of the underlined word from the words surrounding it.

Step IV.  *Practice.*
  Use the words in several different practices to ensure overlearning. After every three exercises, you will be challenged to put chapter words into sentences as well as a paragraph; analogies are provided for the given combining forms and words. A multiple-choice vocabulary test and a true/false vocabulary test are supplied for Step II words. Scoring scales are given so that you will know where you stand. If you score below a certain level, you are provided with additional practice sets. In these "Additional Practice Sets" you are directed to restudy only the combining forms and words you have missed. You are provided with different practice exercises to help you learn the words you have missed.


[2]*Derived* means "made up from."

# Special Features

## Special Notes

A "Special Notes" boxed-in section includes special information about words that might cause you unusual difficulty.

## Extra Word Power

The combining forms presented in the "Extra Word Power" section are those often used with thousands of words. For this reason they are presented in a special boxed section. The "Extra Word Power" section will give additional help to your vocabulary growth.

## Additional Words

The "Additional Words" section presents some more difficult words. You can unlock their meanings by using combining forms and context clues. To help you still more, a practice activity is provided for these words.

I have tried to make *Vocabulary Expansion*, Second Edition, a book that will help you gain vocabulary as quickly as possible in an effective, interesting, and enjoyable way. Most importantly, in *Vocabulary Expansion* I present a powerful technique that once learned will be with you for the rest of your life and help make you a more self-reliant reader.

*Dorothy Rubin*

# CONTENTS

Each chapter is organized in a similar manner. For a description of the organization, see pages ix-xi in the section "To the Student." Every exercise features specific combining forms. These are presented in the Table of Contents after each exercise.

# CHAPTER ONE

This chapter introduces you to *Vocabulary Expansion*. It is important that you read Chapter One because it gives you information that you will need to use this book successfully. Let us begin by considering the importance of vocabulary growth.

## THE IMPORTANCE OF VOCABULARY GROWTH

A good vocabulary and good reading go hand in hand. Unless you know the meaning of words, you will have difficulty in understanding what is read. And the more you read, the more words you will add to your vocabulary. Read the following statement:

The misanthrope was apathetic to the sufferings of those around him.

Do you understand it? Unless you know the meaning of *misanthrope* and *apathetic*, you are not able to read the statement. In order to read, you must know the meanings of words and the way words are used in sentences.

Acquiring word meanings is an important reading skill. Because of its importance, this skill is being presented in a text by itself.

## INTRODUCTION TO COMBINING FORMS AND VOCABULARY DERIVED FROM COMBINING FORMS

As a means of helping you to use combining forms to increase your vocabulary, some terms should be defined. There are a great number of words that combine with other words to form new words, for example, *grandfather* (*grand+father*) and *policeman* (*police+man*)—both compound words. Many words are combined with a letter or a group of letters—either at the beginning (prefix) or at the end (suffix) of the root word—to form a new, related word, for example, *replay* (*re+play*) and *played* (*play+ed*).

In the words *replay* and *played*, play is a root, *re* is a prefix, and *ed* is a suffix. A *root* is the smallest unit of a word that can exist and retain its basic meaning. It cannot be divided further. *Replay* is not a root word because it can be divided into *re* and *play*. *Play* is a root word because it cannot be divided further and still keep a meaning related to the root word.

Combining forms are usually defined as roots borrowed from another language that join together or that join with a prefix, a suffix, or both a prefix and a suffix to form a word. Often the English combining forms are derived from Greek and Latin roots. Because the emphasis in this book is on the building of vocabulary meanings rather than on the naming of word parts, prefixes, suffixes, English roots, and combining forms will *all* be referred to as combining forms. *A combining form in this book is defined as any word part that can join with another word or word part to form a word or a new word.* Examples: *aqua + naut = aquanaut* (a word); *re + turn = return* (a new word); *aqua + duct =* aqueduct (a new word).

The exercises in this book build on previously learned combining forms. Care is taken not to present combining forms that are similar in appearance in the same exercise.

Knowledge of the most common combining forms is valuable in helping you to learn the meaning of an unfamiliar word. For example, knowing that *pseudo* means "false" helps you to "unlock" *pseudoscience*, which means "false science." Knowing that *bi* means "two" and *ped* means "foot" helps you to determine the meaning of *biped* as a two-footed animal.

As an indication of the power of knowing a few combining forms, it has been estimated that with the knowledge of thirty combining forms (which are included in this text), one can unlock the meanings of as many as 14,000 words. Thus, familiarity with a mere thirty forms is a quick way to learn a large number of words. It is also a method that, once learned, helps you to unlock new words all through your life.

# UNDERSTANDING THE TERM
# *OVERLEARNING*

Although you may have at one time or another met many of the vocabulary words presented in this book, you may not be able to read or use the words because you have not *overlearned* them. Throughout this book, the emphasis is on the overlearning of vocabulary. *Overlearning* is not bad like *overcooking* the roast. Overlearning will help you to hold on to information over a long period of time. To overlearn the material, concentrate on the words to be learned, memorize them, and do all the exercises. Overlearning will take place only if practice is continued even after you think you have learned the information. The additional practice you engage in after you think you have mastered the material is called *overlearning*. As practice is the key to overlearning, you will continue to meet in the practice sets of later exercises many words that you have learned earlier.

# SUGGESTIONS ON HOW TO
# STUDY VOCABULARY

1. You should choose a time best for you so that you do not feel pressured.

2. You should try to find a place free of things that may disturb your studying.

3. You shouldn't try to do all the exercises in one sitting. Studies have shown that you will remember your material better if you space your studying over a period of time. The thing to do is to find and work at a pace that is good for you.

4. *Recall*, which refers to how much you remember, is very important in learning. Recall is used as part of the teaching method in this book. After the presentation of the word and its meaning(s), you should cover the meaning(s) to see if you can recall it (or them).

5. When the entire exercise is completed, go over the words you have learned. In addition, take a few minutes before a new exercise to *review* the previous exercise.

6. To make sure you remember the vocabulary words, try to·use them daily in your written work or speech. In addition, see how many times you meet these words in your classroom lectures and readings.

© 1965 United Feature Syndicate, Inc.

# UNDERSTANDING ANALOGIES

Because analogy practice is presented after every three exercises, it is important that you have some understanding of analogies. Analogies have to do with relationships. They are relationships between words or ideas. In order to make the best use of analogies or to supply the missing term in an analogy proportion, you must know not only the meanings of the words, but also the relationship of the words or ideas to one another. For example, "*doctor* is to *hospital* as *minister is to* _____." Yes, the answer is *church*. The relationship has to do with specialized persons and the places with which they are associated. Let's try another one: "*beautiful* is to *pretty* as _____ is to *decimate*." Although you know the meanings of *beautiful* and *pretty* and you can figure out that beautiful is more than pretty, you will not be able to arrive at the correct word to complete the analogy if you do not know the meaning of *decimate*. *Decimate* means "to reduce by one tenth" or "to destroy a considerable part of." Because the word that completes the analogy must express the relationship of more or greater than, the answer could be *eradicate* or *annihilate*, because these words mean "to destroy completely."

The relationships that words may have to one another are similar meanings, opposite meanings, classification, going from particular to general, going from general to particular, degree of intensity, specialized labels, characteristics, cause-effect, effect-cause, function, whole-part, ratio, and many more. The preceding relationships do not have to be memorized. You will gain clues to these from the pairs making up the analogies; that is, the words express the relationship. For example: "*pretty* is to *beautiful*"—the relationship is degree of intensity; "*hot* is to *cold*"—the relationship is one of opposites; "*car* is to *vehicle*"—the relationship is classification.

# PRONUNCIATION KEY

The pronunciation (the way a word sounds) of the words in this book is a simplified one based on the key presented on the following page. In order to simplify pronunciation further, the author has given only long vowel markings and included only the primary accent mark (').

The accent mark (′) is used to show which syllable in a word is stressed. This mark comes right after and slightly above the accented syllable. For example:

**pilot** (pī′lot)    **biology** (bī·ol′o·jē)

In the preceding two words, the syllables *pi′* and *ol′* are sounded with more stress and are called the accented syllables. The dot (•) is used to separate syllables. Note that no dot is used between syllables when the syllable is accented. Also note that the *y* in *biology* has been changed to an *ē* and the *g* has been changed to a *j* to aid you in pronunciation.

The long vowel mark (¯) also helps to indicate pronunciation. A vowel that has a long vowel mark sounds like its letter name.

A slash through a letter means that the sound it stands for is silent. For example:

bāk¢  nōt¢  āt¢  bōat

As an aid in pronunciation, the following key may be used:

Words ending in *tion* and *sion* sound like *shun*, as in *nation*.

Words ending in *cian*, *tian*, and *sian* sound like *shin*, as in *Martian*.

Words ending in *cious* sound like *shus*, as in *delicious*.

Words having *ph* sound like *f* in *fat*, *foot*, as in *phone*.

Words ending in *ique* sound like *ēk* in *lēak*, as in *critique*, *unique*.

Words ending in *le* preceded by a consonant sound like *ul* in *bull*, as in *bubble*, *candle*.

Words ending in *cial* sound like *shul*, as in *special*.

Words ending in *ce* sound like *s* in *safe*, *so*, as in *notice*, *sentence*.

Words beginning in *ce* or *ci* sound like *s* in *safe*, *so*, as in *cent*, *cease*, *citizen*.

Words ending in *c* sound like *k* in *like*, as in *picnic*, *traffic*.

Words beginning in *ca*, *cu*, or *co* sound like *k* in *kite*, as in *cat*, *cut*, *cot*.

Words beginning in *qu* sound like *kw* as in *queen*, *quick*.

Words ending in *ture* sound like *chur* as in *adventure*.

# CHAPTER TWO

## EXERCISE 1

### Step I. Combining Forms

**A. Directions:** A list of combining forms with their meanings follows. Look at the combining forms and their meanings. Concentrate on learning each combining form and its meaning. Cover the meanings, read the combining forms, and state the meanings to yourself. Check to see if you are correct. Now cover the combining forms, read the meanings, and state the combining forms to yourself. Check to see if you are correct.

| Combining Forms | Meanings |
| --- | --- |
| 1. anni, annu, enni | year |
| 2. aut, auto | self |
| 3. bio | life |
| 4. bi | two |
| 5. graph | something written; machine |
| 6. ology | the study of; the science of |
| 7. ped,[1] pod | foot |

[1]Only one meaning for the combining form *ped* is presented in Exercise 1. Another meaning will be presented in a later exercise.

**B. Directions:** Do not look at the preceding meanings. Write the meanings of the following combining forms.

Combining Forms                         Meanings

1. anni, annu, enni          _____

2. aut, auto                 _____

3. bio                       _____

4. bi                        _____

5. graph                     _____

6. ology                     _____

7. ped, pod                  _____

# Step II. Words Derived[2] from Combining Forms

1. **biology** (bi·ol·o·gy) (bī·ol′o·jē)[3] *n.* The science of life.
   *Biology helps students to learn about living things.*

2. **biography** (bi·og·ra·phy) (bī·og′ra·fē) *n.* (*pl.* **phies**)[4] An account of a person's life; a person's life story.
   *I learned all about the life of Martin Luther King, Jr., when I read Coretta King's **biography** of him.*

3. **autobiography** (au·to·bi·og·ra·phy) (au·to·bī·og′ra·fē) *n.* (*pl.* **phies**) A person's life story written by himself or herself.
   *Helen Keller, who was deaf, mute, and blind, gives an interesting account of her life in her **autobiography**.*

4. **autograph** (au·to·graph) (au′to·graf) *n.* Signature. *adj.* Written by a person's own hand: an **autograph** letter; containing autographs: an **autograph** album. *v.* To write one's name on or in.
   *After I get the **autograph** of a famous person, I compare that person's signature with other signatures I have collected.*

5. **annual** (an′n̄ū·al) *adj.* Every year; yearly.
   *At the end of every year the stockholders receive their **annual** report concerning the company's progress.*

6. **anniversary** (an·ni·ver·sa·ry) (an·n̄i·ver′sa·rē) *n.* (*pl.* **ries**) The yearly return of a date marking an event or occurrence of some importance. *adj.* Returning or recurring each year.
   *On August 24 I always celebrate the **anniversary** of my marriage.*

7. **biannual** (bi·an′n̄ū·al) *adj.* Twice a year; (loosely) occurring every two years.
   *Our **biannual** block parties, which take place in April and October, are lots of fun.*

8. **biennial** (bi·en·ni·al) (bī·en′n̄ē·al) *adj.* Once every two years; lasting for two years.
   *Our vacation is a **biennial** event because we can afford a vacation only every two years.*

---

[2]*Derived* means "made up from."

[3]When you see two entries in parentheses following the word, the first refers to the syllabication of the word, and the second refers to the phonetic spelling of the word. The syllabication and pronunciation aids are combined in one entry if the phonetic spelling of the word is similar to the regular spelling of the word.

[4]*Pl.* is the abbreviation for *plural*.

9. **biweekly** (bi·week·ly) (bī·wēēk′lē) *adj.* Every two weeks; twice a week.
   *My **biweekly** paycheck is always gone at the end of two weeks.*

10. **bimonthly** (bi·month·ly) (bī·month′lē) *adj.* Every two months; twice a month.
    *I feel we should change our **bimonthly** meetings to monthly meetings because meeting every two months is not often enough.*

11. **biped** (bī′ped) *n.* A two-footed animal.
    *Humans, who are **bipeds**, are not the only two-footed animals.*

12. **pedestrian** (pe·des·tri·an) (pe·des′trē·an) *n.* One who goes on foot.
    ***Pedestrians** as well as motorists should obey traffic laws.*

## SPECIAL NOTES

1. Note that *biannual* almost always means "twice a year," but when *biannual* is used loosely, it can mean "every two years." *Biennial* means "every two years" or "lasting for two years." In botany, a biennial plant is one that lasts for two years.

2. Note that the meanings for *biweekly* and *bimonthly* may at times be almost the same, because *biweekly* can mean "every two weeks" and *bimonthly* can mean "twice a month." However, when a word has more than one meaning, *the sentence usually provides clues for the proper meaning.*
   a. **bimonthly.** Once every two months; twice a month. *The theater group decided to stop giving **bimonthly** plays because two months did not give them enough time to practice.*
   b. **biweekly.** Once every two weeks; twice a week. *The **biweekly** newspaper is very large because it comes out only every two weeks.*

## Step III. Words in Context

A famous athlete recently wrote his **autobiography** because he was furious at what others had said about him in their **biographies** of him. The biographers claimed that he hated to give **autographs** and that he hated his fans. They said that the athlete gave an **annual** party to celebrate the **anniversary** of his divorce. They said that he had been married to a famous actress and their marriage was filled with **biweekly** battles and **bimonthly** separations. Their life together had been very stormy. In addition, they said that he was a **biped** whom the world would have been better off without. They portrayed him as an irresponsible person who got into drunken brawls and who once hit a number of **pedestrians** with his car. They said that he had no understanding of living things, so they suggested he take a course in **biology**. The publication of **biographies** about some well-known person is not a **biennial** event but a **biannual** one. Every time you look around, there's another one out.

## Step IV. Practice

**A. Directions:** Define the underlined word in each of the following sentences.

1. Our company holds its <u>annual</u> dinner dance in the spring; then, I see all the people I haven't seen all year.

2. At the first class meeting, our English instructor asked us to write our <u>autobiographies</u>.

_____

3. The film's star was a car that tried to run down <u>pedestrians</u> while they were trying to cross the street.

_____

4. The actress said that she knew that she had "arrived" when people began to stop her and ask for her <u>autograph</u>.

_____

5. The author of <u>biographies</u> must have a special and continuing interest in his or her subjects.

_____

6. It seems to be taking my nephew a long time to realize that he is not a four-footed animal but a <u>biped</u>, because he is still crawling on all fours.

_____

7. The members of the club voted to meet once a month rather than <u>bimonthly</u>.

_____

8. <u>Biology</u> has helped me have a better understanding of all living things.

_____

9. The employees said that they would prefer to be paid every week rather than <u>biweekly</u>.

_____

10. Inflation has dug such a hole in our monies that going out to eat may become a <u>biennial</u> event for us; it will probably take us two years to save enough money for such a luxury.

_____

11. We celebrated my parents' twenty-fifth wedding <u>anniversary</u> last night.

_____

12. The company I work for is not going to have <u>biannual</u> parties anymore because of the expense; from now on there will be only one party a year.

_____

> **STOP.**  Check answers at the end of this chapter (p. 41).

**B. Directions:**  Match each word with the *best* definition.

_____ 1. autobiography

_____ 2. bimonthly

_____ 3. biweekly

_____ 4. biology

_____ 5. biannual

_____ 6. biography

_____ 7. anniversary

_____ 8. biennial

_____ 9. pedestrian

_____ 10. autograph

_____ 11. biped

_____ 12. annual

a.  every two weeks; twice a week

b.  life story written by oneself

c.  one's signature

d.  twice a year

e.  life story (written)

f.  a two-footed or two-legged animal

g.  the science or study of life

h.  every two years

i.  one who goes on foot

j.  once every two months; twice a month

k.  once a year

l.  yearly return of a date marking an event of some importance

> **STOP.**  Check answers at the end of this chapter (p. 41).

**C. Directions:**  Use the combining forms that follow to build a word from this exercise to fit the blank in the sentence.

Combining Forms

| | |
|---|---|
| anni | graph |
| auto | ology |
| bi | ped |
| bio | pod |

1. January 24 is not a pleasant day for me because it is the _____ of my parents' divorce.

2. People say that I look like a famous movie star, but I never believed them until some people asked me to sign their _____ book.

3. The lecture part of my _____ course is fine, but I am having trouble with the lab part of it because I can't stand to take anything apart that once was alive.

4. My mother convinced me to have _____ physical checkups rather than _____ ones because a lot of problems can arise and go unnoticed in a two-year period.

5. The famous doctor told the interviewer that he knew when he was still a child that he would someday write his _____, so he started keeping a diary at a very early age.

6. What other animals besides humans are _____?

7. Our English instructor asked us to choose a famous person and then to read two different _____ that had been written about that person and to compare them.

8. _____, as well as motorists, should obey safety rules.

9. The employees complained that their _____ checks weren't enough to cover their expenses because of the high inflation and that they wanted to be paid every week.

---

> **STOP.** Check answers at the end of this chapter (p. 42).

---

# EXTRA WORD POWER

> **ar, er, or.** One who; that which. Note the three different spellings. When *ar, er,* or *or* is found at the end of a word, the word concerns a person or thing. For example: *biographer*—a person who writes biographies; *killer*—one who kills; *player*—one who plays; *author*—one who writes; *beggar*—one who begs; *captor*—one who holds someone a prisoner; *prisoner*—one who is kept in prison. How many more words that end in *ar, er,* or *or* can you supply?

## Additional Words Derived from Combining Forms

From your knowledge of combining forms, can you define the following words?

1. **graphology** (gra·phol·o·gy) (gra·fol′o·jē) *n.* *Detectives sometimes use* **graphology** *to learn about the character of a suspect.*

   _____

2. **graphic** (graph·ic) (graf′ik) *adj.* *His description was so* **graphic** *that it left nothing to the imagination.*

   _____

3. **orthography** (or·thog·ra·phy) (or·thog′ra·fē) *n.* (*pl.* **ies**) *Knowledge of the* **orthography** *of words helps in writing.*

_____

4. **annuity** (an·nu·i·ty) (aṅ·nū′i·tē) *n.* *He receives a sizable* **annuity** *each year from his investment.*

_____

5. **bifocals** (bi·fo·cals) (bī·fō′kulz) *n.* (*pl.*) *When my mother's eye doctor recommended* **bifocals** *for her, she felt that it was a sure sign that she was getting old.*

_____

6. **bilateral** (bī·lat′er·al) *adj.* *The two nations began* **bilateral** *talks, hoping to conclude a peace treaty between them.*

_____

7. **bilingual** (bi·lin·gual) (bī·ling′gwal) *adj. n.* *A number of schools are providing* **bilingual** *programs for students who speak a language other than English.*

_____

8. **binary** (bi·na·ry) (bī′na·rē) *adj.* *The* **binary** *system of numbers is used with digital computers.*

_____

9. **biopsy** (bi·op·sy) (bī′op·sē) *n.* *In order to determine whether major surgery is necessary, the surgeon usually takes a* **biopsy** *of the organ in question.*

_____

10. **podium** (po·di·um) (pō′dē·um) *n.* *When the conductor took his position on the* **podium***, all eyes were directed toward him.*

_____

11. **pedestal** (ped′es·tal) *n.* *The newly acquired statue was placed on a special* **pedestal** *for all to view.*

_____

12. **automatic** (au·to·mat·ic) (au·to·mat′ik) *adj.* **Automatic** *washers and dryers have helped to provide more leisure time for persons.*

_____

13. **automaton** (au·tom′a·ton) *n.* *The goose-stepping soldiers in Hitler's army looked like* **automatons***.*

_____

14. **autonomous** (au·ton'o·møus) *adj.  Because education is not mentioned in the Constitution, each state is **autonomous** in this area.*

---

| **STOP.** Check answers at the end of this chapter (p. 42). |
| --- |

## Practice for Additional Words Derived from Combining Forms

***Directions:*** A list of definitions follows. Choose the word from the word list that *best* fits the definition. Try to relate your definition to the meanings of the combining forms.

### Word List

| | | |
| --- | --- | --- |
| annuity | bilateral | graphology |
| automatic | bilingual | orthography |
| automaton | binary | podium |
| autonomous | biopsy | pedestal |
| bifocals | graphic | |

1. Consisting of two parts _____

2. The study of handwriting _____

3. The cutting out of a piece of living tissue for examination _____

4. Using two languages equally well _____

5. Glasses with two-part lenses _____

6. Self-governing _____

7. Moving by itself _____

8. Two-sided _____

9. The art of correct spelling _____

10. Yearly payment of money _____

11. A base or bottom support _____

12. A raised platform for an orchestra conductor _____

13. Marked by realistic and vivid detail _____

14. A person or animal acting in a mechanical way _____

| **STOP.** Check answers at the end of this chapter (p. 42). |
| --- |

# EXERCISE 2

## Step I. Combining Forms

**A. Directions:** A list of combining forms with their meanings follows. Look at the combining forms and their meanings. Concentrate on learning each combining form and its meaning. Cover the meanings, read the combining forms, and state the meanings to yourself. Check to see if you are correct. Now cover the combining forms, read the meanings, and state the combining forms to yourself. Check to see if you are correct.

| Combining Forms | Meanings |
|---|---|
| 1. tele | from a distance |
| 2. scope | a means for seeing, watching, or viewing |
| 3. geo | earth |
| 4. meter | measure |
| 5. micro | very small |
| 6. scrib, scrip | write |
| 7. phon, phono | sound |

**B. Directions:** Do not look at the preceding meanings. Write the meanings of the following combining forms.

| Combining Forms | Meanings |
|---|---|
| 1. tele | _____ |
| 2. scope | _____ |
| 3. geo | _____ |
| 4. meter | _____ |
| 5. micro | _____ |
| 6. scrib, scrip | _____ |
| 7. phon, phono | _____ |

## Step II. Words Derived from Combining Forms

1. **telegraph** (tel·e·graph) (tel′e·graf) *n.* Instrument for sending a message in a code at a distance. *v. To send a message from a distance.*
    *The **telegraph** is not used as much today as it used to be because there are now faster and simpler ways to send messages from a distance.*

2. **telephone** (tel·e·phone) (tel′e·fōne) *n.* Instrument that sends and receives sound, such as the spoken word, over distance. *v. To send a message by telephone.*
    *I use the **telephone** when my girl friend is away and I want to hear the sound of her voice.*

3. **telescope** (tel·e·scope) (tel′e·skōpé) *n.* Instrument used to view distant objects.
   *Standing on the roof of the Empire State Building, he used the **telescope** to view the city.*

4. **microscope** (mi·cro·scope) (mī′kro·skōpé) *n.* Instrument used to make very small things appear larger so that they can be seen.
   *The **microscope** has helped scientists to observe objects too small to be seen with the naked eye.*

5. **geometry** (ge·om·e·try) (jē·om′e·trē) *n.* Branch of mathematics dealing with the measurement of points, lines, and planes, among other things.
   *An engineer uses his knowledge of **geometry** to measure the land for the building of new roads.*

6. **geography** (ge·og·ra·phy) (jē·og′ra·fē) *n.* Study of the earth's surface and life.
   *In **geography** you learn about the earth's surface and about the plant and animal life there.*

7. **geology** (ge·ol·o·gy) (jē·ol′o·jē) *n.* Study of the earth's physical history and makeup.
   ***Geology** helps people learn about the makeup of the earth, especially as revealed by rocks.*

8. **script** (skript) *n.* Writing that is cursive, printed, or engraved; a piece of writing; a written copy of a play for the use of actors.
   *The actors read from the **script** for the first rehearsal, but after that they could not depend on any writing to help them.*

9. **scripture** (scrip·ture) (skrip′chur) *n.* The books of the Old and New Testaments, or either of them; a text or passage from the Bible; the sacred writings of a religion.
   *Some lawyers quote from the Holy **Scriptures** because they feel a reference to the Bible will gain the jury's sympathy.*

10. **description** (de·scrip·tion) (de·skrip′shun) *n.* An account that gives a picture of something in words.
    *Carol's **description** of the college was so graphic that I could actually picture it in my mind.*

"Can you write me a fast, off-beat, 10-second routine for my telephone answering machine?"

From *The Wall Street Journal*—Permission, Cartoon Features Syndicate.

## SPECIAL NOTES

1. Note that in the words *telescope* and *microscope* the meaning of the words includes the term *instrument*. A telescope is an instrument used to view distant objects. A microscope is an instrument used to make small objects appear larger so that they can be seen.

2. The word *script* can refer to typed or printed matter and to a piece of writing, especially a written copy of a play or dramatic role for the use of actors. For example:
   a. *This sentence is in* **script**.
   b. *The researchers were looking for the original ancient* **script**.
   c. *The* **script** *for the new play was not ready.*

3. The term *Scripture* is used chiefly in the plural with the (and often Holy) and has a capital letter when it refers to the books of the Old or New Testament—in short, the Bible.

## Step III. Words in Context

James Williams looked at his schedule. He knew that there had to be something wrong. James wanted to be a geologist because he was interested in learning about the earth's physical history and makeup. He did not have one **geology** course on his schedule. Instead there was a course in advanced **geometry**. He had already had courses dealing with the measurement of points, lines, and planes. It seemed that he had nothing on his schedule that he had requested. He wanted to study about the earth's surface and life so he had signed up for a **geography** course. He had instead another biology course. He enjoyed learning about living things and working with the **microscope**, but he did not want to become a biologist. He also had a drama course dealing with the reading of **scripts**. In addition, he had a course dealing with the study of religion and the reading of **scripture**. He also had a course dealing with the stars and the **telescope**. James read a **description** of each course that was still open. There wasn't one course he needed. James was so upset that he wanted to **telegraph** the president of the college. Instead he rushed to **telephone** his adviser to find out what to do. The adviser blamed it all on the computer and suggested that James see the registrar. James wondered who took the blame years ago when there were no computers.

## Step IV. Practice

**A. Directions:**  Use the combining forms that follow to build a word from this exercise to fit the blank in the sentence.

Combining Forms

| | |
|---|---|
| geo | phono |
| graph | scope |
| meter | scrib |
| micro | scrip |
| ology | tele |
| phon | |

1. In the biology course, we mounted cells from the inside of our mouths on a slide and observed them under the _____.

2. My friend is taking many courses in _____ because he enjoys studying rock formations.

3. In the movie the murderer used a high-powered _____ to spy on his victims.

4. The _____ in the play called for the lead to be a popular, outgoing, attractive, and athletic individual—everything that the lead wasn't.

5. In the play *Inherit the Wind* both attorneys use quotes from _____ to try to prove their points.

6. When something good happens to me, I usually _____ my family and friends to tell them about it and to exchange other news with them.

7. Algebra and _____ are usually required mathematics courses for students planning to go to college.

8. Who would have thought that a course in _____, which taught about the earth's surface, would help the shipwrecked people when they were marooned on an unknown island far from civilization.

9. The clerk said that the _____ was broken and that no messages could be sent over the wires for about two hours.

10. When Jim gave us a(n) _____ of the cave, I started to tremble because I felt as though I had been there before, yet that was impossible.

---

> **STOP.** Check answers at the end of this chapter (p. 42).

---

**B. Directions:** A list of definitions follows. Choose a word from the word list that *best* fits the definition. There are more words in the list than you need.

**Word List**

| | | |
|---|---|---|
| autobiography | geography | script |
| biographer | geology | Scripture |
| biography | geometry | telegraph |
| biology | microscope | telephone |
| description | pedestrian | telescope |

1. Instrument used to view distant objects _____

2. Instrument used for sending coded messages _____

3. Branch of mathematics dealing with measurement _____

4. Study of the earth's physical history and makeup _____

5. A person who writes about the life of another _____

6. Printed matter; a piece of writing _____

7. Instrument that sends sound at a distance _____

8. Instrument used to make very small objects appear larger _____

9. Writings from the Bible _____

10. Study of the earth's surface _____

11. An account that gives a picture of something in words _____

12. A person who goes on foot _____

> **STOP.**  Check answers at the end of this chapter (p. 42).

***C. Directions:***   Define the underlined word in each of the following sentences.

1. The honeymooners decided to give the news of their marriage in person rather than to telegraph it.

   _____

2. After the director read the script that called for so many peculiar characters, he developed a headache.

   _____

3. In geometry we learned that the shortest distance between two points is a straight line.

   _____

4. My brother who is majoring in geology told me that his instructor had found a rare stone that was worth a fortune.

   _____

5. My telephone bills are so high because I talk too long; I intend to use a timer for all my calls, and when the timer buzzer rings, I intend to say "good-bye" and hang up.

   _____

6. Knowledge of geography helped Jim answer some questions on a quiz show.

   _____

7. The description of the attacker that Jim gave was one that the victim had had in one of her recurring nightmares.

   _____

8. In the film a mad scientist, who is always looking at slides under a microscope, develops a monster plant.

   _____

9. On television there was a disabled private eye who spent all his time spying on other people by looking through a <u>telescope</u>.

_____

10. In most motels and hotels you will find that each room is supplied with <u>Scripture</u>.

_____

> **STOP.**  Check answers at the end of this chapter (p. 43).

## EXTRA WORD POWER

> **re.**  Again; back. _Re_ is found at the beginning of many words. For example: _rewrite_ — to write again; _redo_ — to do again; _recomb_ — to comb again; _rerun_ — to run again; _rework_ — to work again; _repay_ — to pay back; _return_ — to go back. How many more words that begin with _re_ can you supply?

### Additional Words Derived from Combining Forms

From your knowledge of combining forms, can you define the following words?

1. **meter** (mē′ter) _n._   _A **meter** is approximately 3.3 feet or 1.1 yards._

_____

2. **telemeter** (te·lem′e·ter) _n._   _The ground crew serving a space station uses a **telemeter** to learn what is happening in the space ship._

_____

3. **micrometer** (mi·crom·e·ter) (mī·krom′e·ter) _n._   _Technicians use a **micrometer** when measuring microscopic material because it helps them to be as accurate as possible._

_____

4. **micrometer** (mi·cro·me·ter) (mī′krō·mē·ter) _n._   _A **micrometer**, which is equal to a micron, is used by scientists in describing lengths of microscopic organisms such as bacteria._

_____

5. **microbe** (mi·crobe) (mī′krōbe) _n._   _Doctors determine through tests what **microbes** in our bodies are causing our diseases._

_____

6. **microorganism** (mi·cro·or·gan·ism) (mī·krō·or′gan·iz·um) _n._   _A virus is a **microorganism** that cannot be seen by the naked eye._

_____

7. **microphone** (mi·cro·phone) (mī′kro·fōné) *n.* *The speaker used the **microphone** to make sure that the people in the rear of the large room could hear the speech.*

8. **microfilm** (mi·cro·film) (mī′kro·film) *n.* *Many of the older copies of newspapers that I needed for my report were on **microfilm** in the library.*

9. **scribe** (skrībé) *n.* *In ancient times a **scribe** was held in very high esteem because not many persons were able to read or write then.*

10. **inscription** (in·scrip·tion) (in·skrip′shun) *n.* *The **inscription** on the Statue of Liberty beckons all to our shores.*

11. **prescription** (pre·scrip·tion) (pre·skrip′shun) *n.* *A patient may endanger his health because he fails to follow his doctor's **prescription**.*

12. **transcript** (tran·script) (tran′skript) *n.* *The lawyer asked for a **transcript** of a court case to review what had taken place during the trial.*

13. **geocentric** (ge·o·cen·tric) (jē·ō·sen′trik) *adj.* *In ancient times man thought that the universe was **geocentric**.*

14. **phonics** (phon·ics) (fon′iks) *n.* *Children who are good in **phonics** are able to figure out many words independently.*

15. **phonetics** (pho·net·ics) (fo·net′iks) *n.* *Many actors and actresses take courses in **phonetics** to learn how to pronounce words better.*

16. **stethoscope** (steth·o·scope) (steth′o·skōpé) *n.* *The doctor used the **stethoscope** to listen to his patient's heartbeat.*

**STOP.** Check answers at the end of this chapter (p. 43).

## SPECIAL NOTE

Note that the words *micrometer* (mī·krom′e·ter) *n.* and *micrometer* (mī′krō·mē·ter) *n.* are spelled identically but are pronounced differently and have different meanings. Although many words have more than one meaning, they are often pronounced the same. Because the words *micrometer* (mī·krom′e·ter) *n.* and *micrometer* (mī′krō·mē·ter) *n.* are pronounced differently and each word has meanings different from those of the other, they are presented separately.

### Practice for Additional Words Derived from Combining Forms

**Directions:** Match the definition that *best* fits to the word.

| | |
|---|---|
| _____ 1. telemeter | a. a brief dedication in a book; something written or engraved on some surface |
| _____ 2. micrometer | |
| _____ 3. microorganism | b. a writer |
| _____ 4. microbe | c. a very small living thing that cannot be seen with the naked eye |
| _____ 5. microphone | |
| _____ 6. microfilm | d. study of the relationship of written symbols to sound symbols |
| _____ 7. transcript | e. relating to the earth as the center |
| _____ 8. scribe | f. a copy of an original |
| _____ 9. prescription | g. one-millionth of a meter; a micron |
| _____ 10. inscription | h. A doctor's instrument used to hear heart, lungs, and so forth |
| _____ 11. phonics | i. a device to magnify weak sounds |
| _____ 12. phonetics | j. an instrument used to measure distance |
| _____ 13. geocentric | k. film on which printed material is reduced in size |
| _____ 14. stethoscope | l. a doctor's written directions for medicine |
| _____ 15. meter | m. an instrument that measures minute distances |
| _____ 16. micrometer | n. a very small living thing that cannot be seen with the naked eye |
| | o. an instrument that measures the amount of something |
| | p. study of speech sounds |

**STOP.** Check answers at the end of this chapter (p. 44).

# EXERCISE 3

## Step I. Combining Forms

**A. Directions:**  A list of combining forms with their meanings follows. Look at the combining forms and their meanings. Concentrate on learning each combining form and its meaning. Cover the meanings, read the combining forms, and state the meanings to yourself. Check to see if you are correct. Now cover the combining forms, read the meanings, and state the combining forms to yourself. Check to see if you are correct.

| Combining Forms | Meanings |
|---|---|
| 1. gram | something written or drawn; a record |
| 2. uni | one |
| 3. dic, dict | say; speak |
| 4. contra | against; opposite |
| 5. spect | see; view; observe |
| 6. phob, phobo | fear |

**B. Directions:**  Do not look at the preceding meanings. Write the meanings of the following combining forms.

| Combining Forms | Meanings |
|---|---|
| 1. gram | _____ |
| 2. uni | _____ |
| 3. dic, dict | _____ |
| 4. contra | _____ |
| 5. spect | _____ |
| 6. phob, phobo | _____ |

## Step II. Words Derived from Combining Forms

1. **telegram** (tel′e·gram) *n.* Message sent from a distance.
   *A **telegram** is usually sent when the message is important.*

2. **uniform** (ū′ni·form) *adj.* Being always the same; alike. *n.* A special form of clothing.
   *Persons in the armed forces wear **uniforms** that have been specially designed for them.*

3. **unique** (u·nique) (ū′nēk) *adj.* Being the only one of its kind.
   *The ancient statue found in a cave was **unique** because there were no others like it.*

4. **union** (un·ion) (ūn′yun) *n.* A joining; a putting together; something formed by joining.
   *A labor **union** is a group of people who have joined together because they have similar interests and purposes.*

5. **universe** (ū′ni·vers\u00e9) *n.* Everything that exists; all creation; all mankind.
   *With space exploration, man has made but a small probe into the vast unknown regions of the universe.*

6. **universal** (ū·ni·ver′sal) *adj.* Applying to all.
   *It is very hard to give universal satisfaction to people because not everyone agrees on what is satisfactory.*

7. **unison** (ū′ni·son) *n.* A harmonious agreement; a saying of something together: in **unison.** *adv.* Precise and perfect agreement.
   *Choral groups speak in unison when they recite.*

8. **diction** (dic·tion) (dik′shun) *n.* Manner of speaking; choice of words.
   *Mrs. Smith's diction is so precise that no one has any difficulty understanding her speech.*

9. **dictation** (dic·ta·tion) (dik·tā′shun) *n.* The act of speaking or reading aloud to someone who takes down the words.
   *On Monday, Mr. Jones sometimes loses his voice because of the great amount of dictation he gives his secretary.*

10. **dictionary** (dic·tion·a·ry) (dik′shun·a·rē) *n.* A book of alphabetically listed words in a language, giving information about their meanings, pronunciations, and so forth.
    *Whenever I don't know the pronunciation or meaning of a word, I look it up in the dictionary.*

11. **dictator** (dic·ta·tor) (dik′tā·tor) *n.* A ruler who has absolute power; a ruler who has complete control and say; one who dictates.
    *Hitler was a dictator who had complete control over the German people.*

12. **contrary** (con·trar·y) (kon′trar·ē) *adj.* Opposite.
    *We disagree because his opinion is contrary to ours.*

13. **contradiction** (con·tra·dic·tion) (kon·tra·dik′shun) *n.* Something (such as a statement) consisting of opposing parts.
    *If I answer yes and no to the same statement, I am making a contradiction.*

14. **contrast** (con·trast) (kon′trast) *n.* Difference between things; use of opposites for certain results.
    *The black chair against the white wall makes an interesting contrast.*

15. **spectacle** (spec·ta·cle) (spek′ta·kul) *n.* Something showy that is seen by many (the public); an unwelcome or sad sight.
    *The drunken man made a terrible spectacle of himself for the crowd of people.*

16. **spectator** (spec·ta·tor) (spek′tā·tor) *n.* An onlooker; one who views something, such as a spectacle.
    *There were many spectators at the fair who enjoyed looking at the sights.*

17. **spectacular** (spec·tac·u·lar) (spek·tak′ū·lar) *adj.* Relating to something unusual, impressive, exciting, or unexpected.
    *The spectacular rescue of the child from the burning house was widely applauded.*

18. **phobia** (pho·bi·a) (fō′bē·a) *n.* Extreme fear.
    *My friend, who has a phobia about cats, is afraid to be in the same room with one.*

## SPECIAL NOTES

1. The term *phobia* is usually used to refer to an extreme fear of something. For example: *The doctors tried to help the man to overcome his* **phobia** *about heights.* Here is a list of some phobias:
   a.   triskadekaphobia = fear of the number thirteen
   b.   ailurophobia = fear of cats
   c.   cynophobia = fear of dogs
   d.   arachniphobia = fear of spiders
   e.   scotophobia = fear of darkness
   f.   astrapophobia = fear of lightning
   g.   agoraphobia = fear of being in open spaces or fear of leaving one's house

2. The term *Union*, which begins with a capital letter, refers to the United States as a national unit or to any other nation that is a unit, such as the USSR.

3. The combining form *gram* means "something written; a record." However, *gram* is also a noun that refers to a measurement of weight in the metric system.

4. The plural of *spectacle* (spectacles) can also refer to eyeglasses.

5. Do not confuse *contradiction* with *contrast*. A contradiction is something that is in disagreement with itself; it is logically incongruous. Contrast, on the other hand, deals with the differences between persons, things, ideas, events, and so on.

## Step III. Words in Context

Last August my buddies and I traveled across the **universe**. Let me explain. We are all members of the school soccer team, and our **union** has made us the best in the state. In April our school received a **telegram** from a school in a country located about 4,000 miles away. The school wanted our soccer team to play its team. It was a **unique** opportunity. All of us wanted to go. The country, however, is run by a **dictator** whose views are completely **contrary** to ours. To go there, we needed special permission from our government. After a great amount of letter writing involving the **dictation** of letters from one big shot to another, telegraphing, and telephoning, we were told that we would be allowed to go. We were overjoyed.

In August we left for what seemed like the ends of the earth. When we arrived at our destination, there were soldiers in **uniform** waiting to greet us and young children singing "God Bless America" in **unison** in English. We were surprised at their excellent **diction**. It was a rather **spectacular** sight. Because we do not speak their language, we had brought a special **dictionary** with us. As soon as the song was over, two soldiers took us on a special bus to our hotel. As we rode in the bus, we were shocked at how bleak everything looked. The **contrast** between their country and ours is very great. You can imagine our surprise when we saw that our hotel was luxurious and thirty stories high.

Our rooms were on the twenty-fifth floor. When Bill, who has a **phobia** of heights, heard this, he went into a shaking fit. We tried to calm Bill, but we seemed to make matters worse. We merely were making a **spectacle** of ourselves. Soon we had many **spectators** staring at us. We explained Bill's problem to a person who spoke English. There was **universal** agreement that we should have our rooms changed to the first floor. This worked. Throughout our visit we felt that everything was a **contradiction**. We thought things would be one way, but they turned out the opposite way.

# Step IV. Practice

**A. *Directions:*** A list of definitions follows. Underline the word that *best* fits the definition.

1. A saying of something together
   a. union
   b. universe
   c. unison
   d. uniform

2. Refers to the Bible
   a. autobiography
   b. Scripture
   c. autograph
   d. script

3. An extreme fear
   a. biology
   b. biped
   c. phobia
   d. pedestrian

4. Being the same
   a. union
   b. unique
   c. universe
   d. uniform

5. Applying to all
   a. unique
   b. union
   c. unison
   d. universal

6. A joining together
   a. unique
   b. union
   c. universal
   d. uniform

7. Something (such as a statement) consisting of opposing parts
   a. unique
   b. unison
   c. contradiction
   d. uniform

8. The science of life
   a. geology
   b. geography
   c. biography
   d. biology

9. Being unlike anything else
   a. phobic
   b. unique
   c. telegraphic
   d. contrasting

10. Message from a distance
    a. telegraph
    b. telegram
    c. telescope
    d. autograph

11. One who views something
    a. spectator
    b. spectacle
    c. spectacular
    d. script

12. Relating to something impressive
    a. spectator
    b. Scripture
    c. spectacular
    d. spectacle

13. Something showy
    a. spectacular
    b. spectator
    c. phobia
    d. spectacle

14. A ruler with complete control
    a. dictation
    b. diction
    c. autobiography
    d. dictator

15. Manner of speaking
    a. dictionary
    b. dictation
    c. diction
    d. dictator

16. The act of speaking to someone who takes it down
    a. dictation
    b. dictionary
    c. diction
    d. dictator

---

**STOP.**  Check answers at the end of this chapter (p. 44).

---

**B. Directions:**  Twelve sentences follow. Define the underlined word.

1. It's a <u>contradiction</u> to be happy and unhappy at the same time.

_____

2. He is making a <u>spectacle</u> of himself by behaving that way in front of so many people.

_____

3. Although it is a statement <u>contrary</u> to the opinions of other people, I will stick to it.

   _____

4. You have such a <u>unique</u> way of holding your tennis racket.

   _____

5. If that is a <u>universal</u> belief, everyone should agree with it.

   _____

6. Because I am still afraid to go in the water, my doctor has not cured me of my <u>phobia</u>.

   _____

7. The color of your blouse makes a good <u>contrast</u> to your skirt.

   _____

8. The <u>spectators</u> were not able to believe their eyes.

   _____

9. The two feuding organizations decided to join together into one strong <u>union</u>.

   _____

10. Although the trapped men seemed surely doomed, the firemen made a <u>spectacular</u> rescue at the last minute.

    _____

11. John behaves like a <u>dictator</u> in class because he likes to have everyone do what he wants.

    _____

12. Instructors' <u>diction</u> must be excellent if many students are to listen to their lectures

    _____

---

**STOP.**  Check answers at the end of this chapter (p. 44).

---

**C. Directions:**  Use the combining forms that follow to build a word from this exercise to fit the blank in the sentence.

Combining Forms

| | |
|---|---|
| contra | phob |
| dic | spec |
| gram | uni |

1. In colonial days children recited their lessons in _____.

2. The _____ ruled his country with an iron hand.

3. If you have such a severe _____ of cats, why do you have one?

4. Please look up the meaning of this word in the _____.

5. It's a _____ to say that you are well and ill at the same time.

6. It was very embarrassing when _____ gathered to view the sight of us in our ridiculous costumes.

7. There was _____ agreement among us that we would not allow ourselves to be made fools of anymore.

8. There is too much of a _____ with that color and the other.

9. The politician's _____ was so poor that it was difficult to understand what he was saying.

10. Why is Mike's opinion always _____ to ours?

---

**STOP.**  Check answers at the end of this chapter (p. 44).

---

# EXTRA WORD POWER

**ion, sion, tion.**   State of; act of; result of. Note the three spellings. When *ion, sion,* or *tion* is found at the end of a word, it means that the word is a noun. For example: *diction*—the act of speaking in a certain manner; *dictation*—the act of speaking to someone who takes it down; *question*—the act of asking; *description*—the act of describing.

## Additional Words Derived from Combining Forms

From your knowledge of combining forms, can you define the following words?

1. **Dictaphone** (dic·ta·phone) (dĭk′tȧ·fōné) *n.   Sometimes Mr. Jones used a **Dictaphone** to record his letters for his secretary.*

_____

2. **dictum** (dic·tum) (dik′tum) *n.* *(pl.* **dicta** or **dictums**)   The union leaders impressed the strikers with their **dictum** *of nonviolence.*

   _____

3. **indictment** (in·dīċt′ment) *n.*   *The jury felt that the prosecutor had enough evidence to warrant an* **indictment** *against the defendant.*

   _____

4. **unilateral** (ū·ni·lat′er·al) *adj.*   *There is a tendency today in corporations toward consensus decisions by management rather than* **unilateral** *ones by individual executives.*

   _____

5. **unify** (u·ni·fy) (ū′ni·fī) *v.*   *After the strike it was difficult to* **unify** *the different groups because there was still resentment against those who had crossed the picket lines.*

   _____

6. **acrophobia** (ac·ro·pho·bi·a) (ak·ro·fō′bē·a) *n.*   *You would not find a person with* **acrophobia** *at the top of the World Trade Center.*

   _____

7. **hydrophobia** (hy·dro·pho·bi·a) (hī·dro·fō′bē·a) *n.*   *I know someone who developed* **hydrophobia** *after being thrown in the water as a child.*

   _____

8. **claustrophobia** (claus·tro·pho·bi·a) (klaus·tro·fō′bē·a) *n.*   *How horrible to get stuck in an elevator when you have* **claustrophobia***!*

   _____

9. **grammar** (gram′mar) *n.*   *Studies have shown that a knowledge of* **grammar** *does not help students to speak or write better because grammar merely describes the way an individual speaks.*

   _____

10. **speculate** (spec·u·late) (spek′yu·lātė) *v.*   *I do not like to* **speculate** *in the stock market because I like only sure things.*

    _____

---

**STOP.**  Check answers at the end of this chapter (p. 44).

## SPECIAL NOTES

1. Note that the word *dictum* is pronounced (dik′tum) and the word *Dictaphone* is pronounced (dik′ta·fōnè), but the word *indictment* is pronounced (in·dīćt′ment). Unfortunately, in the English language, perfect uniformity of word pronunciations does not exist. It is possible to have two words that are spelled exactly the same but are pronounced differently. Remember, in Exercise 2, you met the words *micrometer* (mī·krom′e·ter) and *micrometer* (mī′krō·mē·ter)? They are spelled the same but have different pronunciations and meanings.

2. *Dictaphone* begins with a capital letter because it is a trademark. Trademarks, which are words or symbols that are developed by owners to identify their products and are legally reserved for their exclusive use, are capitalized.

### Practice for Additional Words Derived from Combining Forms

***Directions:***  Match each word with the best definition.

_____ 1. Dictaphone

_____ 2. dictum

_____ 3. indictment

_____ 4. unilateral

_____ 5. unify

_____ 6. acrophobia

_____ 7. hydrophobia

_____ 8. claustrophobia

_____ 9. grammar

_____ 10. speculate

a.  a fear of heights

b.  that part of the study of language dealing with structure and word forms

c.  to think about from all sides; take part in any risky venture

d.  a fear of closed-in places

e.  a machine for recording speech

f.  a charge

g.  form into one

h.  an authoritative statement

i.  one-sided

j.  a fear of water

> **STOP.**  Check answers at the end of this chapter (p. 45).

# CHAPTER WORDS IN SENTENCES

***Directions:***  Use the given words to write a sentence that makes sense. Also, try to illustrate the meaning of the words without actually defining the words.

*Example* (autobiography; script)  The *script* for the movie is based on a famous actress's *autobiography*, which she wrote because she wanted the world to know the truth about her.

1. (biography; unique)

_____

2. (dictator; contradiction)

_____

3. (anniversary; spectacular)

_____

4. (phobia; description)

_____

5. (biology; microscope)

_____

# CHAPTER WORDS IN A PARAGRAPH

Here is a list of words from this chapter. Write a paragraph using at least 5 of these words. The paragraph must make sense and be logically developed.

**Word List**

| | | |
|---|---|---|
| anniversary | contrast | spectacle |
| annual | description | spectacular |
| autobiography | diction | spectators |
| biennial | general | union |
| biography | pedestrian | unison |
| biped | phobia | unique |
| contradiction | script | |

# ANALOGIES 1

**_Directions:_** Find the word from the following list that _best_ completes each analogy. There are more words in the list than you need. The symbol : means "is to," and the symbol :: means "as."

    _Example_    Brutal is to savage as viewer is to _spectator_.
                  Brutal : savage :: viewer : _spectator_.

**Word List**

| | | |
|---|---|---|
| annually | biweekly | prescription |
| autograph | contradict | spectacle |
| automatic | contrast | spectacular |
| automation | hydrophobia | spectator |
| automaton | indictment | telescope |
| bicyclist | microbe | transcript |
| biennial | orthography | uniform |
| bifocals | pedestrian | unique |
| biography | phobia | unite |
| biped | podium | |

1. Riding : walking :: motorist : _____.

2. Accessory : scarf :: instrument : _____.

3. Height : acrophobia :: water : _____.

4. Hear : racket :: view : _____.

5. Solo : duet :: weekly : _____.

6. Snow : blizzard :: interesting : _____.

7. Groomed : disheveled :: common : _____.

8. Hamper : hinder :: same : _____.

9. Arrest : stop :: dais : _____.

10. Primary : first :: signature : _____.

11. Automobile : vehicle :: robot : _____.

12. Pretty : beautiful :: fear : _____.

13. Smooth : wrinkled :: agree : _____.

14. Dress : gown :: spectacles : _____.

15. Hate : detest :: join : _____.

16. Structure : grammar :: spelling : _____.

17. End : beginning :: original : _____.

18. Advice : counsel :: charge : _____.

19. One : two :: annual : _____.

20. Rule : law :: microorganism : _____.

---

**STOP.** Check answers at the end of this chapter (p. 45).

# MULTIPLE CHOICE
# VOCABULARY TEST 1

**Directions:** This is a test on words in Exercises 1–3. Words are presented according to exercises. *Do all exercises before checking answers.* Underline the meaning that *best* fits the word.

## Exercise 1

1. biology
   a. study of earth
   b. study of people
   c. study of life
   d. science

2. biography
   a. life story written by oneself
   b. a science
   c. life story
   d. some writing

3. autograph
   a. life story
   b. a machine that writes
   c. some writing
   d. signature

4. annual
   a. money
   b. every year
   c. every two years
   d. twice a year

5. biennial
   a. every two years
   b. twice a year
   c. celebration of birthday
   d. once a year

6. autobiography
   a. life story
   b. life story written by oneself
   c. writing machine
   d. science of writing

7. anniversary
   a. refers to annual
   b. every two years
   c. yearly return of a date marking an important event
   d. a celebration

8. biannual
   a. lasting for two years
   b. yearly
   c. twice a year
   d. once a year

9. biweekly
   a. every two weeks
   b. once a week
   c. every four weeks
   d. two weeks every year

10. bimonthly
    a. every two months
    b. every month
    c. four times yearly
    d. two times yearly

11. biped
    a. feet
    b. two socks for feet
    c. two-footed animal
    d. two-footed human

12. pedestrian
    a. one who goes on foot
    b. a foot rest
    c. a foot doctor
    d. refers to two feet

## Exercise 2

13. telescope
    a. an instrument used to view small objects
    b. an instrument used to see large objects
    c. an instrument used for viewing distant objects
    d. an instrument used to record sound

14. geology
    a. science of life
    b. study of the earth
    c. study of the earth's surface and life
    d. study of the earth's physical makeup

15. telegraph
    a. instrument used to see from a distance
    b. a machine used to send messages
    c. a machine that measures distance
    d. a message

16. microscope
    a. an instrument that makes things appear small
    b. an instrument used to make small objects appear larger
    c. an instrument that grows small things
    d. something small

17. telephone
    a. a sounding machine
    b. a recording machine
    c. an instrument that sends sound at a distance
    d. an instrument that measures sound at a distance

18. geography
    a.  a branch of mathematics
    b.  study of the earth
    c.  study of the earth's physical makeup
    d.  study of the earth's surface and life

19. geometry
    a.  study of earth's physical makeup
    b.  study of the earth's surface and life
    c.  a branch of mathematics
    d.  measurement

20. Scripture
    a.  refers to any writings
    b.  the Bible
    c.  refers to a script
    d.  refers only to the Old Testament

21. script
    a.  a piece of writing
    b.  a part in a play
    c.  a writer
    d.  the Bible

22. description
    a.  an account that gives a picture of something in words
    b.  some writing
    c.  your signature
    d.  a play script

## Exercise 3

23. telegram
    a.  a message sent from a distance
    b.  a machine used to send a message
    c.  something from a distance
    d.  a record

24. phobia
    a.  a disease
    b.  refers to hate
    c.  extreme fear
    d.  refers to sound

25. uniform
    a.  joining together
    b.  clothing
    c.  special form of clothing
    d.  all

26. unique
    a.  only one of its kind
    b.  all
    c.  the same
    d.  joining together

27. union
    a.  all
    b.  refers to only one
    c.  the act of putting together
    d.  complete agreement

28. universal
    a.  applying to none
    b.  putting together
    c.  applying to all
    d.  only one of a kind

29. universe
    a.  complete agreement
    b.  similar
    c.  everything that exists
    d.  together

30. unison
    a.  a saying of something together
    b.  manner of speaking
    c.  similar
    d.  all

31. dictionary
    a.  study of words
    b.  a book on speech
    c.  a book of alphabetically listed words in a language
    d.  study of speaking

32. dictator
    a.  ruler
    b.  a ruler without power
    c.  a person who speaks
    d.  a ruler with absolute power

33. dictation
    a.  act of speaking
    b.  act of writing
    c.  act of speaking to someone who takes down the words
    d.  a ruler with absolute power

34. diction
    a.  manner of speaking
    b.  a ruler
    c.  act of writing
    d.  act of speaking to someone who takes down the words

35. contrary
    a.  no agreement
    b.  opposite
    c.  use of opposites for effect
    d.  against someone

36. contradiction
    a.  something (such as a statement) consisting of opposing parts
    b.  something not in complete agreement
    c.  use of opposites for effect
    d.  against

37. contrast
    a. difference between things
    b. against someone
    c. no agreement
    d. against everything

38. spectacle
    a. one who views something
    b. glasses
    c. something showy seen by the public
    d. a place to see things

39. spectator
    a. one who wears glasses
    b. one who views something
    c. a place for seeing
    d. something unusual

40. spectacular
    a. a person who sees things
    b. one who wear glasses
    c. a shameful sight
    d. refers to something unusual

# TRUE/FALSE TEST 1

**Directions:** This is a true/false test on Exercises 1–3. Read each sentence carefully. Decide whether it is true or false. Put a *T* for *true* or an *F* for *false* in the blank. If the answer is false, change a word or part of the sentence to make it true. The number after the sentence tells you if the word is from Exercise 1, 2, or 3.

_____ 1. When something is done in <u>unison</u>, it is done together. 3

_____ 2. In <u>geology</u> class you learn about plants and animals. 2

_____ 3. When something is a <u>contradiction</u> of something else, it is in agreement with it. 3

_____ 4. A <u>biographer</u> would write your autobiography. 1

_____ 5. A <u>pedestrian</u> is one who goes on a bicycle. 1

_____ 6. When something is <u>unique</u>, it is the same for all persons. 3

_____ 7. If everyone were to agree, there would be a <u>universal</u> agreement. 3

_____ 8. If I receive interest <u>biennially</u>, I receive it twice a year. 1

_____ 9. Not all animals are <u>bipeds</u>. 1

_____ 10. The <u>telescope</u> helped me to get a better view of the one-celled animals. 2

_____ 11. If you had a <u>phobia</u> concerning water, you would fear going into deep water. 3

_____ 12. A <u>spectator</u> is one who watches others. 3

_____ 13. When something is <u>spectacular</u>, it is very exciting to observe. 3

_____ 14. <u>Scripture</u> refers to a play script. 2

_____ 15. When you give your <u>autograph</u>, you are giving your life story. 1

_____ 16. A <u>dictator</u> is not an <u>autonomous</u> ruler. 3, 1

> **STOP.**  Check answers for both tests at the end of this chapter (pp. 45–46).

# SCORING OF TESTS

| MULTIPLE-CHOICE VOCABULARY TEST | | TRUE/FALSE TEST* | |
| --- | --- | --- | --- |
| Number Wrong | Score | Number Wrong | Score |
| 0–3 | Excellent | 0–1 | Excellent |
| 4–6 | Good | 2 | Good |
| 7–9 | Weak | 3–4 | Weak |
| Above 9 | Poor | Above 4 | Poor |
| Score _____ | | Score _____ | |

1. If you scored in the excellent or good range on _both tests_, you are doing well. Go on to Chapter Three.

2. If you scored in the weak or poor range on either test, look below and follow directions for Additional Practice. Note that the words on the tests are arranged so that you can tell in which exercise to find them. This will help you if you need additional practice.

# ADDITIONAL PRACTICE SETS

**A. Directions:**  Write the words you missed on the tests from the three exercises in the space provided. Note that the tests are presented so that you can tell to which exercises the words belong.

Exercise 1 Words Missed

1. _____     6. _____

2. _____     7. _____

3. _____     8. _____

4. _____     9. _____

5. _____     10. _____

*When the answer is false, you must get both parts of the true/false question correct in order to receive credit.

Exercise 2 Words Missed

1. _____     6. _____
2. _____     7. _____
3. _____     8. _____
4. _____     9. _____
5. _____    10. _____

Exercise 3 Words Missed

1. _____     6. _____
2. _____     7. _____
3. _____     8. _____
4. _____     9. _____
5. _____    10. _____

**B. Directions:**   Restudy the missed words from the three exercises. Study the combining forms from which those words are derived. Do Step I and Step II for those you missed. Note that Step I and Step II of the combining forms and vocabulary derived from these combining forms are on the following pages:

Exercise 1—pp. 5–7

Exercise 2—pp. 13–15

Exercise 3—pp. 21–23

**C. Directions:**   Do Additional Practice 1 below if you missed words from Exercise 1. Do Additional Practice 2 on pp. 39–40 if you missed words from Exercise 2. Do Additional Practice 3 on pp. 40–41 if you missed words from Exercise 3. Now go on to Chapter Three.

# Additional Practice 1 for Exercise 1

**A. Directions:**   The combining forms presented in Exercise 1 follow. Match each combining form with its meaning.

_____ 1. aut, auto          a.  the study of or science of

_____ 2. bi                 b.  something written; machine

_____ 3. bio                c.  self

_____ 4. graph              d.  life

_____ 5. ology              e.  foot

_____ 6. ped, pod           f.  two

_____ 7. anni, annu, enni   g.  year

---

**STOP.**   Check answers at the end of this chapter (p. 46).

**B. Directions:**  The words presented in Exercise 1 follow. Match each word with its meaning.

_____ 1. biennial

_____ 2. biology

_____ 3. biography

_____ 4. autobiography

_____ 5. autograph

_____ 6. bimonthly

_____ 7. biweekly

_____ 8. pedestrian

_____ 9. biped

_____ 10. annual

_____ 11. anniversary

_____ 12. biannual

a.  study or science of life

b.  yearly

c.  life story

d.  every two years

e.  one who goes on foot

f.  signature

g.  yearly return of a date marking an event

h.  two-footed animal

i.  every two weeks; twice a week

j.  every two months; twice a month

k.  life story written by oneself

l.  twice a year

---

**STOP.**  Check answers at the end of this chapter (p. 46).

---

## Additional Practice 2 for Exercise 2

**A. Directions:**  The combining forms presented in Exercise 2 follow. Match each combining form with its meaning.

_____ 1. tele

_____ 2. scope

_____ 3. geo

_____ 4. meter

_____ 5. micro

_____ 6. scrib, scrip

_____ 7. phon, phono

a.  a means for seeing, watching, or viewing

b.  sound

c.  very small

d.  earth

e.  write

f.  measure

g.  from a distance

---

**STOP.**  Check answers at the end of this chapter (p. 46).

**B. Directions:**    The words presented in Exercise 2 follow. Match each word with its meaning.

_____ 1. telescope

_____ 2. geology

_____ 3. microscope

_____ 4. geography

_____ 5. geometry

_____ 6. telegraph

_____ 7. Scripture

_____ 8. telephone

_____ 9. script

_____ 10. description

a.  instrument for sending a message in code at a distance

b.  a piece of writing

c.  branch of mathematics dealing with the measurement of points, lines, and planes, among other things.

d.  study of the earth's surface and life

e.  instrument that sends sound at a distance

f.  study of the earth's physical makeup

g.  instrument used to make very small objects appear larger so that they can be seen

h.  instrument used for viewing distant objects

i.  Bible

j.  an account that gives a picture of something in words

---

**STOP.**  Check answers at the end of this chapter (p. 46).

---

# Additional Practice 3 for Exercise 3

**A. Directions:**    The combining forms presented in Exercise 3 follow. Match each combining form with its meaning.

_____ 1. spect

_____ 2. uni

_____ 3. phob, phobo

_____ 4. gram

_____ 5. contra

_____ 6. dic, dict

a.  against; opposite

b.  say; speak

c.  one

d.  fear

e.  something written or drawn; a record

f.  see; view; observe

---

**STOP.**  Check answers at the end of this chapter (p. 46).

---

**B. Directions:** The words presented in Exercise 3 follow. Match each word with its meaning.

| | |
|---|---|
| _____ 1. dictionary | a. manner of speaking |
| _____ 2. spectator | b. being the only one of its kind |
| _____ 3. telegram | c. the act of putting together |
| _____ 4. phobia | d. something (such as a statement) con- sisting of opposing parts |
| _____ 5. uniform | e. everything that exists |
| _____ 6. unique | f. applying to all |
| _____ 7. union | g. message sent from a distance |
| _____ 8. universe | h. being always the same |
| _____ 9. universal | i. extreme fear |
| _____ 10. unison | j. act of speaking to someone who takes down the words |
| _____ 11. contrary | k. a saying of something together |
| _____ 12. contradiction | l. book of alphabetically listed words in a language |
| _____ 13. contrast | m. one who views something |
| _____ 14. dictator | n. referring to something unusual; exciting |
| _____ 15. diction | o. opposite |
| _____ 16. dictation | p. difference between things |
| _____ 17. spectacle | q. something showy |
| _____ 18. spectacular | r. a ruler with absolute power |

---

**STOP.** Check answers at the end of this chapter (p. 46).

---

# ANSWERS: Chapter Two

## Exercise 1 (pp. 5–12)

Practice A

(1) yearly, (2) own life stories, (3) walkers, (4) signature, (5) life stories, (6) two-footed animal, (7) every two months, (8) the study of life, (9) every two weeks, (10) every two years, (11) the yearly return of a date marking an occurrence of some importance, (12) twice a year.

Practice B

(1) b, (2) j, (3) a, (4) g, (5) d, (6) e, (7) l, (8) h, (9) i, (10) c, (11) f, (12) k.

## Practice C

(1) anniversary, (2) autograph, (3) biology, (4) annual, biennial, (5) autobiography, (6) bipeds, (7) biographies, (8) Pedestrians, (9) biweekly.

## Additional Words Derived from Combining Forms (pp. 10–12)

1. **graphology.** The study of handwriting, especially for character analysis.
2. **graphic.** Marked by realistic and vivid detail; related to pictorial arts.
3. **orthography.** The part of language study that deals with correct spelling; the art of writing words with correct spelling.
4. **annuity.** An investment yielding a fixed sum of money, payable yearly, to continue for a given number of years or for life; a yearly payment of money.
5. **bifocals.** A pair of glasses with two-part lenses, with one part helping you see what is near and one part helping you see from a distance.
6. **bilateral.** Involving two sides.
7. **bilingual.** Having or using two languages equally well; a bilingual person.
8. **binary.** Made up of two parts; twofold; relating to base two.
9. **biopsy.** In medicine, the cutting out of a piece of living tissue for examination.
10. **podium.** A low wall serving as a foundation; a raised platform for the conductor of an orchestra; a dais.
11. **pedestal.** A base or bottom support; any foundation or support; to put or set on a pedestal; to regard with great admiration.
12. **automatic.** Moving by itself; performed without thinking about it.
13. **automaton.** Anything that can move or act by itself; a person or animal acting in an automatic or mechanical way.
14. **autonomous.** Self-governing; functioning independently of other parts.

## Practice for Additional Words Derived from Combining Forms (p. 12)

(1) binary, (2) graphology, (3) biopsy, (4) bilingual, (5) bifocals, (6) autonomous, (7) automatic, (8) bilateral, (9) orthography, (10) annuity, (11) pedestal, (12) podium, (13) graphic, (14) automaton.

# Exercise 2 (pp. 13–20)

## Practice A

(1) microscope, (2) geology, (3) telescope, (4) script, (5) Scripture, (6) telephone, (7) geometry, (8) geography, (9) telegraph, (10) description.

## Practice B

(1) telescope, (2) telegraph, (3) geometry, (4) geology, (5) biographer, (6) script, (7) telephone, (8) microscope, (9) Scripture, (10) geography, (11) description, (12) pedestrian.

## Practice C

(1) send a message from a distance, (2) a written copy of a play, (3) branch of mathematics dealing with the measurement of points, lines, and planes, among other things, (4) the study of the earth's physical history and makeup, (5) instrument that sends and receives sound, (6) study of the earth's surface and life, (7) account, (8) instrument used to make small things appear larger so that they can be seen, (9) instrument used to view distant objects, (10) the books of the Old and New Testaments.

## Additional Words Derived from Combining Forms (pp. 18–19)

1. **meter.**  In the metric system, a unit of length equal to approximately 39.37 inches; an instrument for measuring the amount of something (as water, gas, electricity); an instrument for measuring and recording distance, time, weight, speed, and so forth; a measure of verse.

2. **telemeter.**  An instrument that measures distance; an instrument that sends information to a distant point.

3. **micrometer.**  An instrument used with a microscope or telescope to measure accurately very minute distances.

4. **micrometer.**  A unit of length equal to one millionth of a meter, also called *micron*.

5. **microbe.**  A very small living thing, whether plant or animal; a microorganism.

6. **microorganism.**  Any organism that is so small that it can be seen only under a microscope—protozoa, bacteria, viruses, and the like; a microbe.

7. **microphone.**  A device that magnifies weak sounds (nontechnical definition used as shorthand for the entire sound amplification system); a device to convert sound waves to electrical waves (technical definition).

8. **microfilm.**  Film on which documents, printed pages, and so forth, are photographed in a reduced size for storage convenience.

9. **scribe.**  A writer, author; a public writer or secretary; in Scripture and Jewish history, a man of learning.

10. **inscription.**  Something written or engraved (words, symbols) on some surface; a brief or informal dedication in a book to a friend.

11. **prescription.**  A doctor's written directions for the preparation and use of medicine; an order; direction; rule.

12. **transcript.**  A written or typewritten copy of an original; a copy or reproduction of any kind.

13. **geocentric.**  Relating to the earth as the center.

14. **phonics.**  Study of the relationship between letter symbols of a written language and the sounds they represent; a method used in teaching word recognition in reading.

15. **phonetics.**  A study dealing with speech sounds and their production.

16. **stethoscope.**  A hearing instrument used in examining the heart, lungs, and so on.

Practice for Additional Words Derived from Combining Forms (p. 20)

(1) j, (2) m or g, (3) c, n, (4) c, n, (5) i, (6) k, (7) f, (8) b, (9) l, (10) a, (11) d, (12) p, (13) e, (14) h, (15) o, (16) g or m.

# Exercise 3 (pp. 21–29)

## Practice A

(1) c, (2) b, (3) c, (4) d, (5) d, (6) b, (7) c, (8) d, (9) b, (10) b, (11) a, (12) c, (13) d, (14) d, (15) c, (16) a.

## Practice B

(1) something consisting of opposites, (2) something showy, (3) opposite, (4) being the only one of its kind, (5) referring to all, (6) extreme fear, (7) use of opposites for certain results, (8) onlookers, (9) a joining, a putting together, (10) unusual, exciting, impressive, (11) a ruler who has absolute power, (12) manner of speaking.

## Practice C

(1) unison, (2) dictator, (3) phobia, (4) dictionary, (5) contradiction, (6) spectators, (7) universal, (8) contrast, (9) diction, (10) contrary.

## Additional Words Derived from Combining Forms (pp. 27–28)

1. **Dictaphone.** A machine for recording and reproducing words spoken into its mouthpiece (differs from a tape recorder because it has controls that fit into use in transcription). *Dictaphone* is capitalized because it is a trademark.

2. **dictum.** An authoritative statement; a saying.

3. **indictment.** A charge; an accusation.

4. **unilateral.** Occurring on one side only; done by one only; one-sided.

5. **unify.** To make or form into one.

6. **acrophobia.** An abnormal fear of high places.

7. **hydrophobia.** An abnormal fear of water; rabies, a viral infectious disease of the central nervous system whose symptoms include an inability to swallow. (Because of the association of water with the act of swallowing, the term *hydrophobia* is used for rabies.)

8. **claustrophobia.** An abnormal fear of being confined, as in a room or a small place.

9. **grammar.** That part of the study of language that deals with the construction of words and word parts (morphology) and the way in which words are arranged relative to each other in utterances (syntax); the study or description of the way language is used.

10. **speculate.** To think about something by turning it in the mind and viewing it in all its aspects and relations; to take part in any risky business venture.

Practice for Additional Words Derived from Combining Forms (p. 29)

(1) e, (2) h, (3) f, (4) i, (5) g, (6) a, (7) j, (8) d, (9) b, (10) c.

## Chapter Words in Sentences (pp. 29–30)

Sentences will vary.

## Chapter Words in a Paragraph (p. 30)

Paragraphs will vary.

## Analogies 1 (pp. 30–31)

(1) pedestrian, (2) telescope, (3) hydrophobia, (4) spectacle, (5) biweekly, (6) spectacular, (7) unique, (8) uniform, (9) podium, (10) autograph, (11) automaton, (12) phobia, (13) contradict, (14) bifocals, (15) unite, (16) orthography, (17) transcript, (18) indictment, (19) biennial, (20) microbe.

## Multiple-Choice Vocabulary Test 1 (pp. 32–36)

Exercise 1

(1) c, (2) c, (3) d, (4) b, (5) a, (6) b, (7) c, (8) c, (9) a, (10) a, (11) c,[5] (12) a.

Exercise 2

(13) c, (14) d, (15) b, (16) b, (17) c, (18) d, (19) c, (20) b, (21) a, (22) a.

Exercise 3

(23) a, (24) c, (25) c,[6] (26) a, (27) c, (28) c, (29) c, (30) a, (31) c, (32) d,[7] (33) c, (34) a, (35) b, (36) a,[8] (37) a, (38) c, (39) b, (40) d.

---

[5] *Two-footed animal* is a better answer than *two-footed human* because there are animals other than humans who are bipeds.

[6] *Special form of clothing* is a better answer than *clothing* because clothing refers to all that you wear. Not all clothing is a uniform; a uniform is a special form of clothing.

[7] *A ruler with absolute power* is a better answer than *a ruler* because not all rulers are dictators.

[8] A contradiction refers to something, such as *two statements about the same thing that are complete opposites.* It is not the use of opposites for effect.

## True/False Test 1[9] (pp. 36–37)

(1) T; (2) F, geology to biology; (3) F, agreement to disagreement; (4) F, autobiography to biography; (5) F, goes on a bicycle to walks; (6) F, same to different or unique to uniform or universal; (7) T; (8) F, twice a year to every two years or biennially to biannually; (9) T; (10) F, telescope to microscope; (11) T; (12) T; (13) T; (14) F, a play script to the Bible; (15) F, life story to signature; (16) F, is not to is.

> **STOP.**  Turn to page 37 for the scoring of the tests.

## Additional Practice Sets (pp. 37–41)

Additional Practice 1

A. (1) c, (2) f, (3) d, (4) b, (5) a, (6) e, (7) g.
B. (1) d, (2) a, (3) c, (4) k, (5) f, (6) j, (7) i, (8) e, (9) h, (10) b, (11) g, (12) l.

Additional Practice 2

A. (1) g, (2) a, (3) d, (4) f, (5) c, (6) e, (7) b.
B. (1) h, (2) f, (3) g, (4) d, (5) c, (6) a, (7) i, (8) e, (9) b, (10) j.

Additional Practice 3

A. (1) f, (2) c, (3) d, (4) e, (5) a, (6) b.
B. (1) l, (2) m, (3) g, (4) i, (5) h, (6) b, (7) c, (8) e, (9) f, (10) k, (11) o, (12) d, (13) p, (14) r, (15) a, (16) j, (17) q, (18) n.

[9]Answers for *false* are suggested answers.

# CHAPTER THREE

# EXERCISE 4

## Step I. Combining Forms

**A. Directions:** A list of combining forms with their meanings follows. Look at the combining forms and their meanings. Concentrate on learning each combining form and its meaning. Cover the meanings, read the combining forms, and state the meanings to yourself. Check to see if you are correct. Now cover the combining forms, read the meanings, and state the combining forms to yourself. Check to see if you are correct.

| Combining Forms | Meanings |
|---|---|
| 1. cent, centi | hundred; hundredth part |
| 2. dec, deca | ten |
| 3. milli | thousand; thousandth part |
| 4. port | carry |
| 5. cred | believe |

**B. Directions:** Do not look at the preceding meanings. Write the meanings of the following combining forms.

Combining Forms                                                    Meanings

  1. cent, centi                              _____

  2. dec, deca                               _____

  3. milli                                   _____

  4. port                                    _____

  5. cred                                    _____

# Step II. Words Derived from Combining Forms

1. **century** (cen·tu·ry) (sen'chu·rē) *n.* (*pl.* **ies**) Period of one hundred years.
   *A man who is 110 years old has lived more than a whole century.*

2. **centennial** (cen·ten·ni·al) (sen·ten'ñē·al) *adj.* Pertaining to a period of one hundred years; lasting one hundred years. *n.* A one-hundredth anniversary.
   *The centennial celebration for the United States took place in 1876.*

3. **bicentennial** (bi·cen·ten·ni·al) (bī·sen·ten'ñē·al) *adj.* Pertaining to or in honor of a two-hundredth anniversary; consisting of or lasting two hundred years; occurring once in two hundred years. *n.* A two-hundredth anniversary.
   *The United States celebrated its bicentennial in 1976.*

4. **million** (mil·lion) (mil'yun) *n.* One thousand thousands (1,000,000); a very large or indefinitely large number. *adj.* Being one million in number; very many; one thousand thousands.
   *A million years equals ten thousand centuries.*

5. **millennium** (mil·len·ni·um) (mil·len'ñē·um) *n.* (*pl.* **niums, nia**) Period of one thousand years; a one-thousandth anniversary; a period of great happiness (the millennium).
   *When the millennium arrives, there will be great happiness on earth.*

6. **decade** (dec·ade) (dek'ādé) *n.* Period of ten years.
   *I can't believe that ten years have passed and that it's already a decade since I last saw my married brother.*

7. **credible** (cred·i·ble) (kred'i·bul) *adj.* Believable.
   *I doubt if anyone will believe you because that is not a credible story.*

8. **credit** (cred·it) (kred'it) *n.* Belief in something; trust; faith; good name; a recognition by name of a contribution to a performance; something that adds to a person's reputation; in an account, the balance in one's favor; an amount of goods or money a person receives and pays for in the future; a unit of academic study. *v.* To supply something on credit to.
   *Because of his strong financial position, he can receive as much credit as he needs from the bank.*

9. **credential** (cre·den·tial) (kre·den'shul) *n.* Something that entitles one to credit or confidence; something that makes others believe in a person; a document such as a degree, diploma, or certificate; *pl.* **credentials**: testimonials entitling a person to credit or to exercise official power.
   *His credentials for the job were so good that everyone felt he would do the work very well.*

"I just met the most incredible aluminum siding salesman . . . ."

From *The Wall Street Journal*–Permission, Cartoon Features Syndicate.

10. **incredible** (in·cred·i·ble) (in·kred′i·bul) *adj.* Not believable.
   *It is not believable that you could have gotten yourself into such an **incredible** situation.*

11. **porter** (por′ter) *n.* A person who carries things; one who is employed to carry baggage at a hotel or transportation terminal.
   *At the airport, I always tip the **porter** who carries my luggage.*

12. **reporter** (rē·port′er) *n.* A person who gathers information and writes reports for newspapers, magazines, and so on.
   *I have always wanted to be a **reporter** because I like to gather information and write reports.*

13. **port** (port) *n.* Place to or from which ships carry things; place where ships may wait.
   *When a ship comes to **port**, its cargo is usually unloaded immediately.*

14. **export** (ex·port) (ek·sport′) *v.* To carry away; to transport or send something to another country. *n.* Something that is exported.
   *The United States **exports** wheat to many nations.*

15. **import** (im·port′) *v.* To carry in; bring in goods from another country. *n.* Something that is imported.
   *The United States **imports** coffee from South America.*

16. **portable** (port·a·ble) (port′a·bul) *adj.* Can be carried; easily or conveniently transported.
   ***Portable** goods are those that you can easily take from one place to another.*

## SPECIAL NOTES

1. The combining form *centi* meaning "hundredth part" is used chiefly in terms belonging to the metric system ( *centimeter*).

2. The combining form *deci* means "tenth part."

3. The combining form *kilo* means "thousand."

4. The combining form *hect* or *hecto* means "hundred." In the metric system *hectometer* is a unit of measure equal to 100 meters.

## Step III. Words in Context

The reporters claimed that at least a **million** people in some large cities crowded the streets at the **bicentennial** to catch a glimpse of the **incredible** parade. It was obviously the event of the **century**. One reporter claimed that he had not seen anything like it since about a **decade** ago. He said that ten years ago in France he had seen something almost as spectacular. Another reporter wrote that a hundred years before at the **centennial** celebration, only a few hundred people witnessed the event rather than one million in one city.

The **reporters** said that they felt the **millennium** must have arrived. They never saw so many people together in one place being so polite to one another. They gave **credit** for the smoothness of the event to the organizers. The organizers had **porters** available to help carry heavy items for people. They made sure that everything used in the parade was easily **portable**. The special items they borrowed from other nations were **imported** with extreme care. Also, they took care to see to it that the items would be **exported** to the other nations in the same condition. They hired special people to watch all these items when they were delivered to and from the **port**. No one could enter the dock to take an item unless he or she had the proper **credentials**. A number of persons tried to con the security guards with stories that sounded **credible**. However, unless they had papers that were signed and that had their photos on them, they were not allowed to remove anything from the dock.

## Step IV. Practice

**A. Directions:**   Underline the word that *best* fits the meaning given for each group of words.

1. A hundredth anniversary
   a. century
   b. centennial
   c. bicentennial
   d. decade

2. A period of ten years
   a. centennial
   b. century
   c. million
   d. decade

3. Believable
   a. credit
   b. credential
   c. credible
   d. incredible

4. Place where ships wait
   a. port
   b. porter
   c. import
   d. deport

5. A person who gathers information for newspapers
   a. port
   b. import
   c. deport
   d. reporter

6. A document such as a degree or diploma
   a. credit
   b. credential
   c. credible
   d. incredible

7. Period of one hundred years
   a. decade
   b. century
   c. bicentennial
   d. millennium

8. Someone who carries things
   a. reporter
   b. port
   c. porter
   d. import

9. One thousand thousands
   a. millennium
   b. centennial
   c. bicentennial
   d. million

10. Period of a thousand years
    a. century
    b. millennium
    c. million
    d. bicentennial

11. Not believable
    a. credit
    b. credential
    c. incredible
    d. credible

12. Can be carried
    a. porter
    b. import
    c. deport
    d. portable

13. Two-hundredth anniversary
    a. bicentennial
    b. millennium
    c. centennial
    d. century

14. Bring in goods from another country
    a. import
    b. export
    c. portable
    d. porter

15. Balance in one's favor
    a. credential
    b. credit
    c. credible
    d. incredible

16. To carry or send something to another country or region
   a. port
   b. import
   c. reporter
   d. export

---

**STOP.** Check answers at the end of this chapter (p. 82).

---

**B. Directions:** A few paragraphs with missing words follow. Fill in the blanks with the word that *best* fits. Words may be used more than once.

**Word List**

| | | |
|---|---|---|
| credential | export | port |
| credible | import | portable |
| credit | incredible | reporter |
| decade | million | |

As a **1**_____ for a large newspaper, I am always looking for a good story. Approximately nine and one-half years ago, almost a whole **2**_____ ago, a lot of drugs were stolen right under the noses of the police. Only persons with proper **3**_____s were allowed to handle the drugs. It just did not seem possible that the drugs could be stolen. It seemed **4**_____. The amount of money involved was said to be thousands of thousands of dollars, over a(n) **5**_____ dollars.

Recently, **6**_____ for this **7**_____ robbery was given to insiders who had proper police **8**_____s. The informer's story about the robbery is a(n) **9**_____ one, and everyone seems to believe it. It seems that persons with **10**_____s were able to get into the place where the drugs were stored. They were able to place the drugs on a **11**_____ table and calmly walk out with them. They replaced the drugs with a mixture of sugar and salt. The robbers then took the drugs to the **12**_____, where they had a ship waiting for them. The drugs were **13**_____ed to another country. When things quieted down, the drugs were **14**_____ed to the United States and sold for **15**_____s of dollars.

---

**STOP.** Check answers at the end of this chapter (p. 83).

---

**C. Directions:** Use the combining forms that follow to build a word from this exercise to fit the blank in the sentence.

**Combining Forms**

cent    milli
cred    port
dec

1. My great-grandparents lived in my home, which is over a _____ old.

2. The United States _____ grain to a number of countries.

3. Many people do not want the United States to _____ as many products as it does.

4. The _____ wrote the incredible story of the politician's early life and his years in reform school.

5. A great amount of _____ was given to one of his counselors for helping him turn his life around.

6. A _____ equals a thousand thousands.

7. A meter equals a thousand _____.

8. A _____ is a period of ten years.

9. I will know that the _____ has arrived when there is absolute peace on earth.

10. No one believed the witness at the murder trial because her story was just not

_____.

---

**STOP.**   Check answers at the end of this chapter (p. 83).

---

## *EXTRA WORD POWER*

**able, ible.**  Can do; able. When *able* or *ible* is found at the end of a word, the word is an adjective meaning "able" or "can do." For example: *portable*—able to be carried; *incredible*—not able to be believed; *credible*—able to be believed; *manageable*—able to be managed; *laughable*—able to be laughed at; *enjoyable*—able to be enjoyed. How many more *able* or *ible* words can you think of?

### Additional Words Derived from Combining Forms

From your knowledge of combining forms, can you define the following words?

1. **decimal** (dec·i·mal) (des'i·mal) *adj. n.   Most of the world's currency uses the **decimal** system, which divides the prime unit of money (such as dollars) into tenths or hundredths.*

_____

2. **decimate** (dec·i·mate) (des'i·maté) *v.   If you have to lose a battle, it is better to be **decimated** than obliterated because in the former case, nine tenths of your troops will survive.*

_____

3. **decameter** (dec·a·me·ter) (dek′a·mē·ter) *n.   Because most countries in the Western world except the United States use the metric system, people should become familiar with such terms as **decameter**.*

_____

4. **decimeter** (dec·i·me·ter) (des′i·mē·ter) *n.   A **decimeter** is approximately 4 inches, so it would take about 3 decimeters to equal 1 foot.*

_____

5. **millimeter** (mil′li·mē·ter) *n.   Microorganisms are even smaller than a **millimeter**.*

_____

6. **centimeter** (cen·ti·me·ter) (sen′ti·mē·ter) *n.   I measured the distance in **centimeters** because I needed to know it to the nearest hundredth of a meter.*

_____

7. **kilometer** (ki·lo·me·ter) (ki·lom′e·ter) *n.   There are approximately 1.6 **kilometers** to a mile.*

_____

8. **centipede** (cen·ti·pede) (sent′i·pēde) *n.   The **centipede** crawled along on its many legs.*

_____

9. **creed** (krēed) *n.   The **creed** "All men are created equal" is found in our Constitution.*

_____

10. **accreditation** (ac·cred·i·ta·tion) (ak·kred·i·tā′shun) *n.   If a college does not have the proper **accreditation**, students might have difficulty in getting jobs or getting into graduate schools.*

_____

11. **creditor** (cred·i·tor) (kred′it·or) *n.   Savings and loan associations are more likely to be large **creditors** to the public through home purchase loans than are commercial banks.*

_____

12. **deportment** (dē·port′ment) *n.   Because his **deportment** has always been above question, everyone is confused by his present behavior.*

_____

---

**STOP.**   Check answers at the end of this chapter (p. 83).

Practice for Additional Words Derived from Combining Forms

**Directions:**   Match each word with the *best* definition.

_____ 1. decimal

_____ 2. decimate

_____ 3. decameter

_____ 4. millimeter

_____ 5. centimeter

_____ 6. centipede

_____ 7. accreditation

_____ 8. creed

_____ 9. creditor

_____ 10. deportment

_____ 11. decimeter

_____ 12. kilometer

a.  statement of belief

b.  one to whom something is due

c.  conduct

d.  1/100 of a meter

e.  wormlike animal with many legs

f.  1/1,000 of a meter

g.  to destroy one tenth of; to destroy but not completely

h.  ten meters

i.  numbered by ten

j.  a giving authority to

k.  1,000 meters

l.  1/10 of a meter

---

**STOP.**   Check answers at the end of this chapter (p. 83).

---

# EXERCISE 5

## Step I. Combining Forms

**A. Directions:**   A list of combining forms with their meanings follows. Look at the combining forms and their meanings. Concentrate on learning each combining form and its meaning. Cover the meaning, read the combining forms, and state the meanings to yourself. Check to see if you are correct. Now cover the combining forms, read the meanings, and state the combining forms to yourself. Check to see if you are correct.

| Combining Forms | Meanings |
|---|---|
| 1. agog, agogue | leading; directing; inciting |
| 2. arch | rule; chief |
| 3. ali | other |
| 4. dem, demo | people |
| 5. mon, mono | one |
| 6. theo | God |

**B. Directions:**   Do not look at the preceding meanings. Write the meanings of the following combining forms.

| Combining Forms | Meanings |
|---|---|
| 1. agog, agogue | _____ |
| 2. arch | _____ |
| 3. ali | _____ |
| 4. dem, demo | _____ |
| 5. mon, mono | _____ |
| 6. theo | _____ |

# Step II. Words Derived from Combining Forms

1. **monarchy** (mon·ar·chy) (mon′ar·kē) *n.* A government or state headed by a single person, who is usually a king, queen, or emperor; called absolute (or despotic) when there is no limitation on the monarch's power and constitutional (or limited) when there is such limitation.
   *Although England is a **monarchy**, the king or queen does not exercise any power at all.*

2. **autocracy** (au·toc·ra·cy) (au·tok′ra·sē) *n.* A form of government in which one person possesses unlimited power.
   *In any **autocracy** the head of government has absolute control of the country.*

3. **autocrat** (au·to·crat) (au′to·krat) *n.* A ruler who has absolute control of a country.
   *The head of government who has absolute control in an autocracy is called an **autocrat**.*

4. **anarchy** (an·ar·chy) (an′ar·kē) *n.* No rule; disorder; the absence of government; chaos.
   *In the West, years ago, **anarchy** existed in many towns because there were no laws.*

5. **atheist** (ā′thē·ist) *n.* One who does not believe in the existence of God.
   *An **atheist** does not believe in the existence of God.*

6. **theocracy** (the·oc·ra·cy) (thē·ok′ra·sē) *n.* Government by a religious group.
   *A country ruled by clergy (persons allowed to preach the gospel) would be called a **theocracy**.*

7. **theology** (the·ol·o·gy) (thē·ol′o·jē) *n.* The study of religion.
   *Ministers, priests, and rabbis must take courses in **theology** to learn about religion.*

8. **democracy** (de·moc·ra·cy) (de·mok′ra·sē) *n.* A form of government in which there is rule by the people either directly or through elected representatives.
   *In a **democracy** the people, through their voting power, have a say in who the leaders of the government will be.*

9. **demagogue** (dem′a·gogue) *n.* A person who stirs up the emotions of people in order to become a leader and achieve selfish ends.
   *A **demagogue** is usually a highly persuasive speaker who plays on the emotions of the crowds for his own ends.*

10. **alias** (a·li·as) (ā′lē·as) *n.* (*pl.* **ses**) Another name taken by a person, often a criminal.
    *A person who uses an **alias** doesn't want others to know what his or her real name is.*

11. **alien** (al·ien) (ā′lē·un) *n.* A foreigner; a person from another country. *adj.* Foreign.
    *If **aliens** in the United States neglect to register as aliens, they may be deported to their country of origin.*

12. **alienate** (al·ien·ate) (ā′lē·a·nāté) *v.* To make others unfriendly to one; to estrange (to remove or keep at a distance).
    *The politicians try not to **alienate** any voters.*

## SPECIAL NOTES

1. The word *demagogue* is a little more difficult to define even though you know the meanings of the combining forms. A demagogue is a person who stirs the emotions of people to become a leader and gain selfish ends. A demagogue appeals usually to popular passion, especially by making extravagant promises or charges. The word is used to refer to leaders who use people for their own ends. *Hitler is probably the most hated demagogue of the twentieth century.*

2. The word *autocrat* means "a ruler in absolute control." An autocrat does not have to be a king or a queen. The word *autocracy* means "government by an autocrat." A *monarchy*, which is rule by a monarch, be it a king, queen, or emperor, does not have to be an autocracy; that is, a country can have a king or a queen, but the king or queen does not necessarily have absolute control of the government. The king or queen usually gains his or her position by inheritance and retains it for life.

3. When the combining form *arch* is the final element of a word, it means "rule." When *arch* is used at the beginning of a word (such as *archbishop, archfiend*), it means "chief."

## Step III. Words in Context

Carlos had lived in an **autocracy** all his life. The **monarchy** in which he lived was ruled by a cruel and selfish **autocrat**. The king had supreme power, and no one dared defy him. The people lived in poverty while the king lived in a spectacular palace. Every week the king gave speeches to the people. He would stir up their emotions and make it seem as though he were doing things for them. However, everyone knew that he was doing everything for his own selfish good. The king was a **demagogue**. The people knew this, but they could do nothing. The king had complete control, and everyone was afraid to do anything. Also, the king had the people believing that if he were not in control there would be **anarchy**.

Carlos had heard stories of a country where people were free and ruled the government. The stories said that the people had a form of government called a **democracy**. Carlos dreamed of one day leaving his small country and going there. He felt that it was better to be an **alien** than to live in your own country under such terrible conditions. Carlos talked about his feelings to his friends, but this **alienated** him from them. They were afraid to be seen with him. They told him that he had to stop talking the way he did. Even his family was afraid that Carlos would get them into trouble. They wanted Carlos to change his name, that is, to take an **alias**. Carlos was not an **atheist**, nor did he know much about **theology**. However, he said that he was sure that God would not have wanted them to live the way they did. When people heard this, they said that he did not believe in God. Carlos was **alienated** even more from his friends and family. Centuries ago, this small country had been a **theocracy**, and the people were still very religious. They felt that things were the way they were because God willed it so. Carlos did not feel this way. One day he would show them.

## Step IV. Practice

**A. Directions:**   The words presented in Exercise 5 follow. Match each word with its meaning. Put the letter of the meaning in the space before the word.

Words

_____ 1. theocracy

_____ 2. theology

_____ 3. atheist

_____ 4. alien

_____ 5. alienate

_____ 6. monarchy

_____ 7. autocrat

_____ 8. anarchy

_____ 9. democracy

_____ 10. autocracy

_____ 11. demagogue

_____ 12. alias

Meanings

a.  a person who stirs emotions of people in order to become a leader and achieve selfish ends

b.  a ruler in absolute control

c.  to make others unfriendly to one

d.  another name, usually used by criminals

e.  one who does not believe in God

f.  a government headed by a king, queen, or emperor

g.  the study of religion

h.  a foreigner

i.  the absence of government

j.  a form of government in which one person possesses unlimited power

k.  government of a state by a religious group

l.  a form of government in which there is rule by the people

---

**STOP.**   Check answers at the end of this chapter (p. 83).

---

**B. Directions:**   A number of sentences with missing words follow. Underline the word that *best* fits the sentence. Two choices are given for each sentence.

1. When there are no laws or government, a state of (autocracy, anarchy) usually exists.

2. Huey Long, a former governor of Louisiana, was known to be a(n) (autocrat, demagogue) because he was able to stir persons' emotions to achieve his own selfish ends.

3. In a (monarchy, democracy) there is rule by the people directly or through elected representatives.

4. A monarchy that is also a(n) (theocracy, autocracy) is one in which the ruler has supreme and unlimited power.

5. A country that is headed by a king, a queen, or an emperor is called an absolute (democracy, monarchy) when there are no limitations on the ruler's powers.

6. A person who does not believe in the existence of God is called an (atheist, anarchist).

7. An (atheist, autocrat) is a ruler who has absolute power in his or her government.

8. John used an (autograph, alias) when he didn't want people at the hotel to recognize his famous name.

9. Every year (autocrats, aliens) living in the United States must register as citizens of another country.

10. I never (alienate, describe) anyone on purpose because I don't like to have enemies.

11. In a(n) (autocracy, theocracy) God is recognized as the ruler.

**STOP.**   Check answers at the end of this chapter (p. 83).

**C. Directions:**   Use the combining forms that follow to build a word from this exercise to fit the blank in the sentence.

**Combining Forms**

| | |
|---|---|
| agog | dem |
| ali | mon |
| arch | theo |

1. There are a number of illegal _____ in this country who work for very low wages.

2. The criminal used a(n) _____ instead of his real name.

3. Priests take a number of courses in _____.

4. People who do not believe in the existence of God are called

    _____.

5. A(n) _____ uses his powers of persuasion to make the people feel he is interested in them, even though he isn't.

6. The _____ has supreme control of his government.

7. It is hard to find a _____ today in which a king or queen has real power.

8. After the violent hurricane, there seemed to be _____ throughout the city.

9. In a(n) _____, people exercise their power when they vote.

10. It's sad when children _____ themselves from their parents.

**STOP.**   Check answers at the end of this chapter (p. 84).

# *EXTRA WORD POWER*

**a.** Without; not. *A* is used in front of some words and means "without" or "not." For example: *anarchy*—without rule; *atheist*—one who is without belief in God; *amoral*—without morals, not being able to tell right from wrong. An amoral person does not have a sense of right or wrong. However, an *immoral* person does know the difference between right and wrong, but he or she chooses to do wrong.

## Additional Words Derived from Combining Forms

From your knowledge of combining forms, can you define the following words?

1. **apodal** (ap′o·dal) *adj.* *The snake is an **apodal** animal.*

_____

2. **demography** (de·mog·ra·phy) (de·mog′ra·fē) *n.* *Demographers study the **demography** of a population to determine the trends of vital statistics.*

_____

3. **archetype** (ar·che·type) (ar′ke·tīpe) *n.* *The architect showed an **archetype** of the building to the interested spectators.*

_____

4. **monotone** (mon′o·tōne) *n.* *When a lecturer speaks in a **monotone**, listeners have difficulty paying attention to what is being said.*

_____

5. **monotonous** (mo·not′o·nøus) *adj.* *Doing the same things over and over again is very **monotonous**.*

_____

6. **monorail** (mon′o·rāil) *n.* *When you ride on the **monorail** at Walt Disney World, everything on the ground appears to be so small.*

_____

7. **monophobia** (mon·o·pho·bi·a) (mon·o·fō′bē·a) *n.* *I can't imagine a person who is suffering from **monophobia** living alone in the mountains.*

_____

8. **monoglot** (mon′o·glot) *n. adj.* *There are probably more* **monoglots** *in the United States than in Europe because Europe does not have a single dominant language.*

_____

9. **monopoly** (mo·nop·o·ly) (mo·nop′o·lē) *n.* (*pl.* **ies**). *Because the company had a* **monopoly** *on the grain market, they were able to charge whatever they wanted for grain.*

_____

10. **oligarchy** (ol·i·gar·chy) (ol′i·gar·kē) *n.* (*pl.* **ies**). **Oligarchy,** *as a form of government, usually fails because each of the rulers generally competes with the others to try to gain more power for himself or herself.*

_____

---

**STOP.** Check answers at the end of this chapter (p. 84).

---

## Practice for Additional Words Derived from Combining Forms

**Directions:** Match each word with the *best* definition.

_____ 1. apodal

_____ 2. demography

_____ 3. archetype

_____ 4. monophobia

_____ 5. monoglot

_____ 6. monorail

_____ 7. monotone

_____ 8. monotonous

_____ 9. monopoly

_____ 10. oligarchy

a. cars suspended from a single rail

b. a form of government in which there is rule by a few

c. dull; changeless

d. speech not having any change in pitch

e. being without feet

f. the exclusive control of something

g. the first of its kind; model

h. study of populations

i. the fear of being alone

j. a person who knows only one language

---

**STOP.** Check answers at the end of this chapter (p. 84).

---

# EXERCISE 6

## Step I. Combining Forms

**A. Directions:**    A list of combining forms with their meanings follows. Look at the combining forms and their meanings. Concentrate on learning each combining form and its meaning. Cover the meanings, read the combining forms, and state the meanings to yourself. Check to see if you are correct. Now cover the combining forms, read the meanings, and state the combining forms to yourself. Check to see if you are correct.

| Combining Forms | Meanings |
|---|---|
| 1.  mis, miso[1] | hate; wrong |
| 2.  poly | many |
| 3.  gamy | marriage |
| 4.  hom, homo[1] | same; man; human |
| 5.  gen, geno | race; kind; descent |
| 6.  anthrop, anthropo | man; human; mankind |
| 7.  leg, legis, lex | law |

**B. Directions:**    Do not look at the preceding meanings. Write the meanings of the following combining forms.

| Combining Forms | Meanings |
|---|---|
| 1. mis, miso | _____ |
| 2. poly | _____ |
| 3. gamy | _____ |
| 4. hom, homo | _____ |
| 5. gen, geno | _____ |
| 6. anthrop, anthropo | _____ |
| 7. leg, legis, lex | _____ |

## Step II. Words Derived from Combining Forms

1. **monogamy** (mo·nog·a·my) (mo·nog′a·mē) *n.* Marriage to one spouse at a time.
   *In the United States, **monogamy** is practiced, so you can be married to only one spouse (husband or wife) at a time.*

2. **bigamy** (big·a·my) (big′a·mē) *n.* Marriage to two spouses at the same time.
   *Because **bigamy** is not allowed in the United States, you will not find many persons who are married to two spouses at the same time.*

3. **polygamy** (po·lyg·a·my) (po·lig′a·mē) *n.* Marriage to more than one spouse at the same time; marriage to many spouses at the same time.
   *Because **polygamy** is allowed in some Middle Eastern countries, you will find some persons with many spouses in such countries.*

[1]When words combine with *mis* in this exercise, *mis* means "hate." When words combine with *homo* in this exercise, *homo* means "same." You will meet words with the other meanings for *mis* and *homo* in a later exercise.

4. **anthropology** (an·thro·pol·o·gy) (an·thro·pol′o·jē) *n.* The study of mankind; the study of the cultures and customs of people.
   *In **anthropology** we studied about a tribe of people who had an entirely different way of life from ours.*

5. **misanthrope** (mis′an·thrōpe) *n.* Hater of humankind.
   *Although Jim does not like women, he is not a **misanthrope** because he doesn't hate all people.*

6. **legal** (lē′gal) *adj.* Referring to law; lawful.
   *Although the business deal was **legal**, it did not sound lawful to me.*

7. **legislature** (leg·is·la·ture) (lej′is·lā·chur) *n.* Body of persons responsible for law-making.
   *The **legislature** is the body of persons given the power to write laws for a state or nation.*

8. **homosexual** (ho·mo·sex·u·al) (hō·mo·sek′shū·al) *adj.* Referring to the same sex or to sexual desire for those of the same sex. *n.* A homosexual individual.
   *A **homosexual** is one who prefers a relationship with an individual of the same sex.*

9. **homograph** (hom·o·graph) (hom′o·graf) *n.* A word spelled the same way as another but having a different meaning.
   *The verb* saw *and the noun* saw *are **homographs**.*

10. **homogeneous** (ho·mo·ge·ne·ous) (hō·mo·jē′nē·ŏus) *adj.* Being the same throughout; being uniform.
    *It is difficult to have a **homogeneous** group of students because students are not all the same.*

11. **general** (gen·er·al) (jen′er·al) *adj.* Referring to all. *n.* In the U.S. Army and Air Force, an officer of the same rank as an admiral in the U.S. Navy.
    *The statement "All humans are equal" is a **general** statement.*

12. **generic** (ge·ner·ic) (je·ner′ik) *adj.* Referring to all in a group or class.
    *When one uses the term* you *in the **generic** sense, one is referring to all who are present.*

# SPECIAL NOTES

1. A *homograph* is a word written the same way as another but having a different meaning. *General* and *general* are two words in this exercise that are *homographs* because they are spelled alike but have different meanings.

2. The term *generic* means "general," "referring to all in a group or class." Persons use the word *generic* in order to make their statements more clear. For example: *I am speaking in the **generic** sense when I use the word* mankind *because* mankind *refers to both males and females.* When the word *chairman* is used, it is used in the *generic* sense; that is, a person can be *chairman* and be either a man or a woman. Today the word *chairperson* is used more often because it is more general. The term *humankind* is also often used in place of *mankind*.

3. There are two kinds of polygamy: *polygyny* is the marriage of one man to two or more women at the same time and *polyandry* is the marriage of one woman to two or more men at the same time. (You will meet the combining form *gyn* meaning "woman" in Exercise 11.)

4. Bigamy is unlawful polygamy.

## Step III. Words in Context

In our society the state **legislatures** have passed many laws concerning marriage. For example, they have outlawed the marriage of **homosexuals**, that is, the marriage of people of the same sex. Also, they have outlawed the practice of having more than one spouse at the same time. **Monogamy**, not **bigamy** nor **polygamy**, is legal. Some people joke about the many marriages and divorces of certain well-known people and claim that this is really legalized **polygamy**. However, it isn't. These people do not have many spouses at the same time. Even though **bigamy** is not **legal**, there are some people who do have more than one spouse at the same time. There have been a number of cases where a person has been married to as many as a dozen spouses at the same time.

It's incredible that some of these people were able to get away with it for so long. You certainly can't call such a person a **misanthrope**. The person's problem may be that he or she loves people too much. It is difficult to make a **general** statement about the people who are bigamists. They are not a **homogeneous** group of people. For example, recently there was a case of a polygamist who was married to five women at the same time. When he was asked why he did this, he said that it made him feel good to make others happy. Another example is that of a woman who had studied **anthropology** all her life. She felt that if in other cultures people could have more than one spouse, she could too. She used the word "you" a lot and said that she was speaking in the **generic** sense. She also used **homographs** often. She seemed to be highly educated and verbal. Her husbands obviously found her quite attractive and interesting. When they found out that she was a **polygamist**, they each wanted to stay married to her.

## Step IV. Practice

**A. Directions:**   A number of sentences with missing words follow. Choose the word that best fits the sentence. Put the word in the blank. There are more words in the list than you need.

**Word List**

| | | |
|---|---|---|
| alien | biology | homosexual |
| alienate | centennial | incredible |
| anthropologist | century | legal |
| anthropology | decade | legislative |
| atheist | generic | misanthrope |
| autocracy | geology | misogamist |
| bicentennial | homogeneous | monogamy |
| bigamy | homograph | |

1. Because I am interested in learning about other cultures and the way man lives,

   I studied _____ in college.

2. The term *man* in sentence 1 is used in the _____
   sense because it refers to both men and women.

3. In 1976, America celebrated its _____.

4. It is not _____ to practice _____
   in the United States.

5. In the United States _____ is practiced because
   it's not legal to have more than one spouse at the same time.

6. The terms *spring* meaning "season" and *spring* meaning "to leap" are

   _____s.

7. A person who hates people would be called a(n) _____.

8. We will be entering another _____ in the
   year 2000.

9. The _____ has voted on a number of issues.

10. Margaret Mead, who studied about other people around the world, is known as a

    famous _____.

11. Margaret Mead wrote about the customs of other people, and these may appear

    _____ to people in the Western world.

> **STOP.**   Check answers at the end of this chapter (p. 84).

**B. Directions:**   A list of definitions follows. Choose the word that *best* fits the definition. Try to relate your definition to the meanings of the combining forms. All the words are used. (One word is used twice.)

**Word List**

| | | |
|---|---|---|
| anthropologist | decade | legal |
| anthropology | generic | legislative |
| bicentennial | homogeneous | misanthrope |
| bigamy | homograph | monogamy |
| centennial | homosexual | polygamist |

1. Hater of mankind                              _____

2. One who is married to many spouses
   at the same time                              _____

3. Hundredth anniversary                         _____

4. Being of the same kind                        _____

5. Lawful                                        _____

6. A period of one hundred years                 _____

7. Word spelled the same as another but
   having a different meaning                     _____

8. Every two hundred years                       _____

9. Referring to a relationship with the
   same sex                                      _____

10. The study of mankind or different cul-
    tures                                         _____

11. Marriage to one spouse at a time             _____

12. Referring to all in a group or class         _____

13. Marriage to two spouses at the same
    time                                          _____

14. One who studies different cultures _____

15. Body of persons responsible for law-making _____

16. A period of ten years _____

> **STOP.** Check answers at the end of this chapter (p. 84).

*C. Directions:* Use the combining forms that follow to build a word from this exercise to fit the blank(s) in the sentence.

**Combining Forms**

| | |
|---|---|
| anthrop | leg |
| gamy | mis |
| gen | poly |
| hom | |

1. In the United States _____ rather than

   _____ is practiced.

2. The _____ is responsible for developing the laws of our country.

3. The mass murderer turned out to be a _____, who had lived in seclusion all his life to avoid people.

4. The word *mean* is a _____.

5. In some countries it is _____ for a woman or man to have more than one spouse.

6. Politicians often make very _____ rather than specific statements about most issues.

7. _____ grouping according to ability is practiced in some schools.

8. I am studying _____ because I am interested in learning about the customs of various cultures.

9. It's cheaper to buy _____ brands than name brands because a lot of money isn't spent on advertising.

10. After a man appeared on television claiming that he practiced

    _____, he was arrested because it's against the law to have two spouses at the same time in our country.

> **STOP.** Check answers at the end of this chapter (p. 84).

# *EXTRA WORD POWER*

> **ist.** One who. When *ist* is found at the end of a noun, it means "one who" and changes the word to a certain type of person. For example, let's add *ist* to a number of words you have met: *geologist*—one who is in the field of geology; *biologist*—one who is in the field of biology; *anthropologist*—one who is in the field of anthropology; *theologist*—one who is in the field of theology; *bigamist*—one who is married to two spouses at the same time; *polygamist*—one who is married to more than one spouse at the same time; *monogamist*—one who believes in or practices monogamy; *anarchist*—one who believes that there should be no government. How many more words with *ist* can you add to this list?

## Additional Words Derived from Combining Forms

From your knowledge of combining forms, can you define the following words?

1. **polyglot** (pol·y·glot) (pol′ē·glot) *n. adj.*   *It's helpful for ambassadors to be **polyglots**.*

   _____

2. **polygon** (pol·y·gon) (pol′ē·gon) *n.*   *In geometry I always had difficulty solving problems involving **polygons** because they have so many angles.*

   _____

3. **podiatrist** (po·dī′a·trist) *n.*   *After I went on a ten-mile hike, my feet hurt so much that I needed to visit a **podiatrist**.*

   _____

4. **bisexual** (bi·sex·u·al) (bī·sek′shū·al) *adj. n.*   ***Bisexual** plants can fertilize themselves to reproduce the next generation.*

   _____

5. **misogamist** (mi·sog′a·mist) *n.*   *Although Jim has never married, I do not think he is a **misogamist**.*

   _____

6. **anthropomorphic** (an·thro·po·mor·phic) (an·thro·po·mor′fik) *adj.*   *In Walt Disney films, all of the animals have **anthropomorphic** characteristics.*

   _____

7. **anthropoid** (an′thro·poid) *n. adj.*   *The gorilla, orangutan, and chimpanzee are **anthropoids**.*

   _____

8. **genealogy** (ge·ne·al·o·gy) (jē·nē·al′o·jē) *n.* (*pl.* **ies**)   *Mrs. Smith went to England to acquire certain documents that would help her in tracing the **genealogy** of her family.*

_____

9. **genus (ge·nus)** (jē′nus) *n.* (*pl.* **genera**) (jen′er·a)   *In biology, when plants or animals are classified according to common characteristics, the name of the **genus** begins with a capital letter.*

_____

10. **generate** (gen·er·ate) (jen′er·āt̸e) *v.*   *Every animal **generates** its own species or kind.*

_____

> **STOP.**   Check answers at the end of this chapter (p. 85).

# SPECIAL NOTE

The following cartoon is a good illustration of the term *anthropomorphic.*

"Think about it, Ed. ... The class Insecta contains 26 orders, almost 1,000 families, and over 750,000 described species — but I can't shake the feeling we're all just a bunch of bugs."

THE FAR SIDE. Copyright 1986 Universal Press Syndicate. Reprinted with Permission. All Rights Reserved.

Practice for Additional Words Derived from Combining Forms

**Directions:** Match each word with the best definition.

| | |
|---|---|
| _____ 1. polyglot | a. hater of marriage |
| _____ 2. polygon | b. resembling or suggesting an ape |
| _____ 3. podiatrist | c. speaking many languages |
| _____ 4. bisexual | d. class, kind, or group marked by common characteristics |
| _____ 5. misogamist | e. to produce |
| _____ 6. anthropomorphic | f. foot doctor |
| _____ 7. anthropoid | g. described in human terms |
| _____ 8. genealogy | h. study of one's descent |
| _____ 9. genus | i. a many-sided plane figure |
| _____ 10. generate | j. of both sexes |

> **STOP.** Check answers at the end of this chapter (p. 85).

# CHAPTER WORDS IN SENTENCES

**Directions:** Use the given words to write a sentence that makes sense. Also, try to illustrate the meaning of the words without actually defining the words.

*Example* (demagogue; anarchy) Everyone knew that he was a *demagogue* who was only interested in fulfilling his own selfish desires and that there would be chaos or *anarchy* if he were elected.

1. (reporter; incredible)

   _____

2. (alien; credentials)

   _____

3. (bigamy; legal)

   _____

4. (autocracy; monarchy)

   _____

5. (misanthrope: atheist)

   _____

# CHAPTER WORDS IN A PARAGRAPH

Here is a list of words from this chapter. Write a paragraph using at least 5 of these words. The paragraph must make sense and be logically developed.

**Word List**

| | | |
|---|---|---|
| alias | bigamy | democracy |
| alien | century | million |
| alienate | credible | misanthrope |
| anarchy | credit | monarchy |
| atheist | decade | reporter |
| autocrat | demagogue | |

# ANALOGIES 2

**Directions:** Find the word from the following list that *best* completes each analogy. There are more words in the list than you need.

**Word List**

| | | |
|---|---|---|
| alias | cent | incredible |
| alien | century | millennium |
| alienate | credential | milli |
| anarchy | credit | millimeter |
| anthropoid | creditor | million |
| anthropologist | deca | penny |
| arch | decade | physician |
| archetype | decameter | podiatrist |
| atheist | decimal | polyglot |
| autocracy | decimate | polygon |
| bigamy | export | reporter |

1. Scientist: biologist : : doctor : _____.

2. Mono : poly : : monoglot : _____.

3. Millimeter : centimeter : : meter : _____.

4. Vehicle : automobile : : writer : _____.

5. Pepper : spice : : hexagon : _____.

6. Milli : cent : : cent : _____.

7. Pedestal : base : : foreigner : _____.

8. Two : binary : : ten : _____.

9. Democracy : autocracy : : import : _____.

10. None : universal : : credible : _____.

11. Decade : century : : century : _____.

12. Beautiful : pretty : : obliterate : _____.

13. One : ten : : decade : _____.

14. Conduct : deportment : : disorder : _____.

15. Earth : geology : : man : _____.

16. Genus : kind : : model : _____.

17. Week : fortnight : : monogamy : _____.

18. Same : unique : : debtor : _____.

19. Glasses : spectacles : : separate : _____.

20. Suit : clothing : : degree : _____.

---

**STOP.**  Check answers at the end of this chapter (p. 85).

---

# MULTIPLE-CHOICE VOCABULARY TEST 2

**Directions:**  This is a test on words in Exercises 4–6. Words are presented according to exercises. *Do all exercises before checking answers.* Underline the meaning that *best* fits the word.

## Exercise 4

1. century
   a. a hundredth anniversary
   b. period of one hundred years
   c. period of ten years
   d. period of one thousand years

2. million
   a. one thousand thousands
   b. period of one thousand years
   c. period of one hundred years
   d. period of great happiness

3. millennium
   a. one thousand thousands
   b. period of two thousand years
   c. period of great happiness
   d. a hundredth anniversary

4. centennial
   a. two thousand years
   b. one thousand thousands
   c. one thousand years
   d. a hundredth anniversary

5. decade
   a. period of ten years
   b. one hundred years
   c. twenty years
   d. one thousand years

6. bicentennial
   a. one thousand years
   b. a two-hundredth anniversary
   c. one hundred years
   d. period of great happiness

7. credible
   a. good faith
   b. a balance
   c. good name
   d. believable

8. incredible
   a. believable
   b. not faithful
   c. not a good reputation
   d. not believable

9. porter
   a. a person who gathers information
   b. something that can be carried
   c. one who carries things
   d. place for ships

10. port
    a. to carry out
    b. to carry in
    c. place where ships may wait
    d. able to be carried

11. import
    a. able to be carried
    b. place where ships wait
    c. to carry out goods
    d. to carry in goods from other areas or countries

12. export
    a. carry in goods
    b. carry out goods to other areas or countries
    c. able to be carried
    d. one who carries things

13. reporter
    a. person who carries things
    b. able to be carried
    c. place where ships wait
    d. person who gathers information for newspapers

14. portable
    a. carry in goods
    b. able to be carried
    c. carry out goods
    d. one who carries things

15. credit
    a. balance in one's favor in an account
    b. owe money
    c. believable
    d. something that gives someone authority

16. credential
    a. good name
    b. owe money
    c. something that entitles someone to credit or confidence
    d. believable

## Exercise 5

17. monarchy
    a. rule by many
    b. rule by a few
    c. rule by king, queen, or emperor
    d. absolute rule

18. autocracy
    a. absolute rule by one
    b. a country headed by a king
    c. rule by a few
    d. no rule

19. autocrat
    a. one who does not believe in rule
    b. absolute ruler
    c. ruler who shares power
    d. one who does not believe in God

20. anarchy
    a. without belief in God
    b. no rule
    c. absolute rule
    d. rule by one

21. atheist
    a. one who believes in no rule
    b. one who believes in absolute rule
    c. one who believes in rule by a religious group
    d. one who does not believe in God

22. theocracy
    a. belief in God
    b. rule by a religious group
    c. the study of religion
    d. absolute rule

23. theology
    a. rule by a religious group
    b. belief in God
    c. absolute rule
    d. the study of religion

24. democracy
    a. absolute rule
    b. leader who influences persons for his own purposes
    c. rule by the people
    d. the study of people

25. demagogue
    a. ruler of people
    b. rule by the people
    c. leader who influences persons for his own purposes
    d. leader of people

26. alias
    a. a foreigner
    b. unfriendly
    c. another name
    d. turns people away

27. alien
    a. another name
    b. a foreigner
    c. turns people away
    d. unfriendly

28. alienate
    a. make others unfriendly
    b. a foreigner
    c. another name
    d. makes friends

## Exercise 6

29. monogamy
    a. hater of marriage
    b. no belief in marriage
    c. marriage to one spouse at a time
    d. the study of marriage

30. bigamy
    a. something not lawful
    b. marriage to two spouses at the same time
    c. having been married twice
    d. marriage to one spouse at a time

31. polygamy
    a. marriage to many spouses at one time
    b. many marriages
    c. something not legal
    d. the study of many marriages

32. misanthrope
    a. hater of marriage
    b. married to a man
    c. hater of mankind
    d. the study of mankind

33. anthropology
    a. marriage to men
    b. the study of mankind
    c. a science
    d. hater of mankind

34. legal
    a. person responsible for law
    b. body of persons responsible for lawmaking
    c. lawful
    d. a person who defends others

35. legislature
    a. lawful
    b. person responsible for laws
    c. body of persons responsible for lawmaking
    d. persons who defend others

36. homosexual
    a. same kind
    b. referring to man
    c. one who prefers relationships with the same sex
    d. one who prefers relationships with the opposite sex

37. homogeneous
    a. being of the same kind
    b. the same sex
    c. referring to man
    d. one who prefers relationships with the same sex

38. homograph
    a. the study of man
    b. the study of graphs
    c. the same word
    d. a word spelled the same as another but having a different meaning

39. general
    a. referring to the same
    b. referring to all
    c. referring to a group of people
    d. referring to kinds of people

40. generic
    a. referring to all in a group or class
    b. referring to people
    c. referring to a group
    d. referring to generals in the army

# TRUE/FALSE TEST 2

**Directions:** This is a true/false test on Exercises 4–6. Read each sentence carefully. Decide whether it is true or false. Put a *T* for *true* or an *F* for *false* in the blank. If the answer is false, change a word or part of the sentence to make it true. The number after the sentence tells you if the word is from Exercise 4, 5, or 6.

_____ 1. One who hates mankind is called a misanthrope. 6

_____ 2. A misogamist must also be a misanthrope. 6

_____ 3. Ten hundred thousand equals one million. 4

_____ 4. Ten decades do not equal a century. 4

_____ 5. An anthropologist is interested in studying ants. 6

_____ 6. An atheist believes in God. 5

_____ 7. A bachelor must be a misogamist. 6

_____ 8. When you import something, you send it out of the country. 4.

_____ 9. A centennial celebration takes place every one thousand years. 4

_____ 10. If you have a good credit rating, you have a good financial reputation. 4

_____ 11. Your credentials are what you have that makes people believe you can do a certain job. 4

_____ 12. An autocrat is a ruler in a democracy. 5

_____ 13. An anarchist is one who believes in no government. 5, 6

_____ 14. An anarchist must be an atheist. 5, 6

_____ 15. A demagogue uses people for his or her own selfish ends. 5

_____ 16. An alien is someone who enters another country not legally. 5, 6

_____ 17. When you use an alias, you are using your given name. 5

_____ 18. *Saw* (the past tense of *to see*) and *saw* (something that you cut with) are examples of homographs. 6

_____ 19. Persons with homogeneous tastes are persons who must like men. 6

_____ 20. In the word *mankind*, "man" is used in the generic sense because it refers to both men and women. 6

_____ 21. Someone who commits bigamy may be jailed because this is not legal in the United States. 6

_____ 22. The legislature is responsible for making laws for the state or federal government. 6

**STOP.** Check answers for both tests at the end of this chapter (pp. 85–86).

# SCORING OF TESTS

| MULTIPLE-CHOICE VOCABULARY TEST | | TRUE/FALSE TEST* | |
|---|---|---|---|
| Number Wrong | Score | Number Wrong | Score |
| 0-3 | Excellent | 0-1 | Excellent |
| 4-6 | Good | 2-3 | Good |
| 7-9 | Weak | 4-5 | Weak |
| Above 9 | Poor | Above 5 | Poor |
| Score _____ | | Score _____ | |

1. If you scored in the excellent or good range on *both tests*, you are doing well. Go on to Chapter Four.

2. If you scored in the weak or poor range on either test, look below and follow directions for Additional Practice. Note that the words on the test are arranged so that you can tell in which exercise to find them. This will help you if you need additional practice.

# ADDITIONAL PRACTICE SETS

**A. Directions:**   Write the words you missed on the tests from the three exercises in the space provided. Note that the tests are presented so that you can tell to which exercises the words belong.

Exercise 4 Words Missed

1. _____    6. _____
2. _____    7. _____
3. _____    8. _____
4. _____    9. _____
5. _____    10. _____

Exercise 5 Words Missed

1. _____    6. _____
2. _____    7. _____
3. _____    8. _____
4. _____    9. _____
5. _____    10. _____

*When the answer is false, you must get both parts of the true/false question correct in order to receive credit.

Exercise 6 Words Missed

1. _____    6. _____

2. _____    7. _____

3. _____    8. _____

4. _____    9. _____

5. _____   10. _____

**B. Directions:**   Restudy the missed words from the three exercises. Study the combining forms from which those words are derived. Do Step I and Step II for those you missed. Note that Step I and Step II of the combining forms and vocabulary derived from these combining forms are on the following pages:

Exercise 4—pp. 47–49

Exercise 5—pp. 55–57

Exercise 6—pp. 62–63

**C. Directions:**   Do Additional Practice 1 below if you missed words from Exercise 4. Do Additional Practice 2 on pp. 80–81 if you missed words from Exercise 5. Do Addition Practice 3 on pp. 81–82 if you missed words from Exercise 6. Now go on to Chapter Four.

# Additional Practice 1 for Exercise 4

**A. Directions:**   The combining forms presented in Exercise 4 follow. Match each combining form with its meaning.

_____ 1. cent, centi         a.  carry

_____ 2. dec, deca           b.  hundred; hundredth part

_____ 3. milli               c.  believe

_____ 4. port                d.  thousand; thousandth part

_____ 5. cred                e.  ten

---

**STOP.**   Check answers at the end of this chapter (p. 86).

**B. Directions:**   Sentences containing the meanings of vocabulary presented in Exercise 4 follow. Choose the word that best fits the meaning of the word or phrase underlined in the sentence.

**Word List**

| | | |
|---|---|---|
| bicentennial | decade | million |
| centennial | export | port |
| century | imports | portable |
| credentials | incredible | porter |
| credible | millennium | reporter |
| credits | | |

1. It is <u>not believable</u> that you are able to do all that. _____

2. In a <u>period of one hundred years</u> many changes have taken place in the United States. _____

3. What do you call <u>the place where a ship waits</u>? _____

4. <u>The one-hundredth anniversary</u> of the first spaceship's landing on the moon will be in 2069. _____

5. When complete peace comes to earth, <u>a period of great happiness</u> will exist.

   _____

6. That is a <u>believable</u> statement. _____

7. How many <u>academic units</u> have you earned toward your degree?

   _____

8. <u>One thousand thousands</u> is a large number. _____

9. The man's <u>college degree</u>, as well as his <u>work experiences</u>, helped him to get the job. _____

10. <u>The person who carried my baggage</u> was very strong. _____

11. My television set is on a table that <u>can be moved very easily</u> to any part of the room. _____

12. She is a <u>person who gathers information and writes articles</u> for the magazine.

    _____

13. When will you <u>take the goods out of the country</u>? _____

14. The year 1976 was <u>the two-hundredth anniversary</u> of the United States.

    _____

15. Every year the United States <u>brings into the country</u> many goods made by foreign countries. _____

16. In a ten-year period clothing styles may change from one extreme to

    another. _____

---

**STOP.** Check answers at the end of this chapter (p. 86).

---

## Additional Practice 2 for Exercise 5

**A. Directions:**    The combining forms presented in Exercise 5 follow. Match each combining form with its meaning.

| | | |
|---|---|---|
| _____ | 1. agog, agogue | a. rule; chief |
| _____ | 2. arch | b. other |
| _____ | 3. ali | c. God |
| _____ | 4. dem, demo | d. leading, directing; inciting |
| _____ | 5. mon, mono | e. people |
| _____ | 6. theo | f. one |

---

**STOP.** Check answers at the end of this chapter (p. 87).

---

**B. Directions:**    A number of sentences with missing words follow. Fill in the blank with the word that *best* fits.

**Word List**

| | | |
|---|---|---|
| alias | atheist | democracy |
| alien | autocracy | monarchy |
| alienate | autocrat | theocracy |
| anarchy | demagogue | theology |

1. You will _____ a lot of people by the way you are acting.

2. As I did not want to be recognized when I traveled, I wore a disguise and used a(n) _____.

3. A(n) _____ is a person who belongs to another country.

4. In a(n) _____ a king or queen may be at the head of government but not necessarily have any power.

5. A(n) _____ has absolute power in his country.

6. I would not like to live in a(n) _____ because one does not have any freedom to disagree with the ruler.

7. In our _____ all persons over eighteen except felons have the right to vote, and the government is ruled by the people through elected representatives.

8. In a state of _____ there is confusion because there are no laws.

9. A(n) _____ would not be a churchgoer because he or she does not believe in the existence of God.

10. _____ does not exist any more, as it did in the Middle Ages, when the Church ruled a large part of Europe.

11. People who study _____ are interested in religion.

12. Hitler is a good example of a(n) _____ because he could stir persons' emotions and get them to do what he wanted.

---

**STOP.** Check answers at the end of this chapter (p. 87).

---

# Additional Practice 3 for Exercise 6

**A. Directions:** The combining forms presented in Exercise 6 follow. Match each combining form with its meaning.

| | | | |
|---|---|---|---|
| _____ | 1. mis, miso | a. | law |
| _____ | 2. poly | b. | many |
| _____ | 3. gamy | c. | kind; race, descent |
| _____ | 4. hom, homo | d. | marriage |
| _____ | 5. gen, geno | e. | hate; wrong |
| _____ | 6. anthrop, anthropo | f. | man; human; mankind |
| _____ | 7. leg, legis, lex | g. | same; man; human |

---

**STOP.** Check answers at the end of this chapter (p. 87).

**B. Directions:** The words presented in Exercise 6 follow. Match each word with its meaning.

_____ 1. hater of mankind

_____ 2. a high-ranking office in the army; refer-ring to all

_____ 3. marriage to many spouses at the same time

_____ 4. marriage to one spouse at a time

_____ 5. one who is married to two spouses at the same time

_____ 6. referring to all in a group or class

_____ 7. being of the same kind

_____ 8. lawful

_____ 9. body of persons who make laws

_____ 10. referring to sexual desire for the same sex

_____ 11. the study of mankind

_____ 12. a word spelled in the same way as another but having a different meaning

a. homograph

b. bigamist

c. monogamy

d. legislature

e. legal

f. homogeneous

g. misanthrope

h. homosexual

i. generic

j. anthropology

k. general

l. polygamy

---

**STOP.** Check answers at the end of this chapter (p. 87).

---

# ANSWERS: *Chapter Three*

## Exercise 4 (pp. 47–55)

Practice A

(1) b, (2) d, (3) c, (4) a, (5) d, (6) b, (7) b, (8) c, (9) d, (10) b, (11) c, (12) d, (13) a, (14) a, (15) b, (16) d.

## Practice B

(1) reporter, (2) decade, (3) credential, (4) incredible, (5) million, (6) credit, (7) incredible, (8) credential, (9) credible, (10) credential, (11) portable, (12) port, (13) export, (14) import, (15) million.

## Practice C

(1) century, (2) exports, (3) import, (4) reporter, (5) credit, (6) million, (7) millimeters, (8) decade, (9) millennium, (10) credible.

## Additional Words Derived from Combining Forms (pp. 53–54)

1. **decimal.**  Numbered by tens; based on 10; pertaining to tenths or the number 10; a decimal fraction.
2. **decimate.**  To take or destroy a tenth part of; to destroy but not completely; to destroy a great number or proportion of.
3. **decameter.**  In the metric system, a measure of length containing 10 meters, equal to 393.70 inches or 32.81 feet.
4. **decimeter.**  In the metric system, a unit of length equal to 1/10 meter.
5. **millimeter.**  In the metric system, a unit of length equal to 1/1,000 meter (0.03937 inch).
6. **centimeter.**  In the metric system, a unit of measure equal to 1/100 meter (0.3937 inch).
7. **kilometer.**  In the metric system, a unit of length equal to 1,000 meters.
8. **centipede.**  Wormlike animal with many legs.
9. **creed.**  A statement of religious belief; a statement of belief, principles.
10. **accreditation.**  The act of bringing into favor; a vouching for; a giving authority to.
11. **creditor.**  One to whom a sum of money or other thing is due.
12. **deportment.**  The manner of conducting or carrying oneself; behavior; conduct.

## Practice for Additional Words Derived from Combining Forms (p. 55)

(1) i, (2) g, (3) h, (4) f, (5) d, (6) e, (7) j, (8) a, (9) b, (10) c, (11) l, (12) k.

# Exercise 5 (pp. 55–61)

## Practice A

(1) k, (2) g, (3) e, (4) h, (5) c, (6) f, (7) b, (8) i, (9) l, (10) j, (11) a, (12) d.

## Practice B

(1) anarchy, (2) demagogue, (3) democracy, (4) autocracy, (5) monarchy, (6) atheist, (7) autocrat, (8) alias, (9) aliens, (10) alienate (11) theocracy.

Practice C

(1) aliens, (2) alias, (3) theology, (4) atheists, (5) demagogue, (6) autocrat, (7) monarchy, (8) anarchy, (9) democracy, (10) alienate.

## Additional Words Derived from Combining Forms (pp. 60–61)

1. **apodal.** Having no feet.
2. **demography.** The statistical study of human populations, including births, deaths, marriages, population movements, and so on.
3. **archetype.** The original pattern or model of a work from which something is made or developed.
4. **monotone.** A single unchanging tone; speech not having any change in pitch; to speak in an unvaried tone.
5. **monotonous.** Changeless; having no variety; uniform; dull.
6. **monorail.** A single rail serving as a track for trucks or cars suspended from it or balanced on it.
7. **monophobia.** An abnormal fear of being alone.
8. **monoglot.** A person who knows, speaks, or writes only one language; speaking or writing only one language.
9. **monopoly.** Exclusive control of a commodity or service in a given market; control that makes possible the fixing of prices and the elimination of free competition.
10. **oligarchy.** A form of government in which there is rule by a few (usually a privileged few).

## Practice for Additional Words Derived from Combining Forms (p. 61)

(1) e, (2) h, (3) g, (4) i, (5) j, (6) a, (7) d, (8) c, (9) f, (10) b.

# Exercise 6 (pp. 62–69)

Practice A

(1) anthropology, (2) generic, (3) bicentennial, (4) legal, bigamy, (5) monogamy, (6) homograph, (7) misanthrope, (8) century, (9) legislature, (10) anthropologist, (11) incredible.

Practice B

(1) misanthrope, (2) polygamist, (3) centennial, (4) homogeneous, (5) legal, (6) century, (7) homograph, (8) bicentennial, (9) homosexual, (10) anthropology, (11) monogamy, (12) generic, (13) bigamy, (14) anthropologist, (15) legislature, (16) decade.

Practice C

(1) monogamy; bigamy or polygamy, (2) legislature, (3) misanthrope, (4) homograph, (5) legal, (6) general, (7) Homogeneous, (8) anthropology, (9) generic, (10) bigamy or polygamy.

Additional Words Derived from Combining Forms (pp. 67–68)

1. **polyglot.** A person who knows, speaks, or writes several languages; speaking or writing many languages.

2. **polygon.** A closed plane figure with several angles and sides.

3. **podiatrist.** Foot doctor.

4. **bisexual.** Of both sexes; having both male and female organs, as is true of some plants and animals; a person who is sexually attracted by both sexes.

5. **misogamist.** Hater of marriage.

6. **anthropomorphic.** Giving human shape or characteristics to gods, objects, animals, and so on.

7. **anthropoid.** A person resembling an ape either in stature, walk, or intellect; resembling man—used especially of apes such as the gorilla, chimpanzee, and orangutan; resembling or suggesting an ape.

8. **genealogy.** The science or study of one's descent; a tracing of one's ancestors.

9. **genus.** A class, kind, or group marked by shared characteristics or by one shared characteristic.

10. **generate.** To produce; to cause to be; to bring into existence.

Practice for Additional Words Derived from Combining Forms (p. 69)

(1) c, (2) i, (3) f, (4) j, (5) a, (6) g, (7) b, (8) h, (9) d, (10) e.

# Chapter Words in Sentences (p. 69)

Sentences will vary.

# Chapter Words in a Paragraph (p. 70)

Paragraphs will vary.

# Analogies 2 (pp. 70–71)

(1) podiatrist, (2) polyglot, (3) decameter, (4) reporter, (5) polygon, (6) deca, (7) alien, (8) decimal (9) export, (10) incredible, (11) millennium, (12) decimate, (13) century, (14) anarchy, (15) anthropology (16) archetype, (17) bigamy, (18) creditor, (19) alienate, (20) credential.

# Multiple-Choice Vocabulary Test 2 (pp. 71–75)

Exercise 4

(1) b, (2) a, (3) c, (4) d, (5) a, (6) b, (7) d, (8) d, (9) c, (10) c, (11) d, (12) b, (13) d, (14) b, (15) a, (16) c.

Exercise 5

(17) c, (18) a, (19) b, (20) b, (21) d, (22) b, (23) d, (24) c, (25) c, (26) c, (27) b, (28) a.

Exercise 6

(29) c, (30) b, (31) a, (32) c, (33) b,[2] (34) c, (35) c, (36) c, (37) a, (38) d, (39) b, (40) a.

## True/False Test 2[3] (p. 76)

(1) T; (2) F,[4] <u>must also be</u> to <u>does not have to be</u>; (3) T[5]; (4) F, <u>do not</u> to <u>do</u>; (5) F, <u>ants</u> to <u>the culture and customs of people</u>; (6) F, <u>believes</u> to <u>does not believe</u>; (7) F,[6] <u>must be</u> to <u>does not have to be</u>; (8) F, <u>import</u> to <u>export</u> or <u>send it out of the country</u> to <u>bring it into the country</u>; (9) F, <u>thousand</u> to <u>hundred</u>; (10) T; (11) T; (12) F, <u>a democracy</u> to <u>an autocracy</u>; (13) T; (14) F,[7] <u>must</u> to <u>need not</u>; (15) T; (16) F,[8] <u>enters another country not legally</u> to <u>comes from another country</u>; (17) F, <u>your given name</u> to <u>another name</u>; (18) T; (19) F, <u>persons who must like men</u> to <u>persons who have similar tastes</u>; (20) T; (21) T; (22) T.

---

**STOP.**    Turn to page 77 for the scoring of the tests.

---

## Additional Practice Sets (pp. 77–82)

Additional Practice 1

A. (1) b, (2) e, (3) d, (4) a, (5) c.
B. (1) incredible, (2) century, (3) port, (4) centennial, (5) millennium, (6) credible, (7) credits, (8) million, (9) credentials, (10) porter, (11) portable, (12) reporter, (13) export, (14) bicentennial, (15) imports, (16) decade.

---

[2]Although anthropology is a science, the better answer is *study of mankind*, which describes what kind of science anthropology is and gives more information.

[3]Answers for false are suggested answers.

[4]Even if someone hates marriage, it does not mean that he or she must also hate people.

[5]Ten times 100 equals 1,000. One thousand thousands equals 1 million.

[6]Not necessarily.

[7]Not so. Persons who believe in no government rule *may* believe in God.

[8]An *alien* is a foreigner. He or she can legally come to this or any other country. Although there are aliens who enter a country illegally, this is not part of the definition of alien.

Additional Practice 2

A. (1) d, (2) a, (3) b, (4) e, (5) f, (6) c.
B. (1) alienate, (2) alias, (3) alien, (4) monarchy, (5) autocrat, (6) autocracy,
(7) democracy, (8) anarchy, (9) atheist, (10) Theocracy, (11) theology, (12) demagogue.

Additional Practice 3

A. (1) e, (2) b, (3) d, (4) g, (5) c, (6) f, (7) a.
B. (1) g, (2) k, (3) l, (4) c, (5) b, (6) i, (7) f, (8) e, (9) d, (10) h, (11) j, (12) a.

# CHAPTER FOUR

# EXERCISE 7

## Step I. Combining Forms

**A. Directions:** A list of combining forms with their meanings follows. Look at the combining forms and their meanings. Concentrate on learning each combining form and its meaning. Cover the meanings, read the combining forms, and state the meanings to yourself. Check to see if you are correct. Now cover the combining forms, read the meanings, and state the combining forms to yourself. Check to see if you are correct.

| Combining Forms | Meanings |
| --- | --- |
| 1. vid, vis | see |
| 2. sci, scio | know |
| 3. poten | powerful |
| 4. omni | all |
| 5. aqua, aqui | water |
| 6. astro | star |
| 7. naut | sailor |
| 8. ven, veni, vent | come |

***B. Directions:***   Do not look at the preceding meanings. Write the meanings of the following combining forms.

Combining Forms                                    Meanings

  1. vid, vis          _____

  2. sci, scio         _____

  3. poten             _____

  4. omni              _____

  5. aqua, aqui        _____

  6. astro             _____

  7. naut              _____

  8. ven, veni, vent    _____

*"I don't listen to the evidence. I like to make up my own mind."*

Drawing by P. Barlow; © 1954, 1982 The New Yorker Magazine, Inc.

## Step II. Words Derived from Combining Forms

  1. **vision** (vi·sion) (vizh′un) *n.* The sense of sight.
     *Because the man's **vision** was blocked by the screen, he could not see what the spectators were looking at.*

  2. **visible** (vis·i·ble) (viz′i·bul) *adj.* Able to be seen; evident; apparent; on hand.
     *On a clear day the skyline of the city is **visible**.*

  3. **invisible** (in·vis·i·ble) (in·viz′i·bul) *adj.* Not able to be seen.
     *In the film, the **invisible** man was able to appear in many prohibited places because no one was able to see him.*

4. **television** (tel·e·vi·sion) (tel'e·vizh'un) *n.* An electronic system for the transmission of visual images from a distance; a television receiving set.

   *Television is viewed by so many people all over the country that sponsors pay millions of dollars to advertise their products on it.*

5. **provision** (pro·vi·sion) (pro·vizh'un) *n.* The act of being prepared beforehand; preparation; something made ready in advance. *pl.* **provisions:** needed materials, especially a supply of food for future needs; a part of an agreement referring to a specific thing.

   *The army was running out of **provisions**, and the men were beginning to complain that they did not have enough supplies to carry on their operations.*

6. **evident** (ev'i·dent) *adj.* Obvious; clearly seen; plain.

   *From everything that you have said, it is **evident** that he is lying about where he was on the night of the murder.*

7. **evidence** (ev'i·dence) (ev'i·densé) *n.* That which serves to prove or disprove something.

   *The **evidence** was so strong against the defendant that it didn't seem possible that he could prove his innocence.*

8. **science** (sci·ence) (scī'ensé ) *n.* Any area of knowledge in which the facts have been investigated and presented in an orderly manner.

   *New **sciences** develop as we learn more and more about the universe.*

9. **astrology** (as·trol·o·gy) (a·strol'o·jē) *n.* The art or practice that claims to tell the future and interpret the influence of the heavenly bodies on the fate of people; a reading of the stars.

   *There are a large number of people who believe in **astrology's** ability to predict their futures.*

10. **astronomy** (as·tron·o·my) (a·stron'o·mē) *n.* The science that deals with stars, planets, and space.

    *When I studied **astronomy**, I used a very high-powered telescope to view the stars and planets.*

11. **astronaut** (as'tro·naut) *n.* One who travels in space, that is, beyond the earth's atmosphere; a person trained to travel in outer space.

    *The Apollo **astronauts** shook hands with the Russian **astronauts** in space during a special space flight in 1975.*

12. **aquanaut** (aq·ua·naut) (ak'wa·naut) *n.* One who travels undersea; a person trained to work in an underwater chamber.

    *Jacques Cousteau has many **aquanauts** on his team who explore the wonders under the seas.*

13. **aquatic** (a·quat·ic) (a·kwat'ik) *adj.* Living or growing in or near water; performed on or in water.

    *The best swimmers performed in our **aquatic** ballet.*

14. **aquarium** (a·quar·i·um) (a·kwar'ē·um) *n.* A pond, a glass bowl, a tank, or the like, in which aquatic animals and/or plants are kept; a place in which aquatic collections are shown.

    *The aquatic plants and animals in my **aquarium** are specially chosen to make sure that they can live together.*

15. **convene** (con·vene) (kon·vēné') *v.* To come together, to assemble.

    *The assemblymen were waiting for everyone to arrive so that they could **convene** for their first meeting of the year.*

16. **convention** (con·ven·tion) (kon·ven'shun) *n.* A formal meeting of members for political or professional purposes; accepted custom, rule, or opinion.
    *The teachers hold their **convention** annually to exchange professional views and learn about new things.*

17. **convenient** (con·ven·ient) (kon·vēn'yent) *adj.* Well suited to one's purpose, personal comfort, or ease; handy.
    *The professional and political conventions are held in cities that have **convenient** hotels and halls to take care of a great number of people.*

18. **potent** (po·tent) (pōt'ént) *adj.* Physically powerful; having great authority; able to influence; strong in chemical effects.
    *The drug was so **potent** that it actually knocked out John, who is over 6 feet tall and weighs almost 200 pounds.*

19. **impotent** (im'po·tent) *adj.* Without power to act; physically weak; incapable of sexual intercourse (said of males).
    *The monarch in England is politically **impotent** because he or she has hardly any power in the governing of the country.*

20. **potential** (po·ten·tial) (po·ten'shul) *n.* The possible ability or power one has. *adj.* Having force or power to develop.
    *The acorn has the **potential** to become a tree.*

21. **omnipresent** (om·ni·pres·ent) (om·ni·prez'ent) *adj.* Being present everywhere at all times.
    *The **omnipresent** toothpaste commercial was annoying because it seemed to be on all the channels at the same time.*

## SPECIAL NOTES

1. When the term *potential* is used, it refers to "possible ability." This means that potential is something that a person may have within him or her, but it may or may not necessarily come out. The following cartoon illustrates this idea very nicely.

   Understanding the Term *Potential*

   © 1959 United Feature Syndicate, Inc.

2. *Astrology* is concerned with the reading of the stars. Astrologists use the stars to try to predict the future. Do not confuse astrology, which is a false science, with astronomy, which is a science that deals with the study of stars, planets, and space.

## Step III. Words in Context

There is an incredible show on **television** that is helping the police catch criminals. Last week it featured a person who uses **astrology** to help police find needed **evidence** and wanted criminals. The astrologist, who reads the stars to forecast events, seems to have some special **vision**. She has helped **astronauts** in trouble in space and **aquanauts** having difficulty undersea. She is often called in when the police feel **impotent**. **Science** does not have an explanation as to why she has the **potential** to do things that the police can't. The police call her their most **potent** weapon. Many people feel she is a quack, but it is **evident** that she does have the **potential** to find escaped or wanted criminals better than others. It is difficult to **convene** any meeting dealing with crime, unless **provisions** have been made to have her as one of the speakers. She gives talks at numerous **conventions** and is seen often on **television**. You can see her at a time **convenient** for you because she is **omnipresent**. This astrologist has also taken a number of **astronomy** courses to study the stars, planets, and space. She feels that this has helped her. She says also that she has always had an interest in **aquatic** animals. She claims that her large **aquarium** filled with exotic fish helps calm her and sharpen her concentration. She learned certain secrets as a young child and can actually make things appear **visible** or **invisible** at will. The police feel fortunate that she is on their side.

## Step IV. Practice

**A. Directions:** A number of sentences with missing words follow. Choose the word that *best* fits the sentence. Put the word in the blank. There are more words in the list than you need.

**Word List**

| | | |
|---|---|---|
| aquanaut | convenient | potent |
| aquarium | convention | potential |
| aquatic | evidence | provision |
| astrology | evident | science |
| astronaut | impotent | scientist |
| astronomy | invisible | television |
| convene | omnipresent | vision |

1. All _____s must be in top physical shape in order to travel in space.

2. If you love swimming and diving and you're very interested in sea life, you may want to be a(n) _____.

3. You find _____ plants in the ocean.

4. Some poisons are so _____ that a one-quarter teaspoon dose will kill you.

5. One of the fish in my _____ grew at an incredible rate.

6. The fortune-teller used her knowledge of _____ to predict my future.

7. I want to study _____ in college because I enjoy learning about stars and planets.

8. Because the stop sign was not clearly _____, the driver went right past it.

9. Have you made any special _____s for
   yourself for when you retire?

10. Although he is the head of government, he is politically _____
    because he has no say in anything.

11. The district attorney must have some _____
    to support his case before he can try to prove the guilt of someone.

12. Astronomy, biology, and geology are all _____s.

13. _____s are formal meetings, which are usually
    held annually.

14. With your good _____, you should be able to see
    the board from where you're sitting.

15. The _____ warriors seemed to be everywhere.

16. If that time is not _____ for you, we'll change it
    for a better one.

17. It is difficult to talk about John's ability level, for we do not know what his

    _____ is.

18. The judge said that the court would _____ in one
    hour to continue the trial.

---

> **STOP.**  Check answers at the end of this chapter (p. 139.)

---

**B. Directions:**  A few paragraphs with missing words follow. Fill the blanks with the
words that *best* fit. Words may be used more than once.

**Word List**

| | | |
|---|---|---|
| anniversary | decade | omnipresent |
| aquanauts | evidence | provision |
| aquatic | evident | reporter |
| astrologist | impotent | scientists |
| astronauts | incredible | television |
| convenient | invisible | visible |
| convention | | |

As a(n) **1**_____ I get to investigate and write stories. I especially remember one story I wrote about a(n) **2**_____ ago. I
remember it was ten years ago because my wife and I were celebrating our first

wedding **3**_____ with a special dinner, when the phone rang.
It was my boss. His excitement was clearly **4**_____. "Joe, did
you see what just happened on **5**_____?" he asked. "No, we
didn't have the **6**_____ . . ." Before I could finish answering, he
said, "Well, get down here immediately. I want you to cover a special story that just
broke." Although it was not a(n) **7**_____ time for me, I went to
meet him.

It seemed that a group of well-known **8**_____, such as
biologists, geologists, astronomists, and so on, were meeting at a national
**9**_____ held in our city. At the **10**_____
there were exhibits of materials that **11**_____ had brought back
from space. There were also special **12**_____ plants that
**13**_____ had found underseas.

At about ten in the morning, a woman phoned the editor in the newspaper office.
She said she was a(n) **14**_____ who could foretell the future.
She told the editor to watch the **15**_____ exhibits that were
being shown on **16**_____ to people all over the country. She
knew that something **17**_____ was going to take place shortly
and that it would be **18**_____ to all who were watching. The
editor felt that from the way the woman was talking it was **19**_____
she was a "crackpot." He receives so many calls from people telling about things that
would happen that never did. There are so many crackpots around that they seem to
be **20**_____.

Well, at eight that night, in plain view of all who had their
**21**_____s tuned to the channel covering the exhibits, a(n)
**22**_____ robbery took place. The people watching the robbery
must have felt **23**_____ because they had no power to do anything about it.

Persons dressed as **24**_____ who were going on a space
flight and **25**_____ who were going to explore the ocean, stole
the priceless materials on display.

Nobody could figure out how they got into the special room. It was as if they
were **26**_____, and at the proper moment they materialized and
became **27**_____ for all to see. They seemed to have had all the
**28**_____s they needed to carry out the robbery. The crime was
so well planned that no **29**_____ as to who they were or why
they did it has ever been found.

**STOP.**  Check answers at the end of this chapter (pp. 139–140).

**C. Directions:** Use the combining forms that follow to build a word from this exercise to fit the blank(s) in the sentence. A word may be used once only.

Combining Forms

| | |
|---|---|
| aqua | sci |
| astro | ven |
| naut | vid |
| omni | vis |
| poten | |

1. Mr. Jackson, who is 84 years old, is still driving his car even though he has extremely poor _____.

2. People from all across the country joined in to send _____ to the flood victims.

3. The _____ would remain for a week in an underwater chamber.

4. The detectives said that they did not have enough _____ to hold the suspect.

5. The witness to the crime said that it wasn't _____ for her to come to the district attorney's office then.

6. It is _____ from what the person said that he is quite biased.

7. The mayor knew that he had made many _____ enemies in the election, which would eventually hurt him.

8. The _____ commercial, which was on every channel, was beginning to get annoying.

9. It's difficult for young people to realize their _____ if they come from an educationally deprived area.

10. The rioters were in control, and the leaders were completely _____.

---

**STOP.** Check answers at the end of this chapter (p. 140).

# EXTRA WORD POWER

**less.** Without. When *less* is placed at the end of a word, it means "without." *Less* changes a noun into an adjective. For example: the word *mother* becomes *motherless*—without a mother; *father* becomes *fatherless*—without a father; *blame* becomes *blameless*—without blame or without fault; *harm* becomes *harmless*—without harm or without hurting. For example: *How lucky you are that you have both a mother and a father. Mary is a **motherless** child.* How many more words with *less* can you supply?

**con, co, cor, com, col.** Together; with. When *con* is placed at the beginning of some words, the *n* may change to an *l, m,* or *r.* The *n* in some words may be left out altogether. However, *con, com, cor, col,* and *co* all mean "together" or "with." Examples: *co-worker*—someone working with you; *convene*—come together, assemble; *convention*—a meeting where persons come together; *combine*—to join together, unite; *collect*—to gather together; *correspond*—to be equivalent, to write letters to one another.

## Additional Words Derived from Combining Forms

From your knowledge of combining forms, can you define the following words?

1. **omnipotent** (om·nip′o·tent) *adj.* *No matter how much wealth, power, and prestige someone has, he or she is not **omnipotent**.*

    _____

2. **omniscient** (om·nis·cient) (on·nish′ent) *adj.* *With the rapid increase of knowledge, it is not possible for someone to be **omniscient**.*

    _____

3. **omnibus** (om′ni·bus) *n.* *Because we had a large group, we chartered an **omnibus** to take us to our destination.*

    _____

4. **visage** (vis·age) (viz′ij) *n.* *His wolfish **visage** warned me about what he might be thinking.*

    _____

5. **visor** (vi·sor) (vī′zor) *n.* *Baseball players wear hats with **visors** because the game is often played in bright sunlight.*

    _____

6. **visa** (vi·sa) (vē′za) *n.* .We need a **visa** to visit Russia.

_____

7. **envision** (en·vi·sion) (en·vizh′un) *v.* The shipwrecked crew, who had been drifting on the raft for two days, deliriously **envisioned** a banquet.

_____

8. **visionary** (vi·sion·ar·y) (vizh′un·er·ē) *n.* (*pl.* **ies**)  The leader of the newly formed religious group claims that he is a **visionary** who has seen visions of things to come.

_____

9. **nautical** (nau·ti·cal) (nau′ti·kul) *adj.* Because John has a **nautical** bent, he wants to become a sailor.

_____

10. **venture** (ven·ture) (ven′chur) *n.* Because the business **venture** involved a great amount of speculation, I did not want to become a part of it.

_____

11. **potentate** (pō′ten·tāte) *n.* The **potentate** of that country is an autocrat whom I would not want as my enemy.

_____

---

**STOP.** Check answers at the end of this chapter (p. 140).

---

"But if nobody needs a Grand Illustrious Potentate, what else will you consider?"

From *The Wall Street Journal*—Permission, Cartoon Features Syndicate.

Practice for Additional Words Derived from Combining Forms

***Directions:*** Match each word with the *best* definition.

| | |
|---|---|
| _____ 1. omnipotent | a. a risky, dangerous undertaking |
| _____ 2. omniscient | b. the face |
| _____ 3. omnibus | c. person possessing great power |
| _____ 4. visage | d. pertaining to seamen, ships |
| _____ 5. visa | e. all-powerful |
| _____ 6. envision | f. large bus |
| _____ 7. visionary | g. the projecting front brim of a cap |
| _____ 8. nautical | h. all-knowing |
| _____ 9. visor | i. a person who sees visions |
| _____ 10. venture | j. to imagine something |
| _____ 11. potentate | k. something granting entrance to a country |

**STOP.** Check answers at the end of this chapter (p. 140).

# EXERCISE 8

## Step I. Combining Forms

**A. Directions:** A list of combining forms with their meanings follows. Look at the combining forms and their meanings. Concentrate on learning each combining form and its meaning. Cover the meanings, read the combining forms, and state the meanings to yourself. Check to see if you are correct. Now cover the combining forms, read the meanings, and state the combining forms to yourself. Check to see if you are correct.

| Combining Forms | Meanings |
|---|---|
| 1. cide | murder; kill |
| 2. pathy | feeling; suffering |
| 3. syl, sym, syn | same; with; together; along with |
| 4. frater, fratr | brother |
| 5. mors, mort | death |
| 6. capit | head |
| 7. corp, corpor | body |
| 8. em, en | into; in |

**B. Directions:**   Do not look at the preceding meanings. Write the meanings of the following combining forms.

| Combining Forms | Meanings |
|---|---|
| 1.  cide | _____ |
| 2.  pathy | _____ |
| 3.  syl, sym, syn | _____ |
| 4.  frater, fratr | _____ |
| 5.  mors, mort | _____ |
| 6.  capit | _____ |
| 7.  corp, corpor | _____ |
| 8.  em, en | _____ |

# Step II. Words Derived from Combining Forms

1. **homicide** (hom·i·cide) (hom′i·sīdé) *n.* Any killing of one human being by another.
   *The spectator witnessed a horrible **homicide** in which the victim was beaten to death.*

2. **suicide** (su·i·cide) (sū′i·sīdé) *n.* The killing of oneself.
   *I wonder if persons who try to kill themselves know that it is against the law to commit **suicide**.*

3. **genocide** (gen·o·cide) (jen′o·sīdé) *n.* The systematic and deliberate killing of a whole racial group or a group of people bound together by customs, language, politics, and so on.
   *During World War II, Hitler attempted to commit **genocide** against the Jewish people because he wanted to wipe them out completely.*

4. **sympathy** (sym·pa·thy) (sim′pa·thē) *n.* (*pl.* **ies**) Sameness of feeling with another; ability to feel pity for another.
   *When Mary lost both her parents in an automobile accident, we all felt deep **sympathy** for her.*

5. **empathy** (em·pa·thy) (em′pa·thē) *n.* (*pl.* **ies**) The imaginative putting of oneself into another person's personality; ability to understand how another feels because one has experienced it firsthand or otherwise.
   *I felt **empathy** for the boy with the broken arm because the same thing had happened to me.*

6. **apathy** (ap·a·thy) (ap′a·thē) *n.* Lack of feeling; indifference.
   *He had such **apathy** regarding the sufferings of persons around him that he didn't care one way or the other what happened to the hurt people.*

7. **fraternity** (fra·ter·ni·ty) (fra·ter′ni·tē ) *n.* (*pl.* **ies**) A group of men joined together by common interests for fellowship; a brotherhood; a Greek letter college organization.
   *In college I decided to join a **fraternity** so that I could make a lot of new friends.*

8. **capital punishment** (cap·i·tal pun·ish·ment) (kap′i·tal pun′ish·ment) *n.* The death penalty.
   ***Capital punishment** has been outlawed in many countries because it is felt that the death penalty is a punishment that is too extreme.*

9. **capitalism** (cap·i·tal·ism) (kap′i·tal·iz·um) *n.* The economic system in which all or most of the means of production, such as land, factories, and railroads, are privately owned and operated for profit.

> Because **capitalism** *is practiced in the United States, individuals privately own and operate their businesses for profit.*

10. **capital** (cap·i·tal) (kap′i·tal) *n.* City or town that is the official seat of government; money or wealth; first letter of a word at the beginning of a sentence. *adj.* Excellent.

> *The* **capital** *of the United States is Washington, D.C.*

11. **corpse** (korpsé) *n.* Dead body.

> *After the detective examined the* **corpse**, *he was told that there was another dead body in the next room.*

12. **corporation** (cor·po·ra·tion) (kor·po·rā′shun) *n.* A group of people who get a charter granting them as a body certain of the powers, rights, privileges, and liabilities (legal responsibilities) of an individual, separate from those of the individuals making up the group.

> *The men formed a* **corporation** *so that they would not individually be liable (legally responsible) for the others.*

13. **incorporate** (in·cor·po·rate) (in·kor′po·rāté) *v.* To unite; combine.

> *The men decided to* **incorporate** *because by joining together they could be a more potent company.*

14. **corporal punishment** (cor·po·ral pun·ish·ment) (kor′po·ral pun′ish·ment) *n.* Bodily punishment; a beating.

> *Because New Jersey is a state that outlaws* **corporal punishment** *in the schools, it is illegal for teachers to hit students.*

15. **mortal** (mor·tal) (mor′tul) *adj.* Referring to a being who must eventually die; causing death; ending in death; very grave; said of certain sins; to the death, as mortal combat; terrible, as mortal terror. *n.* A human being.

> *Because he still advanced, after being shot six times, everyone began to wonder whether he was a* **mortal**.

16. **immortal** (im·mor·tal) (im·mor′tul) *adj.* Referring to a being who never dies; undying. *n.* One who never dies.

> *Because a human being must eventually die, he or she is not* **immortal**.

17. **mortality** (mor·tal·i·ty) (mor·tal′i·tē) *n.* The state of having to die eventually; proportion of deaths to the population of the region, nation, and so on; death rate; death on a large scale, as from disease or war.

> *The* **mortality** *of children among minority groups is decreasing because the living conditions of such groups are improving.*

18. **mortician** (mor·ti·cian) (mor·ti′shin) *n.* A funeral director; undertaker.

> **Morticians** *are accustomed to handling corpses because their job is to prepare the dead for burial.*

19. **mortgage** (mort·gage) (mor′gij) *n.* The pledging of property to a creditor (one to whom a sum of money is owed) as security for payment. *v.* To put up property as security for payment; to pledge.

> *Most people who buy homes obtain a* **mortgage** *from a bank.*

20. **morgue** (morgué) *n.* Place where dead bodies (corpses) of accident victims and unknown persons found dead are kept; for reporters it refers to the reference library of old newspaper articles, pictures, and so on.

> *The police took the accident victim's body to the* **morgue** *because they could find no identification on it.*

## SPECIAL NOTES

1. *empathy* and *sympathy*.

   **empathy:** The imaginative putting of oneself into another in order to better understand him or her; putting oneself into the personality of another. *When people feel* **empathy** *for another, they know how the other person feels because they have had the same experience or can put themselves imaginatively into the personality of the other.*

   **sympathy:** Sameness of feeling with another; ability to feel pity for another. *When you have* **sympathy** *for someone, you feel pity for him or her. You do not have to go through the same experience as the person.* Empathy is a stronger feeling than sympathy. When you say that you *sympathize* with someone's views, it means that you have the same feeling about the views as the person.

2. *apathy.* Lack of feeling; indifference. *He felt complete* **apathy** *for the whole situation.* The term *apathy* means that someone has no feeling one way or another. Such a person is indifferent.

3. The term *homicide* is used in the generic sense. You met the term *generic* in an earlier exercise. *Generic* means "referring to all within a group." Therefore, when someone says that *homicide* is used in the generic sense, he or she means that the combining form *homo* (meaning "man" in the word *homocide*) refers to both men and women, not just to males.

4. Remember the term *misanthrope? Misanthrope* means "hater of mankind." The word is also used in the generic sense in that *mankind* refers to both men and women, not just to men.

5. There are a number of words that are derived from the combining form *cide* with which you may be familiar. For example: *insecticide* means "an agent that destroys insects"; *germicide* means "an agent that destroys germs"; *herbicide* means "an agent that destroys or holds in check plant growth." In Exercises 16 and 17, you will also meet the terms *patricide* and *matricide*.

6. Do not confuse *capitol* with *capital*. *Capitol* refers to the building in which a legislative body meets.

## Step III. Words in Context

Last month John, a college student, fell from a ten-story building. The police did not know whether it was a **suicide** or **homicide**. The young men in the **fraternity** he belonged to said that lately he had a lot of **apathy** toward everything; however, they didn't think he would kill himself. The police took John's **corpse** to the **morgue**. Words cannot describe how John's parents felt when they had to view their son's body there. They couldn't believe that they would be contacting a **mortician** to handle their child's funeral.

When John's parents arrived on campus, everyone felt great **sympathy** for them. Of course, only those parents who have lost children in the same way could feel **empathy** for them. Needless to say, his parents were in shock. They said that it couldn't be **suicide**. They had been loving parents, and their son had been a good, moral, and religious person. It was against his religious beliefs to commit **suicide**. John hated all violence. He didn't believe in either **corporal** or **capital punishment**. John would react very strongly when he read about such crimes as **genocide**. He couldn't believe that dictators could try to wipe out a whole race or religious group of people. At the funeral, the priest said that John was a sensitive **mortal**, and even though he was dead, his soul would be **immortal**. The **mortality** of each person was certain, but John's death was too soon. His parents and friends sobbed uncontrollably. They kept saying that he had so much to live for. He was going to work in a large **corporation** or bank. He had studied about various economic systems and was very knowledgeable of our economic system, **capitalism**. He had done very well in courses dealing with **mortgages** and finance. One day he hoped to **incorporate** all his background and experiences and start his own firm. John's death was a tragedy.

## Step IV. Practice

**A. Directions:**  A number of sentences with missing words follow. Choose the word that *best* fits the sentence. Put the word in the blank. Words may be used in more than one sentence.

**Word List**

| | | |
|---|---|---|
| apathy | fraternity | mortal |
| capital | genocide | mortality |
| capitalism | homicide | mortgage |
| capital punishment | immortal | mortician |
| corporal punishment | incorporate | suicide |
| corporation | morgue | sympathy |
| empathy | | |

1. The _____ of New York State is Albany, the

   _____ of Tennessee is Nashville, and the

   _____ of California is Sacramento.

2. The five businessmen decided to form a _____ so that each would not be legally responsible for the debts of others.

3. Under _____ persons can own their businesses and work for a profit.

4. In order to start a business, you need _____

   because without _____ you cannot purchase the things you need.

5. As most people do not have enough money to pay for a house, they try

   to secure a(n) _____ from a bank.

6. We had to go to the _____ to identify a relative who had been killed in an accident.

7. We went to a(n) _____ to arrange for the funeral of our relative.

8. The men were happy they had decided to _____, joining in a business venture, because together they were doing better than they had alone.

9. The way George drives his car, he must think that he is _____ and that nothing can kill him.

10. Now that women are more involved in careers, they may be more subject to heart attacks and ulcers, and, as a result, their _____ will increase.

11. On earth only _____s exist because no one has yet been able to cheat death.

12. More people are trying to get their legislatures to pass a law to bring back _____ _____ because people feel that fear of death will prevent some crimes.

13. When a(n) _____ is committed, the police try to find a suspect who had a motive, the opportunity, and the means to kill the person.

14. Some persons would choose _____ _____ over lesser _____ _____ because they cannot stand beatings.

15. I felt great _____ for the person whose mother died in an automobile accident because I had experienced the same thing a decade ago.

16. I have no _____ for Alice because I told her beforehand that she would fail if she didn't do any work.

17. It seems incredible that one man was almost able to commit _____ and wipe out a whole race of people.

18. What seems even more incredible is that some people had such _____ about what was going on that they did not care one way or the other.

19. No one could understand why he committed _____ because he seemed to have everything to live for.

20. Many students join a(n) _____ in college in order to be with lots of friendly people and to have a place to go.

---

> **STOP.** Check answers at the end of this chapter (p. 140).

---

**B. Directions:** A list of definitions follows. Underline the word that *best* fits the definition.

1. The killing of a whole racial, political, or cultural group
   a. homicide
   b. suicide
   c. genocide
   d. fratricide

2. Lack of feeling
   a. sympathy
   b. empathy
   c. fraternity
   d. apathy

3. Dead body
   a. mortal
   b. corpse
   c. mortality
   d. immortal

4. Death rate
   a. mortal
   b. immortal
   c. mortality
   d. corpse

5. Ability to put oneself into another's personality
   a. empathy
   b. apathy
   c. fraternity
   d. sympathy

6. A brotherhood
   a. fraternity
   b. corporation
   c. capitalism
   d. capital

7. The feeling of pity for another
   a. empathy
   b. sympathy
   c. apathy
   d. fraternity

8. Killing of one person by another
   a. homicide
   b. suicide
   c. mortality
   d. genocide

9. Killing of oneself
   a. genocide
   b. homicide
   c. mortality
   d. suicide

10. To unite
    a. incorporate
    b. corporation
    c. convene
    d. fraternity

11. Money or wealth
    a. capitalism
    b. corporation
    c. capital
    d. incorporate

12. Bodily punishment
    a. corporal punishment
    b. capital punishment
    c. corpse
    d. corporation

13. Death penalty
    a. capital punishment
    b. corporal punishment
    c. mortality
    d. capitalism

14. Place where unidentified dead are held
    a. mortality
    b. mortal
    c. corpse
    d. morgue

15. Economic system based on profit
    a. capital
    b. corporation
    c. incorporate
    d. capitalism

16. An undertaker
    a. mortician
    b. mortal
    c. mortality
    d. immortal

17. Referring to one who never dies
    a. mortal
    b. immortal
    c. mortality
    d. corpse

18. One who must die
    a. immortal
    b. corpse
    c. mortal
    d. immoral

19. The pledging of property to a creditor
    a. morgue
    b. mortgage
    c. mortician
    d. mortality

---

**STOP.**  Check answers at the end of this chapter (p. 140).

---

**C. Directions:**  Fifteen sentences follow. Define the underlined word or phrase.

1. Very often a <u>homicide</u> is the result of an argument among people who know each other.

_____

2. People who commit <u>suicide</u> have usually given others around them warnings that they were going to <u>kill</u> themselves.

   _____

3. Meg's <u>apathy</u> toward the upcoming dance was obvious, and she couldn't have cared less whether she went or not.

   _____

4. I felt great <u>sympathy</u> for Jack when he had to drop out of college to help support his family after his <u>father</u> died.

   _____

5. Not everyone likes to join a <u>fraternity</u> because if a person does join one, he tends to spend most of his time with only those fellows in the <u>fraternity</u>.

   _____

6. The idea of anyone's attempting <u>genocide</u> to get rid of a whole racial, political, or cultural group seems incredible.

   _____

7. In geography, when we had to list all the <u>capitals</u> of the states, I always listed Washington, D.C., which is, however, the <u>capital</u> of the United States and not a state <u>capital</u>.

   _____

8. Because I can't stand to look at dead bodies, I did not go to the <u>morgue</u> to help to identify the accident victim.

   _____

9. The <u>mortician</u> made the corpse look lifelike.

   _____

10. The men <u>incorporated</u> and formed a <u>corporation</u> so that each would not be liable for the others in their business.

    _____ , _____

11. Because <u>corporal punishment</u> is allowed in many states, school systems have set up regulations regarding when and how a child can be hit.

    _____

12. Do you feel that <u>capital punishment</u> will stop persons from committing horrible crimes because they will be afraid of being put to death?

    _____

13. Some works of art are called <u>immortal</u> because it is thought that they will live forever.

_____

14. I know of no <u>mortal</u> who has lived over 120 years.

_____

15. If you stop paying the money you owe on your <u>mortgage</u>, the bank will be able to take away your house, because your house was put up as security for the loan.

_____

> **STOP.**    Check answers at the end of this chapter (p. 141).

# EXTRA WORD POWER

> **un.**    Not. When _un_ is placed at the beginning of a word, it means "not." _Un_ is used with a very great number of words. Examples: _unwed_—not married; _unaided_—not helped; _unloved_—not loved; _unable_—not able; _uncooked_—not cooked; _unclaimed_—not claimed; _uncaught_—not caught; _uncarpeted_—not carpeted. How many other words can you supply with _un_?
>
> **pre.**    Before. When _pre_ is placed in front of a word it means "before in time" or "before in order." _Pre_, like _un_, is used with a very great number of words. Examples: _prehistoric_—referring to time before history was recorded; _pre-Christian_—referring to time before there were Christians; _prerevolutionary_—referring to time before a revolution; _preheat_—to heat before; _prejudge_—to judge or decide before; _prejudice_—an opinion or judgment made beforehand; _preunite_—to join together before; _preset_—to set before; _premature_—ripened before, developed before the natural or proper period; _predict_—to say before, to foretell, to forecast, to tell what will happen; _prediction_—the act of saying before, the act of forecasting. See how many more words with _pre_ you can supply. Use the dictionary to see the great number of words there are that begin with _un_ and _pre_.

## Additional Words Derived from Combining Forms

From your knowledge of combining forms, can you define the following words?

1. **fratricide** (frat·ri·cide) (frat′ri·sīdé) n.   **Fratricide** _is an especially horrible crime because it involves the murder of a close relative._

_____

2. **corpulent** (cor·pu·lent) (kor′pū·lent) adj.   **Corpulent** _people usually eat a lot._

_____

3. **mortify** (mor·ti·fy) (mor′ti·fī) v.   _The minister was **mortified** that the people in his church had been involved in the riots._

_____

ON THE AIR

O. SOGLOW

*"My next prediction . . ."*

Drawing by O. Soglow; © 1953, 1981 The New Yorker Magazine, Inc.

4. **amortize** (am'or·tīze) *v.   The accountant **amortized** the plant's machinery on a twenty-year schedule.*

_____

5. **caption** (cap·tion) (kap'shun) *n.   By reading chapter **captions**, I am able in a very short time to gain some idea about the chapter.*

_____

6. **capitulate** (ca·pit·u·late) (ka·pich'u·lāte) *v.   With the criminal gang surrounded by the police and having no possible means of escape, they had no choice but to **capitulate**.*

_____

7. **symbol** (sym·bol) (sim'bul) *n.   The dove is a **symbol** of peace, the cross is a **symbol** of Christianity, and the Star of David is a **symbol** of Judaism.*

_____

8. **syllable** (syl·la·ble) (sil'la·bul) *n.   In the word* pilot, *which has two **syllables**,* pi *is the first **syllable** and* lot *is the second syllable.*

_____

9. **monosyllable** (mon·o·syl·la·ble) (mon'o·sil·la·bul) *n.   The word* made *is a **mono-syllable**.*

_____

10. **symphony** (sym·pho·ny) (sim′fo·nē) *n.*   *In the* **symphony** *the instruments blended together in perfect harmony.*

_____

11. **symptom** (symp·tom) (simp′tum) *n.*   *The doctor said that the rash was a definite* **symptom** *of the disease and that there was a cure for it.*

_____

12. **synthesis** (syn·the·sis) (sin′the·sis) *n. (pl.* **theses**)   *The architect was told that his design must be a* **synthesis** *of everyone's ideas.*

_____

13. **symmetry** (sym·me·try) (sim′me·trē) *n. (pl.* **ies**)   *He disliked the disorganized pattern because it lacked* **symmetry**.

_____

---

**STOP.**   Check answers at the end of this chapter (p. 141).

---

## Practice for Additional Words Derived from Combining Forms

**Directions:**   Match each word with the *best* definition.

_____ 1. fratricide

_____ 2. corpulent

_____ 3. mortify

_____ 4. caption

_____ 5. amortize

_____ 6. capitulate

_____ 7. symbol

_____ 8. monosyllable

_____ 9. syllable

_____ 10. symphony

_____ 11. symmetry

_____ 12. synthesis

_____ 13. symptom

a.  heading of a chapter, section, and the like

b.  to cause to feel shame

c.  something that stands for another thing

d.  to cancel a debt by periodic payments

e.  a putting together to form a whole

f.  a vowel or a group of letters with one vowel sound

g.  balanced form or arrangement

h.  harmony of sound

i.  the killing of a brother

j.  to surrender

k.  a condition that results from a disease

l.  word consisting of one syllable

m.  fat

---

**STOP.**   Check answers at the end of this chapter (p. 141).

---

# EXERCISE 9

## Step I. Combining Forms

**A. Directions:**  A list of combining forms with their meanings follows. Concentrate on learning each combining form and its meaning. Cover the meanings, read the combining forms, and state the meanings to yourself. Check to see if you are correct. Now cover the combining forms, read the meanings, and state the combining forms to yourself. Check to see if you are correct.

| Combining Forms | Meanings |
|---|---|
| 1. man, manu | hand |
| 2. fac, fect, fic | make; do |
| 3. loc, loco | place |
| 4. pseudo | false |
| 5. bene | good |
| 6. cura | care |
| 7. aud, audi | hear |
| 8. nomin, onym | name |

**B. Directions:**  Do not look at the preceding meanings. Write the meanings of the following combining forms.

| Combining Forms | Meanings |
|---|---|
| 1. man, manu | _____ |
| 2. fac, fect, fic | _____ |
| 3. loc, loco | _____ |
| 4. pseudo | _____ |
| 5. bene | _____ |
| 6. cura | _____ |
| 7. aud, audi | _____ |
| 8. nomin, onym | _____ |

## Step II. Words Derived from Combining Forms

1. **manual** (man'ū·al) *adj.* Referring to the hand; made, done, or used by the hands. *n.* A handy book used as a guide or source of information.
   *Some persons prefer **manual** labor because they like to work with their hands.*

2. **manicure** (man·i·cure) (man'i·kurė) *n.* Care of the hands and fingernails. *v.* To provide care for hands and nails with a manicure; to cut closely and evenly.
   *Because I like my fingernails to look good, I give myself a **manicure** every week.*

*"Tony asked me to ask you, Mr. Bates—do you know offhand
the whereabouts of your service manual?"*
Drawing by Booth; © 1977. The New Yorker Magazine, Inc.

3. **manuscript** (man·u·script) (man′yu·skript) *adj*. Written by hand or typed; not printed. *n*. A book or document written by hand; a handwritten or typewritten book
   usually sent in for publication; style of penmanship in which letters are not joined
   together, whereas in cursive writing they are.
   *When an author sends a **manuscript** to a publisher, he or she hopes that the editor
   will like it.*

4. **manufacture** (man·u·fac·ture) (man·yu·fak′chur) *v*. To make goods or articles by
   hand or by machinery; to make something from raw materials by hand or machinery. *n*. The act of manufacturing.
   *Some very special and expensive items are still made by hand, but most goods are
   **manufactured** by machine on a large scale.*

5. **factory** (fac·to·ry) (fak′to·rē) *n*. (*pl*. **ies**) A building or buildings in which things are
   manufactured.
   *My mother and father work in a **factory** where automobiles are made.*

6. **benefactor** (ben·e·fac·tor) (ben′e·fak·tor) *n.* One who gives help or confers a benefit; a patron.

   *Many times artists have **benefactors** who help to support them while they are painting.*

7. **beneficiary** (ben·e·fi·ci·ar·y) (ben·e·fish′ē·er·ē) *n.* (*pl.* **aries**) One who receives benefits or advantages; the one to whom an insurance policy is payable.

   *Joyce, as the only **beneficiary** of her husband's insurance policy, did not know that she would receive all the money.*

8. **benefit** (ben′e·fit) *n.* That which is helpful; advantage; a payment; a performance given to raise funds for a worthy cause. *v.* To be helpful or profitable to; to receive benefit; to aid.

   *The actors gave a **benefit** to collect money for the needy children.*

9. **affect** (af·fect) (af·fekt′) *v.* To act upon or to cause something; to influence; to produce an effect or change in.

   *Your poor study habits will definitely begin to **affect** your grades and cause them to go down.*

10. **effect** (ef·fect) (ef·fekt′) *n.* Something brought about by some cause; the result; consequence.

    *I told you what the **effects** of your not studying would be before the results were in.*

11. **effective** (ef·fec·tive) (ef·fek′tive) *adj.* Producing or having the power to bring about an intended result; producing results with the least amount of wasted effort.

    *His way of doing the job is much more **effective** than yours because it takes him so much less time to do the same amount of work.*

12. **audible** (au·di·ble) (au′di·bul) *adj.* Capable of being heard.

    *He spoke so softly that what he had to say was hardly **audible** to anyone.*

13. **auditorium** (au·di·to·ri·um) (au·di·tor′ē·um) *n.* A building or hall for speeches, concerts, public meetings, and so on; the room in a building occupied by an audience.

    *The school **auditorium** was so large that it was able to seat the entire graduating class and their parents.*

14. **audience** (au·di·ence) (au′dē·ense) *n.* An assembly of listeners or spectators at a concert, play, speech, and so on.

    *The **audience** listened to the politicians' speeches to learn what their views were on the income tax.*

15. **audit** (au′dit) *v.* To examine or check such things as accounts; to attend class as a listener. *n.* An examination of accounts in order to report the financial state of a business.

    *Every year banks have their accounts **audited** to check if everything is in order.*

16. **audition** (au·di·tion) (au·dish′un) *n.* A trial hearing, as of an actor or singer; the act of hearing. *v.* To try out for a part in an audition.

    *Carol's first **audition** for the part in the play was so successful that she was told there was no reason to listen to any other person.*

17. **audiovisual** (au·di·o·vis·u·al) (au·dē·ō·vizh′ū·al) *adj.* Of, pertaining to, involving, or directed at both hearing and sight.

    *Many teachers use **audiovisual** aids in the classroom because the added senses of seeing and hearing help in learning.*

18. **local** (lo·cal) (lō′kal) *adj.* Referring to a relatively small area, region, or neighborhood; limited.

    *As a child, I always went to the **local** movie theater because it was close to where I lived.*

19. **location** (lo·ca·tion) (lō·kā′shun) *n.* A place or site; exact position or place occupied; an area or tract of land; a place used for filming a motion picture or a television program (as in the expression *to be on location*).
    *The **location** for our picnic was perfect because it was such a scenic place.*

20. **allocate** (al·lo·cate) (al′lo·kāte) *v.* To set something apart for a special purpose; to divide up something; to divide and distribute something.
    *Each person was **allocated** a certain share of the profits according to the amount of time and work he or she had put into the project.*

21. **antonym** (an·to·nym) (an′to·nim) *n.* A word opposite in meaning to some other word.
    *The words* good *and* bad *are **antonyms** because they are opposite in meaning.*

22. **synonym** (syn·o·nym) (sin′o·nim) *n.* A word having the same or nearly the same meaning as some other word.
    *The words* vision *and* sight *are **synonyms** because they have the same meaning.*

23. **homonym** (hom·o·nym) (hom′o·nim) *n.* A word that agrees in pronunciation with some other word but differs in spelling and meaning.
    *The color* red *and the verb* read *are **homonyms** because they sound alike but are spelled differently and have different meanings.*

24. **pseudonym** (pseu·do·nym) (psēū′do·nim) *n.* False name, used by an author to conceal his or her identity; pen name.
    *Samuel Clemens wrote under the name Mark Twain, his **pseudonym**.*

25. **misnomer** (mis·nō′mer) *n.* A name wrongly applied to someone or something; an error in the naming of a person or place in a legal document.
    *It is a **misnomer** to call a spider an insect.*

26. **anonymous** (a·non·y·mous) (a·non′i·mous) *adj.* Lacking a name; of unknown authorship.
    *As it is the policy of the newspaper to publish signed letters only, the **anonymous** letter was not published.*

## SPECIAL NOTES

1. Note that *alias* (a word from Exercise 5) and *pseudonym* are basically synonyms. However, the term *alias* is usually used when a criminal uses a name other than his or her own, whereas the term *pseudonym* is usually used when an author uses a name other than his or her own.

   Do not confuse *pseudonym* and *alias* with *misnomer*. The term *misnomer* refers to someone's using a wrong name or word accidentally, that is, *not on purpose*. When someone uses an *alias* or *pseudonym*, he or she is doing it *on purpose* and has not made a mistake.

   The term *anonymous* refers to someone who has not signed his or her name, so that the name of the person is unknown. When you see *anonymous* at the end of a poem or story, it means that the author is unknown.

2. *Affect* and *effect* are terms that are used a great deal. However, they are often used incorrectly. Note the way the words are used in the sentences that follow.
   **affect.** *v.* To act upon or to cause something; to influence. *You will probably **affect** your team's chances to win because you seem to have such a great influence on them.*
   **effect.** *n.* Something brought about by some cause; the result. *The **effect** on the team was that they won the game.*

## Step III. Words in Context

Not too long ago there was a big court battle over the will of a very wealthy man. He owned a number of **local factories** that **manufactured** different things. In his **factories** everything was automated; nothing was done by **manual** labor. When the man died, he left all his money to his fifth wife; she was the sole **beneficiary** of his entire will.

Needless to say, the **effect** of this on his children was predictable. Their protests were certainly **audible**; they were furious. They did not expect their father's young wife of only a few months to **benefit** from the will. They had expected that their father would **allocate** his wealth to them. They decided to contest the will. They felt that they had an **effective** case because of a **manuscript** they found in their father's safe that was hidden in a special location on his boat. Even though the **manuscript** was signed with a different name, they felt that it was their father's; he had used a **pseudonym** before. They knew that their father often published things under another name.

In addition, the man's children received an **anonymous** letter from someone saying that he knew that their father had been under some big strain, which could have **affected** his judgment. The **anonymous** letter also stated that his latest wife was concerned about an **audit** of the companies' books. It said further that his latest wife had bought a lot of **audiovisual** equipment lately and had had an **audition** for a play. The writer seemed to know quite a bit about the wife. The writer said that she had performed as a go-go dancer in a certain **auditorium** for many different **audiences**. The children didn't know what to make of the letter. Clearly, the writer had it in for the wife. But the letter was unsigned and full of **misnomers**, wrongly spelled **homonyms**, and **synonyms** that were used as **antonyms** and vice versa. However, this was excellent ammunition for the children.

Most importantly, the **manuscript** that the children had found had a note in it from their father that said that he thought something strange was going on. He felt that he was slowly losing his mind. Also, he said that he intended to leave his entire fortune to his children and to his first wife, who bore his children. He said that the other women he had been married to were more concerned about their **manicures** than about him. He did not want to be their **benefactor** because he knew that they had all married him for his money.

The children felt that their father had met with foul play. They went to the police with their evidence. The police dug up the body and did an autopsy. They found that he had died of a heart attack but that it had been brought on by a special drug. The drug had been given to him in small doses for a number of months. It turned out that his wife and her boyfriend had planned and carried out his murder.

## Step IV. Practice

**A. Directions:** A list of definitions follows. Choose the word that *best* fits the definition. Try to relate your definition to the meanings of the combining forms. All the words are used.

**Word List**

| | | |
|---|---|---|
| affect | auditorium | location |
| allocate | benefactor | manicure |
| anonymous | beneficiary | manual |
| antonym | benefit | manufacture |
| audible | effect | manuscript |
| audience | effective | misnomer |
| audiovisual | factory | pseudonym |
| audit | homonym | synonym |
| audition | local | |

1. A false name _____

2. A name wrongly applied _____

3. A word opposite in meaning to some other word _____

4. A word similar in meaning to some other word _____

5. Lacking a name _____

6. Made by hand _____

7. Written by hand _____

8. Care of the hands and fingernails _____

9. A building in which things are made _____

10. One who gives help _____

11. One who receives aid _____

12. An advantage; payment _____

13. To make goods by hand or machinery _____

14. To influence _____

15. A result _____

16. Producing results with the least amount of wasted effort _____

17. A building or hall for speeches, meetings, and the like _____

18. An assembly of listeners at a concert, play, and so on _____

19. Capable of being heard _____

20. Involving both hearing and sight _____

21. A trial hearing _____

22. To examine or check accounts _____

23. To set apart for a special purpose _____

24. A place or site _____

25. Referring to a relatively small area, region, or neighborhood _____

26. A word that is pronounced the same as some other word but is spelled differently and has a different meaning _____

**STOP.** Check answers at the end of this chapter (p. 141).

**B. Directions:**   A number of sentences with missing words follow. Fill in the word that *best* fits the sentence. Two choices are given for each sentence.

1. As the _____ of the policy, you will receive everything. (benefactor, beneficiary)

2. In the _____ the workers are making a large supply of toy trains. (factory, location)

3. The author did not want to use his own name, so he used a

   _____. (misnomer, pseudonym)

4. The police received a(n) _____ letter that gave them information about the murder. (manual, anonymous)

5. In _____ letters are not joined together. (manual, manuscript)

6. The _____ where the people met to listen to the concert was very large. (factory, auditorium)

7. The _____ you are having on your brother is not the one we wanted. (affect, effect)

8. Try not to _____ your brother as much as you do. (affect, effect)

9. *Alias* and *pseudonym* are _____s. (antonym, synonym)

10. *Happy* and *sad* are _____s. (antonym, synonym)

11. *Sew* and *so* are _____s. (synonym, homonym)

12. When something is _____, it brings about results with the least amount of effort. (effective, anonymous)

13. Each employee of the corporation was _____ a certain share of the profits. (affected, allocated)

14. No one was able to hear it, because it was not _____. (effective, audible)

15. Because I like to stay close to my home, I shop in _____ places. (audiovisual, local)

16. The company decided to _____ its accounts to check for errors. (allocate, audit)

17. If Jennifer doesn't get a(n) _____ soon for a play, she will give up trying to be an actress. (location, audition)

---

**STOP.**   Check answers at the end of this chapter (p. 142).

**C. Directions:**  A few paragraphs with missing words follow. Fill in the blanks with the word that *best* fits. Words may be used more than once.

**Word List**

| | | |
|---|---|---|
| audible | benefit | location |
| audience | effect | manicure |
| audition | effective | manual |
| benefactor | factory | manufacture |
| beneficiary | local | pseudonym |

Because Mary Brown enjoys making things and working with her hands, she doesn't mind **1**_____ labor even though she's a woman. However, her parents want her to have lots of **2**_____s. They feel that the only way she can get the advantages they want her to have is by finishing college. In order to go to college, she works in a **3**_____ in which clothing is **4**_____d on a large scale. She has no **5**_____ to help her, and she is not the **6**_____ of any rich old uncle's insurance policy.

This summer they used the **7**_____ where she is working as the **8**_____ for a movie. It was very exciting! Every day they had a large **9**_____ watch the making of the film. The spectators came from all over. The movie people were so **10**_____ in getting the **11**_____s they wanted for the film that very little time was wasted. When they worked, no outside sounds were **12**_____ because they told the spectators to be silent.

They were going to use a number of **13**_____ people in some of the mob scenes. As Mary Brown lived in the neighborhood, she was chosen for a(n) **14**_____. Mary was told that if they liked what they saw and heard, they would use her in the movie. Well, Mary tried to make herself look as glamorous as possible. She even decided to give her hands a(n) **15**_____.

When the day for her **16**_____ came, she was so excited that she could hardly talk. By the time she got to the **17**_____ for her test, her voice was not **18**_____.

The director told all the people in the mob scene that they were to be in a scene where they all fall into mud. Ugh! And for this Mary Brown had made herself glamorous and given herself a(n) **19**_____. For this role she would probably use a(n) **20**_____ rather than her real name.

---

**STOP.**  Check answers at the end of this chapter (p. 142).

## *EXTRA WORD POWER*

---

**anti.** Against; opposed to. *Anti*, meaning "against," is found at the beginning of a great number of words. For example: *antiwar*—against war; *antigambling*—against gambling; *antimachine*—against machines; *antimen*—against men; *antiwomen*—against women; *antilabor*—against labor. Note that *anti* changes to *ant* before words that begin with a vowel, as in *antacid*—something that acts against acid; *antonym*—a word opposite in meaning to some other word. As you can see, you can place *anti* at the beginning of a lot of words. Can you think of some words to which you might add *anti*? Use the dictionary to see the great number of words there are with *anti*.

**non.** Not. When *non* is placed in front of a word, it means a simple negative or the absence of something. The number of words beginning with *non* is so large that the dictionary has them listed in a special section. Check your dictionary to see how many it has. Following are some words with *non*: *nonbeliever*—not a believer; *non-Arab*—not an Arab; *non-Catholic*—not Catholic; *noncapitalist*—not a capitalist; *non-Communist*—not a Communist; *nonefficient*—not efficient; *noncriminal*—not criminal; *non-English*—not English. How many more can you supply?

---

### Additional Words Derived from Combining Forms

From your knowledge of combining forms, can you define the following words?

1. **audiometer** (au·di·om·e·ter) (au·dē·om′e·ter) *n.   The doctor used the **audiometer** to determine if John had a hearing problem.*

   _____

2. **audiology** (au·di·ol·o·gy) (au·dē·ol′o·jē) *n.   Sally decided to major in **audiology** in college because she wanted to help children who had hearing problems.*

   _____

3. **benediction** (ben·e·dic·tion) (ben·e·dik′shun) *n.   At the end of the church service the minister gave the **benediction**.*

   _____

4. **antipathy** (an·tip·a·thy) (an·tip′a·thē) *n.   Mary had great **antipathy** toward the persons who injured her brother.*

   _____

5. **pseudopodium** (pseu·do·po·di·um) (psēū·do·pō′dē·um) *n. (pl. **dia**) Some one-celled animals have **pseudopodia**, which are used for taking in food and for movement.*

   _____

6. **curator** (cu·ra·tor) (kū·rā′tor) *n.*   *A good **curator** of a museum should know every-thing that is going on in the museum.*

   _____

7. **pedicure** (ped·i·cure) (ped′i·kurė) *n.*   *I always have a **pedicure** before I wear open sandals.*

   _____

8. **pseudoscience** (pseu·do·sci·ence) (psėū·dō·sėī′ensė) *n.*   *Astrology is a **pseudoscience** because it involves only the reading of the stars to foretell the future and is not based on rational principles.*

   _____

9. **manipulation** (ma·nip·u·la·tion) (ma·nip′yu·lā·shun) *n.*   *By his clever **manipulation** of all those around him, he was able to gain the position he desired.*

   _____

10. **emancipate** (e·man·ci·pate) (ē·man′si·pātė) *v.*   *After enslaved people have been **eman-cipated**, they must learn how to live like free people.*

    _____

11. **personification** (per·son·i·fi·ca·tion) (per·son·i·fi·kā′shun) *n.*   *"The clouds wept a tor-rent of tears that almost flooded the city" is an example of **personification**.*

    _____

12. **facsimile** (fac·sim·i·le) (fak·sim′i·lē) *n. v.*   *The little girl was the **facsimile** of her mother at the same age.*

    _____

13. **faction** (fac·tion) (fak′shun) *n.*   *There was a special **faction** in the union that was trying to gain power so that its members could further their own desires.*

    _____

---

**STOP.**   Check answers at the end of this chapter (p. 142).

Practice for Additional Words Derived from Combining Forms

***Directions:*** Match each word with the *best* definition.

_____ 1. audiometer

_____ 2. audiology

_____ 3. benediction

_____ 4. antipathy

_____ 5. pseudopodia

_____ 6. curator

_____ 7. pedicure

_____ 8. pseudoscience

_____ 9. manipulation

_____ 10. emancipate

_____ 11. personification

_____ 12. facsimile

_____ 13. faction

a. a blessing

b. an exact copy

c. to free from servitude or slavery

d. a figure of speech in which human qualities are given to nonliving things

e. a dislike for someone

f. a group in an organization or government, often self-seeking, with common ends

g. one in charge, as of a department in a museum

h. an instrument used to measure hearing

i. the study of hearing

j. a false science

k. the skillfull handling of something

l. false feet

m. care or treatment of the feet

---

**STOP.** Check answers at the end of this chapter (p. 142).

---

# CHAPTER WORDS IN SENTENCES

***Directions:*** Use the given words to write a sentence that makes sense. Also, try to illustrate the meaning of the words without actually defining the words.

*Example* (audience; pseudonym)  The *audience* was stunned to learn that Nancy Gray was a *pseudonym* for Mary Brown and that Mary Brown, who was eighty years old, had been writing sexy romance novels for forty years.

1. (evident; effect)

_____

2. (homicide; affect)

_____

3. (potent; evidence)

_____

4. (omnipresent; apathy)

_____

5. (potential; immortal)

_____

# CHAPTER WORDS
# IN A PARAGRAPH

Here is a list of words from this chapter. Write a paragraph, using at least 8 of these words. The paragraph must make sense and be logically developed.

**Word List**

| | | |
|---|---|---|
| affect | corpse | mortal |
| allocate | effect | omnipresent |
| anonymous | effective | potent |
| apathy | empathy | potential |
| aquanaut | evidence | provision |
| astronaut | fraternity | suicide |
| audit | homicide | sympathy |
| benefit | immortal | television |
| capitalism | impotent | visible |
| convene | local | vision |
| convenient | morgue | |

# ANALOGIES 3

**_Directions:_** Find the word from the following list that _best_ completes each analogy. There are more words in the list than you need.

**Word List**

| | | |
|---|---|---|
| affect | convention | mortify |
| anonymous | corpulent | omnipotent |
| antipathy | creditor | omnipresent |
| apathy | creed | omniscient |
| audible | deny | pedestrian |
| audiology | effect | potential |
| audiometer | empathy | pseudopodal |
| audition | facsimile | pseudoscience |
| capital | feel | stars |
| capitulate | genocide | suicide |
| caption | homicide | sympathy |
| convene | impotent | underwater |
| convenient | love | visage |

1. Astronaut : space : : aquanaut : _____.

2. Visible : evident : : everywhere : _____.

3. Incredible : credible : : potent : _____.

4. Mortal : immortal : : adjourn : _____.

5. Astronomy : science : : astrology : _____.

6. Snake : apodal : : amoeba : _____.

7. Incorporate : unite : : humiliate : _____.

8. Benediction : blessing : : heading : _____.

9. Pseudonym : alias : : face : _____.

10. Autograph : signature : : copy : _____.

11. Life : biology : : hearing : _____.

12. Vest : clothing : : fratricide : _____.

13. Deny : contradict : : fleshy : _____.

14. Symmetry : balance : : dislike : _____.

15. Assembly : meeting : : handy : _____.

16. Benefit : advantage : : indifference : _____.

17. Noise : clamor : : faith : _____.

18. Handbook : manual : : result : _____.

19. Location : site : : nameless : _____.

20. Anarchy : order : : resist : _____.

> **STOP.**   Check answers at the end of this chapter (p. 143).

# MULTIPLE-CHOICE VOCABULARY TEST 3

**Directions:**   This is a test on words in Exercises 7–9. Words are presented according to exercises. *Do all exercises before checking answers.* Underline the meaning that *best* fits the word.

Exercise 7

1. vision
   a. able to be seen
   b. system for the transmission of visual images from a distance
   c. sense of sight
   d. easily recognized

2. visible
   a. sense of sight
   b. system for the transmission of visual images from a distance
   c. able to be seen
   d. not seen

3. television
   a. sense of sight
   b. system for the transmission of visual images from a distance
   c. able to be seen
   d. plain

4. invisible
   a. not able to be seen
   b. in disguise
   c. out of sight
   d. to view from inside

5. provision
   a. something made ready in advance
   b. something to see from a distance
   c. something to see
   d. to see for someone

6. evident
   a. clearly seen
   b. sense of sight
   c. able to see from a distance
   d. to view

7. evidence
   a. that which seems to prove or disprove something
   b. able to see clearly
   c. that which is seen from a distance
   d. that which shows something

8. science
   a. a knowing person
   b. able to know
   c. the sense of knowing
   d. area of ordered and investigated knowledge

9. astrology
   a. the study of heavenly bodies
   b. the reading of the stars to foretell the future
   c. a true science
   d. refers to stars

10. astronomy
    a. the study of stars, planets, and space
    b. the reading of the stars
    c. a true science
    d. refers to stars

11. astronaut
    a. refers to space
    b. refers to stars
    c. one who travels underwater
    d. one who travels in space

12. aquanaut
    a. refers to undersea
    b. one who travels undersea
    c. refers to water
    d. refers to one who travels in space

13. aquatic
    a. referring to a water plant
    b. referring to a water flower
    c. referring to water
    d. referring to undersea plants

14. aquarium
    a. a water bowl
    b. refers to water
    c. a globelike bowl or rectangular container for water plants and animals
    d. an area of study

15. convene
    a. something suitable
    b. a meeting
    c. to come together
    d. to call a special meeting

16. convention
    a. a friendly get-together
    b. a formal meeting of members for professional purposes
    c. something suitable
    d. to come together

17. convenient
    a. suited to one's purpose
    b. a get-together
    c. joining together
    d. a special meeting

18. potent
    a. a drug
    b. a perfume
    c. powerful
    d. refers to money

19. impotent
    a. refers to sex
    b. without power
    c. refers to power
    d. refers to males only

20. potential
    a. the ability or power one may have
    b. refers to sex
    c. refers to males only
    d. refers to feeling

21. omnipresent
    a. referring to a gift
    b. referring to all
    c. referring to everyone
    d. being present everywhere at all times

Exercise 8

22. homicide
    a.  killing of a brother
    b.  killing of oneself
    c.  killing of one person by another
    d.  killing of a whole group of people

23. suicide
    a.  killing of oneself
    b.  killing of a whole group of people
    c.  killing of a brother
    d.  killing of one person by another

24. genocide
    a.  killing of man
    b.  killing of a whole racial, political, or cultural group
    c.  killing of a brother
    d.  killing of oneself

25. sympathy
    a.  feeling sad
    b.  ability to put onself into the personality of another
    c.  self-pity
    d.  ability to feel pity for another

26. empathy
    a.  ability to feel pity for
    b.  ability to imaginatively put oneself into the personality of another
    c.  self-pity
    d.  feeling sad

27. apathy
    a.  refers to pity
    b.  self-pity
    c.  lack of feeling
    d.  feeling sad

28. fraternity
    a.  a Greek letter college organization
    b.  a brother
    c.  killing of a brother
    d.  refers to friends and relatives

29. capital punishment
    a.  bodily harm
    b.  head punishment
    c.  death penalty
    d.  beatings

30. capitalism
    a.  refers to profit
    b.  an economic system in which all or most of the means of production are privately owned
    c.  an economic system in which all or most of the means of production are not privately owned
    d.  an economic system in which all or most of the means of production are privately owned and operated for profit

31. capital
    a. official seat of government
    b. relevant
    c. refers to an economic system
    d. refers to death

32. corpse
    a. a body
    b. a dead body
    c. a group of people
    d. refers to beatings

33. corporation
    a. men getting together
    b. a business
    c. a group of people with a charter granting them certain powers and making them not legally responsible for each other
    d. a group of people with a charter granting them certain powers to rule

34. incorporate
    a. to unite
    b. to join a club
    c. refers to a body
    d. men getting together

35. corporal punishment
    a. death penalty
    b. a beating
    c. refers to the body
    d. refers to punishment of an officer in the service

36. mortal
    a. referring to death
    b. referring to a dead person
    c. referring to any dead animal
    d. referring to someone who must die

37. immortal
    a. referring to all living persons
    b. referring to all dead persons
    c. referring to death
    d. referring to a being who never dies

38. mortality
    a. dead persons
    b. death rate
    c. one who never dies
    d. one who must die

39. mortician
    a. a dead man
    b. one who must die
    c. a person who counts the dead
    d. an undertaker

40. mortgage
    a. refers to death
    b. pledging property
    c. giving up your property
    d. pledging property to a creditor as security for payment

41. morgue
    a. refers to the dead
    b. place to keep all dead bodies
    c. an undertaker's office
    d. place where unidentified dead bodies are kept

## Exercise 9

42. manual
    a. referring to the hands
    b. referring to manly work
    c. referring to men
    d. referring to help

43. manicure
    a. refers to cure
    b. refers to hands
    c. the curing of hand problems
    d. the care of the hands and fingernails

44. manuscript
    a. a newspaper
    b. a role in a play
    c. written by hand
    d. a letter

45. manufacture
    a. to make machinery
    b. to store in a factory
    c. to make by hand or machine from raw material
    d. made to sell

46. factory
    a. a building
    b. a house
    c. a place for storing things only
    d. a place for manufacturing things

47. benefactor
    a. one who gets help
    b. one who gives help
    c. someone good
    d. a blessing

48. beneficiary
    a. one who gives help
    b. one who needs help
    c. one who gets help
    d. a blessing

49. benefit
    a. a performance for some charity or cause
    b. a blessing
    c. a performance
    d. charity

50. affect
    a.  the result
    b.  to bring
    c.  an action
    d.  to influence

51. effect
    a.  to influence
    b.  the result
    c.  the action
    d.  to bring something

52. effective
    a.  producing no results after a while
    b.  producing
    c.  making something do
    d.  producing results in a minimum of time

53. audible
    a.  referring to hearing
    b.  referring to a listener
    c.  capable of being heard
    d.  not heard

54. auditorium
    a.  a building in which things are made
    b.  a special building
    c.  a place for workers
    d.  a place for speeches, concerts, and so on

55. audience
    a.  a group of listeners or spectators at a play, concert, and so on
    b.  spectacles
    c.  people
    d.  a building

56. audit
    a.  to hear
    b.  to examine accounts
    c.  to examine
    d.  to be a spectator

57. audition
    a.  an examination of books
    b.  an examination
    c.  a hearing for a jury trial
    d.  a trial hearing for an actor or singer

58. audiovisual
    a.  instruction using books
    b.  instruction using printed matter
    c.  instruction using only television
    d.  pertaining to hearing and seeing

59. local
    a.  referring to a neighborhood area
    b.  referring to a distant place
    c.  referring to a place
    d.  referring to a situation

60. location
    a. in the neighborhood
    b. a place or site
    c. a situation
    d. any place close

61. allocate
    a. to place
    b. to set
    c. to divide and distribute
    d. to put together

62. antonym
    a. a word similar to another in meaning
    b. a word opposite in meaning to another
    c. a word that is pronounced the same as another
    d. a word that is spelled like another

63. synonym
    a. a word similar in pronunciation to another
    b. a word opposite in meaning to another
    c. a word similar to another in spelling
    d. a word similar to another in meaning

64. homonym
    a. a word similar to another in spelling
    b. a word similar to another in pronunciation
    c. a word different from another in meaning and spelling but similar in pronunciation
    d. a word different in meaning from another

65. pseudonym
    a. wrong name
    b. same name
    c. lacking a name
    d. false name

66. misnomer
    a. false name
    b. lacking a name
    c. same name
    d. wrong name

67. anonymous
    a. wrong name
    b. false name
    c. lacking a name
    d. same name

# TRUE/FALSE TEST 3

**Directions:** This is a true/false test on Exercises 7–9. Read each sentence carefully. Decide whether it is true or false. Put a *T* for *true* or an *F* for *false* in the blank. If the answer is false, change a word or part of the sentence to make it true. The number after the sentence tells you if the word is from Exercise 7, 8, or 9.

_____ 1. A fratricide would also be a homicide. 8

_____ 2. A suicide is also a homicide. 8

_____ 3. Corporal punishment refers to a beating. 8

_____ 4. Some mortals are able to survive forever. 8

_____ 5. If the proportion of minority group children who die is higher, then the mortality of such children is lower than that for children as a whole. 8

_____ 6. A person who receives capital punishment is not executed. 8

_____ 7. Astrology is a science. 7

_____ 8. Astronauts travel undersea. 7

_____ 9. If something is convenient for you, it occurs at a bad time. 7

_____ 10. Your potential is your ability. 7

_____ 11. An omnipresent thing is present everywhere all the time. 7

_____ 12. You can have sympathy for someone even if you can't experience how he or she feels. 8

_____ 13. Genocide is a fatal illness. 8

_____ 14. The words *antipathy* and *apathy* are synonyms. 8, 9

_____ 15. The words *synonym* and *antonym* are antonyms. 9

_____ 16. To audit the books means to examine them. 9

_____ 17. The words *alias* and *pseudonym* are synonyms. 9

_____ 18. Man is immortal. 8

_____ 19. A morgue is where all dead bodies are stored. 8

_____ 20. A manuscript can refer to a book written by hand and sent in for publication. 9

_____ 21. Something audible can be heard. 9

_____ 22. The words *pseudonym* and *misnomer* are synonyms. 9

_____ 23. The words *bury* and *berry* are synonyms. 9

_____ 24. The words *fat* and *corpulent* are synonyms. 8, 9

_____ 25. The words *anonymous* and *alias* are synonyms. 9

**STOP.** Check answers for both tests at the end of this chapter (p. 143).

# SCORING OF TESTS ═══════════════════

| MULTIPLE-CHOICE VOCABULARY TEST | | TRUE/FALSE TEST* | |
|---|---|---|---|
| Number Wrong | Score | Number Wrong | Score |
| 0–4 | Excellent | 0–2 | Excellent |
| 5–10 | Good | 3–5 | Good |
| 11–14 | Weak | 6–7 | Weak |
| Above 14 | Poor | Above 7 | Poor |
| Score _____ | | Score _____ | |

1. If you scored in the excellent or good range on *both tests*, you are doing well. Go on to Chapter Five.

2. If you scored in the weak or poor range on either test, look below and follow directions for Additional Practice. Note that the words on the tests are arranged so that you can tell in which exercise to find them. This will help you if you need additional practice.

# ADDITIONAL PRACTICE SETS ═══════════

**A. Directions:**  Write the words you missed on the tests from the three exercises in the space provided. Note that the tests are presented so that you can tell to which exercises the words belong.

## Exercise 7 Words Missed

1. _____     6. _____
2. _____     7. _____
3. _____     8. _____
4. _____     9. _____
5. _____    10. _____

## Exercise 8 Words Missed

1. _____     6. _____
2. _____     7. _____
3. _____     8. _____
4. _____     9. _____
5. _____    10. _____

*When the answer is false, you must get both parts of the true/false question correct in order to receive credit.

Exercise 9 Words Missed

1. _____    6. _____
2. _____    7. _____
3. _____    8. _____
4. _____    9. _____
5. _____    10. _____

**B. Directions:**   Restudy the missed words from the three exercises. Study the combining forms from which those words are derived. Do Step I and Step II for those you missed. Note that Step I and Step II of the combining forms and vocabulary derived from these combining forms are on the following pages:

Exercise 7—pp. 89–92

Exercise 8—pp. 99–102

Exercise 9—pp. 111–114

**C. Directions:**   Do Additional Practice 1 below if you missed words from Exercise 7. Do Additional Practice 2 on pp. 135–137 if you missed words from Exercise 8. Do Additional Practice 3 on pp. 137–139 if you missed words from Exercise 9. Now go on to Chapter Five.

## Additional Practice 1 for Exercise 7

**A. Directions:**   Following are the combining forms presented in Exercise 7. Match each combining form with its meaning.

_____ 1. vid, vis          a. star
_____ 2. sci, scio         b. all
_____ 3. poten            c. see
_____ 4. omni             d. come
_____ 5. aqua, aqui        e. sailor
_____ 6. astro            f. water
_____ 7. naut             g. powerful
_____ 8. ven, veni, vent    h. know

**STOP.**   Check answers at the end of this chapter (p. 144).

**B. Directions:**   Sentences containing the meanings of vocabulary presented in Exercise 7 follow. Choose the word that *best* fits the meaning of the word or phrase underlined in the sentence. A word may be used only once.

**Word List**

| | | |
|---|---|---|
| aquanauts | convenient | potent |
| aquarium | conventions | potential |
| aquatic | evidence | provisions |
| astrology | evident | science |
| astronauts | impotent | television |
| astronomy | invisible | visible |
| convene | omnipresent | vision |

1. If you are blind, you do not have your <u>sense of sight</u>. _____

2. In the film, a man played a ghost who was <u>not able to be seen</u>.

   _____

3. I enjoy <u>visual image shows that come from New York and California</u> in my own home. _____

4. The sign was <u>able to be seen</u>, but I went past it. _____

5. We will take enough <u>supplies</u> for our trip. _____

6. I am studying astronomy, which is <u>a field of organized knowledge</u> concerning heavenly bodies. _____

7. The lawyer needed <u>something that would prove</u> that his client was innocent of the charges. _____

8. It is <u>plain</u> from the way you are acting that you want me to leave.

   _____

9. Some people believe that <u>a reading of the stars</u> will predict their futures.

   _____

10. What do you call <u>men who travel in space</u>? _____

11. What do you call <u>men who travel undersea</u>? _____

12. My favorite course is <u>the study of stars, planets, and space</u>. _____

13. I enjoy studying about <u>water</u> plants and animals. _____

14. I keep my water plants and animals in <u>a large tank</u> where I can watch them.

    _____

15. The judge said that the people in court should <u>come together</u> again at two in the afternoon. _____

16. I enjoy attending <u>formal professional meetings</u>. _____

17. Attending classes in the afternoon is not <u>suitable</u> for me because I work in the afternoon. _____

18. That is <u>powerful</u> medicine you are taking. _____

19. The person in charge was merely a figurehead who was <u>without power</u>. _____

20. If I knew what my <u>possible ability</u> was, I would try to do something with it. _____

21. The bandits seemed to be <u>present everywhere at all times</u>. _____

---

**STOP.**  Check answers at the end of this chapter (p. 144).

---

## Additional Practice 2 for Exercise 8

**A. Directions:**  The combining forms presented in Exercise 8 follow. Match each combining form with its meaning.

| | | |
|---|---|---|
| _____ 1. cide | a. | into; in |
| _____ 2. pathy | b. | kill; murder |
| _____ 3. syl, sym, syn | c. | death |
| _____ 4. frater, fratr | d. | same; with; together; along with |
| _____ 5. mors, mort | e. | brother |
| _____ 6. capit | f. | feeling; suffering |
| _____ 7. corp, corpo | g. | head |
| _____ 8. em, en | h. | body |

---

**STOP.**  Check answers at the end of this chapter (p. 144).

**B. Directions:**  Sentences containing the meanings of vocabulary presented in Exercise 8 follow. Choose the word that *best* fits the meaning of the word or phrase underlined in the sentence.

**Word List**

| | | |
|---|---|---|
| apathy | empathy | mortality |
| capital | fraternity | mortals |
| capitalism | genocide | mortgage |
| capital punishment | homicide | mortician |
| corporal punishment | immortals | suicide |
| corporation | incorporate | sympathy |
| corpse | morgue | |

1. More and more people are involved in <u>the act of killing others</u>.

   _____

2. Only a madman would attempt <u>the destruction of a whole race of people</u>.

   _____

3. I have <u>the ability to understand how you feel</u> because I had the same experience. _____

4. I have <u>no feeling</u> about that. _____

5. I have <u>pity</u> for the child who lost both parents in an accident.

   _____

6. The man resorted to <u>the act of killing himself</u> when he lost all his money.

   _____

7. I am joining <u>a Greek letter college organization</u> next semester.

   _____

8. My father's friends formed <u>an association of a number of businessmen, which took out a special charter granting it certain rights</u>. _____

9. In the United States we have <u>an economic system based on private ownership and profit</u>. _____

10. Are you and the other men going to <u>join together to form a business</u>?

    _____

11. All <u>human beings</u> must eventually die. _____

12. <u>Undying beings</u> do not exist on earth. _____

13. We found <u>a dead body</u> in the woods. _____

14. I wonder if <u>the death penalty</u> will return. _____

15. Many persons believe that children should not be subjected to <u>a beating</u> in school. _____

16. Do you know <u>the death rate</u> of teenagers involved in automobile accidents? _____

17. Because it was unidentified, the body was taken to <u>a special place where unidentified bodies are held</u> until it could be claimed. _____

18. They had difficulty paying off <u>the loan on their property</u> because of other very large unexpected expenses. _____

19. She went to <u>an undertaker</u> to arrange for her father's funeral. _____

20. Do you have enough <u>money</u> to start such a business venture? _____

---

**STOP.**  Check answers at the end of this chapter (p. 144).

---

# Additional Practice 3 for Exercise 9

**A. Directions:**  The combining forms presented in Exercise 9 follow. Match each combining form with its meaning.

| | | |
|---|---|---|
| _____ 1. man, manu | a. | make; do |
| _____ 2. fac, fect, fic | b. | place |
| _____ 3. loc, loco | c. | hear |
| _____ 4. pseudo | d. | care |
| _____ 5. bene | e. | name |
| _____ 6. aud, audi | f. | false |
| _____ 7. cura | g. | good |
| _____ 8. nomin, onym | h. | hand |

---

**STOP.**  Check answers at the end of this chapter (p. 144).

---

**B. Directions:** Sentences containing the meanings of vocabulary presented in Exercise 9 follow. Choose the word that *best* fits the meaning of the word or phrase underlined in the sentence.

**Word List**

| | | |
|---|---|---|
| affect | auditorium | location |
| allocate | benefactor | manicure |
| anonymous | beneficiary | manual |
| antonyms | benefit | manufacture |
| audible | effect | manuscript |
| audience | effective | misnomer |
| audiovisual | factory | pseudonyms |
| audit | homonyms | synonyms |
| audition | local | |

1. She goes to the beauty shop for <u>the care of her fingernails.</u> _____

2. We learned <u>the style of writing our letters without joining them together.</u>

   _____

3. The <u>building in which furniture is made</u> burned to the ground.

   _____

4. Many artists have <u>a person who supports them</u> so that they do not have to worry about money. _____

5. <u>Hand</u> labor does not bother me. _____

6. The speaker was just <u>capable of being heard.</u> _____

7. When they <u>examine the accounts</u>, they had better balance, or you will be in trouble. _____

8. There will be <u>a tryout</u> for the new play next week. _____

9. In my school we use a lot of <u>television, radio, records, and picture</u> aids.

   _____

10. The method you have for studying is really <u>productive in getting results</u> for you.

    _____

11. The concert is being held in <u>a large special room</u> used for such performances in the school. _____

12. In this day and age we <u>make goods by machinery</u> on a large scale in order to have enough available for so many people. _____

13. What <u>result</u>, if any, did you find? _____

14. I just found out that I am <u>the receiver of a large amount of money</u> that was left to me by an old uncle who recently died. _____

15. What is the major <u>advantage</u> of going to college? _____

16. <u>The group of listeners at the concert</u> was so quiet that you could hear a pin drop. _____

17. I am not going to <u>influence</u> your brother in any way. _____

18. *Bear* and *bare* are <u>words that sound alike but are spelled differently and have different meanings.</u> _____

19. *Corpulent* and *fat* are <u>words similar in meaning.</u> _____

20. *Antonym* and *synonym* are <u>words opposite in meaning.</u> _____

21. Some authors use <u>pen names or names other than their own names.</u>

_____

22. When I used the term *misanthrope* to mean a hater of marriage, I was using <u>a wrong word.</u> _____

23. The poem was <u>without an author's name.</u> _____

24. I shop only in <u>neighborhood</u> stores. _____

25. The men will <u>set aside</u> a certain number of tickets for us.

_____

26. Our house is in a lovely <u>place.</u> _____

> **STOP.** Check answers at the end of this chapter (p. 144).

# ANSWERS: *Chapter Four*

## Exercise 7 (pp. 89–99)

### Practice A

(1) astronaut, (2) aquanaut, (3) aquatic, (4) potent, (5) aquarium, (6) astrology, (7) astronomy, (8) evident, (9) provision, (10) impotent, (11) evidence, (12) science, (13) Convention, (14) vision, (15) omnipresent, (16) convenient, (17) potential, (18) convene.

### Practice B

(1) reporter, (2) decade, (3) anniversary, (4) evident, (5) television, (6) television, (7) convenient, (8) scientists, (9) convention, (10) convention, (11) astronauts, (12) aquatic, (13) aquanauts, (14) astrologist, (15) convention, (16) television,

(17) incredible, (18) visible,[1] (19) evident, (20) omnipresent, (21) television, (22) incredible, (23) impotent, (24) astronauts, (25) aquanauts, (26) invisible, (27) visible, (28) provision, (29) evidence.

## Practice C

(1) vision, (2) provisions, (3) aquanauts, (4) evidence, (5) convenient, (6) evident, (7) potent, (8) television, omnipresent, (9) potential, (10) impotent.

## Additional Words Derived from Combining Forms (pp. 97–98)

1. **omnipotent.**  All-powerful.

2. **omniscient.**  All-knowing.

3. **omnibus.**  A large bus designed to carry a number of people as passengers. An *omnibus* bill is a legislative bill that carries a mixture of provisions.

4. **visage.**  The face; the appearance of the face or its expression.

5. **visor.**  The projecting front brim of a cap for shading the eyes.

6. **visa.**  Something stamped or written on a passport that grants an individual entry to a country.

7. **envision.**  To imagine something; to picture in the mind.

8. **visionary.**  A person who sees visions.

9. **nautical.**  Pertaining to seamen, ships, or navigation.

10. **venture.**  A risky or dangerous undertaking, especially a business enterprise in which there is a danger of loss as well as a chance for profit.

11. **potentate.**  A person possessing great power; a ruler; a monarch.

## Practice for Additional Words Derived from Combining Forms (p. 99)

(1) e, (2) h, (3) f, (4) b, (5) k, (6) j, (7) i, (8) d, (9) g, (10) a, (11) c.

# Exercise 8 (pp. 99–110)

## Practice A

(1) capital, (2) corporation, (3) capitalism, (4) capital, (5) mortgage, (6) morgue, (7) mortician, (8) incorporate, (9) immortal, (10) mortality, (11) mortal, (12) capital punishment, (13) homicide, (14) capital punishment, corporal punishment, (15) empathy, (16) sympathy, (17) genocide, (18) apathy, (19) suicide, (20) fraternity.

## Practice B

(1) c, (2) d, (3) b, (4) c, (5) a, (6) a, (7) b, (8) a, (9) d, (10) a, (11) c, (12) a, (13) a, (14) d, (15) d, (16) a, (17) b, (18) c, (19) b.

---

[1]Answer can be either *evident* or *visible*.

## Practice C

(1) killing of one person by another, (2) killing of oneself, (3) lack of feeling, (4) ability to feel sorry for, (5) a men's organization at college, (6) the killing of a whole group of people, (7) city or town that is the official seat of government, (8) place where unidentified dead are kept, (9) undertaker, (10) joined together; group of people who get a charter granting them certain rights as a body, (11) a beating, (12) death penalty, (13) that which never dies, (14) person who must die or human being, (15) pledge of property as security with a creditor.

## Additional Words Derived from Combining Forms (p. 108–110)

1. **fratricide.** The killing of a brother; may also refer to the killing of a sister.
2. **corpulent.** Fat; fleshy; obese.
3. **mortify.** To cause to feel shame; to punish (one's body) or control (one's physical desires or passions) by self-denial, fasting, and the like, as a means of religious or ascetic (severe) discipline.
4. **amortize.** The gradual extinction of a debt such as a mortgage or a bond issue by payment of a part of the principal at the time of each periodic interest payment.
5. **caption.** The head of a chapter, section, or page in a book; a title or subtitle of a picture.
6. **capitulate.** To give up; surrender.
7. **symbol.** Something that stands for or represents another thing; an object used to represent something abstract.
8. **syllable.** A vowel or a group of letters with one vowel sound.
9. **monosyllable.** A word consisting of a single syllable.
10. **symphony.** Harmony of sound; harmony of any kind.
11. **symptom.** In medicine, a condition that results from a disease and serves as an aid in diagnosis; a sign or token that indicates the existence of something else.
12. **synthesis.** A putting together of two or more things to form a whole.
13. **symmetry.** Balanced form or arrangement; balance on both sides.

## Practice for Additional Words Derived from Combining Forms (p. 110)

(1) i, (2) m, (3) b, (4) a, (5) d, (6) j, (7) c, (8) l, (9) f, (10) h, (11) g, (12) e, (13) k.

# Exercise 9 (pp. 111–121)

## Practice A

(1) pseudonym, (2) misnomer, (3) antonym, (4) synonym, (5) anonymous, (6) manual, (7) manuscript, (8) manicure, (9) factory, (10) benefactor, (11) beneficiary, (12) benefit, (13) manufacture, (14) affect, (15) effect, (16) effective, (17) auditorium, (18) audience, (19) audible, (20) audiovisual, (21) audition, (22) audit, (23) allocate, (24) location, (25) local, (26) homonym.

## Practice B

(1) beneficiary, (2) factory, (3) pseudonym, (4) anonymous, (5) manuscript, (6) auditorium, (7) effect, (8) affect, (9) synonym, (10) antonym, (11) homonym, (12) effective, (13) allocated, (14) audible, (15) local, (16) audit, (17) audition.

## Practice C

(1) manual, (2) benefit, (3) factory, (4) manufacture, (5) benefactor, (6) beneficiary, (7) factory, (8) location, (9) audience, (10) effective, (11) effect, (12) audible, (13) local, (14) audition, (15) manicure, (16) audition, (17) location, (18) audible, (19) manicure, (20) pseudonym.

## Additional Words Derived from Combining Forms (pp. 119–120)

1. **audiometer.**  An instrument used to measure hearing.

2. **audiology.**  The study of hearing.

3. **benediction.**  A blessing; the expression of good wishes.

4. **antipathy.**  A dislike for someone.

5. **pseudopodium.**  False foot.

6. **curator.**  Head of a museum or head of a department of a museum; one in charge.

7. **pedicure.**  Care of the feet, toes, and nails.

8. **pseudoscience.**  A false science.

9. **manipulation.**  The act of handling or operating; the act of managing or controlling skillfully or by shrewd use of influence; the act of changing or falsification for one's own purposes or profit.

10. **emancipate.**  To set free from servitude or slavery; to set free.

11. **personification.**  A figure of speech in which a nonliving thing or idea is made to appear as having the qualities of a person.

12. **facsimile.**  An exact copy; to make an exact copy of.

13. **faction.**  A number of persons in an organization, group, government, party, and so on, having a common goal, often self-seeking and reckless of the common good.

## Practice for Additional Words Derived from Combining Forms (p.121)

(1) h, (2) i, (3) a, (4) e, (5) l, (6) g, (7) m, (8) j, (9) k, (10) c, (11) d, (12) b, (13) f.

# Chapter Words in Sentences (pp. 121–122)

Sentences will vary.

# Chapter Words in a Paragraph (p.122)

Paragraphs will vary.

## Analogies 3 (pp. 121–123)

(1) underwater, (2) omnipresent, (3) impotent, (4) convene, (5) pseudoscience, (6) pseudopodal, (7) mortify, (8) caption, (9) visage, (10) facsimile, (11) audiology, (12) homicide, (13) corpulent, (14) antipathy, (15) convenient, (16) apathy, (17) creed, (18) effect, (19) anonymous, (20) capitulate.

## Multiple-Choice Vocabulary Test 3 (pp. 123–130)

### Exercise 7

(1) c, (2) c, (3) b, (4) a, (5) a, (6) a, (7) a, (8) d, (9) b, (10) a, (11) d, (12) b, (13) c, (14) c, (15) c, (16) b, (17) a, (18) c, (19) b, (20) a, (21) d.

### Exercise 8

(22) c, (23) a, (24) b, (25) d, (26) b, (27) c, (28) a, (29) c, (30) d, (31) a, (32) b, (33) c, (34) a, (35) b, (36) d, (37) d, (38) b, (39) d, (40) d, (41) d.

### Exercise 9

(42) a, (43) d, (44) c, (45) c, (46) d, (47) b, (48) c, (49) a,[2] (50) d, (51) b, (52) d, (53) c, (54) d, (55) a, (56) b, (57) d, (58) d, (59) a, (60) b, (61) c, (62) b, (63) d, (64) c, (65) d, (66) d, (67) c.

## True/False Test 3[3] (p. 131)

(1) T;[4] (2) F,[5] also a homicide to a murder by oneself; (3) T; (4) F, Some to No; (5) F,[6] lower to higher; (6) F, is not to is; (7) F, science to pseudoscience; (8) F, Astronauts to Aquanauts or undersea to in space; (9) F, bad time to good time; (10) T; (11) T; (12) T;[7] (13) F, is a fatal illness to a murdering of a whole race of people; (14) F, are to are not or antipathy to indifference or apathy to dislike; (15) T; (16) T; (17) T; (18) F, is to is not or immortal to mortal; (19) F,[8] all dead bodies to unidentified dead bodies or accident victims; (20) T; (21) T; (22) F, are to are not or misnomer to alias; (23) F, are to are not or synonyms to homonyms; (24) T; (25) F, are to are not or anonymous to pseudonym.

---

> **STOP.** Turn to page 132 for the scoring of the tests.

---

[2] *Performance* or *charity* is not specific enough by itself. A benefit performance is a performance for some charity or cause. Not *all* performances are for benefits.

[3] Answers for *false* are suggested answers.

[4] Although a fratricide is the killing of a brother or a sister, it is also a homicide.

[5] A suicide is *not* a homicide because it does not involve another person.

[6] As proportionally more minority group children die than children as a whole, the mortality or death rate for minority group children would be *higher*.

[7] Only for empathy must you experience how the other person feels.

[8] A morgue is a place where only accident victims and other unidentified bodies are kept.

# Additional Practice Sets (pp. 132–139)

### Additional Practice 1

A. (1) c, (2) h, (3) g, (4) b, (5) f, (6) a, (7) e, (8) d.
B. (1) vision, (2) invisible, (3) television, (4) visible,[9] (5) provisions, (6) science, (7) evidence, (8) evident,[9] (9) astrology, (10) astronauts, (11) aquanauts, (12) astronomy, (13) aquatic, (14) aquarium, (15) convene, (16) conventions, (17) convenient, (18) potent, (19) impotent, (20) potential, (21) omnipresent.

### Additional Practice 2

A. (1) b, (2) f, (3) d, (4) e, (5) c, (6) g, (7) h, (8) a.
B. (1) homicide, (2) genocide, (3) empathy, (4) apathy, (5) sympathy, (6) suicide, (7) fraternity, (8) corporation, (9) capitalism, (10) incorporate, (11) mortals, (12) Immortals, (13) corpse, (14) capital punishment, (15) corporal punishment, (16) mortality, (17) morgue, (18) mortgage, (19) mortician, (20) capital.

### Additional Practice 3

A. (1) h, (2) a, (3) b, (4) f, (5) g, (6) c, (7) d, (8) e.
B. (1) manicure, (2) manuscript, (3) factory, (4) benefactor, (5) manual, (6) audible, (7) audit, (8) audition, (9) audiovisual, (10) effective, (11) auditorium, (12) manufacture, (13) effect, (14) beneficiary, (15) benefit, (16) audience, (17) affect, (18) homonyms, (19) synonyms, (20) antonyms, (21) pseudonyms, (22) misnomer, (23) anonymous, (24) local, (25) allocate, (26) location.

---

[9]Although *visible* and *evident* are synonyms, *visible* is the more specific and therefore *better* answer for 4; *evident* is the *better* answer for 8.

# CHAPTER FIVE

# EXERCISE 10

## Step I. Combining Forms

**A. Directions:**  A list of combining forms with their meanings follows. Look at the combining forms and their meanings. Concentrate on learning each combining form and its meaning. Cover the meanings, read the combining forms, and state the meanings to yourself. Check to see if you are correct. Now cover the combining forms, read the meanings, and state the combining forms to yourself. Check to see if you are correct.

| Combining Forms | Meanings |
| --- | --- |
| 1. dia | through |
| 2. cata | down |
| 3. log, logo | speech; word |
| 4. fin | end |
| 5. biblio | book |
| 6. fer | bring; bear; yield (give up) |
| 7. epi | upon; beside; among |
| 8. pro | before; forward |

**B. Directions:**   Do not look at the preceding meanings. Write the meanings of the following combining forms.

| Combining Forms | Meanings |
|---|---|
| 1. dia | _____ |
| 2. cata | _____ |
| 3. log, logo | _____ |
| 4. fin | _____ |
| 5. biblio | _____ |
| 6. fer | _____ |
| 7. epi | _____ |
| 8. pro | _____ |

## Step II. Words Derived from Combining Forms

1. **logical** (log·i·cal) (loj′i·kal) *adj.* Relating to the science concerned with correct reasoning.

   *The arguments that you are giving are not very **logical** because the reasoning is faulty.*

2. **prologue** (prō′logúé) *n.* An introduction, often in verse (poetry), spoken or sung before a play or opera; any introductory or preceding event; a preface.

   *The **prologue** of the play comes at the beginning and sometimes introduces the characters or sets the mood for the play.*

3. **epilogue** (ep′i·logúé) *n.* A short section added at the end to a book, poem, and so on; a short speech added to a play and given at the end.

   *We were very moved by the actor's **epilogue** at the end of the play.*

4. **catalog** (cat·a·log) (kat′a·log) *n.* A listing of names, titles, and so on, in some order; a book containing such a list. *v.* To make a catalog.

   *The card **catalog** in the library lists books in alphabetical order according to topics, authors, and titles.*

5. **dialogue** (dī′a·logúé) *n.* A conversation in which two or more take part; the conversation in a play.

   *John and Mary had such a good **dialogue** going that, when the bell rang, they still continued their conversation.*

6. **diagram** (dī′a·gram) *n.* An outline figure that shows the relationship among parts or places; a graph or chart.

   *The **diagram** showing the circulatory system of the body helped me to see the relationship between the veins and arteries.*

7. **diameter** (dī·am′e·ter) *n.* A straight line passing through the center of a circle.

   *The **diameter** of a circle divides the circle in half because it passes through the center of it from one end to the other.*

8. **bibliography** (bib·li·og·ra·phy) (bib·lē·og′ra·fē) *n.* (*pl.* **phies**) A listing of books on a subject or by an author (the description includes author's name, title, publisher, date of publication, and so on).

   *The **bibliography** for my paper was large because our teacher wanted us to list at least twenty books on the topic we were writing about.*

9. **final** (fī′nal) *adj.* Conclusive; last; coming at or relating to the end.

   *Most instructors give a **final** examination at the end of the semester.*

10. **finite** (fī′nīte) *adj.* Having a limit or end; able to be measured.

    *Because there are a **finite** number of places where the missing item can be, we'll find it.*

11. **infinite** (in′fi·nite) *adj.* Having no limit or end; not able to be measured.

    *If the universe is **infinite**, it has no beginning or end.*

12. **fertile** (fer′tile) *adj.* Able to produce a large crop; able to produce; capable of bearing offspring, seeds, fruit, and so on; productive in mental achievements; inventive; having abundant resources.

    *The land was so **fertile** that each year it produced a very large crop*

13. **fertilization** (fer·til·i·za·tion) (fer·til·i·zā′shun) *n.* The act of making something able to produce; in biology, the union of a male and female germ cell; impregnation.

    *Human **fertilization** takes place when a sperm cell and egg cell unite.*

14. **reference** (ref·er·ence) (ref′er·ense) *n.* A referring or being referred; the giving of a problem to a person, a committee, or an authority for settlement; a note in a book that sends the reader for information to another book; the name of another person who can offer information or recommendation; the mark or sign, as a number or letter, directing the reader to a footnote, and so on; a written statement of character, qualification, or ability; testimonial.

    *My biology and geology instructors said that they would give me good **references** for a job after college.*

15. **preference** (pref·er·ence) (pref′er·ense) *n.* The choosing of one person or thing over another; the valuing of one over another; a liking better.

    *Her **preference** for science courses is obvious, for she chooses those over all others.*

16. **transfer** (trans′fer) *v.* To carry or send from one person or place to another; to cause to pass from one person or place to another. *n.* An act of transferring or being transferred.

    *When my boss said he would **transfer** me to another department, I was very pleased because I wanted to go to the other place.*

17. **conference** (con·fer·ence) (kon′·fer·ense) *n.* A discussion or meeting on some important matter.

    *Because the dean wanted a **conference** with the students involved in the fight, he asked his secretary to call in the students for a meeting with him.*

18. **suffer** (suf′·fer) *v.* To feel pain or distress.

    *The woman who lost five sons in World War II must have **suffered** a great deal.*

19. **circumference** (cir·cum·fer·ence) (sir·kum′fer·ense) *n.* The distance around a circle; a boundary line of any rounded area.

    *When we speak of the **circumference** of the globe, we refer to the distance around the globe.*

## SPECIAL NOTES

1. *Prologue* and *preface* are both introductory statements. However, a *prologue* is usually found at the beginning of a play or poem but usually not in a book such as a novel or textbook. In a book, article, or speech, the introduction found at the beginning is usually called a *preface*. The preface sets forth the plan, purpose, and so on, of the book, article, or speech.

2. *logical*. Relating to correct reasoning. A person who is *logical* is able to present arguments in a carefully thought out manner so that each statement correctly follows the other.

## Step III. Words in Context

Writing has never been easy for me. Maybe I don't have a **fertile** brain; maybe I don't have the sitting power; maybe I can't **transfer** my thoughts very well to a blank sheet of paper that is staring at me. Whatever the reasons, and these may be **infinite**, I **suffer** a great amount of anxiety when I have to write anything. You can imagine my state of mind when our professor, Dr. Percy, said that one of the class requirements was to write a short play and that this would count very heavily toward the **final** grade. My **preference** originally had been for a literature course, but it was full. My heart sank further as the professor's voice droned on with all the other requirements. We needed to include a **prologue** or introduction, as well as an **epilogue**. Dr. Percy wanted good **dialogue**, and the play had to develop in a **logical** fashion. She also wanted us to write a paper on the type of play we had chosen to write. She wanted us to use **references** and to read a number of plays by different playwrights and list them in a formal **bibliography**.

Dr. Percy suggested we become familiar with the card **catalog** in the library. She said also that she would have an individual **conference** with each of us to discuss our progress. I couldn't believe my ears! I have only a **finite** amount of time to work in this course. Dr. Percy must think that her course is the only one that we are taking. In addition, she told us that during the semester we would be going to see three plays in the local theater. She showed us a **diagram** of it and said that the theater was very unusual because it was round and the stage was in the center of the theater right on its **diameter**. She asked us to guess the **circumference** of the theater. She then told us that the first play we would see dealt with a couple's problems with **fertilization**.

## Step IV. Practice

**A. Directions:** A number of sentences with missing words follow. Fill in the word that *best* fits the sentence. Two choices are given for each sentence.

1. _____ in plants also involves the union of egglike and spermlike cells. (Circumference, Fertilization)

2. A _____ is an outline figure that shows the relationship between parts or places. (diameter, diagram)

3. A(n) _____ is found at the end of a book. (prologue, epilogue)

4. In order to engage in a _____, you need two or more people interested in the topic of discussion. (dialogue, prologue)

5. When a limited number of something exists, it means that the number is

_____. (final, finite)

6. The biologists held a number of _____s to discuss important topics. (conference, circumference)

7. The _____ is a listing of books that usually comes at the end of a research paper, a report, or an essay. (bibliography, catalog)

8. When someone has a _____ for something, he or she usually chooses that thing over another. (reference, preference)

9. An introduction to a play or poem is called a _____. (dialogue, prologue)

10. The _____ exam will come on the last day of class. (finite, final)

11. Time is considered _____ because it goes on without end. (infinite, final)

12. A(n) _____ lists items in some kind of order. (epilogue, catalog)

13. Both lawyers presented arguments that sounded reasonable and appeared

_____. (logical fertile)

14. The author of the book I am reading made a _____ to another author who has written on the same topic. (reference, preference)

15. When a tomato plant is _____, it can produce a lot. (fertile, finite)

---

**STOP.**   Check answers at the end of this chapter (p. 193).

---

***B. Directions:***   A number of sentences with missing words follows. Choose the word that *best* fits the sentence. Put the word in the blank. All words are used.

**Word List**

| | | |
|---|---|---|
| bibliography | epilogue | logical |
| catalog | fertile | preference |
| circumference | fertilization | prologue |
| conference | final | reference |
| diagram | finite | suffer |
| dialogue | infinite | transfer |
| diameter | | |

1. At the beginning of some plays there is a(n) _____.

2. The _____ between the main characters in the play was interesting to listen to.

3. Some authors add a(n) _____ at the end of their books.

4. _____s have always helped me in learning something because I can understand better when I see an outline picture.

5. Our instructor asked us to list at least twenty-five books for our topic and to make sure that we gave the author, name of book, publisher, and date in the proper form for our _____.

6. As a senior, do you have to take _____s at the end of the semester?

7. Only a(n) _____ number of people can attend the jazz concert because there is limited seating.

8. The number system is _____ because you can go on counting numbers without end.

9. At the science convention, a group of scientists had _____s to discuss some important matters.

10. The _____ cuts a circle in half.

11. The boundary of a circle is called its _____.

12. I am going to _____ my funds from the State National Bank to the Security Bank because the Security Bank pays more interest.

13. Because your argument is full of holes, it is not very _____.

14. A file clerk has to _____ things in some order.

15. The soil in our garden is so _____ that we can grow practically anything.

16. I asked Professor Jones, from whom I received an *A*, if I could use his name as a(n) _____ for a job.

17. Because she has a(n) _____ for certain kinds of clothing, I know exactly what she will choose.

18. He was willing to _____ and bear the pain of another operation if it meant that he would walk again.

19. In the process of sexual reproduction, the union of sperm and egg is called _____.

---

**STOP.** Check answers at the end of this chapter (p. 193).

**C. Directions:**  Fill in each blank with the word that matches the meaning. Some words are from other exercises.

1. Endless _____

2. A listing of books _____

3. Last _____

4. Killing of oneself _____

5. An introduction _____

6. Not believable _____

7. Not legal _____

8. Able to produce _____

9. Able to be measured; having an end _____

10. Relating to correct reasoning _____

11. A listing of names, titles, and so on, in some order _____

12. A conversation _____

13. The act of making something able to produce _____

14. The distance around a circle _____

15. A straight line passing through the center of a circle _____

16. A short section added to the end of a book _____

17. An outline figure that shows the relationship among parts _____

18. To feel pain or distress _____

19. A note in a book that sends the reader to another book _____

20. The choosing of one person or thing over another _____

21. A discussion or meeting of some important matter _____

22. To carry from one place to another _____

**STOP.**  Check answers at the end of this chapter (p. 193).

# EXTRA WORD POWER

**im, in.** Into. **in, im, il, ir.** Not.   Note that when *in* is placed at the beginning of a word, it can mean either "into" or "not." Note also that the *n* changes to an *m* when *in* is added to a word beginning with an *m*, *b*, or *p*. Example of *in* meaning "into": *inspection* — the act of looking into something. *The inspector gave the restaurant a careful* **inspection** *to see if everything was in order.* Examples of *in* meaning "not": *infinite* — not ending; *ineffectual* — not being able to bring about results. *The lifeguard was* **ineffectual** *in his efforts to save the drowning child.* Examples of *in* meaning "into" changing to *im*: *import* — to carry in; *important* — deserving of notice, of great value. *The materials being* **imported** *were so* **important** *that fifteen extra guards were hired to watch them as they came off the ship.* Examples of *in* meaning "not" changing to *im*: *imperfect* — not perfect; having a fault. Note that *in* meaning "not" also changes to *il* and *ir* when *in* is added to words beginning with *l* or *r*. For example: *illegal* — not legal; *irregular* — not uniform, not the same.

**trans.** Across; beyond; through; on the other side of; over. When *trans* is placed at the beginning of a word such as the following, it means "across," "beyond," "through," "on the other side of." For example: *transatlantic* — across the Atlantic, on the other side of the Atlantic; *transhuman* — beyond human limits; *transport* — to carry from one place to another; *transparent* — able to be seen through; *transfer* — to move from one place to another.

## Additional Words Derived from Combining Forms

From your knowledge of combining forms, can you define the following words?

1. **inference** (in·fer·ence) (in′fer·ens*ě*) *n.*   *Although he did not say it exactly, the* **inference** *I got was that he was quitting his job.*

   _____

2. **proficient** (pro·fi·cient) (pro·fish′ent) *adj.*   *It was obvious that he was a* **proficient** *skier because he was able to ski from the highest and steepest mountain paths with ease.*

   _____

3. **dialect** (di·a·lect) (dī′a·lekt) *n.*   *It's evident that Jane comes from the South because she speaks a Southern* **dialect**.

   _____

4. **monologue** (mon′o·logu*ě*) *n.*   *Jim's* **monologue** *was so long that after a while nobody was listening to what he was saying.*

   _____

5. **definitive** (de·fin′i·tiv*ě*) *adj.*   *The results from the studies are not* **definitive** *because there are too many different conclusions.*

   _____

6. **finale** (fi·na′lē) *n.*   *The play's **finale** was completely unexpected on the basis of everything that went before.*

_____

7. **affinity** (af·fin·i·ty) (af·fin′i·tē) *n.*   *We knew that our relationship would grow into more than just being acquaintances, because of the **affinity** we had for one another when we first met.*

_____

8. **infinitesimal** (in·fin·i·tes′i·mal) *adj.*   *The size of the microorganism was almost **infinitesimal** because it could be seen only with the most high-powered microscope.*

_____

9. **deference** (def·er·ence) (def′er·ensé) *n.*   *In **deference** to his age and position, the group decided to give him a chance to speak.*

_____

10. **defer** (de·fer′) *v.*   *I will **defer** to my partner because he has studied the matter very closely.*

_____

**STOP.**   Check answers at the end of this chapter (p. 193).

## Practice for Additional Words Derived from Combining Forms

***Directions:***   Match each word with the *best* definition.

_____ 1. inference
_____ 2. proficient
_____ 3. dialect
_____ 4. monologue
_____ 5. infinitesimal
_____ 6. affinity
_____ 7. definitive
_____ 8. finale
_____ 9. deference
_____ 10. defer

a. respect
b. too small to be measured
c. able to do something very well
d. a conclusion drawn from statements
e. to leave to another's opinion
f. conclusive
g. long speech by one person
h. close relationship
i. the last part
j. a variety of speech

**STOP.**   Check answers at the end of this chapter (p. 193).

© 1960 United Feature Syndicate, Inc.

# EXERCISE 11

## Step I. Combining Forms

**A. Directions:**   A list of combining forms with their meanings follows. Look at the combining forms and their meanings. Concentrate on learning each combining form and its meaning. Cover the meanings, read the combining forms, and state the meanings to yourself. Check to see if you are correct. Now cover the combining forms, read the meanings, and state the combining forms to yourself. Check to see if you are correct.

| Combining Forms | Meanings |
|---|---|
| 1. cap, cep | take, receive |
| 2. gnosi, gnosis | knowledge |
| 3. ped, pedo | child |
| 4. tox, toxo | poison |
| 5. gyn, gyno | woman |
| 6. temp, tempo, tempor | time |
| 7. hypo | under |
| 8. derm, dermo | skin |
| 9. ri, ridi, risi | laughter |

**B. Directions:**   Do not look at the preceding meanings. Write the meanings of the following combining forms.

| Combining Forms | Meanings |
|---|---|
| 1. cap, cep | _____ |
| 2. gnosi, gnosis | _____ |
| 3. ped, pedo | _____ |
| 4. tox, toxo | _____ |
| 5. gyn, gyno | _____ |

6. temp, tempo, tempor  _____

7. hypo  _____

8. derm, dermo  _____

9. ri, ridi, risi  _____

## Step II. Words Derived from Combining Forms

1. **capable** (ca·pa·ble) (kā′pa·bul) *adj.* Able to be affected; able to understand; having ability; having qualities that are able to be developed.

   *Although he is **capable** of many things, time will tell whether he will use all his abilities.*

2. **captive** (cap·tive) (kap′tivé) *n.* One who is taken prisoner; one who is dominated.

   *When the daughter of a wealthy man was held a **captive** by dangerous criminals, one million dollars was paid to the criminals to release the girl.*

3. **conceive** (con·ceive) (kon·sēivé′) *v.* To become pregnant with; to form in the mind; to understand; to think; to believe; to imagine; to develop mentally.

   *I cannot **conceive** of him as a scientist because the image I have of him is as a playboy.*

4. **deceive** (de·ceive) (de·sēivé′) *v.* To mislead by lying; to lead into error.

   *I couldn't believe that my best friend told all those lies to **deceive** me.*

5. **reception** (re·cep·tion) (re·sep′shun) *n.* The act of receiving or being received; a formal social entertainment; the manner of receiving someone; the receiving of a radio or television broadcast.

   *I received a warm **reception** when I attended Laura's wedding **reception**, which was the social event of the year.*

6. **exception** (ex·cep·tion) (ek·sep′shun) *n.* The act of taking out; something that is taken out or left out; an objection.

   *In English spelling there always seems to be an **exception** to which the rule does not apply.*

7. **perception** (per·cep·tion) (per·sep′shun) *n.* The act of becoming aware of something through the senses of seeing, hearing, feeling, tasting, or smelling.

   *If you have something wrong with your senses, your **perception** will be faulty.*

8. **capsule** (cap·sule) (kap′sulé) *n.* A small container made of gelatin (or other material that melts) that holds a dose of medicine; a special removable part of an airplane or rocket.

   *Each **capsule** contained the exact amount of medicine the doctor wanted me to take.*

9. **ridiculous** (ri·dic·u·lous) (ri·dik′yu·lóus) *adj.* Unworthy of consideration; absurd (senseless); preposterous.

   *His suggestion was so **ridiculous** that no one would even consider it.*

10. **ridicule** (rid·i·cule) (rid′i·kūlé) *n.* The language or actions that make a person the object of mockery or cause one to be laughed at or scorned. *v.* To mock or view someone in a scornful way; to hold someone up as a laughingstock; to make fun of.

    *I think it is cruel when someone **ridicules** another person and holds him or her up as a laughingstock.*

11. **diagnose** (dī·ag·nōsé′) *v.* To determine what is wrong with someone after an examination.

    *It is very important for a doctor to be able to **diagnose** a person's illness correctly so that the doctor will know how to treat it.*

12. **prognosis** (prog·nō′sis) *n.* (*pl.* **ses**) (sēz) A prediction or conclusion regarding the course of a disease and the chances of recovery; a prediction.

    *Because the doctor's **prognosis** regarding John's illness was favorable, we knew that he would recover.*

13. **pediatrician** (pe·di·a·tri·cian) (pē·dē·a·trish′un) *n.* A doctor who specializes in children's diseases.

    *I like to take my children to a **pediatrician** for a checkup rather than to a general doctor because a **pediatrician** deals only with children's diseases.*

BLOOM COUNTY. © 1985, Washington Post Writers Group. Reprinted with permission.

14. **gynecologist** (gyn·e·col·o·gist) (gī·ne·kol′o·jist) *n.* A doctor dealing with women's diseases, especially in reference to the reproductive organs.

    *Many women go to a **gynecologist** for an annual checkup even if they have no symptoms of anything wrong.*

15. **toxic** (tox·ic) (tok′sik) *adj.* Relating to poison.

    *Children should not be allowed to lick painted walls because some paints have **toxic** materials in them.*

16. **dermatologist** (der·ma·tol·o·gist) (der·ma·tol′o·jist) *n.* A doctor who deals with skin disorders.

    *When I broke out in a rash, I went to a **dermatologist** to find out what was wrong with me.*

17. **hypodermic** (hy·po·der·mic) (hī·po·der′mik) *adj.* Referring to the area under the skin; used for injecting under the skin. *n.* A hypodermic injection; a hypodermic syringe or needle.

    *The doctor injected the **hypodermic** needle so far under my skin that my arm hurt all day.*

18. **hypothesis** (hy·poth·e·sis) (hī·poth′e·sis) *n.* (*pl.* **ses**) (sēz) An unproved scientific conclusion drawn from known facts; something assumed as a basis for argument; a possible answer to a problem that requires further investigation.

    *The **hypothesis** that was put forth as the solution to the problem seemed logical, but it required further investigation to prove whether it was correct.*

19. **temporary** (tem·po·rar·y) (tem′po·rar·ē) *adj.* Lasting for a short period of time.

    *I was not upset when I was dismissed from my job because I had been told, when hired, that it was only a **temporary** position.*

20. **contemporary** (con·tem·po·rar·y) (kon·tem′po·rar·ē) *adj.* Belonging to the same age; living or occurring at the same time; current. *n.* (*pl.* **ies**) One living in the same period as another or others; a person or thing of about the same age or date of origin.

    *Even though they act like **contemporaries**, they are a generation apart.*

## SPECIAL NOTES

1. The term *exception*, meaning "something or one that is left out," has a special meaning when it is used in the phrase *to take exception*. *To take exception* means "to disagree," "to object." For example: *I take exception to what you are saying.*

2. *Hypothesis* is a term that is much used in the area of logic and science. Hypothesis may be defined as an unproved scientific conclusion drawn from known facts and used as a basis for further investigation. In science, *hypothesis* is a possible explanation of observed facts and must be found true or false by more experiments.

3. You met the combining forms *ped, pod* in Exercise 1 of Chapter Two. *Ped, pod* mean "foot" in such words as *biped, pedestrian, apodal, pseudopodia,* and *podiatrist. Ped, pedo* means "child" in such words as *pediatrician* and *pedagogue.*

4. *Capsule* can also mean "something extremely brief" such as an outline or survey. When *capsule* is used as an adjective, it means "extremely brief or small and very compact." When someone asks for a capsule report of something, he or she wants a very brief report.

## Step III. Words in Context

In **contemporary** times life can be rather confusing. For example, it may sound **ridiculous**, but I don't know what to eat anymore. Everything seems to have something **toxic** in it. A **pediatrician diagnosed** my child's problem recently and said it was due to what he was eating. He told me to make sure I do not give my child anything that has artificial color in it because it makes him overactive. I don't think you can **conceive** of how may foods have artificial color in them. We are really **captives** of the food manufacturers. Just read some of the labels. Often the advertisers try to **deceive** us into thinking that their foods are pure when they are not. They package them in such a way that we get a deceptive **perception** of the item.

Recently, my **gynecologist** told me that I should not drink coffee any more because it was bad for me; it could cause lumps in the breast. Also, since my cholesterol is very high, my family doctor suggested that I avoid beef and fatty foods. He also said that this should not be a **temporary** measure but a permanent one. He said that these foods are **capable** of clogging my arteries. Without **exception** there seems to be some food that is bad for you. When my husband broke out in hives, the **dermatologist** said it was due to something he had eaten. I just do not feel I am **capable** of figuring out what foods to buy anymore.

Have you ever noticed how most of the commercials deal with yummy junk food? Yet we live in a society where everyone wants to be thin. Have you also ever noticed how on television shows the people are always eating three full meals and go to fancy **receptions** and still stay slim? Amazing! Have you also seen how television shows usually **ridicule** fat people?

I believe in the **hypothesis** that much of our ills is due to what we eat. I do not believe, however, in some people's **prognosis** that soon many of us, instead of eating, will just take various food **capsules** three times a day or give ourselves **hypodermic** injections that will have all the vitamins and nutrients that we require based on our body weight and height.

## Step IV. Practice

**A. Directions:**   The words presented in Exercise 11 follow. Match each word with its meaning.

| | |
|---|---|
| _____ 1. diagnose | a.  having ability |
| _____ 2. prognosis | b.  a small container that holds a dose of medicine |
| _____ 3. pediatrician | c.  the act of taking out |
| _____ 4. gynecologist | d.  to become pregnant with; to think |
| _____ 5. toxic | e.  a prisoner |
| _____ 6. dermatologist | f.  a formal social entertainment; act of receiving |
| _____ 7. capable | g.  the act of becoming aware of something through the senses |
| _____ 8. captive | h.  to mislead by lying |
| _____ 9. deceive | i.  referring to the area under the skin |
| _____ 10. reception | j.  an unproved scientific conclusion |
| _____ 11. conceive | |
| _____ 12. perception | |

_____ 13. exception

_____ 14. ridicule

_____ 15. capsule

_____ 16. ridiculous

_____ 17. hypodermic

_____ 18. hypothesis

_____ 19. temporary

_____ 20. contemporary

k.  to mock or view someone in a scornful way

l.  absurd; beyond belief

m.  a doctor who specializes in skin diseases

n.  referring to poison

o.  a doctor who specializes in children's diseases

p.  a prediction

q.  to determine what is wrong with someone after an examination

r.  a doctor who specializes in women's diseases

s.  of the same age; current

t.  for a short period of time

---

**STOP.**  Check answers at the end of this chapter (p. 194).

---

**_B. Directions:_**  Each sentence has a missing word. Choose the word that _best_ completes the sentence. Write the word in the blank.

**Word List**

| | | |
|---|---|---|
| capable | diagnose | prognosis |
| capsule | exception | reception |
| captive | gynecologist | ridicule |
| conceive | hypodermic | ridiculous |
| contemporary | hypothesis | temporary |
| deceive | pediatrician | toxic |
| dermatologist | perception | |

1. The scientists came up with a(n) _____, which they felt needed further testing to determine if it was the solution to their problem.

2. It is _____ to believe that an eighty-five-year-old man can ride a bicycle across the whole United States, so I will not even consider the idea.

3. As I don't know what these spots on my face and hands are, I'm going to visit a(n) _____.

4. The space _____ left the rocket at the proper time.

5. Because the patient could not take any medicine by mouth, the doctor told the nurse to give the patient the medicine using a(n) _____ needle.

6. When I am ill, I want a doctor who is able to _____
   what is wrong with me.

7. After being _____s for three years or more, some
   prisoners of war had a difficult time adjusting to normal life.

8. The help I need is _____ because we are leaving
   in a short period of time.

9. The doctor's _____ for the patient's recovery was
   favorable.

10. _____ materials are dangerous and should be
    clearly marked as poisonous.

11. It's a shame that someone who is as _____ as you
    are is not doing anything with his ability.

12. I dislike people who _____ others by making fun
    of them.

13. It is incredible that in _____ times there are
    still people in the United States who do not have indoor bathrooms and other
    modern conveniences.

14. A(n) _____ to a rule is something that does
    not fit in.

15. The wedding _____ of the two wealthiest persons
    in the world was held in the largest ballroom the reporters ever saw, and it was
    a spectacular affair.

16. Many parents like to take their young children to _____s
    because they prefer doctors who specialize in children's diseases.

17. Nobody was able to _____ of a plan that was
    agreeable to all because everyone thought of a different one.

18. Some husbands or wives _____ their spouses by
    telling them lies.

19. Because I prefer a doctor who specializes in women's diseases, I go to a(n)
    _____.

20. A person who is deaf has no _____ of what it
    is to hear.

---

**STOP.**   Check answers at the end of this chapter (p. 194).

**C. Directions:**   Twenty sentences containing the meanings of vocabulary presented in Exercise 11 follow. Choose the word that *best* fits the meaning of the word or phrase underlined in the sentence.

**Word List**

| | | |
|---|---|---|
| capable | diagnose | prognosis |
| capsules | exception | reception |
| captive | gynecologist | ridicule |
| conceive | hypodermic | ridiculous |
| contemporaries | hypothesis | temporary |
| deceive | pediatrician | toxic |
| dermatologist | perception | |

1. As a person <u>having ability</u>, you should do well in college.

   _____

2. I knew they were happy to see us because of the <u>manner in which they received us</u> when we visited them.

   _____

3. I become very upset when I learn how some leaders of our country <u>mislead us by lying</u> to us.

   _____

4. I can't <u>think</u> of you as someone interested in astrology.

   _____

5. What you have said is so <u>unworthy of consideration</u> that I will not even repeat it to anyone.

   _____

6. How cruel of those children to <u>make fun of</u> the poor man.

   _____

7. Would you believe that I have to take ten <u>tiny containers of medicine</u> like this every day?

   _____

8. Blind persons seem to have a more developed <u>sense</u> of hearing because they seem to be able to hear things that others can't.

   _____

9. Almost every general rule has <u>an example that does not belong.</u>

   _____

10. When I received <u>an injection by needle under my skin</u>, I broke out in a cold sweat.

_____

11. The geologist has come up with <u>a possible solution to a problem</u> he has been working on, and now he would like to test it to determine if it is correct.

_____

12. At the political rally, I met a lot of <u>people of my same age group</u>.

_____

13. We waited anxiously to hear what the doctor's <u>prediction</u> would be concerning our
mother's heart condition.

_____

14. <u>After an examination</u>, the doctor was able <u>to tell what was wrong</u> with our mother.

_____

15. I feel that it's best to take a child to <u>a doctor who specializes in children's diseases</u>.

_____

16. I feel that <u>a doctor who specializes in women's diseases</u> would know more about
problems with women's reproductive organs than other doctors.

_____

17. When I have a skin problem, I go to <u>a doctor who specializes in skin disorders</u>.

_____

18. Parents should keep <u>poisonous</u> materials out of the reach of children.

_____

19. Although this job will be <u>lasting for a short period of time</u> only, I will still try to
do my best at it.

_____

20. The warden of the jail was held <u>a prisoner</u> by three men who were trying to escape.

_____

**STOP.**   Check answers at the end of this chapter (p. 194).

# EXTRA WORD POWER

**e, ex.**  Out of; from; lacking. When *ex* or *e* is placed at the beginning of a word, it means "out of" or "from." When *ex* is placed at the beginning of a word and a hyphen (-) is attached to the word, *ex* means "former" or "sometime." For example: *ex-president*—former president; *ex-wife*—former wife. Examples of *ex* meaning "out of" or "from": *exclude*—to keep from; *exit*—to go out of; *expect*—to look out for; *excuse*—to forgive, to apologize for; *exhale*—to breathe out.

**de.**  Away; from; off; completely. *De* is found at the beginning of many words. For example: *deport*—to send someone away. *An alien who was involved in many holdups was* **deported** *to his own country.* Other words with *de*: *deflea*—to take off fleas; *delouse*—to free from lice; *decolor*—to take color away; *decode*—to change from code to plain language; *detoxify*—to take away poison, to destroy the poison; *decapitate*—to take off the head, to kill; *deprive*—to take something away from; *denude*—to strip the covering from completely. Can you supply more words with *ex, e,* or *de?*

## Additional Words Derived from Combining Forms

From your knowledge of combining forms, can you define the following words?

1. **misogynist** (mi·sog·y·nist) (mi·soj'i·nist) *n.*  *Although Tom is a misogamist, he isn't a* **misogynist** *because he likes women.*

   _____

2. **agnostic** (ag·nos·tic) (ag·nos'tik) *adj. n.*  *Pat must be an* **agnostic** *because she believes that there is no way for anyone to know for sure about the existence of God.*

   _____

3. **epidermis** (ep·i·der'mis) *n.*  *The* **epidermis** *is the layer of skin that is the most exposed.*

   _____

4. **pedagogue** (ped'a·gogúé) *n.*  *A* **pedagogue** *is a person who teaches students.*

   _____

5. **antitoxin** (an·ti·tox·in) (an·ti·tok'sin) *n.*  *The doctor injected my brother with an* **antitoxin** *in order to prevent his getting a certain disease.*

   _____

6. **toxicologist** (tox·i·col·o·gist) (tok·si·kol'o·jist) *n.*  *A* **toxicologist** *was called in to help in the homicide investigation because all symptoms pointed to a possible death by poisoning.*

   _____

7. **derisive** (de·rī'sivé) *adj.*  *The* **derisive** *laughter of the class toward all student comments kept me from saying anything because I did not want to be ridiculed.*

   _____

8. **intercept** (in·ter·cept) (in·ter·sept′) *v.*   *When the ball was* **intercepted** *before a goal could be made, the home team audience screamed with delight.*

      —————————————————————————————

9. **susceptible** (sus·cep·ti·ble) (sus·sep′ti·bul) *adj.*   *When he heard that he was* **susceptible** *to tuberculosis, he asked the doctor to help him to prevent the onset of the disease.*

      —————————————————————————————

10. **perceptive** (per·cep·tive) (per·sep′tive) *adj.*   *Being a* **perceptive** *individual, she knew that this was not the right time to ask her father for use of the car.*

      —————————————————————————————

11. **tempo** (tem′pō) *n.* (*pl.* **tempi**)   *The* **tempo** *of modern living is very fast.*

      —————————————————————————————

12. **extemporaneous** (ex·tem·po·ra·ne·ous) (ek·stem·po·rā′nē·ous) *adj.*   *When she was called upon to express her views, her* **extemporaneous** *talk was so logical and well expressed that she couldn't have done better if she had spent hours preparing it.*

      —————————————————————————————

> **STOP.**   Check answers at the end of this chapter (p. 194).

## Practice for Additional Words Derived from Combining Forms

***Directions:***   Match each word with the best definition.

| | | |
|---|---|---|
| _____ 1. misogynist | a. | outermost layer of skin |
| _____ 2. agnostic | b. | rate of speed |
| _____ 3. pedagogue | c. | being aware |
| _____ 4. antitoxin | d. | hater of women |
| _____ 5. epidermis | e. | mocking; jeering |
| _____ 6. toxicologist | f. | something used against poison |
| _____ 7. derisive | g. | done or spoken without preparation |
| _____ 8. intercept | h. | professing uncertainty about ultimates |
| _____ 9. susceptible | i. | specialist in poisons |
| _____ 10. perceptive | j. | a teacher |
| _____ 11. extemporaneous | k. | especially liable to |
| _____ 12. tempo | l. | to stop or interrupt the course of |

> **STOP.**   Check answers at the end of this chapter (p. 194).

# EXERCISE 12

## Step I. Combining Forms

**A. Directions:**  A list of combining forms with their meanings follows. Look at the combining forms and their meanings. Concentrate on learning each combining form and its meaning. Cover the meanings, read the combining forms, and state the meanings to yourself. Check to see if you are correct. Now cover the combining forms, read the meanings, and state the combining forms to yourself. Check to see if you are correct.

| Combining Forms | Meanings |
|---|---|
| 1. tain, ten, tent | hold |
| 2. cede, ceed | go; give in; yield (give in) |
| 3. sequi | follow |
| 4. cycl, cyclo | circle; wheel |
| 5. chron, chrono | time |
| 6. archae, archaeo | ancient |
| 7. crypt, crypto | secret; hidden |
| 8. duc | lead |
| 9. brevi | short; brief |

**B. Directions:**  Do not look at the preceding meanings. Write the meanings of the following combining forms.

| Combining Forms | Meanings |
|---|---|
| 1. tain, ten, tent | _____ |
| 2. cede, ceed | _____ |
| 3. sequi | _____ |
| 4. cycl, cyclo | _____ |
| 5. chron, chrono | _____ |
| 6. archae, archaeo | _____ |
| 7. crypt, crypto | _____ |
| 8. duc | _____ |
| 9. brevi | _____ |

## Step II. Words Derived from Combining Forms

1. **tenant** (ten′ant) *n.* A person who holds property; one who lives in property belonging to another; one who rents or leases from a landlord; one who lives in a place. *The **tenants** told the landlord, who owned the building, that they would not pay the rent unless the landlord made the needed repairs to their apartments.*

2. **content** (con·tent) (kon'tent) *n.* What something holds (usually plural in this sense); subject matter; the material that something is made up of; the main substance or meaning.

    *The course **content** was supposed to deal with the earth's crust or makeup, but the instructor had not yet covered any subject matter related to geology.*

3. **content** (con·tent) (kon·tent') *adj.* Satisfied; not complaining; not desiring something else.

    *It is obvious that Sally is **content** with her life because she never complains and always seems free from worry.*

4. **maintain** (māin·tāin') *v.* To carry on or continue; to keep up; to keep in good condition.

    *When Mr. Jones lost his job, he found that he could not **maintain** his house because the needed repairs were too costly.*

5. **sequence** (se·quence) (sē'kwensé) *n.* The following of one thing after another; order; a continuous or related series, with one thing following another.

    *The detectives investigating the suicide were trying to get the **sequence** of events, step-by-step and in order, to try to figure out why the man took his life.*

6. **consequence** (con·se·quence) (kon'se·kwensé) *n.* That which follows from any act; a result; an effect.

    *I had no idea what the **consequence** of my leaving home would be until I found out that my mother became ill as a result of it.*

7. **subsequent** (sub·se·quent) (sub'se·kwent) *adj.* Following soon after; following in time, place, or order; resulting.

    *The **subsequent** chapter, which follows this one, is Chapter Six.*

8. **cycle** (cy·cle) (sī'kul) *n.* A period that keeps coming back, in which certain events take place and complete themselves in some definite order; a round of years or ages; a pattern of regularly occurring events; a series that repeats itself.

    *We seem to be going through an economic **cycle** that is similar to one we had a decade ago.*

9. **cyclone** (cy·clone) (sī'klōné) *n.* A system of violent and destructive whirlwinds.

    *When the **cyclone** hit the small town, its winds were so strong that it destroyed everything in its path.*

10. **archaeology** (ar·chae·ol·o·gy) (ar·kē·ol'o·jē) *n.* The study of the life and culture of ancient people, as by the digging up of old settlements, ruins from the past, and old man-made or other objects.

    *I knew that I'd enjoy studying **archaeology** because I have always loved to dig in old places and hunt for things from the past so that I could learn more about ancient times.*

11. **archaic** (ar·cha·ic) (ar·kā'ik) *adj.* Belonging to an earlier period; ancient; old-fashioned; no longer used.

    *It is surprising to find someone in our times who believes in such an **archaic** practice as bloodletting for curing disease.*

12. **chronological** (chron·o·log·i·cal) (kron·o·loj'i·kal) *adj.* Arranged in time order (earlier things or events precede later ones).

    *In order to arrange our outline on wars in the United States in **chronological** order, we needed to know the dates of the wars.*

13. **chronic** (chron·ic) (kron'ik) *adj.* Continuing for a long time; prolonged; recurring.

    *Because he had a **chronic** cough, it lasted for a long period of time and always came back.*

14. **concede** (con·cede) (kon·sēdé') *v.* To give in; surrender; yield; grant; admit.
    *After a long discussion and debate on an issue, the union said it would* **concede** *on this particular issue because the employers had given in on other issues.*

15. **precede** (pre·cede) (prē·sēdé') *v.* To go or come before.
    *In the circus parade the clowns were to* **precede** *the others because, by entering first, they would put the spectators in a good mood for the rest of the show.*

16. **proceed** (pro·ceed) (prō·sēéd') *v.* To go on; to go forward; to carry on an action.
    *We will* **proceed** *the way we have been going unless someone knows some reason why we should not continue.*

17. **succeed** (suc·ceed) (suk·sēéd') *v.* To accomplish what is attempted; to come next in order; to come next after or replace another in an office or position.
    *The people who* **succeed** *seem to be those who do not stop until they have accomplished what they set out to do.*

18. **abbreviation** (ab·bre·vi·a·tion) (ab·brē·vē·ā'shun) *n.* A shortened form of a word or phrase.
    *It is usual to give an* **abbreviation** *of the spelling of the states rather than write them out completely because it's much faster and easier.*

19. **conductor** (con·duc·tor) (kon·duk'tor) *n.* One who guides or leads; a guide or director; one who has charge of a railroad train; the director of an orchestra or chorus; any substance that conducts electricity, heat, and so on.
    *You could tell from the applause that the* **conductor** *of the orchestra was greatly admired by the large audience that had come to see him lead the orchestra.*

"Mr. Bailey? There's a gentleman here who claims an ancestor of yours once defiled his crypt, and now you're the last remaining Bailey and ... oh, something about a curse. Should I send him in?"

THE FAR SIDE. Copyright 1986 Universal Press Syndicate. Reprinted with Permission. All Rights Reserved.

20. **deduction** (de·duc·tion) (de·duk'shun) *n.* The act of drawing a conclusion by reasoning or reasoning that goes from the general to the particular; the subtraction of something; an inference or conclusion.

    *How much money are you able to get back by having so many **deductions** on your income tax?*

21. **cryptic** (cryp·tic) (krip'tik) *adj.* Having a hidden or secret meaning; mysterious.

    *The **cryptic** message was very difficult to decode because no one was familiar with the meanings of the letters used in the code.*

22. **crypt** (kript) *n.* An underground vault.

    *The **crypt** was buried fifty feet underground in a special cave.*

# SPECIAL NOTES

1. Note that the terms *content* (con'tent) *n.* and *content* (con·tent') *adj.* are spelled identically but are *pronounced differently* and have *different meanings.* Many of the words you have met have had more than one meaning. However most of them were *pronounced identically.* Because *content* (con'tent) *n.* and *content* (con·tent') *adj.* are pronounced differently and each word has meanings different from those of the other, they are presented separately.

    a. **content** (con'tent) *n.* What something holds (usually plural in this sense). *The **contents** of the box contained all her childhood toys.*

    b. **content** (con'tent) *n.* Subject matter. *The course **content** was so boring that I decided not to take any other courses in that subject.*

    c. **content** (con'tent) *n.* The material that something is made up of. *When I checked the **content** of the ice cream I was eating, I found that it was made up almost completely of artificial products.*

    d. **content** (con·tent') *adj.* Satisfied; not complaining; not desiring something else. *I am **content** with my job, so there is no need for me to look for another.*

2. You probably know that the term *bicycle* means "two-wheeler." You can now see that *cycle* in *bicycle* comes from the combining form *cyclo* meaning "wheel."

3. The term *deduction* has a few meanings.

    a. **deduction.** A subtraction; something taken away. A *deduction* refers to your being able to subtract or take away a certain amount from something else. This meaning of *deduction* is much used in relation to the income tax. You can subtract or take away a certain amount of money from your income taxes on the basis of the number of *deductions* you have.

    b. **deduction.** Reasoning from the general to the particular or reasoning from given statements to conclusions. This meaning of *deduction* is used in *logic,* which is the *science of correct reasoning.* You met the term *logical,* which deals with correct reasoning, in Exercise 10. An example of deduction—going from the general to the specific—follows:

       All men are good.
       Arthur is a man.
       Therefore, Arthur is good.

    In the preceding example, we can decide, on the basis of a general statement that all men are good, that a particular man, Arthur, must be good.

    c. **deduction.** An inference; a conclusion. It is important for readers to be able to make *deductions* in reading because many times writers do not directly state what they mean but present ideas in a more "roundabout" way, or *indirectly.*

In Exercise 10 you met the word *inference* in the section entitled Additional Words Derived from Combining Forms. *Deduction* and *inference* have the same meaning. Remember that an *inference* is drawn from information that is not directly stated. The same is true of *deduction*. When all the information is given in statements but the information is given indirectly, you must make *deductions* or *inferences*. In order to get the information, you must "read between the lines." Mystery writers often use *inference* to make their stories more interesting and enjoyable. Following is an example of inference. Can you draw the proper inferences or make the correct deductions from the information given?

Read the following short selection, and answer the two questions.

> The six remaining boys were worn out from walking all day with such heavy knapsacks. They headed toward the mountain range, hoping to reach it before the sun finally set behind it. One third of their original number had turned back earlier.

1. In what direction were the six boys headed?

2. How many boys had there been at the beginning of the trip?

In order to answer the first question, you must collect the following clues:

1. Boys walking toward mountain range.

2. Sun sets behind the mountain range.

From this information you should conclude that the answer to the first question is "west" because the sun sets in the West and the boys were heading toward the setting sun.

To answer the second question, you must collect the following clues:

1. Six boys remaining.

2. One third had turned back.

From this information you should conclude that the answer to the second question is "nine" because two thirds of the boys equals six, one third must be three, and six plus three equals nine.

## Step III. Words in Context

Jeff Hanes and Sally Bailey had both majored in **archaeology** in the same school and had been in the college orchestra under the same **conductor**. They had also been **tenants** in the same apartment building, but they met in Egypt while working on ancient ruins. On the dig they discovered a strange **crypt**, which had a **cryptic** inscription. After the **crypt** was brought to the surface, the archaeologists **proceeded** to open it. Just then a strange little man dressed in an **archaic** costume jumped forth and yelled, "No! No! It is forbidden! Do so at great risk!" Before anyone could say anything, he disappeared as quickly as he had appeared. **Subsequent** to this, the sky clouded up and a **cyclone** struck as if from nowhere. The whirlwinds were so forceful that no one was able to **maintain** his or her balance. Everyone **conceded** that what had happened was strange, but their **deduction** was that it was merely a coincidence; the cyclone was not a **consequence** of the little man's message. Everyone, except Sally, was **content** that there was nothing to any of it.

The **archaeologists**, therefore, **proceeded** to open the **crypt** to determine its **contents**. Just as they began, another **cyclone** hit the area. It was as if the **cycle** was starting all over again. The **sequence** was similar. The attempt to open the **crypt preceded** the **cyclone**. "This is a bad omen!" said the guide. "I will not remain here anymore. The gods wish for you to return the **crypt** to its sacred burial grounds. You will never **succeed** in opening the **crypt**. If you continue you will have **chronic** bad luck. This **crypt** was placed here thousands of years ago. The inscription is an **abbreviation** of the message contained inside. Everything is done in some kind of **chronological** order. You cannot disturb this order." With these words, the guide left the archaeologists.

If you were they, would you have opened the **crypt**?

## Step IV. Practice

**A. Directions:** Each sentence has a missing word. Choose the word that *best* completes the sentence. Write the word in the blank. Note that one word is used in two sentences, once as a noun and once as an adjective.

**Word List**

| | | |
|---|---|---|
| abbreviation | consequence | maintain |
| archaeology | content | precede |
| archaic | crypt | proceed |
| chronic | cryptic | sequence |
| chronological | cycle | subsequent |
| concede | cyclone | succeed |
| conductor | deduction | tenant |

1. As that is a(n) _____ word, it is not used anymore.

2. Whenever I have an argument with anyone, it always seems that I'm the one to _____, because the other person just won't give in.

3. The _____ writing that they found on the box has still not been decoded because no one can figure out the code.

4. I've heard that some banks store their gold in a(n) _____ that is buried so far in the ground that it is almost impossible for robbers to get to it.

5. A(n) _____ is a person who usually pays rent to occupy property.

6. I am perfectly _____ with the place where I live, so there is no reason for me to complain about it.

7. Because our landlord will not _____ the property and keep it in good condition, we are withholding our rent.

8. The _____ of events was easy to follow because there was a definite order to the events.

9. After the fire it was difficult to tell what the

_____s of the house had been because everything
in the house was so badly burned.

10. The doctor told my friend that unless he followed the doctor's orders, the

_____s would be bad, and he might have to go to
the hospital.

11. How many _____s will you be able to subtract
from your income tax this year?

12. Because _____ deals with ancient cultures, we
are going to visit an ancient cave and dig for things from the past for our

_____ class.

13. The dates were listed in _____ order, starting with
ancient times and continuing to contemporary times.

14. I can tell that I'm starting my losing _____ all
over again because the events that happened before seem to be repeating themselves.

15. The problem with a(n) _____ illness is that even
though it may go away, it always comes back.

16. When the _____ hit our area, we were lucky that
our house was not in the path of the violent winds because it would have been
completely destroyed.

17. I attempt to do only things that I feel I can accomplish because I like to

_____ in what I do.

18. You usually use a(n) _____ for name titles rather
than write out the whole word.

19. _____ with your work because you seem to be
doing it correctly.

20. I was surprised that you did not _____ him in the
lineup of players because you always go up to bat before he does.

21. The audience was quiet when the _____ came on
stage to begin directing the orchestra.

22. The _____ chapters should be easier for you because they come after the more difficult material.

---

**STOP.**  Check answers at the end of this chapter (p. 195).

**B. Directions:** A short story with missing words follows. Fill in the blanks with the words that *best* fit. Words are used only once. Note that *content* is given twice because it is used in two different ways.

**Word List**

| | | |
|---|---|---|
| abbreviation | cycle | maintain |
| chronic | cyclone | morgue |
| concede | deduction | proceed |
| conductor | description | sequence |
| consequence | homicide | subsequent |
| content | hypothesis | succeed |
| content | illegal | television |
| corpse | local | tenant |
| cryptic | | |

I am a(n) **1**_____ in a large apartment building. I have been **2**_____ living there and really had nothing much to complain about until last month. A(n) **3**_____ of events took place that has made it very difficult for me to **4**_____ my former way of living. What I am saying is that as a(n) **5**_____ of one particular night my whole life has changed.

I remember the night very well for three reasons. First, we had such a violent **6**_____ during the day that some of my windows had been broken. Second, the night was very dark because the moon was completing its monthly **7**_____ just before the new moon. Third, a(n) **8**_____ took place right outside my broken window.

I should tell you that I live on the ground floor in a rather quiet neighborhood. My building is across the street from a large park, and during the summers we have many famous **9**_____s leading orchestras in outdoor concerts. I live on the ground floor because I have a(n) **10**_____ back problem, and I never know when it will give me trouble.

Let me **11**_____ with my story of the murder. At about 10 P.M. I thought I heard some sounds from outside, but I had the **12**_____ on so I wasn't sure. The third time I thought I heard something, I went to my broken window to look outside. It was so dark that I saw nothing. However, on my floor I found a paper attached to a broken piece of glass. Although I tried to read it, I did not **13**_____ in figuring out the **14**_____s of the paper. The paper contained a(n) **15**_____ message, which I could not decode. The only thing I could make out was *Dr.*, a(n) **16**_____ of the word *doctor*.

I immediately phoned the police. While waiting for the police, I again tried to decode the message. I finally had to **17**_____ to myself that I could not figure it out. The police arrived. I told them my story. They went out to investigate. It was then that they found the **18**_____. I was asked to look at the body. Frightened and trembling, I did. However, I had never seen the person before. The dead body was then taken to the **19**_____ because there was no identification on it. **20**_____ to that, the

police came to question me. They wanted to know if I had any **21** _____
that might be a possible explanation for the murder. I stated that I had none and
that I knew nothing.

I told them that the only **22** _____ I could make or conclude
was that the person couldn't have died right away because he had time to pick up a
piece of broken glass, attach some paper to it, and throw it through my already
broken window.

The police were able to decode the message. The message gave such a good
**23** _____ of the murderer that the police were able to have a picture drawn of him. It turned out to be a(n) **24** _____ doctor
from the neighborhood who was involved with the **25** _____ sale
of drugs.

> **STOP.**   Check answers at the end of this chapter (p. 195).

**C. Directions:**   Write the words from this exercise that go with the meanings.

1. Satisfied; not complaining _____

2. To continue; to keep up; to keep in good condition _____

3. A continuous series _____

4. A result; an effect _____

5. A person who rents or leases from a landlord _____

6. Following soon after _____

7. The study of the life and culture of ancient people _____

8. Referring to what is ancient _____

9. A round of years or ages _____

10. A violent, destructive whirlwind _____

11. Arranged in time order _____

12. To go forward _____

13. To give in _____

14. To go or come before _____

15. Continuing for a long time and coming back _____

16. To accomplish what is attempted; to come after _____

17. A shortened form of a word or phrase _____

18. One who guides or leads _____

19. The act of drawing a conclusion by reasoning; an inference _____

20. Having a hidden meaning _____

21. An underground vault _____

22. Subject matter _____

---

**STOP.**   Check answers at the end of this chapter (p. 195).

---

# EXTRA WORD POWER

**dis.**   Away from; apart; not. When *dis* is placed in front of a word, it may give it the opposite meaning. It may result in undoing something that was done. It may take away some quality, power, rank, and so on. For example: *disrobe* — take off clothes; *disband* — break up the group; *disable* — make an object or someone not able to do something; *disloyal* — not loyal; *disapprove* — to not approve of, to regard as not worthy; *dishonest* — not honest, not to be trusted. How many more words with *dis* can you supply?

**sub.**   Under; beneath; below; lower in rank. *Sub* is added to the beginning of many words. For example: *submarine* — undersea ship; *subfloor* — floor beneath; *subtraction* — the act of taking something away; *subset* — something that is under the larger set; *subcommittee* — a committee under the original committee. Check your dictionary to find many more words beginning with *sub*.

## Additional Words Derived from Combining Forms

From your knowledge of combining forms, can you define the following words?

1. **chronometer** (chro·nom·e·ter) (kro·nom′e·ter) *n.*   *As the car's **chronometer** was always correct, I usually went by that time.*

   _____

2. **anachronism** (a·nach·ro·nism) (a·nak′ro·niz·um) *n.*   *An example of an **anachronism** in a film would be to have an automobile present in a set representing the Middle Ages.*

   _____

3. **synchronize** (syn·chro·nize) (sin′kro·nīze) *v.*   *We **synchronized** our watches to make sure that we all had the same time.*

   _____

4. **concession** (con·ces·sion) (kon·sesh'un) *n.*    *In order to settle the strike, both sides had to make a number of* **concessions**.

_____

5. **procession** (pro·ces·sion) (pro·sesh'un) *n.*    *The* **procession** *continued to move forward in an orderly manner even though it was raining very hard.*

_____

6. **recession** (re·ces·sion) (re·sesh'un) *n.*    *During a* **recession**, *when unemployment is high, economists try to figure out ways to stimulate the economy.*

_____

7. **secede** (se·cede) (se·sēdé') *v.*    *During the Civil War, the South* **seceded** *from the Union.*

_____

8. **subscription** (sub·scrip·tion) (sub·skrip'shun) *n.*    *Each year when I take out a* **subscription** *for my favorite magazine, I sign a form promising to pay a certain amount of money for the delivery of the magazine.*

_____

9. **untenable** (un·ten·a·ble) (un·ten'a·bul) *adj.*    *Her position on the issue was such an* **untenable** *one that we all agreed not to support her.*

_____

10. **detain** (de·tāin') *v.*    *The man at the airport was* **detained** *by the police because they thought that he was a criminal attempting to flee the country.*

_____

11. **retentive** (re·ten'tivé) *adj.*    *Arthur has such a* **retentive** *memory that he can recall details from things he studied or read over twenty years ago.*

_____

12. **tenacious** (te·na·cious) (te·nā'shus) *adj.*    *He had such* **tenacious** *feelings on that issue that no one could change his mind.*

_____

**STOP.**  Check answers at the end of this chapter (p. 195).

© 1966 United Feature Syndicate, Inc.

## Practice for Additional Words Derived from Combining Forms

***Directions:*** Match each word with the *best* definition.

_____ 1. chronometer

_____ 2. concession

_____ 3. anachronism

_____ 4. recession

_____ 5. synchronize

_____ 6. untenable

_____ 7. tenacious

_____ 8. retentive

_____ 9. secede

_____ 10. subscription

_____ 11. procession

_____ 12. detain

a. having the ability to keep things in

b. to withdraw from

c. an instrument used to measure time

d. the act of going back

e. a parade

f. an act of giving in

g. something out of time order

h. to cause to agree in rate or speed

i. an agreement to pay some money for something

j. to stop; to delay

k. stubborn

l. not able to be held or defended

---

**STOP.** Check answers at the end of this chapter (p. 196).

# CHAPTER WORDS IN SENTENCES

**Directions:** Use the given words to write a sentence that makes sense. Also, try to illustrate the meaning of the words without actually defining the words.

*Example* (dialogue; ridicule) It is difficult to carry on a *dialogue* with someone who tries to *ridicule* everything you say.

1. (logical; deduction)

   _____

2. (conceive; contemporary)

   _____

3. (pediatrician; prognosis)

   _____

4. (consequence; subsequent)

   _____

5. (dermatologist; diagnose)

   _____

# CHAPTER WORDS IN A PARAGRAPH

Here is a list of words from this chapter. Write a paragraph using at least 8 of these words. The paragraph must make sense and be logically developed.

**Word List**

| | | |
|---|---|---|
| archaic | diagnose | preference |
| capable | dialogue | proceed |
| chronic | exception | prognosis |
| concede | fertile | ridicule |
| conceive | final | ridiculous |
| contemporary | finite | sequence |
| content | hypothesis | suffer |
| cycle | infinite | temporary |
| cyclone | logical | toxic |
| deceive | maintain | transfer |
| deduction | perception | |

# ANALOGIES 4

**Directions:** Find the word from the following list that best completes each analogy. There are more words in the list than you need.

**Word List**

| | | |
|---|---|---|
| adult | deceive | infinitesimal |
| agnostic | decimate | mouth |
| ancient | deride | pedagogue |
| archaic | diagnosis | pediatrician |
| bibliography | diagram | preface |
| biography | dialect | procession |
| captor | dialogue | prognosis |
| catalog | diameter | reference |
| chronometer | epilogue | tenacious |
| consequence | fertile | toxicologist |
| contemporary | finite | transparent |
| content | inference | visage |
| cyclone | infinite | |

1. Clock : chronometer :: stubborn : _____.

2. Beginning : end :: prologue : _____.

3. Enthusiasm : apathy :: immeasurable : _____.

4. Deference : respect :: ridicule : _____.

5. Skin : dermatologist :: poison : _____.

6. Limp: wilted :: parade : _____.

7. Extemporaneous : prepared :: dissatisfied : _____.

8. Woman : gynecologist :: child : _____.

9. Lawyer : counselor :: teacher : _____.

10. Potentate : monarch :: current : _____.

11. Deportment : behavior :: effect : _____.

12. Snow : blizzard :: wind : _____.

13. Wrist : arm :: nose : _____.

14. Archaic : ancient :: bluff : _____.

15. Salary : employee :: ransom : _____.

16. Alarm : warn :: dynamite : _____.

17. Sheer : opaque :: sterile : _____.

18. God : atheist :: knowing : _____.

19. Shawl : scarf :: deduction : _____.

20. Gait : trot :: speech : _____.

---

> **STOP.**  Check answers at the end of this chapter (p. 196).

---

# MULTIPLE-CHOICE VOCABULARY TEST 4

**Directions:**   This is a test on words in Exercises 10–12. Words are presented according to exercises. *Do all exercises before checking answers.* Underline the meaning that *best* fits the word.

Exercise 10

1. prologue
   a.  added to the end of a book
   b.  introduction to a play
   c.  correct reasoning
   d.  conversation

2. logical
   a.  relating to correct reasoning
   b.  relating to an introduction
   c.  a listing of names
   d.  added to the end of a book

3. catalog
   a.  added to the end of a book
   b.  an introduction
   c.  conversation
   d.  a listing of names, titles, and so on, in some order

4. epilogue
   a.  conversation
   b.  a listing of books
   c.  addition to the end of a book
   d.  an introduction

5. dialogue
   a.  introduction
   b.  conversation
   c.  at the end of a book
   d.  refers to reasoning

6. diagram
   a.  divides circle in half
   b.  conversation
   c.  outline figure showing relationships
   d.  introduction

7. diameter
   a. line dividing a circle in half
   b. an outline showing relationships in a circle
   c. an outline
   d. a map

8. bibliography
   a. a listing of books on a subject
   b. a note in a book
   c. refers to books
   d. the study of spelling

9. final
   a. able to produce
   b. limited number
   c. last
   d. refers only to tests

10. finite
    a. the end of a play
    b. at the end of a book
    c. added to a book
    d. having a limit or an end

11. infinite
    a. ends in time
    b. endless
    c. ends
    d. certain number

12. fertile
    a. a producer
    b. able to produce a large crop
    c. refers to soil
    d. refers to children

13. fertilization
    a. a producer
    b. what one puts on soil
    c. union of sperm and egg
    d. refers to childern

14. reference
    a. a person who sends things
    b. a chapter in a book
    c. a recommendation from a person
    d. a letter

15. preference
    a. a note in a book
    b. a note in a book sending you for information
    c. a recommendation
    d. someone or something you choose over another

16. transfer
    a. to carry or send from one place to another
    b. a sender
    c. a carrier
    d. to cross

17. conference
    a. a convention
    b. a friendly get-together
    c. a discussion or meeting on some important matters
    d. refers to science meetings

18. suffer
    a. to be able to take pain
    b. to put up with pain
    c. to feel pain
    d. refers to pain

19. circumference
    a. the distance across a circle
    b. refers to measurement
    c. the distance around a circle
    d. refers to a globe

## Exercise 11

20. capable
    a. something for the head
    b. able to wear hats
    c. refers to power
    d. having ability

21. captive
    a. a prisoner
    b. a hunter
    c. a kidnapper
    d. a searcher

22. conceive
    a. to learn
    b. to conceal
    c. to teach
    d. to think

23. deceive
    a. to believe
    b. to lead
    c. to mislead by lying
    d. to tell

24. reception
    a. to receive something
    b. the manner of receiving someone
    c. the manner of thinking
    d. the act of taking

25. exception
    a. something or one that is left out
    b. being included
    c. being invited
    d. refers to leaving

26. perception
    a. a sense
    b. senses of seeing and hearing
    c. act of knowing something
    d. act of becoming aware of something through the senses

27. capsule
    a. a spaceship
    b. a rocket
    c. an instrument
    d. a removable part of a rocket or an airplane

28. ridiculous
    a. funny
    b. unworthy of consideration
    c. something not nice
    d. something not helpful

29. ridicule
    a. to laugh
    b. to joke
    c. to make someone the object of mockery
    d. to be cruel

30. diagnose
    a. to make a prediction
    b. to make a prediction concerning someone's illness
    c. to give an examination
    d. to determine what is wrong with someone after an examination

31. prognosis
    a. refers to recovery
    b. refers to illness
    c. refers to knowing what is wrong
    d. a prediction concerning an illness

32. pediatrician
    a. a woman who is a doctor
    b. a doctor
    c. a doctor who specializes in foot diseases
    d. a children's doctor

33. gynecologist
    a. a woman who is a doctor
    b. a doctor
    c. a doctor who is a specialist
    d. a doctor who specializes in women's diseases

34. toxic
    a. deadly
    b. poisonous
    c. unsafe
    d. unclear

35. dermatologist
    a. a skin disease
    b. a doctor
    c. a skin doctor
    d. refers to skin

36. hypodermic
    a. a needle
    b. referring to the area under the skin
    c. area above the skin
    d. skin

37. hypothesis
    a. any guess
    b. any idea
    c. an unproved conclusion
    d. an unproved conclusion drawn from known facts

38. temporary
    a. referring to time
    b. referring to a waiting period
    c. referring to a short time period
    d. referring to a time period

39. contemporary
    a. referring to what is ancient
    b. referring to a time period
    c. referring to a short period of time
    d. referring to what is modern

## Exercise 12

40. tenant
    a. one who takes care of apartments for a salary
    b. one who lives on property belonging to another
    c. one who takes care of buildings for a salary
    d. one who holds things

41. content
    a. subject matter
    b. refers to courses
    c. refers to teaching
    d. refers to learning

42. maintain
    a. to keep up in good repair
    b. to help someone
    c. to carry
    d. to hold

43. content
    a. worried
    b. unsure
    c. unhappy
    d. satisfied

44. sequence
    a. coming before
    b. coming after
    c. following
    d. following one after the other

45. consequence
    a. an arrangement
    b. in order
    c. an effect
    d. following

46. subsequent
    a. in order
    b. following
    c. a result
    d. an arrangement

47. cycle
    a. refers to time
    b. refers to the wind
    c. refers to the mind
    d. a round of years or ages

48. cyclone
    a. a wind
    b. a rainstorm
    c. system of violent and destructive whirlwinds
    d. a round of years or ages

49. archaeology
    a. study of rocks
    b. study of rulers
    c. ancient life
    d. study of the life and culture of ancient people

50. archaic
    a. refers to rulers
    b. the study of ancient cultures
    c. ancient
    d. a time period

51. chronological
    a. referring to disease
    b. arranged in time order
    c. referring to an outline
    d. referring to an ancient time

52. chronic
    a. time
    b. time period
    c. continuing for a long time
    d. not returning

53. concede
    a. going before
    b. coming after
    c. to accomplish what one started to do
    d. to give in

54. precede
    a. to go forward
    b. to come before
    c. to give in
    d. to accomplish things

55. proceed
    a. to come before
    b. to go forward
    c. to go back
    d. to give in

56. succeed
    a. to accomplish what one started out to do
    b. to give in
    c. to go forward
    d. to go back

57. abbreviation
    a. a short person
    b. a shortened form of a word or phrase
    c. refers to short
    d. a cutoff of something

58. conductor
    a. head of a company
    b. an orchestra leader
    c. one who takes
    d. one who takes away

59. deduction
    a. act of leading away
    b. act of leading
    c. a conclusion
    d. act of leading to

60. cryptic
    a. a hidden vault
    b. a mysterious vault
    c. an underground vault
    d. having a hidden or secret meaning

61. crypt
    a. having a hidden meaning
    b. having a secret meaning
    c. a vault
    d. an underground vault

# TRUE/FALSE TEST 4

**Directions:** This is a true/false test on Exercises 10–12. Read each sentence carefully. Decide whether it is true or false. Put a T for *true* or an F for *false* in the blank. If the answer is false, change a word or part of the sentence to make it true. The number after the sentence tells you if the word is from Exercise 10, 11, or 12.

_____ 1. A bibliography is a listing of reference words. 10

_____ 2. *Prologue* and *dialogue* are antonyms. 10

_____ 3. A diagram helps to give a description of something by using an outline figure to show relationships among things. 10

_____ 4. *Podiatrist* and *pediatrician* are synonyms. 11

_____ 5. Something contemporary must be archaic. 11, 12

_____ 6. *Content* meaning "subject matter" and *content* meaning "satisfied" are homographs. 12

_____ 7. When I was preceded by Alan in the parade, Alan came after me. 12

_____ 8. The number of deductions on my paycheck refers to money I get from savings bonds. 12

_____ 9. Antitoxin is used by scientists to diagnose a patient's condition. 11

_____ 10. A prognosis is usually based on a doctor's diagnosis and makes a prediction about a patient's recovery. 11

_____ 11. An agnostic is one who is sure of his or her beliefs. 11

_____ 12. *Demagogue* and *pedagogue* are synonyms. 11

_____ 13. A pediatrician is a foot doctor. 11

_____ 14. A misanthrope is also a misogynist. 11

_____ 15. A bachelor must be a misogynist. 11

_____ 16. An archaeologist is one who is ancient. 12

_____ 17. The word *conceive* can mean "to become pregnant" and "to think of." 11

_____ 18. Something that is finite must end. 10

_____ 19. When something is an exception to a rule, it means that it belongs to the rule. 11

_____ 20. *Crypt* refers to a hidden message. 12

_____ 21. In order to be logical, you must use correct reasoning. 10

_____ 22. An epilogue is what is sometimes given at the beginning of a play to the audience. 10

_____ 23. A capable person is one with ability. 11

_____ 24. *Consequence* and *affect* are synonyms. 12

_____ 25. When something is subsequent to something else, it comes before it. 12

_____ 26. Chronological order does not have to refer to time order. 12

_____ 27. When someone maintains something, he or she keeps it up. 12

_____ 28. It is logical to assume that if *A* is taller than *B* and *B* is taller than *C*, then *A* is taller than *C*. 10

_____ 29. The consequences of actions would be the results of them. 12

_____ 30. The terms *deduction* and *inference* can be synonyms. 12, 10

_____ 31. When someone is able to make a conclusion from the general to the particular, that is a deduction. 12

_____ 32. When someone is able to gain information from statements that are indirectly stated, that is a deduction. 12

_____ 33. When you are a <u>captive</u>, you are always a prisoner in jail. 11

_____ 34. Something <u>temporary</u> can last for an infinite time period. 11

_____ 35. When <u>fertilization</u> takes place, it means a woman has <u>conceived</u>. 10, 11

---

**STOP.** Check answers for both tests at the end of this chapter (pp. 196–197).

---

# SCORING OF TESTS

| MULTIPLE-CHOICE VOCABULARY TEST | | TRUE/FALSE TEST* | |
|---|---|---|---|
| Number Wrong | Score | Number Wrong | Score |
| 0–4 | Excellent | 0–4 | Excellent |
| 5–9 | Good | 5–7 | Good |
| 10–13 | Weak | 8–10 | Weak |
| Above 13 | Poor | Above 10 | Poor |
| Score _____ | | Score _____ | |

1. If you scored in the excellent or good range on *both tests*, you are doing well. Go on to Chapter Six.

2. If you scored in the weak or poor range on either test, look below and follow directions for Additional Practice. Note that the words on the test are arranged so that you can tell in which exercise to find them. This will help you if you need additional practice.

# ADDITIONAL PRACTICE SETS

**A. Directions:** Write the words you missed on the tests from the three exercises in the space provided. Note that the tests are presented so that you can tell to which exercises the words belong.

Exercise 10 Words Missed

1. _____        6. _____

2. _____        7. _____

3. _____        8. _____

4. _____        9. _____

5. _____        10. _____

*When the answer is false, you must get both parts of the true/false question correct in order to receive credit for it.

Exercise 11 Words Missed

1. _____    6. _____
2. _____    7. _____
3. _____    8. _____
4. _____    9. _____
5. _____   10. _____

Exercise 12 Words Missed

1. _____    6. _____
2. _____    7. _____
3. _____    8. _____
4. _____    9. _____
5. _____   10. _____

**B. Directions:**   Restudy the missed words from the three exercises. Study the combining forms from which those words are derived. Do Step I and Step II for those you missed. Note that Step I and Step II of the combining forms and vocabulary derived from these combining forms are on the follwoing pages:

    Exercise 10 — pp. 145–148

    Exercise 11 — pp. 154–157

    Exercise 12 — pp. 165–169

**C. Directions:**   Do Additional Practice 1 below if you missed words from Exercise 10. Do Additional Practice 2 on pp. 190–191 if you missed words from Exercise 11. Do Additional Practice 3 on pp. 191–192 if you missed words from Exercise 12. Now go on to Chapter Six.

## Additional Practice 1 for Exercise 10

**A. Directions:**   The combining forms presented in Exercise 10 follow. Match each combining form with its meaning.

_____ 1. dia          a.  end

_____ 2. cata         b.  down

_____ 3. log, logo    c.  through

_____ 4. fin          d.  book

_____ 5. biblio       e.  speech; word

_____ 6. fer          f.  before; forward

_____ 7. epi          g.  bring; bear; yield (give up)

_____ 8. pro          h.  upon; beside; among

**STOP.**   Check answers at the end of this chapter (p. 197).

**B. Directions:**   The words presented in Exercise 10 follow. Match each word with its meaning.

_____ 1. prologue

_____ 2. logical

_____ 3. catalog

_____ 4. epilogue

_____ 5. dialogue

_____ 6. diagram

_____ 7. diameter

_____ 8. bibliography

_____ 9. final

_____ 10. finite

_____ 11. infinite

_____ 12. fertile

_____ 13. reference

_____ 14. fertilization

_____ 15. preference

_____ 16. transfer

_____ 17. conference

_____ 18. suffer

_____ 19. circumference

a.  to feel pain

b.  outline figure showing relationships

c.  last

d.  someone or something chosen over another

e.  a listing of books on a subject

f.  endless

g.  a discussion or meeting on an important matter

h.  section added to the end of a book

i.  a listing of names, titles, and so on, in some order

j.  distance around a circle

k.  having an end

l.  the union of sperm and egg

m.  able to produce

n.  referring to correct reasoning

o.  a recommendation

p.  introduction to a play

q.  to carry or send from one place to another

r.  a line that divides a circle in half

s.  conversation

---

**STOP.**   Check answers at the end of this chapter (p. 197).

## Additional Practice 2 for Exercise 11

**A. *Directions:*** The combining forms presented in Exercise 11 follow. Match each combining form with its meaning

_____ 1. cap, cep      a. skin

_____ 2. gnosi, gnosis      b. laughter

_____ 3. ped, pedo      c. under

_____ 4. tox, toxo      d. take; receive

_____ 5. gyn, gyno      e. child

_____ 6. temp, tempo, tempor      f. woman

_____ 7. hypo      g. knowledge

_____ 8. derm, dermo      h. time

_____ 9. ri, ridi, risi      i. poison

---

**STOP.** Check answers at the end of this chapter (p. 197).

---

**B. *Directions:*** The words presented in Exercise 11 follow. Match each word with its meaning.

_____ 1. capable      a. to mock or view in a scornful way

_____ 2. captive      b. modern

_____ 3. conceive      c. a children's doctor

_____ 4. deceive      d. prediction concerning an illness

_____ 5. reception      e. poisonous

_____ 6. exception      f. having ability

_____ 7. perception      g. doctor who specializes in women's diseases

_____ 8. capsule

_____ 9. ridiculous      h. an unproved conclusion drawn from known facts

_____ 10. ridicule      i. to think

_____ 11. diagnose      j. something that is left out

_____ 12. prognosis      k. to mislead by lying

_____ 13. pediatrician

_____ 14. gynecologist

_____ 15. toxic

_____ 16. dermatologist

_____ 17. hypodermic

_____ 18. hypothesis

_____ 19. temporary

_____ 20. contemporary

l.  referring to the area under the skin

m.  unworthy of consideration

n.  a becoming aware of something through the senses

o.  a prisoner

p.  manner of receiving someone

q.  lasting for a short period of time

r.  to determine what is wrong with someone after an examination

s.  a removable part of a rocket or airplane

t.  a skin doctor

---

**STOP.** Check answers at the end of this chapter (p. 197).

---

# Additional Practice 3 for Exercise 12

**A. Directions:** The combining forms presented in Exercise 12 follow. Match each combining form with its meaning.

_____ 1. tain, ten, tent

_____ 2. cede, ceed

_____ 3. sequi

_____ 4. cycl, cyclo

_____ 5. chron, chrono

_____ 6. archae, archaeo

_____ 7. crypt, crypto

_____ 8. duc

_____ 9. brevi

a.  short; brief

b.  ancient

c.  hold

d.  lead

e.  circle; wheel

f.  secret; hidden

g.  follow

h.  go; give in; yield (give in)

i.  time

---

**STOP.** Check answers at the end of this chapter (p. 197).

**B. Directions:**    The words presented in Exercise 12 follow. Match each word with its meaning.

_____ 1. tenant

_____ 2. content

_____ 3. content

_____ 4. maintain

_____ 5. sequence

_____ 6. consequence

_____ 7. subsequent

_____ 8. cycle

_____ 9. cyclone

_____ 10. archaeology

_____ 11. archaic

_____ 12. chronological

_____ 13. chronic

_____ 14. concede

_____ 15. precede

_____ 16. proceed

_____ 17. succeed

_____ 18. abbreviation

_____ 19. conductor

_____ 20. deduction

_____ 21. cryptic

_____ 22. crypt

a.  the study of the life and culture of ancient people

b.  to go forward

c.  to come before

d.  to give in

e.  one who lives on property belonging to another

f.  a result

g.  satisfied

h.  a round of years or ages

i.  the following of one thing after another

j.  a system of violent and destructive whirlwinds

k.  subject matter

l.  to keep up

m.  following

n.  a shortened form of a word or phrase

o.  ancient

p.  having a hidden meaning

q.  a conclusion

r.  underground vault

s.  continuing for a long time

t.  orchestra leader; one in charge of a train

u.  arranged in time order

v.  to accomplish what one started out to do

**STOP.**   Check answers at the end of this chapter (p. 197).

# ANSWERS: Chapter Five

## Exercise 10 (pp.145-154)

### Practice A

(1) Fertilization, (2) diagram, (3) epilogue, (4) dialogue, (5) finite, (6) conference, (7) bibliography, (8) preference, (9) prologue, (10) final, (11) infinite, (12) catalog, (13) logical, (14) reference, (15) fertile.

### Practice B

(1) prologue, (2) dialogue, (3) epilogue, (4) Diagram, (5) bibliography, (6) final, (7) finite, (8) infinite, (9) conference, (10) diameter, (11) circumference, (12) transfer, (13) logical, (14) catalog, (15) fertile, (16) reference, (17) preference, (18) suffer, (19) fertilization.

### Practice C

(1) infinite, (2) bibliography, (3) final, (4) suicide, (5) prologue, (6) incredible, (7) illegal, (8) fertile, (9) finite, (10) logical, (11) catalog, (12) dialogue, (13) fertilization, (14) circumference, (15) diameter, (16) epilogue, (17) diagram, (18) suffer, (19) reference, (20) preference, (21) conference, (22) transfer.

### Additional Words Derived from Combining Forms (pp. 152–153)

1. **inference.**   Something derived by reasoning; something that is not directly stated but suggested in the statement; a logical conclusion that is drawn from statements; a deduction.

2. **proficient.**   Knowing something very well; able to do something very well.

3. **dialect.**   A variety of speech; a regional form of a standard language.

4. **monologue.**   A long speech by one person; a dramatic sketch performed by one actor.

5. **definitive.**   Conclusive; final; most nearly complete or accurate.

6. **finale.**   The last part; end; the concluding movement of a musical composition; the last scene of an entertainment.

7. **affinity.**   Close relationship; attraction to another.

8. **infinitesimal.**   Too small to be measured; very minute.

9. **deference.**   Respect; a giving in to another's opinion or judgment.

10. **defer.**   To leave to another's opinion or judgment; to delay; to postpone; to put off for a future time.

### Practice for Additional Words Derived from Combining Forms (p. 153)

(1) d, (2) c, (3) j, (4) g, (5) b, (6) h, (7) f, (8) i, (9) a, (10) e.

## Exercise 11 (pp. 154–164)

Practice A

(1) q, (2) p, (3) o, (4) r, (5) n, (6) m, (7) a, (8) e, (9) h, (10) f, (11) d, (12) g, (13) c, (14) k, (15) b, (16) l, (17) i, (18) j, (19) t, (20) s.

Practice B

(1) hypothesis, (2) ridiculous, (3) dermatologist, (4) capsule, (5) hypodermic, (6) diagnose, (7) captive, (8) temporary, (9) prognosis, (10) Toxic, (11) capable, (12) ridicule, (13) contemporary, (14) exception, (15) reception, (16) pediatrician, (17) conceive, (18) deceive, (19) gynecologist, (20) perception.

Practice C

(1) capable, (2) reception, (3) deceive, (4) conceive, (5) ridiculous, (6) ridicule, (7) capsules, (8) perception, (9) exception, (10) hypodermic, (11) hypothesis, (12) contemporaries, (13) prognosis, (14) diagnose, (15) pediatrician, (16) gynecologist, (17) dermatologist, (18) toxic, (19) temporary, (20) captive.

### Additional Words Derived from Combining Forms (pp. 163–164)

1. **misognyist.**   Hater of women.
2. **agnostic.**   Professing uncertainty; one who is not for or against; one who doubts that the ultimate cause (God) and the essential nature of things are knowable.
3. **epidermis.**   Outermost layer of skin.
4. **pedagogue.**   A teacher.
5. **antitoxin.**   Something used against bacterial poison; a substance formed in the body that counteracts a specific toxin; the antibody formed in immunization with a given toxin, used in treating certain infectious diseases or in immunizing against them.
6. **toxicologist.**   One who specializes in the study of poisons.
7. **derisive.**   Mocking; jeering.
8. **intercept.**   To stop or interrupt the course of.
9. **susceptible.**   Easily influenced by or affected with; especially liable to.
10. **perceptive.**   Being aware; having insight, understanding, or intuition, as a *perceptive* analysis of the problems involved.
11. **tempo.**   The rate of speed at which a musical composition is supposed to be played; rate of activity.
12. **extemporaneous.**   Done or spoken with little or no special preparation; impromptu; makeshift; done or spoken as if without special preparation.

### Practice for Additional Words Derived from Combining Forms (p. 164)

(1) d, (2) h, (3) j, (4) f, (5) a, (6) i, (7) e, (8) l, (9) k, (10) c, (11) g, (12) b.

# Exercise 12 (pp. 165–176)

## Practice A

(1) archaic, (2) concede, (3) cryptic, (4) crypt, (5) tenant, (6) content, (7) maintain, (8) sequence, (9) content, (10) consequence, (11) deduction, (12) archaeology, (13) chronological, (14) cycle, (15) chronic, (16) cyclone, (17) succeed, (18) abbreviation, (19) Proceed, (20) precede, (21 conductor, (22) subsequent.

## Practice B

(1) tenant, (2) content, (3) sequence, (4) maintain, (5) consequence, (6) cyclone, (7) cycle, (8) homicide, (9) conductor, (10) chronic, (11) proceed, (12) television, (13) succeed, (14) content, (15) cryptic, (16) abbreviation, (17) concede, (18) corpse, (19) morgue, (20) Subsequent, (21) hypothesis, (22) deduction, (23) description, (24) local, (25) illegal.

## Practice C

(1) content, (2) maintain, (3) sequence, (4) consequence, (5) tenant, (6) subsequent, (7) archaeology, (8) archaic, (9) cycle, (10) cyclone, (11) chronological, (12) proceed, (13) concede, (14) precede, (15) chronic, (16) succeed, (17) abbreviation, (18) conductor, (19) deduction, (20) cryptic, (21) crypt, (22) content.

## Additional Words Derived from Combining Forms (pp. 174–175)

1. **chronometer.**  A very accurate clock or watch; an instrument used to measure time.

2. **anachronism.**  Something out of time order; an error in chronology (the science of measuring time in fixed periods, and arranging dates in their proper order) in which a person, an object, or an event is assigned an incorrect date or period.

3. **synchronize.**  To cause to agree in rate or speed; to happen or take place at the same time.

4. **concession.**  An act of giving in; a right granted by the government or other authority for a specific purpose.

5. **procession.**  A parade, as a funeral *procession*; any continuous course.

6. **recession.**  The act of going back; in economics, the decline of business activity.

7. **secede.**  To withdraw from.

8. **subscription.**  An agreement; a promise in writing to pay some money; an agreement to receive something and pay for it.

9. **untenable.**  Not able to be held or defended.

10. **detain.**  To stop; to hold; to keep from proceeding; to delay.

11. **retentive.**  Having the ability to retain or keep in things; tenacious, as a *retentive* memory; having a good memory.

12. **tenacious.**  Stubborn; tough; holding or tending to hold strongly to one's views, opinions, rights, and so on; retentive, as a *tenacious* memory.

Practice for Additional Words Derived from Combining Forms (p. 176)

(1) c, (2) f, (3) g, (4) d, (5) h, (6) l, (7) k, (8) a, (9) b, (10) i, (11) e, (12) j.

## Chapter Words in Sentences (p. 177)

Sentences will vary.

## Chapter Words in a Paragraph (p. 177)

Paragraphs will vary.

## Analogies 4 (pp. 178–179)

(1) tenacious, (2) epilogue, (3) finite, (4) deride, (5) toxicologist, (6) procession, (7) content, (8) pediatrician, (9) pedagogue, (10) contemporary, (11) consequence, (12) cyclone, (13) visage, (14) deceive, (15) captor, (16) decimate, (17) fertile, (18) agnostic, (19) inference, (20) dialect.

## Multiple-Choice Vocabulary Test 4 (pp. 179–185)

Exercise 10

(1) b, (2) a, (3) d, (4) c, (5) b, (6) c, (7) a, (8) a, (9) c, (10) d, (11) b, (12) b, (13) c, (14) c, (15) d, (16) a, (17) c, (18) c, (19) c.

Exercise 11

(20) d, (21) a, (22) d, (23) c, (24) b, (25) a, (26) d, (27) d, (28) b, (29) c, (30) d, (31) d, (32) d, (33) d, (34) b, (35) c, (36) b,[1] (37) d,[2] (38) c, (39) d.

Exercise 12

(40) b, (41) a, (42) a, (43) d, (44) d, (45) c, (46) b, (47) d, (48) c,[3] (49) d, (50) c, (51) b, (52) c, (53) d, (54) b, (55) b, (56) a, (57) b, (58) b, (59) c, (60) d, (61) d.

[1]*Referring to the area under the skin* is a better answer than a *needle* because *hypodermic* refers to an area under the skin. The term *hypodermic* also means "a needle that is injected under the skin" or "a hypodermic needle." However, the best answer is *b* because a needle could refer to any needle, including a sewing needle.

[2]*An unproved conclusion drawn from known facts* is a better answer than *an unproved conclusion* because it is a more complete answer.

[3]*System of violent and destructive whirlwinds* is a better answer than *a wind* because it is more complete and less general. This is also true for numbers 32, 33, and 35 in Exercise 11. It is not enough to state *doctor* as the answer. That is too general. You must state the kind of doctor the person is.

## True/False Test 4[4] (pp. 185–187)

(1) F, reference words to books on a subject; (2) F, are to are not or dialogue to epilogue; (3) T; (4) F, are to are not; (5) F, archaic to modern or must to must not be; (6) T; (7) F, after to before; (8) F, money I get from savings bonds to money that is subtracted; (9) F, is used to is not used or by scientists to diagnose a patient's condition to against bacterial poison; (10) T; (11) F, is sure to is not sure; (12) F, are to are not or Demagogue to Teacher; (13) F, pediatrician to podiatrist or foot doctor to children's doctor; (14) T;[5] (15) F, must to must not[6] or bachelor to misanthrope; (16) F, ancient to one who studies the life and culture of ancient people; (17) T; (18) T; (19) F, belongs to does not belong; (20) F, a hidden message to an underground vault; (21) T; (22) F, beginning to end or epilogue to prologue; (23) T; (24) F, affect to effect or are to are not;[7] (25) F, before to after; (26) F, does not to does; (27) T; (28) T; (29) T; (30) T; (31) T; (32) T; (33) F, are to are not or are always a prisoner in jail to are always a prisoner; (34) F, infinite to finite or can to cannot; (35) T.

> **STOP.**  Turn to p. 187 for the scoring of the tests.

## Additional Practice Sets (pp. 187–192)

### Additional Practice 1

A.  (1) c, (2) b, (3) e, (4) a, (5) d, (6) g, (7) h, (8) f.
B.  (1) p, (2) n, (3) i, (4) h, (5) s, (6) b, (7) r, (8) e, (9) c, (10) k, (11) f, (12) m, (13) o, (14) l, (15) d, (16) q, (17) g, (18) a, (19) j.

### Additional Practice 2

A.  (1) d, (2) g, (3) e, (4) i, (5) f, (6) h, (7) c, (8) a, (9) b.
B.  (1) f, (2) o, (3) i, (4) k, (5) p, (6) j, (7) n, (8) s, (9) m, (10) a, (11) r, (12) d, (13) c, (14) g, (15) e, (16) t, (17) l, (18) h, (19) q, (20) b.

### Additional Practice 3

A.  (1) c, (2) h, (3) g, (4) e, (5) i, (6) b, (7) f, (8) d, (9) a.
B.  (1) e, (2) g,[8] (3) k,[9] (4) l, (5) i, (6) f, (7) m, (8) h, (9) j, (10) a, (11) o, (12) u, (13) s, (14) d, (15) c, (16) b, (17) v, (18) n, (19) t, (20) q, (21) p, (22) r.

---

[4]Answers for *false* are suggested answers.

[5]Because a misanthrope is a hater of mankind, in the generic sense, he or she would also have to be a hater of women.

[6]It does not necessarily follow that a man who is not married is a hater of women. He may be unmarried for many reasons—one might be that he likes many women a lot.

[7]*Consequence* and *effect* have the same meanings. *Affect* means "to influence."

[8]The answer for 2 can be either *g* or *k*.

[9]The answer for 3 can be either *k* or *g*.

# CHAPTER SIX

# EXERCISE 13

## Step I. Combining Forms

**A. Directions:** A list of combining forms with their meanings follows. Look at the combining forms and their meanings. Concentrate on learning each combining form and its meaning. Cover the meanings, read the combining forms, and state the meanings to yourself. Check to see if you are correct. Now cover the combining forms, read the meanings, and state the combining forms to yourself. Check to see if you are correct.

| Combining Forms | Meanings |
|---|---|
| 1. tend, tens, tent | stretch; strain |
| 2. belli, bello | war |
| 3. civ, civis | citizen |
| 4. polis | city |
| 5. pac, pax | peace |
| 6. voc, vox | voice; call |
| 7. post | after |
| 8. ambi | both |
| 9. mega | very large |

**B. Directions:**    Do not look at the preceding meanings. Write the meanings of the following combining forms.

Combining Forms                                    Meanings

1. tend, tens, tent                     _____

2. belli, bello                         _____

3. civ, civis                           _____

4. polis                                _____

5. pac, pax                             _____

6. voc, vox                             _____

7. post                                 _____

8. ambi                                 _____

9. mega                                 _____

# Step II. Words Derived from Combining Forms

1. **attention** (at·ten·tion) (at·ten′shun) *n.* Mental concentration; care; a position of readiness; act of courtesy.
   *When children are tired, they cannot pay **attention** because they have lost their ability to concentrate.*

2. **intention** (in·ten·tion) (in·ten′shun) *n.* Aim; goal; purpose.
   *Although, as a child, her **intention** was to become a famous archaeologist, she never thought that she would achieve her goal.*

3. **tension** (ten·sion) (ten′shun) *n.* The act of stretching or the condition of being stretched tight; mental strain.
   *The parents' **tension** was so great when their child was kidnapped that they did not know how long they could stand the mental strain.*

4. **intense** (in·tense′) *adj.* Having great or extreme force; very strong; existing or occurring to a high or extreme degree.
   *The heat was so **intense** from the fire that the firemen could not enter the building.*

5. **belligerent** (bel·lig·er·ent) (bel·lij′er·ent) *adj.* Warlike. *n.* Any nation, person, or group engaged in fighting or war.
   *Because he has such a **belligerent** manner, he gets into a lot of fights.*

6. **civilian** (ci·vil·ian) (si·vil′yun) *n.* One who is not in the military. *adj.* Of civilians; nonmilitary.
   *It is good to be a **civilian** again after spending three years in the army.*

7. **civics** (civ·ics) (siv′iks) *n.* (Used in the singular.) The part of political science dealing with the study of civic affairs and the rights and responsibilities of citizenship.
   *In school I took a course in **civics** because I wanted to learn more about the individual citizen's rights and responsibilities.*

8. **civilization** (civ·i·li·za·tion) (siv'i·li·zā·shun) *n.* A state of human society that has a high level of intellectual, social, and cultural development; the cultural development of a specific people, country, or region.

   *In a **civilization**, a high level of intellectual, social, and cultural development is supposed to exist.*

9. **civil** (siv'il) *adj.* Of a citizen or citizens; relating to citizens and their government; relating to ordinary community life as distinguished from military or church affairs; courteous or polite.

   ***Civil** liberties are the rights that individual citizens have.*

10. **politics** (pol·i·tics) (pol'i·tiks) *n.* (Although plural, it is usually looked upon as singular.) The science or art of government or of the direction and management of public or state affairs.

    *Persons who are in **politics** are interested in the management of public or state affairs.*

11. **politician** (pol·i·ti·cian) (pol'i·tish·un) *n.* A person engaged in politics; a person involved in the science or art of government; a person who seeks advancement or power within an organization by dubious (doubtful) means.

    *The **politicians** met to determine whom they would support for office.*

12. **metropolitan** (met·ro·pol·i·tan) (met·ro·pol'i·tun) *adj.* Referring to a major city center and its surrounding area. *n.* A person who inhabits a metropolis or one who has the manners and tastes associated with a metropolis.

    *I like to live in a **metropolitan** area so that I can be close to the kinds of stores, theaters, and restaurants that are found in large cities.*

13. **vocal** (vo·cal) (vō'kul) *adj.* Referring to the voice; having voice; oral; freely expressing oneself in speech, usually with force; speaking out.

    *When we strained our **vocal** cords from yelling at the basketball game, we could hardly use our voices the next day.*

14. **vocabulary** (vo·cab·u·lar·y) (vō·kab'yu·lar·ē) *n.* (*pl.* **ies**) A list of words and phrases, usually arranged alphabetically, that are defined or translated from another language; a stock of words possessed by an individual or a group.

    *You are gaining a larger **vocabulary** from doing the exercises involving lists of words and their definitions.*

15. **vocation** (vo·ca·tion) (vō·kā'shun) *n.* A calling; a person's work or profession.

    *Sharon chose a **vocation** similar to her father's because she wanted to follow in his footsteps.*

16. **ambiguous** (am·big'·ū·ǿus) *adj.* Having two or more meanings.

    *What he said was so **ambiguous** that I couldn't figure out if he wanted me to stay or go.*

17. **postscript** (post·script) (pōst'skript) *n.* Something added to a letter after the writer's signature; something added to written or printed legal papers.

    *The abbreviation of **postscript**, something added to a letter after the writer has signed his or her name, is P.S.*

18. **pacify** (pac·i·fy) (pas'i·fī) *v.* To bring peace to; to calm; to quiet.

    *The speaker tried to **pacify** the mob, but he could not calm them down.*

19. **megaphone** (meg·a·phone) (meg'a·fōnĕ) *n.* A device used to increase sound.

    *At the county fair, the tradespeople used **megaphones** to try to get people to buy their wares.*

## SPECIAL NOTES

1. The term *civilian*, which refers to someone who is not in the military, is used also by policemen and by others who wear special uniforms to refer to someone out of uniform.

2. The combining form *mega* also means "million."

   Examples:   megabucks = 1,000,000 dollars
   megabit = 1,000,000 bits (A bit is a unit of computer information; 1 byte = 8 bits of data; usually 2 bytes = 1 word.)

## Step III. Words in Context

The **politicians** in this election are more **belligerent** than usual. They must feel that the best way to get the audience's **attention** is to be as **vocal** as possible and not very **civil** to one another. They speak so forcibly and loudly that they certainly don't need a **megaphone**. Also, in one of the primary elections, it seemed as though the **intention** of the two people running for election was to see how **ambiguous** they could be because they used **vocabulary** words that could be taken in more than one way. Furthermore, the **tension** between the two was so great that you thought they might start swinging at one another. The moderator actually tried to **pacify** the two by saying, "Gentlemen, gentlemen, we are all friends here. This is just a friendly debate." It didn't help. Each continued to be very **intense** when he spoke. In addition, each tried to make the audience feel that he was quite different from the other and that a vote for him would save our **civilization**. It's funny because both have such similar backgrounds. They are both **civilians** who never served in the armed forces; they both have taken a number of **civics** courses; they both chose the same **vocation**; they both grew up in a **metropolitan** area; and they both went into **politics** at an early age. There is a **postscript** to this story. Neither one of the men was elected.

## Step IV. Practice

**A. Directions:**   Each sentence has a missing word. Choose the word that *best* completes the sentence. Write the word in the blank.

**Word List**

| | | |
|---|---|---|
| ambiguous | intense | politics |
| attention | intention | postscript |
| belligerent | megaphone | tension |
| civics | metropolitan | vocabulary |
| civil | pacify | vocal |
| civilian | politician | vocation |
| civilization | | |

1. Some people pay a lot of _____ to their appearance because they want to look their best.

2. His _____ is to be on time, but he is always late.

3. Too much _____ gives me a headache because I can't take mental strain.

4. Try to be less _____ about everything you do because your forcefulness is beginning to annoy us.

5. The police used a(n) _____ to talk to the criminals
   who had barricaded themselves in the old factory.

6. The homeowners were so angry at their increase in taxes that it was difficult to

   _____ them.

7. The crowd had become so _____ that the police
   had to call for reinforcements to help control the crowd.

8. My course in _____ helped me gain a better
   understanding of the individual citizen's rights and responsibilities.

9. After being in military service for a decade, I decided to leave and become a(n)

   _____ again.

10. Being in _____ has opened my eyes to a lot of
    problems that exist in the management and direction of state affairs.

11. As a(n) _____ who was elected to office, I hope to
    be able to make some contribution to society.

12. Some people are _____ on purpose because they
    do not want to say exactly how they stand on an issue.

13. This is not the _____ I planned for in school, but
    it's the only work I could get.

14. Although we have reached a high level of _____,
    wars still exist among nations.

15. Persons involved in the _____ rights movement try
    to protect citizens' rights as established in the Constitution.

16. The singer had to cancel her performance because she had something wrong with

    her _____ cords.

17. Because I need a good _____ to read successfully,
    I am studying words and their meanings.

18. After I signed my name to the letter I was writing, I had to add a(n)

    _____ because I thought of something else I
    wanted to say.

19. When we moved to a(n) _____ area, I sold my car
    and decided to become a pedestrian because it was too difficult to keep a car in
    the city.

> **STOP.**  Check answers at the end of this chapter (p. 247).

**B. Directions:**    Underline the word that *best* fits the definition(s).

1. Mental concentration; act of courtesy
   a.  tension
   b.  intense
   c.  attention
   d.  intention

2. Aim; goal
   a.  attention
   b.  intense
   c.  tension
   d.  intention

3. Mental strain
   a.  intense
   b.  tension
   c.  attention
   d.  intention

4. Very strong
   a.  tension
   b.  attention
   c.  intention
   d.  intense

5. Warlike
   a.  intense
   b.  tension
   c.  belligerent
   d.  civil

6. One not in the military
   a.  civil
   b.  civilization
   c.  civilian
   d.  civics

7. Cultural development of a people
   a.  civics
   b.  civilization
   c.  civilian
   d.  civil

8. Polite; of a citizen or citizens
   a.  civics
   b.  politician
   c.  civilian
   d.  civil

9. Science of government dealing with the management of public affairs
   a.  civilization
   b.  civics
   c.  politics
   d.  civilian

10. The part of political science dealing with citizens' rights and responsibilities
    a. civics
    b. politics
    c. civilization
    d. civilian

11. A person involved in the science or art of government
    a. civilian
    b. vocation
    c. politics
    d. politician

12. Referring to a major city center and its surrounding area
    a. civilization
    b. metropolitan
    c. politics
    d. civilian

13. Something added to a letter after the signature
    a. vocabulary
    b. ambiguous
    c. metropolitan
    d. postscript

14. List of words that are defined
    a. vocation
    b. vocabulary
    c. vocal
    d. postscript

15. Referring to the voice
    a. vocal
    b. vocation
    c. vocabulary
    d. ambiguous

16. A person's work
    a. vocation
    b. civilization
    c. politics
    d. vocal

17. To calm
    a. civil
    b. vocal
    c. pacify
    d. postscript

18. Having two or more meanings
    a. vocabulary
    b. attention
    c. vocal
    d. ambiguous

19. Device to increase sound
    a. vocal
    b. intense
    c. megaphone
    d. telephone

---

**STOP.** Check answers at the end of this chapter (p. 247).

---

**C. Directions:** In the following sentences give the meaning that *best* fits the underlined word.

1. During the president's speech we paid very close <u>attention</u> to what he was saying because we did not want to miss one word. _____

2. From his conflicting actions, I can't figure out what his <u>intentions</u> are.

   _____

3. There was considerable <u>tension</u> in the room after the instructor told the students that they needed to do more work. _____

4. The light was so <u>intense</u> that it hurt my eyes. _____

5. Pat avoids <u>belligerent</u> people because she is peaceful. _____

6. How do you feel now that you're out of uniform and a <u>civilian</u> again?

   _____

7. Courses in <u>civics</u> will help me because I want to become a politician.

   _____

8. Western <u>civilization</u> is different from Eastern <u>civilization</u> because the cultural development of the West and that of the East have been different.

   _____

9. There have been so many scandals in <u>politics</u> in the past decade that many people feel that elected officials are more concerned with selfish interests than with the proper management of public affairs. _____

10. It is sometimes difficult to be <u>civil</u> to persons who are rude and impolite.

    _____

11. As a <u>politician</u>, Kim intends to serve wisely the people who elected her to office.

    _____

12. What a change it was when we moved from a rural area, which is all farmland, to a <u>metropolitan</u> area. _____

13. The students were very <u>vocal</u> in their demands. _____

14. After studying so many words and their meanings, I have a larger <u>vocabulary</u>.

    _____

15. Jack's <u>vocation</u> is one that requires a lot of time, effort, and study.

    _____

16. The directions for the exam were so <u>ambiguous</u> that half the class did one thing, and the other half did something else. _____

17. I needed to add a <u>postscript</u> to my letter because I thought of more things to say after I had already signed my letter. _____

18. The mother tried to <u>pacify</u> her screaming child by giving him a toy.

    _____

19. At the company picnic, John used a <u>megaphone</u> to get everyone's attention.

    _____

---

**STOP.**   Check answers at the end of this chapter (p. 247).

---

# EXTRA WORD POWER

**ance, ence.**   Act of; state of; quality of. When *ance* is found at the end of a word, it means "act of," "state of," or "quality of." In an earlier exercise you met *tion*, which also means "state of" or "act of." If *ance* or *ence* is added to a word, the word changes to a noun. For example: **maintain**. To carry on or continue; to keep up. *I will **maintain** your car while you are away so that it will be in good working condition when you get home.* **maintenance**. The act of keeping up. *The **maintenance** of your car is important if it is to stay in good running condition.* Examples of words with *ance, ence: dependence*—act of trusting, act of relying on someone for support; *assistance*—act of helping; *sequence*—the state of following; *conference*—the act of meeting in a group. How many more words can you supply?

**al.**   Relating to. When *al*, meaning "relating to," is added to the end of a word, the word is usually an adjective. For example: *vocal*—relating to the voice; *local*—relating to a place; *manual*—relating to the hand; *annual*—relating to the year; *universal*—relating to all; *legal*—relating to law; *apodal*—relating to being without feet; *nautical*—relating to sailing. How many more words can you supply?

## Additional Words Derived from Combining Forms

From your knowledge of combining forms, can you define the following words?

1. **postmortem** (pōst·mor'tem) *adj. n.* *The doctor performed a* **postmortem** *examination on the victim in order to determine the cause of his death.*

   _____

2. **posterior** (pos·te·ri·or) (pos·tir'ē·or) *adj. n.* *This blueprint shows the* **posterior** *section of the new airplane our company is building.*

   _____

3. **posterity** (pos·ter·i·ty) (pos·ter'i·tē) *n.* *Artists hope that their works will be admired by* **posterity**.

   _____

4. **posthumously** (post·hu·mous·ly) (pos'chū·mous·lē) *adv.* *Many artists gain recognition* **posthumously** *rather than during their lifetime.*

   _____

5. **provoke** (pro·vōke') *v.* *The speaker's words so* **provoked** *some of the people in the audience that they stood up and booed.*

   _____

6. **pacifist** (pac·i·fist) (pas'i·fist) *n.* *As George was a* **pacifist**, *he would not join the armed forces or any other military organization.*

   _____

7. **megalopolis** (meg·a·lop'o·lis) *n.* *The area between Boston and Washington, D.C., is considered one* **megalopolis** *because of the high density of population between these two cities.*

   _____

8. **ambidextrous** (am·bi·dex·trous) (am·bē·dek'strous) *adj.* *Some* **ambidextrous** *people use their left hands for writing and their right hands for everything else.*

   _____

9. **vociferous** (vo·cif·er·ous) (vō·sif'er·ous) *adj.* *The couple in the apartment above us were so* **vociferous** *that the neighbors called the police to complain about the noise.*

   _____

10. **convocation** (con·vo·ca·tion) (kon·vo·kā'shun) *n.* *At the beginning of the college year, a* **convocation** *is held, at which time the president of the college gives his welcoming address.*

    _____

11. **avocation** (av·o·ca·tion) (av·o·kā'shun) *n.    Stamp collecting is my father's **avocation**.*

_____

12. **irrevocable** (ir·rev·o·ca·ble) (if·rev'o·ka·bul) *adj.    My boss said that his decision to fire my friend was an **irrevocable** one.*

_____

13. **detention** (de·ten·tion) (de·ten'shun) *n.    The accused person was held in **detention** until bail was raised for him.*

_____

14. **détente** (de·tente) (dā·tanté') *n.    The President said that **détente** between the two nations would continue if each country lived up to its agreements.*

_____

> **STOP.**  Check answers at the end of this chapter (pp. 247–248).

## Practice for Additional Words Derived from Combining Forms

**Directions:**   Match each word with the *best* definition.

| | | |
|---|---|---|
| _____ 1. postmortem | a. | a group of people called together |
| _____ 2. posterity | b. | easing of strained relations |
| _____ 3. posterior | c. | one very large city |
| _____ 4. provoke | d. | an autopsy |
| _____ 5. pacifist | e. | one who is against war |
| _____ 6. ambidextrous | f. | confinement; a keeping back |
| _____ 7. convocation | g. | not to be recalled |
| _____ 8. détente | h. | after death |
| _____ 9. vociferous | i. | future generations |
| _____ 10. posthumously | j. | to stir up; irritate |
| _____ 11. detention | k. | able to use both hands equally well |
| _____ 12. megalopolis | l. | hobby |
| _____ 13. avocation | m. | clamorous |
| _____ 14. irrevocable | n. | in the rear |

> **STOP.**  Check answers at the end of this chapter (p. 248).

# EXERCISE 14

## Step I. Combining Forms

**A. Directions:**   A list of combining forms with their meanings follows. Look at the combining forms and their meanings. Concentrate on learning each combining form and its meaning. Cover the meanings, read the combining forms, and state the meanings to yourself. Check to see if you are correct. Now cover the combining forms, read the meanings, and state the combining forms to yourself. Check to see if you are correct.

| Combining Forms | Meanings |
|---|---|
| 1. luc, lum | light; clear |
| 2. err | wander |
| 3. soph | wise |
| 4. sist, sta | stand |
| 5. nov | new |
| 6. dorm | sleep |
| 7. peri | around |
| 8. hyper | over; above; excessive (very much) |
| 9. ego | I; me; the self |

**B. Directions:**   Do not look at the preceding meanings. Write the meanings of the following combining forms.

| Combining Forms | Meanings |
|---|---|
| 1. luc, lum | _____ |
| 2. err | _____ |
| 3. soph | _____ |
| 4. sist, sta | _____ |
| 5. nov | _____ |
| 6. dorm | _____ |
| 7. peri | _____ |
| 8. hyper | _____ |
| 9. ego | _____ |

## Step II. Words Derived from Combining Forms

1. **lucid** (lu·cid) (lū′sid) *adj.* Clear; easily understood; bright; shining.
    *When I ask a question about something I don't understand, I like to receive a **lucid** explanation.*

2. **translucent** (trans·lu·cent) (trans·lū′sent) *adj.* Permitting light to go through but not permitting a clear view of any object.
    *We had a **translucent** screen on our window that allowed light to go through, but*

*people looking through the screen would not get a clear view of what was in the room.*

3. **error** (er′ſor) *n.* A mistake; something done, said, or believed incorrectly; a wandering from what is correct.

    *The **error** in judgment seemed like a very small mistake, but it caused a great deal of suffering for others.*

4. **sophisticated** (so·phis·ti·cat·ed) (so·fis′ti·kāt·id) *adj.* Not in a simple, natural, or pure state; worldly-wise; not naive; cultured; highly complicated; complex; experienced.

    *Because she has traveled quite a lot and is very cultured, she always acts in a **sophisticated** manner.*

5. **sophomore** (soph·o·more) (sof′o·morė) *n.* A second-year student in American high schools or colleges; an immature person; one who thinks he or she knows more than is the case.

    *As a college **sophomore**, I have two more years to go before I graduate.*

6. **philosophy** (phi·los·o·phy) (fi·los′o·fē) *n.* (*pl.* **phies**) The study of human knowledge; the love of wisdom and the search for it; a search for the general laws that give a reasonable explanation of something.

    *Students of **philosophy** seek to understand various ideas better.*

7. **circumstance** (cir·cum·stance) (sir′kum·stansė) *n.* Something connected with an act, an event, or a condition; (*often pl.*): the conditions, influences, and so on surrounding and influencing persons or actions; formal display, as in *pomp and circumstance.*

    *The **circumstances** of the suicide were so suspicious that a full-scale investigation was started.*

8. **substitute** (sub′sti·tūtė) *v.* To put in place of another person or thing. *n.* One who takes the place of another person; something that is put in place of something else or is available for use instead of something else.

    *When our teacher was absent, a **substitute** took her place.*

9. **consist** (con·sist) (kon·sist′) *v.* To be made up of.

    *I know what the plan **consists** of because I made it up myself.*

10. **assist** (aſ·sist′) *v.* To give help to. *n.* An act of helping.

    *John **assisted** his friend because his friend had always helped him.*

11. **distant** (dis′tant) *adj.* Separated or apart by space and/or time; away from; far apart; not closely related.

    *A **distant** relative came to visit us, but I had never met her before because I am not closely related to her.*

12. **obstacle** (ob·sta·cle) (ob′sta·kul) *n.* Something that stands in the way or opposes; something that stops progress; an obstruction.

    *There were many **obstacles** that stood in the way of my going to college, but I was able to overcome each of them.*

13. **persist** (per·sist′) *v.* To continue in some course or action even though it is difficult.

    *Even though she knew that it would be difficult to become an actress, she **persisted** in trying.*

14. **innovation** (in·no·va·tion) (in·ńo·vā′shun) *n.* Something newly introduced; a new method; something new.

    *The man's **innovation** saved his company millions of dollars because his new method made it possible to manufacture the product cheaper.*

15. **novel** (nov′el) *n.* A work of fiction of some length. *adj.* New; strange; unusual.

    *It takes some people a while to get used to **novel** ideas because they do not like anything new or different.*

16. **dormitory** (dor·mi·to·ry) (dor′mi·tor·ē) *n.* (*pl.* **ries**) A large room in which many people sleep; a building providing sleeping and living quarters, especially at a school, college, or resort (summer or winter hotel).
     *Our college dormitory houses one hundred students.*

17. **dormant** (dor′mant) *adj.* Asleep or as if asleep; not active.
     *Bears are dormant during the winter.*

18. **period** (pe·ri·od) (pir′ē·od) *n.* A portion of time; a portion of time into which something is divided; a punctuation mark that signals a full stop at the end of a sentence, also used after abbreviations.
     *In high school, the school day was divided into seven class periods.*

19. **periodical** (pe·ri·od·i·cal) (pir·ē·od′i·kul) *adj.* Referring to publications, such as magazines, that appear at fixed time intervals. *n.* A periodical publication.
     *I have a subscription to a periodical that is published every month.*

20. **hypertension** (hy·per·ten·sion) (hī·per·ten′shun) *n.* High blood pressure.
     *When someone is diagnosed as having hypertension, he or she should have his or her blood pressure checked frequently to make sure that it doesn't get too high.*

21. **egocentric** (e·go·cen·tric) (ē·gō·sen′trik) *adj.* Self-centered; relating everything to oneself.
     *He is so egocentric that everything he says seems to start with* I, me, *or* my.

## SPECIAL NOTES

1. *Hyper*, meaning "over," "above," "excessive" (very much), is placed at the beginning of a great number of words. For example: *hypersensitive*—oversensitive; hyperactive—overactive; hyperproductive—over productive.

   Check your dictionary for more words with *hyper*.

2. *Philosophy* is made up of the combining forms *philo* and *soph*. You will meet the combining form *philo* meaning "love" in Exercise 16.

## Step III. Words in Context

Recently, a writer for a widely read **periodical** did an analysis of a well-known author's **novels**. He wrote that the author is a **sophisticated** and attractive woman, who is, however, very **egocentric**. He said that her **novels** seem to **consist** primarily of **circumstances** from her own life and vividly reflect her **philosophy**. She may have **substituted** different names and places, but the story is nevertheless hers. For example, in one **novel**, the main character is an attractive coed who is a **sophomore** at a **distant** college. While there, she goes through a number of difficult **periods**. She is attacked in her **dormitory**, and by the time someone comes to **assist** her, she has been brutally beaten. When the young woman is well enough to speak to the police, she is unable to help them find the attacker because he wore a **translucent** stocking on his face that hid his facial features.

   The coed finally recovers and goes back to school, but life is very difficult for her there. Wherever she goes, people point her out to others and start whispering. Also, she is always afraid. Wherever she goes she feels that she is being watched. She has difficulty studying; she makes stupid **errors** on examinations; she can't give **lucid** explanations or remember even simple messages. At times she feels that she is losing her mind. Other times she feels she is having a heart attack. Her doctor told her that she had developed **hypertension** since her attack and that she had to try to be more calm. This poor young coed seems to go from one disaster to another. Yet despite all these **obstacles**, she **persists** at school and finally graduates.

Graduation seems to bring a major change in this young woman's life. It is as if she had been **dormant** and had finally awakened. Her awakening makes her sensitive to the needs of others around her. She goes to work at a research laboratory which develops new devices or **innovations** that help others. Throughout her life she is always influenced by what happened to her at school.

## Step IV. Practice

**A. Directions:**  A number of sentences with missing words follow. Choose the word that *best* fits the sentence from the following words, and write it in the blank.

**Word List**

| | | |
|---|---|---|
| assist | error | periodical |
| circumstance | hypertension | persist |
| consist | innovation | philosophy |
| distant | lucid | sophisticated |
| dormant | novel | sophomore |
| dormitory | obstacle | substitute |
| egocentric | period | translucent |

1. I make the most _____s when I am very excited about something because I don't stop to think.

2. He was not very _____ when he spoke; so we still do not know what took place.

3. I like the _____ glass we have in our living room because it allows light to come in, but people can't see clearly inside the room.

4. Some scientists may take courses in _____ because they are interested in general laws that give reasonable explanations that apply to the whole field of science.

5. Under what _____s would you consider taking this job?

6. Now that I'm a(n) _____, I have only two more years after this one to graduation.

7. Doctors have more _____ equipment today, which helps them to diagnose illnesses better.

8. We had a(n) _____ in our geometry class because our regular teacher was out ill.

9. The man needed a(n) _____ to get his car started, but no one seemed to want to stop and give help.

10. In the not too _____ future, I intend to become a geologist.

11. Although I will probably meet many _____s in my life, I intend to overcome them.

12. I want to know what the medicine _____s of because I am allergic to some drugs.

13. In the past four decades, many _____s have been developed by man that were never dreamed possible a century ago.

14. Ms. Smith uses _____ approaches in teaching her course because she finds that students enjoy new ways of learning.

15. The doctor said that the disease was _____ at the moment, but it could become active at any time.

16. We have both males and females living in our college _____.

17. I am the kind of person who will _____ until I achieve what I started out to achieve.

18. Some people are so _____ that they talk only about themselves.

19. The doctor's prognosis for Nancy's mother was not too good because her mother suffers from _____ and has already had one stroke.

20. If this _____ of drought does not end, the farmers will not be able to produce the crops that are needed.

21. I receive a few _____s every month, but I don't always have time to read all the articles in them.

---

> **STOP.**  Check answers at the end of this chapter (p. 248).

---

**B. Directions:**  Write the words from this exercise that go with the meanings.

| Meanings | Words |
|---|---|
| 1. Clear; easily understood | _____ |
| 2. Permitting light to go through | _____ |
| 3. A mistake | _____ |
| 4. Worldly-wise | _____ |
| 5. Second-year student | _____ |
| 6. The study of human knowledge | _____ |
| 7. Conditions or influences connected with an act or event | _____ |

8. To put in place of _____

9. To be made up of _____

10. Give help to _____

11. Separated or apart by space and/or time _____

12. Something in the way of _____

13. Continue in some course even though it's difficult _____

14. A new idea _____

15. Strange; unusual; long work of fiction _____

16. Large room in which many people sleep _____

17. Asleep; not active _____

18. Portion of time _____

19. Referring to a publication that is put out at regular intervals _____

20. High blood pressure _____

21. Self-centered _____

---

> **STOP.**   Check answers at the end of this chapter (p. 248).

---

*C. Directions:*   In the following sentences, give the meaning that *best* fits the underlined word.

1. We were able to view a <u>distant</u> star through the telescope. _____

2. The <u>dormant</u> volcano had been inactive for so long that no one expected it to erupt when it did. _____

3. Under what <u>circumstances</u> do you feel we should allow such things to take place? _____

4. The light that shone through the <u>translucent</u> glass made different designs in our room, depending on the time of day. _____

5. Your <u>error</u> in auditing the books is so serious that the mistake could cost you your job. _____

6. Jean was not very <u>lucid</u> when she awakened after having been attacked; so we had to wait until she could be clearer about what had happened. _____

7. Because I don't know what that travel package <u>consists</u> of, I'd like you to tell me exactly what is included. _____

8. I took a course in <u>philosophy</u> because I love to examine ideas and deal with such questions as "What is good?" and "What is truth?"

    _____

9. At college some students live off campus rather than in a <u>dormitory</u>.

    _____

10. What picture will you <u>substitute</u> to take the place of the one you took out?

    _____

11. It gives me a good feeling to be able to <u>assist</u> people when they need help.

    _____

12. Whenever an <u>obstacle</u> is put in my way that makes things difficult for me, I try to think of ways to remove it. _____

13. The doctors were hoping that the <u>innovations</u> in heart surgery that had just been introduced at the hospital would help to save patients' lives.

    _____

14. I will <u>persist</u> in doing my work this way, even though it is more difficult, because I know that it is the correct way. _____

15. I always forget to put a <u>period</u> after abbreviations. _____

16. When my <u>periodical</u> did not arrive for three months in a row, I wrote to the magazine publisher's office to complain. _____

17. <u>Hypertension</u> is called the "silent killer" because many people are not aware that they have high blood pressure. _____

18. It is difficult to carry on a dialogue with an <u>egocentric</u> person because he always seems to be interested only in himself. _____

19. Whenever someone says that I'm behaving like a <u>sophomore</u>, I know that he or she is not giving me a compliment. _____

20. I like to go out with <u>sophisticated</u> people because they are cultured and know how to behave properly. _____

21. I enjoy reading books with <u>novel</u> plots because I like strange or unusual stories.

    _____

---

**STOP.**   Check answers at the end of this chapter (p. 248).

# *EXTRA WORD POWER*

**inter.** Between; among. When *inter* comes at the beginning of a word, it means "between" or "among." Do not confuse *inter* with *intra*. For example: *interdepartmental*—between departments; *interdependent*—dependent upon one another; *interstate*—between states; *intercollegiate*—between colleges.

**intra.** Within; inside of. *Intra* comes at the beginning of a word. It means "within." Do not confuse *intra* with *inter*. For example: *intradepartmental*—within the department; *intracollegiate*—within the college; *intramural*—within a school or an institution. Can you supply more words beginning with *inter* and *intra*? Check your dictionary for a large list of such words.

## Additional Words Derived from Combining Forms

From your knowledge of combining forms, can you define the following words?

1. **perimeter** (pe·rim′e·ter) *n.*   The **perimeter** *of a circle would be its circumference.*

   _____

2. **periphery** (pe·riph·er·y) (pe·rif′er·ē) *n.* (*pl.* **eries**)   **Periphery** *and* perimeter *are synonyms.*

   _____

3. **periscope** (per·i·scope) (per′i·skōpe) *n.*   *The sailor in the submarine used the **periscope** to view the approaching destroyer.*

   _____

4. **hyperbole** (hy·per·bo·le) (hī·per′bo·lē) *n.*   *When Sharon said that she had walked a million miles today, she was using **hyperbole**.*

   _____

5. **illuminate** (il·lū′·mi·nate) *v.*   *The lights so **illuminated** the room that everything could be seen clearly.*

   _____

6. **egotistic** (e·go·tis·tic) (ē·gō·tis′tik) *adj.*   *I do not enjoy being in the company of **egotistic** people because they are too concerned with themselves.*

   _____

7. **novice** (nov·ice) (nov′ise) *n.*   *Everyone thought that he was an expert rather than a **novice** because of the way he handled himself on the tennis court.*

   _____

8. **stamina** (stam′i·na) *n.*   *Professional athletes need a lot of **stamina** in order to keep playing.*

   _____

9. **obstinate** (ob·sti·nate) (ob'sti·nit) *adj.* *My friend is so **obstinate** that once he makes up his mind, he will never change it.*

_____

10. **sophistry** (soph·ist·ry) (sof'ist·rē) *n.* (*pl.* **ies**) *Some persons are so clever in presenting their illogical arguments that it is difficult to recognize that the arguments are filled with **sophistry**.*

_____

11. **erratic** (er·rat·ic) (er·rat'ik) *adj.* *Her behavior was so **erratic** that we wondered if she was mentally ill.*

_____

12. **periodic** (pe·ri·od·ic) (pir·ē·od'ik) *adj.* *The phases of the moon are **periodic**.*

_____

**STOP.** Check answers at the end of this chapter (p. 249).

## Practice for Additional Words Derived from Combining Forms

**Directions:** Match each word with the *best* definition.

| | | |
|---|---|---|
| _____ 1. perimeter | a. | to give light to |
| _____ 2. periphery | b. | a beginner |
| _____ 3. periscope | c. | staying power |
| _____ 4. hyperbole | d. | faulty reasoning |
| _____ 5. egotistic | e. | the outer part or boundary of something |
| _____ 6. illuminate | | |
| _____ 7. novice | f. | conceited |
| _____ 8. erratic | g. | great exaggeration |
| _____ 9. obstinate | h. | an instrument used by a submarine to see all around |
| _____ 10. stamina | i. | a measure of the outer part of a closed plane figure |
| _____ 11. sophistry | j. | not regular; not stable |
| _____ 12. periodic | k. | stubborn |
| | l. | taking place at regular intervals |

**STOP.** Check answers at the end of this chapter (p. 249).

# EXERCISE 15

## Step I. Combining Forms

**A. Directions:** A list of combining forms with their meanings follows. Look at the combining forms and their meanings. Concentrate on learning each combining form and its meaning. Cover the meanings, read the combining forms, and state the meanings to yourself. Check to see if you are correct. Now cover the combining forms, read the meanings, and state the combining forms to yourself. Check to see if you are correct.

| Combining Forms | Meanings |
| --- | --- |
| 1. miss, mitt | send |
| 2. pon, pos | place; set |
| 3. anima, animus | spirit; mind; soul |
| 4. magna | great; large |
| 5. hypn, hypno | sleep |
| 6. feder, fid, fide | trust; faith |
| 7. nasc, nat | born |
| 8. equi | equal |
| 9. pop | people |

**B. Directions:** Do not look at the preceding meanings. Write the meanings of the following combining forms.

| Combining Forms | Meanings |
| --- | --- |
| 1. miss, mitt | _____ |
| 2. pon, pos | _____ |
| 3. anima, animus | _____ |
| 4. magna | _____ |
| 5. hypn, hypno | _____ |
| 6. feder, fid, fide | _____ |
| 7. nasc, nat | _____ |
| 8. equi | _____ |
| 9. pop | _____ |

## Step II. Words Derived from Combining Forms

1. **mission** (mis·sion) (mish'un) *n.* Group or team of persons sent some place to perform some work; the task, business, or responsibility that a person is assigned; the place where missionaries carry out their work; a place where poor people may go for assistance.

    *The astronauts were sent on a special **mission** to try to locate a missing spaceship.*

2. **permission** (per·mis·sion) (per·mish'un) *n.* Act of allowing the doing of something; a consent.
   *I received **permission** from the instructor to audit her class.*

3. **dismiss** (dis·miss') *v.* To tell or allow to go; to discharge, as from a job; to get rid of; to have done with quickly; to reject.
   *The class was **dismissed** when the period was over.*

4. **admission** (ad·mis·sion) (ad·mish'un) *n.* Act of allowing to enter; entrance fee; a price charged or paid to be admitted; acknowledgment; a confession, as to a crime.
   *We did not know we had to pay **admission** to enter the fair.*

5. **submit** (sub·mit') *v.* To give in to another; to surrender; to concede; to present for consideration or approval; to present as one's opinion.
   *I will **submit** my manuscript to a publisher for possible publication.*

6. **transmit** (trans·mit') *v.* To send from one place to another; to pass on by heredity; to transfer; to pass or communicate news, information, and so on.
   *Certain diseases are **transmitted** from the parent to the child through heredity.*

7. **intermission** (in·ter·mis·sion) (in·ter·mish'un) *n.* Time between events; recess.
   *The **intermissions** between acts in the play were each fifteen minutes long.*

8. **position** (po·si·tion) (po·zish'un) *n.* An act of placing or arranging; the manner in which a thing is placed; the way the body is placed, as in *sitting position*; the place occupied by a person or thing; the proper or appropriate place, as *in position*; job; a feeling or stand; social standing.
   *He had been sitting in that **position** for so long that, if he hadn't moved a little, his legs would have fallen asleep.*

9. **postpone** (pōst·pōné') *v.* To put off to a future time; to delay.
   *They had to **postpone** their annual reading convention for another month because many members could not come at the scheduled time.*

10. **positive** (pos·i·tive) (poz'i·tivé) *adj.* Being directly found to be so or true; real; actual; sure of something; definitely set; confident.
    *She was **positive** that she could describe the men who kidnapped her because they hadn't bothered to blindfold her.*

11. **posture** (pos·ture) (pos'chur) *n.* The placing or carriage of the body or parts of the body; a mental position or frame of mind.
    *His sitting **posture** is so poor that after a while it may cause him to have back problems.*

12. **post** (pōst) *n.* A position or employment, usually in government service; an assigned beat; a piece of wood or other material to be used as a support; a place occupied by troops. *v.* To inform; to put up (as on a wall); to mail (as a letter).
    *Do you like the **post** you have with the government?*

13. **proposal** (pro·po·sal) (pro·pō'zul) *n.* An offer put forth to be accepted or adopted; an offer of marriage; a plan.
    *As the governor's **proposal** for a tax plan was not acceptable to the people, the legislators voted against it.*

14. **animosity** (an·i·mos·i·ty) (an·i·mos'i·tē) *n.* (*pl.* **ties**) Hatred; resentment.
    *She felt great **animosity** toward the persons who attacked her father and beat him so badly that he had to go to the hospital.*

15. **magnanimous** (mag·nan'i·møus) *adj.* Forgiving of insults or injuries; high-minded; great of soul.

    *The speaker was very **magnanimous** to overlook the insults that were yelled at him.*

16. **magnify** (mag·ni·fy) (mag'ni·fī) *v.* To increase the size of; to make larger.

    *The microscope **magnifies** very small objects so that they can be viewed easily.*

17. **magnificent** (mag·nif·i·cent) (mag·nif'i·sent) *adj.* Splendid; beautiful; superb.

    *The palace was so **magnificent** that it was difficult to find words to describe its splendor.*

18. **hypnosis** (hyp·no·sis) (hip·nō'sis) *n.* (*pl.* **ses**; sēz) A sleeplike trance that is artificially brought about.

    *I can't believe that I was put in a state of **hypnosis** and did all those silly things, because I do not remember anything that took place.*

19. **federal** (fed'er·al) *adj.* Of or formed by an agreement between two or more states, groups, and so on; relating to a union of states, groups, and so on in which central authority in common affairs is established by consent of its members.

    *All the states in the United States joined to form a **federal** government in which common affairs, such as foreign policy, defense, and interstate commerce, are controlled by the government.*

20. **confide** (con·fīdé') *v.* To tell in trust; to tell secrets trustingly.

    *If you do not want others to know your secrets, **confide** only in people you can trust.*

21. **innate** (in·nāté') *adj.* Inborn; born with; not acquired from the environment; belonging to the fundamental nature of something; beginning in; coming from.

    ***Innate** characteristics are those that cannot be acquired after birth.*

22. **postnatal** (post·na·tal) (pōst·nāt'ul) *adj.* Occurring after birth.

    *It is important that all infants receive good **postnatal** care.*

23. **prenatal** (pre·na·tal) (prē·nāt'ul) *adj.* Being or taking place before birth.

    *A pregnant woman should take good care of herself so that her unborn child will be receiving good **prenatal** care.*

24. **nature** (na·ture) (nā'chur) *n.* The necessary quality or qualities of something; sort; kind; wild state of existence; uncivilized way of life; overall pattern or system; basic characteristic of a person; inborn quality; the sum total of all creation; the whole physical universe.

    *It seems to be his **nature** to behave in such a friendly manner all the time.*

25. **popular** (pop·u·lar) (pop'yu·lar) *adj.* Referring to the common people or the general public; approved of; admired; liked by most people.

    *Jack and Herb were voted the most **popular** boys in their class because they were liked by the most people.*

26. **population** (pop·u·la·tion) (pop·yu·lā'shun) *n.* Total number of people living in a country, city, or any area.

    *Every ten years a census is taken to determine the **population** and other important demographic statistics of the United States.*

27. **equivalent** (e·quiv·a·lent) (e·kwiv'a·lent) *adj.* Equal in value, meaning, force, and so on.

    *The amounts were **equivalent**, so that each person had exactly the same number.*

## SPECIAL NOTES

1. Do not confuse the word *post*, meaning "a position or employment," "a support for a sign," "to inform," and so on, with the combining form *post* meaning "after." The word *post* comes from the combining form *pos, pon,* meaning "place" or "set."

2. The word *innate* meaning "born with" refers to characteristics or qualities with which you are born. You cannot acquire these after birth. The term *innate* can also be applied to things about which you say that something is such an important part of the thing in question that it is necessarily a part of it. For example: the *innate* weakness of certain kinds of government. Note that "innate weakness" does not mean "inborn weakness." *Inborn* can apply only to living beings.

3. When the term *federal* is spelled with a capital letter, it means "relating to or supporting the central government of the United States" or "relating to or loyal to the Union cause in the American Civil War of 1861–1865." It is also capitalized when it is part of the name of an agency.
   a. The *Federal* Bureau of Investigation is an agency of the United States that investigates violations of *federal* criminal laws.
   b. The *Federal* soldiers were those who fought for the Union cause in the Civil War.

"Federal labeling laws don't apply to homemade meat loaf."

From *The Wall Street Journal*—Permission, Cartoon Features Syndicate.

## Step III. Words in Context

When James Jefferson, not a very **popular** employee, was **dismissed** from his **position** at the **federal** government, he said that he would get even. Too bad no one took his threat seriously. Let me explain. James Jefferson was suspected of stealing secrets and **transmitting** them to other governments. Our government did not have **positive** proof of this, so they decided to ask him to **submit** his resignation. James, however, refused to leave his **post**. He felt that this would be an **admission** of guilt or **equivalent** to it. He came up with a **proposal** that he thought was **magnificent** and that would show he was innocent. He said that he would give **permission** to anyone in the government to use **hypnosis** on him and ask him anything he or she wanted. The government officials said that even if he did pass the **hypnosis** test, it would be too risky to **confide** in him again. Too many people in the **population** were at stake. They said that they had no **animosity** toward him, but they felt he had to either resign or be **dismissed**. James's **innate** stubborn **nature** would not allow him to resign, so he was **dismissed**.

After his dismissal, James's **posture** toward his innocence did not change. He became very belligerent; his one **mission** in life was to get even with "those" who had **dismissed** him. He had never been a **magnanimous** person, and his dismissal just **magnified** his **animosity**. He had hatred toward everyone. He hated his mother, who had not given him good **prenatal** or **postnatal** care because she was an alcoholic, and he hated his father, who had walked out on his mother when he was born. As the days passed, James's **animosity** grew and grew. He was obsessed with getting even. He followed his former boss every day. One evening when his ex-boss was at a theater, James waited for the **intermission**. During the **intermission**, James took out a gun and shot his former boss, as well as ten other people.

## Step IV. Practice

**A. Directions:** A number of sentences with missing words follow. Choose the word that *best* fits the sentence. Put the word in the blank. Each word is used only once.

**Word List**

| | | |
|---|---|---|
| admission | magnanimous | positive |
| animosity | magnificent | post |
| confide | magnify | postnatal |
| dismiss | mission | postpone |
| equivalent | nature | posture |
| federal | permission | prenatal |
| hypnosis | popular | proposal |
| innate | population | submit |
| intermission | position | transmit |

1. Tom has to _____ his report to his adviser for approval.

2. The _____ in some cities is so large that there are not enough jobs for all the people.

3. A misanthrope would have _____ toward all people because he or she is a hater of mankind.

4. The men are going on such a secret _____ that even they do not yet know what they are supposed to accomplish.

5. It appears that our jobs are _____ because we have the same duties to perform, and we're getting paid the same.

6. I wonder how it feels to be the most _____ person in school and be admired by practically everyone?

7. Have you gained _____ to the school you want to go to in the fall?

8. Did you know that the company will have to _____ a number of employees because it is not as productive as it was?

9. Tonight the network is going to _____ the television program from England to the United States.

10. Will the _____ between events be long or short?

11. Try to _____ the conference for as long as you can so that we can gather more information.

12. The politician running for office was presenting his _____ on the issue of school busing.

13. If you always sit slouched over and never stand up straight, you will have bad

_____ .

14. I am _____ that the capital of the United States is Washington, D.C.

15. She has been employed in a very important _____ in government service for the past decade.

16. When Ms. Smith was pregnant, she visited her obstetrician every month to make sure that she was receiving proper _____ care.

17. When Jim's third _____ of marriage was turned down, he began to wonder whether there was something wrong with him.

18. Babies who are born prematurely need special _____ care.

19. _____ people are so great of spirit that they can overlook many things that others of us may not be able to overlook.

20. Some people _____ their errors so that they seem larger than they are.

21. One of the wealthiest men in the world built himself the most

_____ mansion that has ever been seen.

22. While under the spell of _____, I did some very embarrassing things that I would not have done if I had been awake.

23. As she was born with that defect, it is _____ .

24. When we went on our camping trip, we went to a place that was away from all civilization, and we lived in a state of _____ .

25. I _____ only in people I know I can trust.

26. Although in a(n) _____ government all states must obey laws that are common to all, each state does have control of its own internal affairs.

27. In many states you need your parents' _____ in order to marry under the age of eighteen.

---

**STOP.**   Check answers at the end of this chapter (p. 249).

---

**B. Directions:**   A list of definitions follows. Give the word that *best* fits the definition. Try to relate the definition to the meanings of the combining forms.

**Word List**

| | | |
|---|---|---|
| admission | magnanimous | positive |
| animosity | magnificent | post |
| confide | magnify | postnatal |
| dismiss | mission | postpone |
| equivalent | nature | posture |
| federal | permission | prenatal |
| hypnosis | popular | proposal |
| innate | population | submit |
| intermission | position | transmit |

1. To send from one place to another _____

2. Sure of something _____

3. A piece of wood or other material to be used as a support

   _____

4. The manner in which a thing is placed _____

5. Forgiving of insults or injuries _____

6. The placing or carriage of the body _____

7. Time between events _____

8. A sleeplike trance that is artificially brought about _____

9. Splendid _____

10. An offer put forth to be accepted or adopted _____

11. Being before birth _____

12. Born with _____

13. Occurring after birth _____

14. The necessary qualities of something _____

15. Relating to or formed by an agreement between two or more states

_____

16. To reveal in trust _____

17. To enlarge _____

18. Hatred _____

19. Total number of people living in a country _____

20. Entrance fee _____

21. Task or responsibility _____

22. Equal in value, meaning, and so on _____

23. Liked by most people _____

24. To delay _____

25. To tell or allow to go _____

26. To give in to another _____

27. A consent _____

---

**STOP.**   Check answers at the end of this chapter (p. 249).

---

*C. Directions:*   Sentences containing the meaning of vocabulary presented in Exercise 15 follow. Choose the word that *best* fits the meaning of the word or phrase underlined in the sentence.

**Word List**

| | | |
|---|---|---|
| admission | magnanimous | positive |
| animosity | magnificent | postnatal |
| confide | magnify | posts |
| dismissed | mission | postpone |
| equivalent | nature | posture |
| federal | permission | prenatal |
| hypnosis | popular | proposal |
| innate | population | submit |
| intermission | position | transmit |

1. Because I did not have the entrance fee, I could not enter the park.

_____

2. I refuse to <u>give in</u> to that group of people's ways of doing things.

   _____

3. After working there for a decade, I was told that I was going to be <u>let go</u>.

   _____

4. I am <u>certain</u> that this is the correct way to put that together.

   _____

5. The city we visited was <u>exceptionally impressive</u>. _____

6. Could you please <u>put off</u> going on that trip for another two weeks?

   _____

7. Your <u>carriage</u> is so poor when you walk. Can't you straighten up?

   _____

8. We used <u>strong timber</u> to hold up our birdhouse. _____

9. Will there be <u>a break between the acts</u> in the show? _____

10. All week the newsreporters had to <u>pass on</u> information about the floods
    so that people would know when they could return to their homes.

    _____

11. It's rare to meet someone who can turn the other cheek and be so <u>forgiving of
    insults</u>. _____

12. I need something that will <u>increase the size of</u> this print so that I can see
    it better. _____

13. The doctor gave me <u>suggestions to induce a sleeplike trance</u> so that he could try
    to cure me of my phobia of heights. _____

14. Have you read my <u>plan</u> in full? _____

15. Children need good <u>after birth</u> care. _____

16. It's difficult to determine <u>the basic characteristic</u> of a person.

    _____

17. The color of your eyes is determined by your genes and is an <u>inborn</u>
    characteristic. _____

18. I always try to give the twins <u>equal</u> attention. _____

19. I am shocked at what my best friend will <u>reveal</u> to me <u>in trust</u>.

    _____

20. In order to have a good start in life, a child needs good <u>before birth</u>

    care. _____

21. What type of government are we talking about when we say "<u>relating to a</u>
    <u>union of states in which central authority in common affairs is established</u>

    <u>by consent of its members</u>"? _____

22. Some leaders tend to be more <u>admired</u> than others. _____

23. Do you know <u>the total number of people</u> in your community?

    _____

24. The government would not give its <u>consent</u> to some aliens to remain in
    this country when it was found out <u>that</u> the aliens had criminal records

    in their own countries. _____

25. Do you have <u>a special task</u> that you must accomplish? _____

26. Is this <u>the proper place</u> for the chair? _____

27. <u>The hatred</u> that the people felt for the demagogue who attempted to deceive

    them was evident in their faces. _____

---

**STOP.**   Check answers at the end of this chapter (p. 249).

---

# *EXTRA WORD POWER*

**mal.**   Bad; ill; evil; wrong; not perfect. *Mal* is found at the beginning of a great number of words. Examples: *malfunction*—to function badly; *malnourished*—badly nourished; *malformed*—abnormally formed; *maltreated*—treated badly. How many more words with *mal* can you supply? Check your dictionary for a list of words beginning with *mal*.

**semi.**   Half; not fully; partly; occurring twice in a period. *Semi* is found at the beginning of a great number of words. For example: *semiblind*—partly blind; *semicircle*—half circle; *semiannual*—twice in a year, every half year; *semistarved*—partly starved; *semiwild*—partly wild. How many more words with *semi* can you supply? Check your dictionary for a long list of words beginning with *semi*.

© 1960 United Feature Syndicate, Inc.

## Additional Words Derived from Combining Forms

From your knowledge of combining forms, can you define the following words?

1. **equivocate** (e·quiv·o·cate) (e·kwiv′o·cāte) *v.  He always seems to **equivocate** when he does not want to commit himself to giving an exact answer.*

   _____

2. **missile** (mis′sile) *n.  That big stone, which he used as a **missile**, hit its target.*

   _____

3. **remission** (re·mis·sion) (re·mish′un) *n.  The doctors were delighted that the disease had reached a state of **remission** and was now dormant.*

   _____

4. **emissary** (em·is·sa·ry) (em′is·sa·rē) *n.  Usually, an **emissary** is sent to another country to try to learn about the other country's plans and to try to influence the plans.*

   _____

5. **intermittent** (in·ter·mit′tent) *adj.  Because the pain was **intermittent**, he had some pain-free moments.*

   _____

6. **intercede** (in·ter·cede) (in·ter·sēde′) *v.  The company's troubleshooter was called upon to **intercede** in the dispute that had hurt relations between the company and the town.*

   _____

7. **intervene** (in·ter·vēne′) *v.  Because the strike had been going on for so long, the courts decided to **intervene** by asking for a "cooling off" period for both sides.*

   _____

8. **proposition** (prop·o·si·tion) (prop·o·zish′un) *n.  His **proposition** sounded like a very sophisticated plan; so we decided to consider it at our next conference.*

   _____

9. **disposition** (dis·po·si·tion) (dis·po·zish'un) *n.   Because he has such a good **disposition**, I'm sure that he will be very nice to you.*

_____

10. **depose** (de·pose) (de·pōzé') *v.   After some monarchs have been **deposed**, they have been executed.*

_____

11. **expound** (ex·pound) (ik·spound') *v.   As the class had difficulty understanding the concept of intelligence, the professor **expounded** further on it.*

_____

12. **infidelity** (in·fi·del·i·ty) (in·fi·del'i·tē) *n.   Both spouses were suing for divorce on the grounds of **infidelity** because each had found that the other had been unfaithful.*

_____

13. **perfidious** (per·fid·i·ous) (per·fid'ē·óus) *adj.   I did not know that I had a **perfidious** friend until I heard from others that my secrets had all been told.*

_____

14. **magnate** (mag'nāté) *n.   Howard Hughes, a **magnate** of considerable wealth, lived in seclusion the last years of his life.*

_____

15. **malediction** (mal·e·dic·tion) (mal·e·dik'shun) *n.   The words **malediction** and bene-diction are antonyms.*

_____

16. **malefactor** (mal·e·fac·tor) (mal'e·fak·tor) *n.   When a **malefactor** is caught by the police, he usually is sent to jail for his crimes.*

_____

17. **animate** (an'i·māté) *v.   When Arthur tells a story, he becomes so **animated** that every part of him is alive and active.*

_____

---

**STOP.**   Check answers at the end of this chapter (p. 250).

Practice for Additional Words Derived from Combining Forms

**Directions:** Match each word with the *best* definition.

| | | |
|---|---|---|
| _____ | 1. equivocate | a. a criminal; one who does something bad |
| _____ | 2. missile | b. breach of trust; adultery |
| _____ | 3. remission | c. a speaking badly of someone |
| _____ | 4. proposition | d. to come between |
| _____ | 5. disposition | e. starting or stopping again |
| _____ | 6. animate | f. a person sent on a special mission |
| _____ | 7. malediction | g. a temporary stopping of a disease |
| _____ | 8. infidelity | h. to remove from a throne or other high position |
| _____ | 9. malefactor | i. to come between |
| _____ | 10. intervene | j. to use ambiguous language on purpose |
| _____ | 11. intercede | k. a very important or influential person |
| _____ | 12. intermittent | l. a plan put forth for consideration |
| _____ | 13. emissary | m. one's usual frame of mind |
| _____ | 14. perfidious | n. to state in detail |
| _____ | 15. depose | o. to make alive |
| _____ | 16. expound | p. a weapon intended to be thrown |
| _____ | 17. magnate | q. treacherous |

> **STOP.** Check answers at the end of this chapter (p. 250).

# CHAPTER WORDS IN SENTENCES ════════════

**Directions:** Use the given words to write a sentence that makes sense. Also, try to illustrate the meaning of the words without actually defining the words.

*Example* (popular; egocentric)  Mike, who is always interested in others, is well liked and *popular*, but his *egocentric* brother is not.

1. (pacify; belligerent)

_____

2. (politician; egocentric)

_____

3. (animosity; tension)

_____

4. (proposal; ambiguous)

_____

5. (vocation; popular)

_____

# CHAPTER WORDS IN A PARAGRAPH

Here is a list of words from this chapter. Write a paragraph using at least 8 of these words. The paragraph must make sense and be logically developed.

**Word List**

| | | | |
|---|---|---|---|
| admission | civilian | lucid | post |
| ambiguous | confide | magnify | posture |
| animosity | dismiss | nature | sophisticated |
| assist | equivalent | novel | submit |
| attention | error | pacify | tension |
| belligerent | hypnosis | permission | transmit |
| circumstances | innate | persist | vocal |
| civil | intense | politician | vocation |

# ANALOGIES 5

**Directions:** Find the word from the following list that _best_ completes each analogy. There are more words in the list than you need.

**Word List**

| | | | |
|---|---|---|---|
| active | contemporary | intense | polite |
| affect | content | intention | politician |
| agnostic | convocation | knowledge | politics |
| aid | cyclone | lucid | procession |
| animosity | decimate | magnificent | proposal |
| antitoxin | dismiss | malediction | sequence |
| attorney | expert | malefactor | stubborn |
| avocation | fertile | nature | tense |
| civilian | fertilization | novel | toxicologist |
| civilization | impolite | novice | vacation |
| concession | inactive | oral | visage |
| confide | infidelity | peace | vocabulary |
| consequence | innate | persist | vocation |

1. Credible : incredible : : benediction : _____.

2. Uniform : same : : criminal : _____.

3. Hyper : hypo : : ambiguous :_____.

4. Admit : deny : : civil : _____.

5. Independent : dependent : : veteran : _____.

6. Intention : aim : : assembly : _____.

7. Quiet : vociferous : : relaxed : _____.

8. Entrance : exit : : dormant : _____.

9. Shy : bashful : : tenacious : _____.

10. Magnify : enlarge : : unfaithfulness : _____.

11. Belligerent : war : : pacifist : _____.

12. Content : dissatisfied : : love : _____.

13. Pine : tree : : banking : _____.

14. Infinite : finite : : military : _____.

15. Unpopular : popular : : weak : _____.

16. Error : mistake : : assist : _____.

17. Monotonous : changeless : : continue : _____.

18. Provoke : irritate : : unusual : _____.

19. Astronomer : stars : : philosopher : _____.

20. Position : post : : vocal : _____.

---

**STOP.**  Check answers at the end of this chapter (p. 251).

---

# MULTIPLE-CHOICE VOCABULARY TEST 5

**Directions:**  This is a test on words in Exercises 13–15. Words are presented according to exercises. *Do all exercises before checking answers.* Underline the meaning that *best* fits the word.

Exercise 13

1. attention
   a. aim
   b. mental strain
   c. mental concentration
   d. very strong

2. intention
   a. mental concentration
   b. extreme force
   c. mental strain
   d. aim

3. tension
   a. mental strain
   b. aim
   c. mental concentration
   d. very strong

4. intense
   a. mental strain
   b. very strong
   c. mental concentration
   d. aim

5. belligerent
   a. aim
   b. very strong
   c. hatred
   d. warlike

6. civilian
   a. polite
   b. a state of human society
   c. refers to citizenship
   d. person not in the military

7. civics
   a. cultural development
   b. not in uniform
   c. polite
   d. the study of the rights and responsibilities of citizenship

8. civilization
   a. dealing with citizens
   b. polite
   c. cultural development, as of a people
   d. not in the military

9. civil
   a. not in uniform
   b. polite
   c. cultural development
   d. the study of the rights and responsibilities of citizens

10. politics
    a. science or art of government
    b. cultural development
    c. rule by people
    d. refers to a city

11. politician
    a. science or art of government
    b. refers to citizens
    c. refers to a city
    d. person engaged in the science or art of government

12. metropolitan
    a. surrounding area
    b. a person involved in city government
    c. city government
    d. referring to a major city center and its surrounding area

13. vocal
    a. manner of speaking
    b. referring to the voice
    c. referring to a person's work
    d. referring to peace

14. vocabulary
    a. refers to work
    b. refers to the voice
    c. refers to new words
    d. list of words that are defined

15. vocation
    a. one's work
    b. voice
    c. outspoken
    d. list of words

16. ambiguous
    a. referring to two
    b. having two or more meanings
    c. referring to many words
    d. referring to words with the same meanings

17. postscript
    a. a letter
    b. something written
    c. a signature
    d. something added to a letter after the writer's signature

18. pacify
    a. an agreement
    b. to calm
    c. to help
    d. to work with

## Exercise 14

19. lucid
    a. a light
    b. clear
    c. permitting light to go through
    d. to view

20. translucent
    a. a clear view
    b. light
    c. permitting light to go through but not allowing a clear view
    d. light can go through and permits a clear view

21. error
    a. to walk around
    b. to wander off walking
    c. a mistake
    d. to lie

22. sophisticated
    a. worldly-wise
    b. very knowledgeable
    c. not clever
    d. to know how to dress

23. sophomore
    a. third-year student
    b. immature person
    c. someone who is knowledgeable
    d. someone not too smart

24. philosophy
    a. refers to knowledge
    b. wise man
    c. the study of human knowledge
    d. charity

25. circumstances
    a. the conditions surrounding an act
    b. the acts
    c. the events
    d. aims

26. substitute
    a. to put in place of
    b. to place
    c. to set
    d. to take

27. consist
    a. to place
    b. to stand
    c. to put together
    d. to be made up of

28. assist
    a. to stand by
    b. to stand off
    c. to help
    d. to place

29. distant
    a. separated by time and/or space
    b. a relation
    c. refers to space
    d. to stand by

30. obstacle
    a. something helpful
    b. something harmful
    c. something that stands in the way
    d. a large rock

31. persist
    a. to stand around
    b. to move on
    c. to stand for
    d. to continue in some course even when it is difficult

32. innovation
    a. a book
    b. a strange idea
    c. something newly introduced
    d. an immunization

33. novel
    a. refers to a nonfiction book
    b. new
    c. something done over
    d. refers to a biography

34. dormitory
    a. a house
    b. a room
    c. a resort
    d. a building providing sleeping and living quarters at a school

35. dormant
    a. active
    b. inactive
    c. awake
    d. referring to door

36. period
    a. a circle
    b. time
    c. portion of time
    d. portion of something

37. hypertension
    a. mental strain
    b. very strong force
    c. very tired
    d. high blood pressure

38. egocentric
    a. not concerned with self
    b. self-centered
    c. self-sufficient
    d. able to help self

Exercise 15

39. mission
    a. the task or responsibility a person is assigned
    b. a vacation trip
    c. a house
    d. atomic particles

40. permission
    a. weekly allowance
    b. a consent
    c. to give in to
    d. to give

41. dismiss
    a. to leave
    b. to let alone
    c. to tell to go
    d. to go

42. admission
    a. act of allowing to enter
    b. allow to do
    c. refers to money
    d. an allowance

43. submit
    a. to allow to do
    b. to let go
    c. to give in to
    d. to help

44. transmit
    a. to send away
    b. to give in
    c. to let go
    d. to send from one place to another

45. intermission
    a. a space
    b. time period
    c. a responsibility
    d. time between events

46. position
    a. place occupied by a thing
    b. to put off
    c. something proper
    d. to put away

47. postpone
    a. to mail
    b. to delay
    c. to put away
    d. to stay

48. positive
    a. the manner of sitting
    b. to put off
    c. sure of
    d. not confident

49. posture
    a. a place
    b. a setting
    c. the manner of carrying the body
    d. mental strain

50. post
    a. a government job
    b. government
    c. to put off
    d. to serve

51. proposal
    a. to put off
    b. to send away
    c. an acceptance
    d. an offer

52. magnanimous
    a. large
    b. highly spirited
    c. forgiving of insults
    d. splendid

53. magnify
    a. to see from
    b. something large
    c. to help
    d. to enlarge

54. magnificent
    a. forgiving of insults
    b. large of spirit
    c. splendid
    d. large

55. animosity
    a. full of spirit
    b. refers to the mind
    c. hatred
    d. large of soul

56. hypnosis
    a. sleep
    b. put to sleep
    c. a sleeplike trance artificially brought on
    d. a drug

57. federal
    a. government
    b. relating to states
    c. faith in government
    d. relating to an agreement between two or more states to join into a union

58. confide
    a. faith in
    b. to tell in trust
    c. to tell everything
    d. to give information

59. innate
    a. not born
    b. acquired after birth
    c. birth
    d. born with

60. postnatal
    a.  refers to nose condition
    b.  occurring before birth
    c.  born with
    d.  occurring after birth

61. prenatal
    a.  refers to birth
    b.  born with
    c.  occurring before birth
    d.  occurring after birth

62. nature
    a.  outside
    b.  flowers
    c.  the necessary qualities of something
    d.  a person

63. popular
    a.  people
    b.  approved of
    c.  the number of people
    d.  lots of people

64. population
    a.  people
    b.  total number of people living in an area
    c.  liked by people
    d.  an area in which people live

65. equivalent
    a.  equal to
    b.  unlike
    c.  a comparison
    d.  a mathematical sign

# TRUE/FALSE TEST 5

***Directions:***  This is a true/false test on Exercises 13–15. Read each sentence carefully. Decide whether it is true or false. Put a *T* for *true* or an *F* for *false* in the blank. If the answer is false, change a word or part of the sentence to make it true. The number after the sentence tells you if the word is from Exercise 13, 14, or 15.

_____ 1. When you pay <u>attention</u> to something, you do not need to concentrate. 13

_____ 2. A <u>pacifist</u> is <u>belligerent</u>. 13

_____ 3. A <u>civilian</u> is a member of the armed forces. 13

_____ 4. *Intense* and *tension* are synonyms. 13

_____ 5. If you live in a <u>metropolitan</u> area, you are in or near a major city. 13

_____ 6. If you <u>postpone</u> something, you are putting it off. 15

_____ 7. A <u>proposal</u> is something you must accept. 15

_____ 8. All <u>intermissions</u> are at least ten minutes. 15

_____ 9. A <u>sophisticated</u> plan is a complex plan. 14

_____ 10. You can clearly see through something <u>translucent</u>. 14

_____ 11. <u>Politics</u> is the science of people. 13

_____ 12. <u>Civilization</u> can exist in the wilderness without people. 13

_____ 13. Your <u>vocation</u> is what you are called. 13

_____ 14. A <u>postscript</u> is the last paragraph of your essay. 13

_____ 15. When you are <u>ambiguous</u>, what you say can be taken two ways. 13

_____ 16. The way you dress would be due to <u>innate</u> factors. 15

_____ 17. *Equivalent* and *similar* are synonyms. 15

_____ 18. An <u>egocentric</u> person is concerned with himself or herself. 14

_____ 19. To <u>persist</u> in a course means you need an <u>assist</u>. 14

_____ 20. *Civil* and *rude* are antonyms. 13

_____ 21. An <u>innovation</u> is an archaic plan. 14

_____ 22. A <u>dormant</u> disease is in <u>remission</u>. 14, 15

_____ 23. To <u>transmit</u> information means that you send it from one place to another. 15

_____ 24. *Hypnosis* and *dormant* are synonyms. 15, 14

_____ 25. *Animosity* and *love* are antonyms. 15

_____ 26. *Submit* and *concede* are synonyms. 15

_____ 27. A person who behaves like a <u>sophomore</u> is someone who is worldly-wise. 14

_____ 28. <u>Federal</u> refers to all unions. 15

_____ 29. Astronauts go on <u>missions</u> in space. 15

_____ 30. A <u>novel</u> can be an autobiography. 14

---

**STOP.**   Check answers for both tests at the end of this chapter (p. 251).

# SCORING OF TESTS

| MULTIPLE-CHOICE VOCABULARY TEST | | TRUE/FALSE TEST* | |
|---|---|---|---|
| Number Wrong | Score | Number Wrong | Score |
| 0–4 | Excellent | 0–3 | Excellent |
| 5–10 | Good | 4–6 | Good |
| 11–14 | Weak | 7–9 | Weak |
| Above 14 | Poor | Above 9 | Poor |
| Score _____ | | Score _____ | |

1. If you scored in the excellent or good range on *both tests*, you are doing well. Go on to Chapter Seven.

2. If you scored in the weak or poor range on either test, look below and follow directions for Additional Practice. Note that the words on the tests are arranged so that you can tell in which exercise to find them. This will help you if you need additional practice.

# ADDITIONAL PRACTICE SETS

**A. Directions:** Write the words you missed on the tests from the three exercises in the space provided. Note that the tests are presented so that you can tell to which exercises the words belong.

## Exercise 13 Words Missed

1. _____   6. _____

2. _____   7. _____

3. _____   8. _____

4. _____   9. _____

5. _____   10. _____

## Exercise 14 Words Missed

1. _____   4. _____

2. _____   5. _____

3. _____   6. _____

*When the answer is false, you must get both parts of the true/false question correct in order to receive credit for it.

7. _____    9. _____

8. _____    10. _____

Exercise 15 Words Missed

1. _____    6. _____

2. _____    7. _____

3. _____    8. _____

4. _____    9. _____

5. _____    10. _____

**B. Directions:**   Restudy the missed words from the three exercises. Study the combining forms from which those words are derived. Do Step I and Step II for those you missed. Note that Step I and Step II of the combining forms and vocabulary derived from these combining forms are on the following pages:

Exercise 13 — pp. 199–202.

Exercise 14 — pp. 210–212.

Exercise 15 — pp. 219–222.

**C. Directions:**   Do Additional Practice 1 below if you missed words from Exercise 13. Do Additional Practice 2 on pp. 244–245 if you missed words from Exercise 14. Do Additional Practice 3 on pp. 246–247 if you missed words from Exercise 15. Now go on to Chapter Seven.

## Additional Practice 1 for Exercise 13

**A. Directions:**   The combining forms presented in Exercise 13 follow. Match each combining form with its meaning.

_____ 1. tend, tens, tent      a.  war

_____ 2. bello, belli          b.  city

_____ 3. civ, civis            c.  stretch; strain

_____ 4. polis                 d.  after

_____ 5. pac, pax              e.  both

_____ 6. voc, vox              f.  peace

_____ 7. post                  g.  voice; call

_____ 8. ambi                  h.  citizen

---

**STOP.**  Check answers at the end of this chapter (p. 252).

**B. Directions:** The words presented in Exercise 13 follow. Match each word with its meaning.

_____ 1. attention

_____ 2. intention

_____ 3. tension

_____ 4. intense

_____ 5. belligerent

_____ 6. civilian

_____ 7. civics

_____ 8. civilization

_____ 9. civil

_____ 10. politics

_____ 11. politician

_____ 12. metropolitan

_____ 13. vocal

_____ 14. vocabulary

_____ 15. vocation

_____ 16. ambiguous

_____ 17. postscript

_____ 18. pacify

a. aim

b. person not in the military

c. cultural development, as of a people

d. mental concentration

e. the science or art of government

f. referring to a major city center and its surrounding area

g. warlike

h. referring to the voice

i. job; profession

j. able to be taken two or more ways

k. having extreme force

l. person engaged in the science or art of government

m. the study of the rights and responsibilities of citizenship

n. to calm

o. something written after signature

p. polite; relating to ordinary community life

q. a list of words with definitions

r. mental strain

---

**STOP.** Check answers at the end of this chapter (p. 252).

---

# Additional Practice 2 for Exercise 14

**A. Directions:** The combining forms presented in Exercise 14 follow. Match each combining form with its meaning.

_____ 1. luc, lum

_____ 2. err

_____ 3. soph

_____ 4. sist, sta

a. wise

b. sleep

c. stand

d. light; clear

_____  5. nov       e.  I; me; the self

_____  6. dorm      f.  over; above; excessive

_____  7. peri       g.  wander

_____  8. hyper     h.  around

_____  9. ego       i.  new

---

**STOP.**  Check answers at the end of this chapter (p. 252).

---

**B. Directions:**  The words presented in Exercise 14 follow. Match each word with its meaning.

_____  1. lucid          a.  second-year student; immature person

_____  2. translucent    b.  to put in place of

_____  3. error         c.  separated by time and/or space

_____  4. sophisticated   d.  work of fiction of some length

_____  5. sophomore    e.  clear

_____  6. philosophy     f.  something newly introduced

_____  7. circumstance   g.  inactive

_____  8. substitute      h.  to continue in some course even when it is difficult

_____  9. assist

_____ 10. consist        i.  the study of human knowledge

_____ 11. distant        j.  mistake

_____ 12. obstacle       k.  to help

_____ 13. persist        l.  worldly-wise

_____ 14. innovation     m.  something in the way of

_____ 15. novel         n.  something connected with an act

_____ 16. dormitory      o.  portion of time

_____ 17. dormant       p.  self-centered

_____ 18. period        q.  permitting light to go through but not allowing a clear view

_____ 19. hypertension   r.  high blood pressure

_____ 20. egocentric     s.  a building providing sleeping quarters

                                    t.  to be made up of

---

**STOP.**  Check answers at the end of this chapter (p. 252).

# Additional Practice 3 for Exercise 15

**A. Directions:** The combining forms presented in Exercise 15 follow. Match each combining form with its meaning.

_____ 1. miss, mitt      a. spirit; mind; soul

_____ 2. pon, pos      b. born

_____ 3. anima, animus      c. place; set

_____ 4. magna      d. people

_____ 5. hypn, hypno      e. trust; faith

_____ 6. feder, fid, fide      f. great; large

_____ 7. nasc, nat      g. equal

_____ 8. equi      h. sleep

_____ 9. pop      i. send

---

**STOP.** Check answers at the end of this chapter (p. 252).

---

**B. Directions:** The words presented in Exercise 15 follow. Match each word with its meaning.

_____ 1. mission      a. place occupied by a thing

_____ 2. dismiss      b. sure of

_____ 3. admission      c. time between events

_____ 4. permission      d. the manner of carrying the body

_____ 5. submit      e. to enlarge

_____ 6. transmit      f. referring to agreement of two or more states to join into a union

_____ 7. intermission

_____ 8. position      g. the task or responsibility of a person

_____ 9. postpone      h. sleeplike trance artificially brought on

_____ 10. positive      i. occurring after birth

_____ 11. posture      j. necessary qualities of something or someone

_____ 12. post      k. to give in to

_____ 13. proposal      l. to tell to go

_____ 14. magnanimous      m. splendid

_____ 15. animosity      n. total number of people in an area

_____ 16. magnify      o. occurring before birth

_____ 17. magnificent      p. forgiving of insults

_____ 18. hypnosis      q. liked by many people

_____ 19. federal      r. government job

_____ 20. confide

_____ 21. innate

_____ 22. postnatal

_____ 23. prenatal

_____ 24. nature

_____ 25. popular

_____ 26. population

_____ 27. equivalent

s. act of allowing to enter

t. to send from one place to another

u. to tell in trust

v. hatred

w. equal to

x. a consent

y. born with

z. to delay

aa. an offer

---

**STOP.** Check answers at the end of this chapter (p. 252).

---

# ANSWERS: Chapter Six

## Exercise 13 (pp. 199–209)

### Practice A

(1) attention, (2) intention, (3) tension, (4) intense, (5) megaphone, (6) pacify,
(7) belligerent, (8) civics, (9) civilian, (10) politics, (11) politician, (12) ambiguous,
(13) vocation, (14) civilization, (15) civil, (16) vocal, (17) vocabulary, (18) postscript,
(19) metropolitan.

### Practice B

(1) c, (2) d, (3) b, (4) d, (5) c, (6) c, (7) b, (8) d, (9) c, (10) a, (11) d, (12) b, (13) d, (14) b,
(15) a, (16) a, (17) c, (18) d, (19) c.

### Practice C

(1) mental concentration, (2) aims, (3) mental strain, (4) very strong, (5) warlike,
(6) one not in the military, (7) the part of political science dealing with the rights and
responsibilities of citizens, (8) cultural development of a people, (9) the science or art
of government, (10) polite, (11) one who is in politics, (12) referring to a major city
center and surrounding area, (13) freely expressive of opinions, (14) stock of words,
(15) work, (16) having two or more meanings, (17) addition to a letter after signature,
(18) calm, (19) a device to increase sound.

### Additional Words Derived from Combining Forms (pp. 208–209)

1. **postmortem.** Happening or performed after death; pertaining to an examination
   of a human body after death; a postmortem examination; autopsy.

2. **posterior.** Located behind; in the rear; later; following after; coming after in
   order; succeeding (sometimes _pl._) the buttocks.

3. **posterity.**   Future generations; all of one's descendants (offspring).

4. **posthumously.**   After death.

5. **provoke.**   To stir up anger or resentment; to irritate.

6. **pacifist.**   One who is against war.

7. **megalopolis.**   One very large city made up of a number of cities; a vast, populous, continuously urban area.

8. **ambidextrous.**   Able to use both hands equally well.

9. **vociferous.**   Of forceful, aggressive, and loud speech; marked by a loud outcry; clamorous.

10. **convocation.**   A group of people called together; an assembly.

11. **avocation.**   Something one does in addition to his or her regular work, usually for enjoyment; a hobby.

12. **irrevocable.**   Not to be recalled, withdrawn, or annulled; irreversible; not able to be changed.

13. **detention.**   A keeping or holding back; confinement; the state of being detained in jail.

14. **détente.**   Easing of strained relations, especially between nations.

## Practice for Additional Words Derived from Combining Forms (p. 209)

(1) d, (2) i, (3) n, (4) j, (5) e, (6) k, (7) a, (8) b, (9) m, (10) h, (11) f, (12) c, (13) l, (14) g.

# Exercise 14  (pp. 210–218)

## Practice A

(1) error, (2) lucid, (3) translucent, (4) philosophy, (5) circumstance, (6) sophomore, (7) sophisticated, (8) substitute, (9) assist, (10) distant, (11) obstacle, (12) consist, (13) innovation, (14) novel, (15) dormant, (16) dormitory, (17) persist, (18) egocentric, (19) hypertension, (20) period, (21) periodical.

## Practice B

(1) lucid, (2) translucent, (3) error, (4) sophisticated, (5) sophomore, (6) philosophy, (7) circumstances, (8) substitute, (9) consist, (10) assist, (11) distant, (12) obstacle, (13) persist, (14) innovation, (15) novel, (16) dormitory, (17) dormant, (18) period, (19) periodical, (20) hypertension, (21) egocentric.

## Practice C

(1) separated by distance, far away, (2) inactive, (3) conditions, (4) permitting light to go through, (5) mistake, (6) clear, (7) is made up of, (8) the study of human knowledge, (9) place that houses people, (10) put in place of, (11) help, (12) obstruction, (13) new methods, (14) continue, (15) punctuation mark that signals a full stop, (16) publication issued at fixed time intervals, (17) high blood pressure, (18) self-centered, (19) immature person, (20) cultured, (21) unusual.

## Additional Words Derived from Combining Forms (pp. 217–218)

1. **perimeter.**  A measure of the outer part or boundary of a closed plane figure; boundary line of a closed plane figure.

2. **periphery.**  The outer part or boundary of something.

3. **periscope.**  An instrument used by a submarine to see all around.

4. **hyperbole.**  Great exaggeration or overstatement.

5. **illuminate.**  To give light to; light up; make clear.

6. **egotistic.**  Conceited; very concerned with oneself; selfish; vain.

7. **novice.**  Someone new at something; a rookie; a beginner.

8. **stamina.**  Staying power; resistance to fatigue, illness, and the like.

9. **obstinate.**  Stubborn; tenacious.

10. **sophistry.**  Faulty reasoning; unsound or misleading but clever and plausible (appearing real) argument or reasoning.

11. **erratic.**  Wandering; not regular; not stable.

12. **periodic.**  Occurring or appearing at regular intervals.

## Practice for Additional Words Derived from Combining Forms (p. 218)

(1) i, (2) e, (3) h, (4) g, (5) f, (6) a, (7) b, (8) j, (9) k, (10) c, (11) d, (12) l.

# Exercise 15  (pp. 219–231)

## Practice A

(1) submit, (2) population, (3) animosity, (4) mission, (5) equivalent, (6) popular, (7) admission, (8) dismiss, (9) transmit, (10) intermission, (11) postpone, (12) position or proposal, (13) posture, (14) positive, (15) post or position, (16) prenatal, (17) proposal, (18) postnatal, (19) Magnanimous, (20) magnify, (21) magnificent, (22) hypnosis, (23) innate, (24) nature, (25) confide, (26) federal, (27) permission.

## Practice B

(1) transmit, (2) positive, (3) post, (4) position, (5) magnanimous, (6) posture, (7) intermission, (8) hypnosis, (9) magnificent, (10) proposal, (11) prenatal, (12) innate, (13) postnatal, (14) nature, (15) federal, (16) confide, (17) magnify, (18) animosity, (19) population, (20) admission, (21) mission, (22) equivalent, (23) popular, (24) postpone, (25)  dismiss, (26) submit, (27) permission.

## Practice C

(1) admission, (2) submit, (3) dismissed, (4) positive, (5) magnificent, (6) postpone, (7) posture, (8) posts, (9) intermission, (10) transmit, (11) magnanimous, (12) magnify, (13) hypnosis, (14) proposal, (15) postnatal, (16) nature, (17) innate, (18) equivalent, (19) confide, (20) prenatal, (21) federal, (22) popular, (23) population, (24) permission, (25) mission, (26) position, (27) animosity.

Additional Words Derived from Combining Forms (pp. 229–230)

1. **equivocate.** To use ambiguous language on purpose.

2. **missile.** An object, especially a weapon, intended to be thrown or discharged, as a bullet, an arrow, a stone, and so on.

3. **remission.** A temporary stopping or lessening of a disease; a pardon.

4. **emissary.** A person or an agent sent on a specific mission.

5. **intermittent.** Starting or stopping again at intervals; not continuous; coming and going at intervals.

6. **intercede.** To come between; to come between as an influencing force; to intervene.

7. **intervene.** To come between; to act as an influencing force; to intercede.

8. **proposition.** A plan or something put forth for consideration or acceptance.

9. **disposition.** One's usual frame of mind or one's usual way of reacting; a natural tendency.

10. **depose.** To remove from a throne or other high position; to let fall.

11. **expound.** To state in detail; to set forth; to explain.

12. **infidelity.** Breach of trust; lack of faith in a religion; unfaithfulness of a marriage partner; adultery.

13. **perfidious.** Violating good trust; treacherous; deceitful; deliberately faithless.

14. **magnate.** A very important or influential person.

15. **malediction.** A speaking badly of someone; slander; a curse.

16. **malefactor.** Someone who does something bad; one who commits a crime; a criminal.

17. **animate.** To make alive; to move to action.

Practice for Additional Words Derived from Combining Forms (p. 231)

(1) j, (2) p, (3) g, (4) l, (5) m, (6) o, (7) c, (8) b, (9) a, (10) d, i, (11) i, d, (12) e, (13) f, (14) q, (15) h, (16) n, (17) k.

# Chapter Words in Sentences (pp. 231–232)

Sentences will vary.

# Chapter Words in a Paragraph (p. 232)

Paragraphs will vary.

## Analogies 5 (pp. 232–233)

(1) malediction, (2) malefactor, (3) lucid, (4) impolite, (5) novice, (6) convocation, (7) tense, (8) active, (9) stubborn, (10) infidelity, (11) peace, (12) animosity, (13) vocation,[1] (14) civilian, (15) intense, (16) aid, (17) persist, (18) novel, (19) knowledge, (20) oral.

## Multiple-Choice Vocabulary Test 5[2] (pp. 233–240)

Exercise 13

(1) c, (2) d, (3) a, (4) b, (5) d, (6) d, (7) d, (8) c, (9) b, (10) a, (11) d, (12) d, (13) b, (14) d, (15) a, (16) b, (17) d, (18) b.

Exercise 14

(19) b, (20) c, (21) c, (22) a, (23) b, (24) c, (25) a, (26) a, (27) d, (28) c, (29) a, (30) c, (31) d, (32) c, (33) b, (34) d, (35) b, (36) c, (37) d, (38) b.

Exercise 15

(39) a, (40) b, (41) c, (42) a, (43) c, (44) d, (45) d, (46) a, (47) b, (48) c, (49) c, (50) a, (51) d, (52) c, (53) d, (54) c, (55) c, (56) c, (57) d, (58) b, (59) d, (60) d, (61) c, (62) c, (63) b, (64) b, (65) a.

## True/False Test 5[2] (pp. 240–241)

(1) F, do not to do; (2) F, is to is not or belligerent to peaceful; (3) F, is to is not; (4) F, are to are not; (5) T; (6) T; (7) F, must to need not or something you must accept to a plan; (8) F, are to are not or at least ten minutes to time between events; (9) T; (10) F, can to cannot; (11) F, is to is not or people to government; (12) F, can to cannot; (13) F, is to is not or what you are called to your profession; (14) F, is to is not or last paragraph of your essay to something added to a letter after the signature; (15) T; (16) F, would be to would not be; (17) T; (18) T; (19) F, means to does not mean or you need an assist to you continue in what you are doing; (20) T; (21) F, is to is not or an archaic plan to a new plan; (22) T; (23) T; (24) F, are to are not or Hypnosis to Inactive;[3] (25) T; (26) T; (27) F, is to is not or worldly-wise to immature; (28) F, refers to does not refer or all unions to a union of states; (29) T; (30) F, can to cannot.

> **STOP.** Turn to page 242 for the scoring of the tests.

---

[1]*Vocation* is the answer because the relationship between *pine* and *tree* is one of *classification.*

[2]Answers for *false* are suggested answers.

[3]Persons can be active while under *hypnosis.* Also, *hypnosis* is a noun and *dormant* is an adjective.

## Additional Practice Sets (pp. 242–247)

Additional Practice 1

A.  (1) c, (2) a, (3) h, (4) b, (5) f, (6) g, (7) d, (8) e.
B.  (1) d, (2) a, (3) r, (4) k, (5) g, (6) b, (7) m, (8) c, (9) p, (10) e, (11) l, (12) f, (13) h, (14) q, (15) i, (16) j, (17) o, (18) n.

Additional Practice 2

A.  (1) d, (2) g, (3) a, (4) c, (5) i, (6) b, (7) h, (8) f, (9) e.
B.  (1) e, (2) q, (3) j, (4) l, (5) a, (6) i, (7) n, (8) b, (9) k, (10) t, (11) c, (12) m, (13) h, (14) f, (15) d, (16) s, (17) g, (18) o, (19) r, (20) p.

Additional Practice 3

A.  (1) i, (2) c, (3) a, (4) f, (5) h, (6) e, (7) b, (8) g, (9) d.
B.  (1) g, (2) l, (3) s, (4) x, (5) k, (6) t, (7) c, (8) a, (9) z, (10) b, (11) d, (12) r, (13) aa, (14) p, (15) v, (16) e, (17) m, (18) h, (19) f, (20) u, (21) y, (22) i, (23) o, (24) j, (25) q, (26) n, (27) w.

# CHAPTER SEVEN

## EXERCISE 16

### Step I. Combining Forms

**A. Directions:** A list of combining forms with their meanings follows. Look at the combining forms and their meanings. Concentrate on learning each combining form and its meaning. Cover the meanings, read the combining forms, and state the meanings to yourself. Check to see if you are correct. Now cover the combining forms, read the meanings, and state the combining forms to yourself. Check to see if you are correct.

| Combining Forms | Meanings |
|---|---|
| 1. pater, patri | father |
| 2. phil, phile, philo | love |
| 3. psych, psyche, psycho | spirit; mind; soul |
| 4. se | apart |
| 5. greg | flock; herd; crowd; mob |
| 6. eu | well; good; pleasant |

**B. Directions:**  Do not look at the preceding meanings. Write the meanings of the following combining forms.

Combining Forms                     Meanings

 1. pater, patri          _____

 2. phil, phile, philo    _____

 3. psych, psyche, psycho _____

 4. se                    _____

 5. greg                  _____

 6. eu                    _____

## Step II. Words Derived from Combining Forms

1. **paternal** (pa·ter′nal) *adj.* Of or like a father; fatherly; related on the father's side of the family; inherited or received from the father.
   *My girlfriend resented her boyfriend's behaving in such a **paternal** manner toward her.*

2. **paternity** (pa·ter·ni·ty) (pa·ter′ni·tē) *n.* Fatherhood; state of being a father; origin or descent from a father; provides for citizenship of the child born out of wedlock if fatherhood is established.
   *The court would try to determine the **paternity** of the child.*

3. **paternalism** (pa·ter·nal·ism) (pa·ter′nal·iz·um) *n.* The principle or practice of managing the affairs of a country or group of employees as a father manages the affairs of children.
   *The employees resented the **paternalism** of their employer.*

4. **patricide** (pat·ri·cide) (pat′ri·sīd́) *n.* The murder of one's own father.
   *The crime was an especially horrible one because it concerned **patricide**; however, when the jurors learned all the circumstances of the crime and how the father had mistreated his children, the crime became more understandable.*

5. **patriotic** (pa·tri·ot·ic) (pā′trē·ot·ik) *adj.* Characteristic of a person who loves his or her country; loving one's country; showing support and loyalty of one's country.
   *Many **patriotic** people were aroused to anger when they saw the American flag being dragged through the mud.*

6. **patron** (pā′tron) *n.* A person who buys regularly at a given store or who goes regularly to a given restaurant, resort, and so on; a regular customer; a wealthy or influential supporter of an artist or writer; one who gives one's wealth or influence to aid an institution, an individual, or a cause; a guardian saint or god.
   *I have been a **patron** of that restaurant for several years.*

7. **philanthropist** (phi·lan·thro·pist) (fi·lan′thro·pist) *n.* A person who shows love toward one's fellow human beings by active efforts to promote their welfare; one who shows good will toward others by practical kindness and helpfulness.
   *The **philanthropist** contributed a great amount of money to the community for worthy causes.*

8. **psychology** (psy·chol·o·gy) (psī·kol′o·jē) *n.* The science of the mind; the science that studies the behavior of humans and other animals; the mental or behavioral characteristics of a person or persons.

    *We took a course in **psychology** because we wanted to learn more about people's behavior and why they act as they do.*

9. **psychiatrist** (psy·chi·a·trist) (psī·kī′a·trist) *n.* A doctor who specializes in the treatment of people with mental, emotional, or behavioral disorders.

    *The court requested that a **psychiatrist** examine the defendant to determine whether he was legally sane and able to stand trial.*

10. **psychotic** (psy·chot·ic) (psī·kot′ik) *adj.* Having to do with or caused by serious mental disease; insane.

    *The psychiatrist said that the defendant was **psychotic** and should not stand trial because he was criminally insane.*

11. **gregarious** (gre·gar·i·ous) (gre·gar′ē·ous) *adj.* Tending to live in a flock, herd, or community rather than alone; marked by a fondness to be with others than alone; outgoing; sociable.

    *Jane, who is shy, is the opposite of her **gregarious** husband, who can't stand being alone.*

12. **congregate** (con·gre·gate) (kon′gre·gāte) *v.* To come together into a group, crowd, or assembly; to assemble; to come together or collect in a particular place or locality.

    *Everyone **congregated** around the famous actor and tried to get his autograph.*

13. **aggregate** (ag·gre·gate) (ag′gre·git) *n.* A mass of separate things joined together; the whole sum or amount; the total. *adj.* Formed by the collection of units or particles into a body, mass, or amount; total. *v.* To amount to; to come to; to total; to come together in a mass or group; to collect; unite; accumulate.

    *Taken separately, the amount was not very much, but in the **aggregate**, it was very high.*

14. **segregate** (seg′re·gāte) *v.* To set apart from others; to separate.

    *Try not to **segregate** yourself from others at the party; be more sociable.*

15. **seclusion** (se·clu·sion) (se·klū′zhun) *n.* The act of keeping apart from others; the act of confining in a place hard to find; the act of segregating or hiding; the act of isolating oneself; isolation.

    *The writer said that she was going into **seclusion** to finish writing her novel because she needed complete quiet and solitude to finish her work.*

16. **seduce** ((se·duce) (se·dūse′) *v.* To tempt to wrongdoing; to persuade into disobedience; to persuade or entice (lead on by exciting desire) into partnership in sexual intercourse.

    *In the film the older man tried to **seduce** the young girl, but she did not allow herself to be enticed by the older man's charm and money.*

17. **sedition** (se·di·tion) (se·dish′un) *n.* Conduct consisting of speaking, writing, or acting against an established government or seeking to overthrow it by unlawful means; incitement to rebellion or discontent.

    *Anyone found guilty of **sedition** can be severely punished by the government, especially in times of war.*

18. **eulogy** (eu·lo·gy) (ēū′lō·gē) *n.* The speaking well of someone; usually a formal speech of high praise for the dead.

    *At the funeral, the minister's **eulogy** for the recently deceased senator was filled with praise for the senator's service to his nation.*

## SPECIAL NOTES

1. Note that the word *philosophy* appears in Exercise 14. *Philosophy* is derived from the combining form *philo* as well as *soph*.

2. Also, the word *eulogy* is made up of the combining forms *eu* and *log, logo*. You met the combining forms *log, logo* meaning "speech, word" in Exercise 10.

# Step III. Words in Context

On Joan Anderson's twenty-first birthday she learned a tragic secret about her **paternal** great-grandfather, John Sloan, who had been a **patriotic** man, a **philanthropist**, and a **patron** of the arts. She learned that her great-grandfather had been the victim of **patricide**. In the **aggregate**, the story seems incredible and very complex, but if we were to look at the specific events that led up to the murder, it might be simpler.

John Sloan's first marriage was one of convenience. His family and his wife's had known each other all their lives and it was expected that the two would marry. They did. The marriage was not a good one, but neither was it a bad one. They both liked each other, but there was no great passion between them. John was a very **gregarious** man who liked to have a good time; his wife was very quiet and liked to stay at home. His wife enjoyed living in the country in **seclusion** and **segregated** from the outside world; John did not like country living. As a result, John had an apartment in the city and usually stayed there during the week. At night he often **congregated** with his friends at nightclubs.

It was there that he met Mary Bates, a singer at the club. The moment he saw her, he fell madly in love with her. He went to hear her sing every night; he showered her with gifts and constantly tried to **seduce** her, but she wouldn't have anything to do with him unless he married her. So John Sloan took her to Reno and married her. He was now a bigamist with two families who knew nothing about each other's existence. He had three children from the marriages—two girls from the first and a boy from the second.

For years everything went along fine. It wasn't until his children were grown that the trouble began. The root of the problem was his son, David, who was always getting into trouble. He would rant and rave against the government and complain that the government was treating everyone with **paternalism**. He was always talking about suicide and homicide. He thought everyone was his enemy. He even felt that his father wasn't really his father; he questioned his **paternity**.

John prided himself on his loyalty to his country, so you can imagine his state of mind when he learned that his son had committed an act of **sedition**. He confronted his son and asked him what had made him try to get people to overthrow the government. David just laughed in his father's face and said that if he wanted to understand him, he should take a course in **psychology**. The federal government issued a warrant for David's arrest. David's parents claimed that their son was **psychotic** and that he needed to see a **psychiatrist** rather than go to prison. Unfortunately, before the federal agents came to arrest David, David went into a rage and committed **patricide**—he killed his father.

An incredible footnote to this story is that it wasn't until after the father's death that his two wives learned of each other. When the two met, the fireworks began. There was no **eulogy** at the funeral for their bigamist husband.

# Step IV. Practice

**A. _Directions:_**  Define the underlined word in each of the following sentences.

1. My <u>paternal</u> grandfather died of a heart attack at an early age, so my father feels that his chances of having one are pretty high. _____

2. The company I work for operates on the principles of <u>paternalism</u>, but many of us resent the company's attitude of always knowing what is best for us.

   _____

3. I read a book recently in which there was so much hatred between the father and his sons that it actually led to <u>patricide</u>. _____

4. I feel that I am as <u>patriotic</u> as the next person, but I don't like to march in parades or wave flags to prove my patriotism. _____

5. At the dance the boys <u>segregated</u> themselves in the left corner of the room, and the girls <u>segregated</u> themselves in the right corner of the room.

   _____

6. At the trial the lawyer was trying to prove that his client had not <u>seduced</u> the young girl but that she had been a willing partner and that she had in fact <u>seduced</u> his client. _____

7. The money collected at the two charity balls amounted in the <u>aggregate</u> to two hundred thousand dollars. _____

8. After the death of her famous husband, she went into <u>seclusion</u> and refused to see or speak to anyone. _____

9. I have been a <u>patron</u> of this restaurant for a long time, but after my treatment today I will no longer frequent this restaurant. _____

10. Today many more fathers are taking <u>paternity</u> more seriously, and in a number of situations fathers rather than mothers are raising the children.

    _____

11. The well-known <u>philanthropist</u> donated his fortune to his university and to a cat.

    _____

12. Because John is such a <u>gregarious</u> person, you almost never find him alone.

    _____

13. When my friend kept having the same nightmare for weeks and weeks and became ill from lack of sleep, we suggested that she seek help from a <u>psychiatrist</u>. _____

14. At our school the students seem to <u>congregate</u> at the student center.

   _____

15. Pat majored in <u>psychology</u> at college because she wanted to be a psychologist.

   _____

16. We knew that the man was peculiar because of his odd behavior, but we didn't realize that he was <u>psychotic</u> until he went on a wild rampage and tried to kill many people. _____

17. In the United States, as well as in other countries, <u>sedition</u> against the government is a serious crime. _____

18. Everyone was amazed and shocked to learn that the deceased's longtime enemy would deliver the <u>eulogy</u>. _____

> **STOP.** Check answers at the end of this chapter (p. 297).

**B. Directions:** Match each word with the *best* definition.

| | |
|---|---|
| _____ 1. paternal | a. one who shows goodwill by giving practical help |
| _____ 2. eulogy | b. insane |
| _____ 3. psychology | c. to come together in a group |
| _____ 4. psychiatrist | d. a wealthy supporter of an artist |
| _____ 5. paternity | e. tending to live in a flock |
| _____ 6. psychotic | f. fatherhood |
| _____ 7. philanthropist | g. fatherly |
| _____ 8. patriotic | h. the total |
| _____ 9. segregate | i. to tempt to wrongdoing |
| _____ 10. congregate | j. the murder of one's own father |
| _____ 11. aggregate | k. the science of the mind |
| _____ 12. sedition | l. the act of keeping apart from others |
| _____ 13. seduce | m. incitement to rebellion |
| _____ 14. patricide | n. to separate |
| _____ 15. paternalism | o. loving one's country |
| _____ 16. gregarious | p. a specialist in the disorders of the mind |
| _____ 17. seclusion | q. the practice of managing a company in a fatherly way |
| _____ 18. patron | r. high praise, especially for the dead |

> **STOP.** Check answers at the end of this chapter (p. 297).

**C. Directions:**  A number of sentences with missing words follow. Choose the word that *best* fits the sentence. All the words are used.

**Word List**

| | | |
|---|---|---|
| aggregate | paternity | psychology |
| congregate | patricide | psychotic |
| eulogy | patriotic | seclusion |
| gregarious | patron | sedition |
| paternal | philanthropist | seduce |
| paternalism | psychiatrist | segregate |

1. Looking at the _____ of my past experiences with the firm, I should have known better and not trusted them.

2. The _____ said that she could not help me unless I trusted her and told her everything that bothered me and shared all my feelings with her.

3. My brother has always behaved in a(n) _____ manner toward me because there is a fifteen-year age span between us.

4. Dennis is taking a lot of _____ courses at school because he is interested in learning about the behavior of people.

5. During the Renaissance, many artists were fortunate to have a person who acted as a(n) _____ to them.

6. A person who is _____ should be confined in a mental institution.

7. My _____ friend is never alone.

8. My friends tend to _____ at my house.

9. There is one group of people at school who tend to _____ themselves from all the other students.

10. Because Joseph is an outgoing person, he does not like _____.

11. No one can _____ me into doing anything I do not want to do.

12. It is difficult to determine the _____ of a child with one hundred percent accuracy.

13. Congress is responsible for passing laws against the crime of _____.

14. _____ is a horrible crime.

15. Some countries govern based on a policy of _____.

16. The _____ was the best I had ever heard because it came from the heart.

17. The _____ man said that he had fought for his country before and that he was ready to fight for it again.

18. There is a(n) _____ in our town who has helped many people and who can always be counted on to give to needy causes.

---

**STOP.**   Check answers at the end of this chapter (p. 297).

---

## *EXTRA WORD POWER*

**ous.**   Full of; having. *Ous* is found at the end of a great number of adjectives. For example: *wondrous* — full of wonder; *joyous* — full of joy; *monogamous* — having to do with monogamy.

**ize.**   To cause to be or become; to be like; to be formed into. *Ize* is found at the end of many verbs. For example: *unionize* — to form into a union; *Americanize* — to become an American; *liquidize* — to cause to be liquid.

Additional Words Derived from Combining Forms

From your knowledge of combining forms, can you define the following words?

1. **expatriate** (ex·pa·tri·ate) (eks·pā′trē·āté) *v.* (eks·pā′trē·it) *n.*   *A number of people have* **expatriated** *themselves from their native countries and fled to the United States.*

   _____

2. **bibliophile** (bib·li·o·phile) (bib′lē·o·fīlé) *n.*   *My brother, who is a* **bibliophile**, *spends all his time reading or taking out books from the library.*

   _____

3. **philanthrope** (phil·an·thrope) (fil′an·thrōpé) *n.*   *It seems incredible that in the same family you can have a person who is a misanthrope and another who is a* **philanthrope**.

   _____

4. **philanderer** (phi·lan·der·er) (fi·lan′der·er) *n.*   *Jane will not marry Jim because she wants to marry someone whom she can trust rather than a* **philanderer**.

   _____

5. **psychosis** (psy·cho·sis) (p̸sī·kō′sis) *n.* (*pl.* **ses**)  *The psychiatrist said that Jim's behavior indicated that he had some form of **psychosis** and that he would have to be hospitalized.*

_____

6. **psychopath** (psy·cho·path) (p̸sī′kō·path) *n.*  *The police felt that the horrible murders were being committed by a **psychopath**.*

_____

7. **psychic** (psy·chic) (p̸sī′kik) *n. adj.*  *My friend went to a psychic because he felt that the **psychic** could help him communicate with his dead fiancée.*

_____

8. **egregious** (e·gre·gious) (e·grē′jus) *adj.*  *The doctor's **egregious** mistake may cost him the life of his patient.*

_____

9. **euphemism** (eu·phe·mism) (e̸ū′fe·miz·um) *n.*  *When we use such terms as* plump, passed away, *and* underprivileged, *for the terms* fat, died *and* poor, *we are using* ***euphemisms**.*

_____

10. **euphoria** (eu·phor·i·a) (e̸ū·for′ē·a) *n.*  *Many drug addicts claim that at first drugs give them a feeling of **euphoria**, that is, of well-being or elation; however, after a while many go into a state of depression and disgust.*

_____

11. **euphonious** (eu·pho·ni·ous) (e̸ū·fō′nē·us) *adj.*  *The **euphonious** sound of the chorus and the orchestra was enjoyed by everyone at the concert.*

_____

12. **euthanasia** (eu·tha·na·sia) (e̸ū·the·nā′zhē·a) *n.*  *Mr. Brown committed **euthanasia** because his hopelessly ill wife begged him to; however, the police arrested him for murder.*

_____

---

**STOP.**  Check answers at the end of this chapter (pp. 297–298).

Practice for Additional Words Derived from Combining Forms

**Directions:**  Match each word with the *best* definition.

_____ 1. expatriate

_____ 2. bibliophile

_____ 3. philanthropist

_____ 4. philanderer

_____ 5. psychosis

_____ 6. psychopath

_____ 7. psychic

_____ 8. egregious

_____ 9. euphonious

_____ 10. euphemism

_____ 11. euphoria

_____ 12. euthanasia

a.  a feeling of well-being

b.  a mental disorder characterized by lost contact with reality

c.  a less harsh way of saying a word

d.  mercy killing

e.  a person sensitive to nonphysical forces

f.  a person who has many love affairs with no intention of marriage

g.  one who has renounced his or her native country

h.  a person who shows his or her love to mankind by helpfulness to mankind

i.  a mentally ill person

j.  harmonious

k.  conspicuously bad

l.  a lover of books

---

**STOP.**  Check answers at the end of this chapter (p. 298).

---

# EXERCISE 17

## Step I. Combining Forms

**A. Directions:**  A list of combining forms with their meanings follows. Look at the combining forms and their meanings. Concentrate on learning each combining form and its meaning. Cover the meanings, read the combining forms, and state the meanings to yourself. Check to see if you are correct. Now cover the combining forms, read the meanings, and state the combining forms to yourself. Check to see if you are correct.

| Combining Forms | Meanings |
| --- | --- |
| 1. matr, matri, matro | mother |
| 2. juris, jus | law |
| 3. di | two |
| 4. vers, vert | turn |
| 5. rog | ask; beg |
| 6. simil, simul | like; resembling |

**B. Directions:** Do not look at the preceding meanings. Write the meanings of the following combining forms.

| Combining Forms | Meanings |
|---|---|
| 1. matr, matri, matro | _____ |
| 2. juris, jur | _____ |
| 3. di | _____ |
| 4. vers, vert | _____ |
| 5. rog | _____ |
| 6. simil, simul | _____ |

# Step II. Words Derived from Combining Forms

1. **maternal** (ma·ter'nal) *adj.* Motherly; having to do with a mother; inherited or derived from a mother; related on the mother's side of the family.
   *My friend behaves in a **maternal** manner toward her boyfriend but he seems to like it.*

2. **maternity** (ma·ter·ni·ty) (ma·ter'ni·tē) *n.* The state of being a mother; motherhood; a hospital or section of a hospital designated for the care of women immediately before and during childbirth and for the care of newborn babies. *adj.* Pertaining to or associated with the period in which a woman is pregnant, and with childbirth.
   *When my sister started to have labor pains, her husband rushed her to the **maternity** ward in the hospital.*

3. **matrimony** (mat·ri·mo·ny) (mat'ri·mō·nē) *n.* The act or state of being married; the union of man and woman as husband and wife; marriage.
   ***Matrimony** is something that should not be gone into lightly.*

4. **justice** (jus·tice) (jus'tisé) *n.* The maintenance of what is reasonable and well founded; the assignment of deserved rewards or punishments; the quality or characteristic of being fair and impartial; rightfulness; correctness.
   *The man said with all **justice** that he had not been treated fairly.*

5. **justification** (jus·ti·fi·ca·tion) (jus·ti·fi·kā'shun) *n.* A reason, circumstance, explanation, or fact that justifies or defends; good reason.
   *Everyone felt that the defendant had great **justification** to do what she did; however, she shouldn't have because it was against the law.*

6. **juror** (ju'ror) *n.* One of a group of persons sworn to deliver a verdict in a case submitted to them; member of a jury.
   *The jury was deadlocked because one **juror** kept voting differently from the other **jurors**.*

7. **divorce** (di·vorce) (di·vorsé') *n.* A legal dissolvement of a marriage relation usually by a court or other body having the authority; the legal ending of a marriage. *v.* To legally end a marriage; separate; disunite.
   *Even though the rate of **divorce** seems to be increasing each year, the institution of marriage is still respected.*

8. **dilemma** (di·lem'ma) *n.* Any situation that necessitates a choice between equally unfavorable or equally unpleasant alternatives; an argument that presents two equally unfavorable alternatives.
   *Jane has a **dilemma** because she didn't study for her exam. If she takes the exam,*

*she will fail it, but if she doesn't take the exam, her instructor will give her an automatic "F."*

9. **divide** (di·vīde′) *v.* To separate into parts.
   *We were trying to figure out how to **divide** the pie when our dog jumped on the table and ate it all up.*

10. **divert** (dī·vert′) *v.* To turn aside or from a path or course; to draw off to a different course, purpose, and so on.
    *The police were trying to **divert** the robbers' attention so that they could sneak to the back of the bank.*

11. **versatile** (ver′sa·tile) *adj.* Capable of turning from one subject, task, or occupation to another; able to do many things well; many-sided; changeable; variable.
    *The **versatile** actor has played many different types of roles.*

12. **converse** (con·verse) (kon′verse) *n.* A thing, especially a statement, that is turned around, usually producing a different idea or meaning; something that is opposite or contrary. *adj.* Opposite; contrary; turned about.
    *The **converse** of "all persons are animals" would not be correct.*

13. **reversible** (re·vers·ible) (re·ver′si·bul) *adj.* Capable of being opposite or contrary to a previous position; having two finished or usable sides (of a fabric, and so on).
    *I have a **reversible** jacket that I wear a lot, but someone thought that I had two different jackets because the sides are so different.*

14. **adverse** (ad·verse′) or (ad′verse) *adj.* Hostile; contrary to one's interest or welfare; unfavorable.
    *Her **adverse** remarks made us realize how hostile she was to our position on the issue.*

15. **controversy** (con·tro·ver·sy) (kon′tro·ver·sē) *n.* (*pl.* **sies**) A dispute, especially a lengthy and public one, between sides holding opposing views; a quarrel; debate; argument.
    *The **controversy** that has been raging for so long between the two opponents may be settled soon.*

16. **advertise** (ad·ver·tise) (ad′ver·tīze) *v.* To give public notice of in newspapers, on radio, on television, and so on; to praise the good qualities of a product, service, and so on; to call attention to; to notify, inform.
    *Sponsors **advertise** their products because they feel that this helps to sell them.*

17. **interrogate** (in·ter′ro·gāte) *n.* To ask questions of formally; to examine by questioning.
    *The police said that everyone in the room would be **interrogated** and that no one could leave because the answer to the mystery was contained in that room.*

18. **arrogant** (ar′ro·gant) *adj.* Full of pride and self-importance; overbearing; haughty.
    *The **arrogant** man made me feel very uncomfortable because I do not like people who are overbearing and impressed with their own importance.*

19. **derogatory** (de·rog·a·to·ry) (de·rog′a·tor·ē) *adj.* Tending to make less well regarded; tending to belittle someone or something; disparaging; belittling.
    *When the hostess kept making **derogatory** remarks about everyone, Sharon stood up, got her hat and coat, and left.*

20. **similar** (sim′i·lar) *adj.* Alike in essentials; having characteristics in common.
    *The identical twins in my class even had **similar** personalities.*

21. **simile** (sim'i·lē) *n.* A figure of speech comparing two unlike things using *like* or *as*. *"The clouds are like marshmallows" is an example of a **simile**.*

## SPECIAL NOTE

The term *converse* (kon·vers̄́') can also be a verb meaning "to talk informally together." This definition is not presented in this lesson.

## Step III. Words in Context

Have you read the newspaper stories about the sensational murder trial? It all started when a middle-aged man answered a personal advertisement in a magazine. It seems that Mary Simms, a middle-aged woman, decided to **advertise** for a husband in the personal section of a magazine. She stated that she was seeking **matrimony** with a gentleman who wanted a mature, **versatile** woman who had **maternal** instincts but was not interested in **maternity**. She stated also that she did not want someone who had been **divorced** and that she was very attractive.

Interestingly, a number of men answered her advertisement. They all seemed **similar**; that is, they all were men who lived in isolated places and did not have opportunities to meet women. There was one, however, who stood out. Jeff Dodds wrote and said that he hadn't married because he hadn't found the kind of old-fashioned girl he wanted. He felt that Mary sounded like that girl. She wasn't **arrogant**, and she was interested in making some lucky man happy. When Mary read that, she answered the letter right away. She said in order that there not be any **adverse** feelings between them, it would be a good idea for them to exchange photos and to write to one another for a while. That way they could see if they had things in common.

To make a long story short, the two finally met and decided to get married. The next part is rather difficult to tell. It seems that Mary Simms was not really a "she" but a "he." How Mary or rather "he" thought he could get away with this is incredible. Anyway, when Jeff found out, he was in a state of shock. He couldn't believe that Mary Simms wasn't a woman. He was in a **dilemma**. He felt he loved her, or rather him, or thought he had, but he felt that he could not stay married to someone who wasn't a she but a he. When Jeff told Mary he was leaving, Mary went crazy. She took out a gun and pointed it at Jeff. Jeff struggled to get the gun from Mary, and in the struggle Mary was fatally wounded.

When the police came, they **interrogated** Jeff and then charged him with the murder of Mary Simms. He told them that it was self-defense, but they said that the **converse** was true. They claimed that there was a **controversy**: Jeff and Mary had both said **derogatory** things to one another, and then Jeff tried to **divert** Mary's attention while he got the gun and shot her.

At the trial, Jeff kept using the same **simile** over and over again to describe Mary. He said that she was like a **reversible** jacket, but he didn't know that she had two sides. He said that he did not murder her and if there was **justice** the **jurors** would realize this. The prosecutor kept saying that what Mary Simms did was despicable but still was no **justification** for murder. Many people were **divided** on whether they thought Jeff was innocent or guilty. However, the **jurors** did find Jeff not guilty. Jeff returned to his hometown and never answered another advertisement as long as he lived.

# Step IV. Practice

**A. Directions:**   A list of definitions follows. Choose the word from the word list that *best* fits the definition.

**Word List**

| | | |
|---|---|---|
| adverse | divert | maternal |
| advertise | divide | maternity |
| arrogant | divorce | matrimony |
| controversy | interrogate | reversible |
| converse | juror | similar |
| derogatory | justice | simile |
| dilemma | justification | versatile |

1. Good reason _____

2. Member of a jury _____

3. The state of being a mother _____

4. The maintenance of what is reasonable _____

5. To ask questions formally _____

6. Tending to belittle someone _____

7. To legally end a marriage _____

8. Overbearing _____

9. The act of being married _____

10. Having two usable sides _____

11. To draw off to a different course _____

12. An argument that presents two equally unfavorable alternatives _____

13. Something that is opposite or contrary _____

14. A dispute _____

15. Hostile _____

16. To praise the good qualities of _____

17. Motherly _____

18. To separate into parts _____

19. Changeable _____

20. Alike in essentials _____

21. A comparison of two unlike things using *like* or *as* _____

---

**STOP.**   Check answers at the end of this chapter (p. 298).

**B. Directions:** A few paragraphs with missing words follow. Fill in the blanks with the word that *best* fits. Words may be used more than once.

**Word List**

| | | |
|---|---|---|
| adverse | divert | maternal |
| advertise | divide | maternity |
| arrogant | divorce | matrimony |
| controversy | interrogated | reversible |
| converse | juror | similar |
| derogatory | justice | simile |
| dilemma | justification | versatile |

My best friend was the first of our group to get a(n) **1**_____.
After having been married for two years, he decided that **2**_____
was not for him. He told us that his wife behaved in a very **3**_____
manner to him and if he wanted someone **4**_____ he could go
back home to his mother. His wife, on the other hand, did not want a(n)
**5**_____. She felt that there was no **6**_____
for one. She wanted them to go to a marriage counselor, but my friend didn't want to.

In all **7**_____, I should say that my friend is a(n)
**8**_____ person, who thinks a lot of himself, and that his wife
would probably be better off without him. He has always made
**9**_____ remarks about his wife, so we didn't know why he
married her in the first place.

When we **10**_____ my friend about this, he said that he had
met her when he was a(n) **11**_____. She, too, was a(n)
**12**_____. It seems that the case was a very complicated one,
and they spent a lot of time together. She had a strong sense of
**13**_____, and during the trial she tried to see to it that
**14**_____ would triumph. The case concerned a(n)
**15**_____ that had been going on for a long time and that finally
ended in violence. However bitter the **16**_____, there was no
**17**_____ for the violence. One **18**_____
always tried to **19**_____ the others from their purpose, but his
wife always got them back on the track. She helped the others to see the
**20**_____ that the defendant had and how he felt that he had no
choice. My friend said that he fell in love with her then and wanted to marry her.

Interestingly, she did not want to enter **21**_____ with him
at that time. She is a nurse who works in the **22**_____ ward
and she didn't feel that she was ready for marriage. My friend pursued her. He actually said that he would **23**_____ his love for her in the papers if
she didn't marry him. We were surprised to hear this since, as I've said, my friend is
such a(n) **24**_____ fellow. It seemed incredible to me that his
position was in the **25**_____ now and that he had such
**26**_____ feelings toward his wife.

My friend said that he did indeed love his wife when they were married, but he doesn't now. She treats him as if he were an infant in the 27_____ ward. She is not very 28_____, so she is not able to change her role from being a nurse to being a wife. He felt that she would not change, so he decided to get a(n) 29_____.

My friend still hasn't gotten the 30_____, because they haven't decided how to 31_____ their property. His wife has refused to discuss it with him or the lawyers. She feels that they have too many things in common and many 32_____ tastes. She uses a 33_____ to express what she feels is wrong with her husband. She says that her husband is like a spoiled baby.

> **STOP.**   Check answers at the end of this chapter (p. 298).

**C. Directions:**   Define the underlined word in each of the following sentences.

1. Jim Sloan must believe in <u>matrimony</u> because he has been married about thirteen times.

   _____

2. Jim Sloan must be an expert on <u>divorce</u> because of his many marriages.

   _____

3. Psychologists claim that a woman does not automatically have <u>maternal</u> instincts and these must be learned.

   _____

4. There is no <u>justification</u> for child abuse.

   _____

5. The boxer knew that he had a <u>dilemma</u> because he would lose whatever his choice.

   _____

6. A <u>reversible</u> coat serves dual purposes.

   _____

7. Please refrain from making <u>derogatory</u> remarks about my friends.

   _____

8. We were in a state of shock when the police stopped our car and said that they were taking us to the police station to <u>interrogate</u> us about a recent robbery. We knew that it was a case of mistaken identity, but how could we prove it?

   _____

9. The <u>arrogant</u> man talked about his ancestors all evening long.

_____

10. No one wanted to say anything <u>adverse</u> to him about his friend, but we felt that he should know that his friend was <u>ridiculing</u> him behind his back.

_____

11. My sister bought some beautiful <u>maternity</u> clothes.

_____

12. When the baby wanted something that we didn't want her to have, we tried to <u>divert</u> her attention away from it.

_____

13. How should we <u>divide</u> the monies that we made?

_____

14. I feel that the more <u>versatile</u> you are, the better able you are to survive in our society.

_____

15. The <u>controversy</u> between the two different factions at our plant is threatening our production.

_____

16. It seems to me that the <u>converse</u> of that statement is true.

_____

17. More work needs to be done on this before we <u>advertise</u> its virtues.

_____

18. The <u>juror</u> said that he could not make up his mind about the guilt of the defendant.

_____

19. We felt that <u>justice</u> had been served when the man who had murdered innocent bystanders was himself murdered by one of his partners.

_____

20. Jim and Mary have been married for so many years that they are even beginning to look <u>similar</u>.

_____

21. The <u>simile</u> "the trees look like tall brides in a chapel" is quite descriptive.

---

| **STOP.**  Check answers at the end of this chapter (pp. 298–299). |
| --- |

## *EXTRA WORD POWER*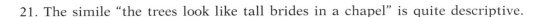

> **tude.**  Condition of; state of. *Tude* is found at the end of a great number of nouns. For example: *gratitude* — the state of being grateful; *solitude* — the state of being alone; *exactitude* — the state of being exact.
>
> **ness.**  Quality of; state of. *Ness* is found at the end of many nouns. For example: *happiness* — the state of being happy; *goodness* — the state of being good; *preparedness* — the state of being prepared or ready.

### Additional Words Derived from Combining Forms

From your knowledge of combining forms, can you define the following words?

1. **matriarch** (ma·tri·arch) (mā′trē·ark) *n.*   *In the novel the main character was a **matriarch** who ruled her family with an iron hand, and no one dared to defy her.*

---

2. **matricide** (ma·tri·cide) (ma′tri·sīdé) *n.*   *In the novel one of the sons commits the horrible crime of **matricide** because he hates his mother so much.*

---

3. **jurisdiction** (ju·ris·dic·tion) (jur·is·dik′shun) *n.*   *The police chief said that he could not help us because he did not have **jurisdiction** in the next county, but he did tell us whom to speak to in the next county.*

---

4. **jurisprudence** (ju·ris·pru·dence) (jur·is·prū′densé) *n.*   *If one were to study the course of court decisions in the United States, one would see that many times **jurisprudence** is influenced by social and economic factors.*

---

5. **dichotomy** (di·chot·o·my) (dī·kot′o·mē) *n.* (*pl.* **mies**)   *The psychiatrist said that the psychopath had been living with the **dichotomy** of good and evil within him.*

---

6. **adversity** (ad·ver·si·ty) (ad·ver′si·tē) *n.*   *From the day that Jill left school, **adversity** seemed to be her constant companion, even though she tried hard to escape from all the misfortunes.*

_____

7. **pervert** (per·vert′) *v.* (per′vert) *n.*   *It seems inconceivable that a teacher would try to **pervert** young people, but in last night's newspaper it was stated that a teacher was arrested for trying to engage young children in pornographic films.*

_____

8. **aversion** (a·ver·sion) (a·ver′zhun) *n.*   *My friend avoids going to seafood restaurants because she has an **aversion** to fish.*

_____

9. **subversion** (sub·ver·sion) (sub·ver′zhun) *n.*   *When the heads of government found out that a group of rebels were attempting the **subversion** of the government, the rebels were arrested and thrown into jail.*

_____

10. **introvert** (in′tro·vert) *n.* (in·tro·vert′) *v.*   *Jim is an **introvert**, yet his friends are outgoing people.*

_____

11. **abrogate** (ab′ro·gāte) *v.*   *The student council passed some new bylaws that **abrogated** some former ones, which were outdated.*

_____

12. **prerogative** (pre·rog′a·tive) *n.*   *Because Marie is a gifted person, she has the **prerogative** to go to any school that she wants to.*

_____

13. **surrogate** (sur′ro·gate) *n.*   *The court appointed a **surrogate** to act in legal matters for the two children whose parents had recently died.*

_____

14. **simultaneously** (sī·mul·tā′nē·ous·lē) *adv.*   *Jim and Helen Jones decided **simultaneously** that the best place for their psychotic son was in an institution where he could get the proper care.*

_____

15. **assimilate** (as·sim′i·late) *v.*   *Many immigrants successfully **assimilate** to their new country and culture.*

_____

16. **simulation** (sim·u·la·tion) (sim·ū·lā′shun) *v.*   *Before the actual moon flights, there were **simulations** of the flights so that the astronauts could gain the experience they needed and learn beforehand about the intricacies of the flights.*

---

**STOP.**   Check answers at the end of this chapter (p. 299).

## Practice for Additional Words Derived from Combining Forms

**Directions:**   Match each word with the *best* definition.

_____ 1. matriarch

_____ 2. matricide

_____ 3. jurisdiction

_____ 4. dichotomy

_____ 5. jurisprudence

_____ 6. adversity

_____ 7. assimilate

_____ 8. aversion

_____ 9. subversion

_____ 10. abrogate

_____ 11. prerogative

_____ 12. surrogate

_____ 13. introvert

_____ 14. simulation

_____ 15. pervert

_____ 16. simultaneously

a.  occurring at the same time

b.  a person drawn inward toward himself or herself

c.  an imitative representation of a process or system

d.  the killing of a mother by a son or daughter

e.  a systematic attempt to overthrow a government

f.  a mother who is ruler of her family

g.  an exclusive or special right or privilege

h.  the limits in which authority may be exercised

i.  to cause to turn away from what is right

j.  the course of court decisions

k.  to invalidate

l.  division into two parts

m.  a hardship

n.  to take in; to absorb

o.  a strong dislike

p.  a substitute

**STOP.**   Check answers at the end of this chapter (p. 299).

# EXERCISE 18

## Step I. Combining Forms

**A. Directions:** A list of combining forms with their meanings follows. Look at the combining forms and their meanings. Concentrate on learning each combining form and its meaning. Cover the meanings, read the combining forms, and state the meanings to yourself. Check to see if you are correct. Now cover the combining forms, read the meanings, and state the combining forms to yourself. Check to see if you are correct.

| Combining Forms | Meanings |
|---|---|
| 1. sphere | ball |
| 2. therm, thermo | heat |
| 3. techni, techno | arts and crafts (especially industrial arts); method; system; skill |
| 4. hydr, hydra, hydro | water |
| 5. fort | strong |
| 6. tract | draw; pull |
| 7. flu, fluc | flowing |

**B. Directions:** Do not look at the preceding meanings. Write the meanings of the following combining forms.

| Combining Forms | Meanings |
|---|---|
| 1. sphere | _____ |
| 2. therm, thermo | _____ |
| 3. techni, techno | _____ |
| 4. hydr, hydra, hydro | _____ |
| 5. fort | _____ |
| 6. tract | _____ |
| 7. flu, fluc | _____ |

## Step II. Words Derived from Combining Forms

1. **sphere** (sfir) *n.* A round geometrical body whose surface is equally distant at all points from the center; any rounded body; a globe, a ball; any of the stars or planets; the place or surroundings in which a person exists, works, lives, and so on.
   *That nation's **sphere** of influence extends across the world.*

2. **hemisphere** (hem·i·sphere) (hem′i·sfir) *n.* A half sphere or globe; half the earth's surface (either the northern or southern half of the earth as divided by the equator or the eastern or western half as divided by a meridian).
   *The United States is in the Northern **Hemisphere**.*

3. **atmosphere** (at·mos·phere) (at'mo·sfir) *n.* The air that surrounds the earth; the mass of gases that surrounds the earth and is held to it by the force of gravity; the air in any given place; a mental or moral environment; surrounding influence; the feeling or coloring that surrounds a work of art.

   *A heavy **atmosphere** seemed to fill the room after Mary spoke to her mother in such harsh and bitter tones.*

4. **thermometer** (ther·mom'e·ter) *n.* An instrument for measuring the temperature of a body or of space, especially one consisting of a graduated glass tube with a bulb, usually mercury, that expands and rises in the tube as the temperature increases.

   *We didn't need our outdoor **thermometer** to tell us that it was 100 degrees outside; we knew it immediately when we stepped out of the house.*

5. **thermostat** (ther'mo·stat) *n.* An automatic device for regulating temperature; any device that automatically responds to temperature changes and activates switches controlling equipment such as furnaces, refrigerators, and air conditioners.

   *We knew that our **thermostat** for regulating heat was broken because we were freezing, yet the **thermostat** was set at 68 degrees.*

6. **thermal** (ther'mal) *adj.* Pertaining to, using, or causing heat.

   *In the winter when Jack goes skiing, he wears **thermal** underwear to keep warm.*

7. **technical** (tech·ni·cal) (tek'ni·kal) *adj.* Having to do with an art, science, discipline, or profession; having to do with industrial arts, applied sciences, mechanical trades or crafts; marked by specialization; meaningful or of interest to persons of specialized knowledge rather than to lay persons; marked by a strict legal interpretation.

   *The document was written in such **technical** language that not one of us understood it, so we had to bring it to a lawyer.*

8. **technique** (tech·nique) (tek·nēk') *n.* The manner in which a scientific or complex task is accomplished; the degree of skill or command of fundamentals shown in any performance.

   *The doctors claimed that they had perfected a new surgical **technique** that should save many lives.*

9. **technician** (tech·ni·cian) (tek·nish'un) *n.* A specialist in the details of a subject or skill, especially a mechanical one; any artist, musician, and so on with skilled technique.

   *The lab **technician** said that my contact lenses would be ready shortly.*

10. **technology** (tech·nol·o·gy) (tek·nol'o·jē) *n.* Applied science; a technical method of achieving a practical purpose; the totality of the means employed to provide objects necessary for human existence and comfort.

    *Life in a world of **technology** has many, many advantages, but there are some drawbacks too, and people must weigh the drawbacks against the advantages in future endeavors.*

11. **hydrant** (hy·drant) (hī'drant) *n.* An upright pipe or street fixture with a valve for drawing water directly from a water main; fireplug.

    *The firefighters said that the pressure from the water **hydrant** was too low and that would make it difficult to put out the fire.*

12. **dehydrate** (de·hy·drate) (dē·hī'drāté) *v.* To remove water from; to lose water or moisture; dry.

    *After being lost in the desert for a few days with nothing to drink, the three men were **dehydrated**.*

13. **fortress** (for·tress) (for'tris) *n.* A large place strengthened against attack; a fort or group of forts, often including a town; any place of security; a stronghold.

    *Some very wealthy people build homes that are like **fortresses** to protect themselves from thieves.*

14. **fortify** (for·ti·fy) (for'ti·fī) *v.* To strengthen against attack; to surround with defenses; to strengthen and secure (as a town) by forts; to give physical strength and courage to; to add mental or moral strength to.

    *In films many people **fortify** themselves with a drink before they attack some problem.*

15. **fortitude** (for'ti·tūd́) *n.* Strength of mind that enables persons to bear pain or encounter danger with courage.

    *The passerby showed great **fortitude** when he tried to help the man who was being mugged.*

16. **contract** (con·tract) (kon'trakt·) *n.* A binding agreement between two or more persons or parties; a covenant.

    *After we signed the **contract**, we shook hands.*

17. **contract** (con·tract) (kon·trakt') *v.* To draw together; to make smaller; shrink; shorten; to shorten a word by omitting one or more sounds or letters; to bring on oneself as an obligation or debt; to get.

    *The doctor isolated the patient who had a contagious disease because he didn't want the other patients to **contract** it.*

18. **detract** (de·tract) (de·trakt') *v.* To draw away or divert; to take away a part, as from quality, value, or reputation.

    *The speaker's mannerisms were so annoying that they **detracted** from what she was saying.*

19. **retract** (re·tract) (re·trakt') *v.* To draw back; to take back; to withdraw.

    *The politician apologized and said that he wanted to **retract** his earlier statements in which he had criticized the mayor of the town.*

20. **traction** (trac·tion) (trak'shun) *n.* The act of drawing; the state of being drawn; the force exerted in drawing; friction; in medicine, a pulling or drawing of a muscle, organ, and so on for healing a fracture, dislocation, and so on.

    *My friend's doctor had to be put in **traction** because he had a slipped disk.*

21. **abstract** (ab·stract) (ab'strakt) *adj.* Thought of apart from any specific object; disassociated from any particular instance; difficult to understand; theoretical; not concrete. *n.* A short statement giving the main points of a book, article, or research paper.

    *Our professor asked us to write an **abstract** of three research articles.*

22. **abstract** (ab·stract) (ab·strakt') *v.* To take away or remove; to withdraw; to take away secretly, slyly, or dishonestly; to divert; to make an abstraction.

    *The company spy was able to **abstract** the information that she wanted without anyone knowing about it.*

23. **fluid** (flū'id) *n.* A substance such as a liquid or gas that flows. *adj.* Employing a smooth easy style; easily convertible into cash; likely to change.

    *I wanted to keep my assets in a **fluid** state in case I needed cash quickly.*

24. **influence** (in·flu·ence) (in'flū·ensé) *n.* The power to produce an effect without the exertion of physical force or authority. *v.* To affect by indirect means; to sway.

    *When the people learned that the judge had used his **influence** to gain his son an important position, they demanded that the judge be impeached.*

25. **affluent** (af·flu·ent) (af'flū·ent) *adj.* Wealthy, rich; having a generous supply of material possessions.

    *John's girlfriend comes from an **affluent** family, so she is used to having nice things.*

## SPECIAL NOTES

1. Note that the words *contract* (kon'trakt) *n.* and *contract* (kon·tract') *v.* are spelled identically but are pronounced differently and have different meanings. Most of the words that you have met have had more than one meaning; however, they were usually pronounced the same. Because the words *contract* (kon'trakt) *n.* and *contract* (kon·trakt') *v.* are usually pronounced differently (pronunciations vary from region to region) and each word has meanings different from those of the other, they are presented separately. The same holds for the words *abstract* (ab'strakt) *adj., n.* and abstract *(ab·strakt')* *v., which are presented in the main part of the exercise, and for the words* forte *(forté)* n. *and* forte *(for'tā)* adj., adv., *which are presented in the Additional Words section.*

2. The word *hydrophobia*, which is derived from the combining forms *hydro* and *phob*, is presented in Exercise 3.

3. The word *subtraction*, which is derived from the combining forms *sub*, *ion*, and *tract*, is presented in the Extra Word Power section of Exercise 12.

## Step III. Words in Context

The movie on the new age of **technology** is rather frightening. In the film, everyone's life on all **hemispheres** in the universe in the twenty-first century is influenced greatly by his or her personal Computer Information Processing System (CIPS). Each person's CIPS determines exactly what he or she will eat, the amount of **fluid** intake, and what he or she will wear. No one does anything without first consulting his or her CIPS. CIPS measures the **atmosphere** to determine weather patterns, checks **thermometers**, and adjusts **thermostats** to make sure the room temperature is optimal for the individual person. At times some CIPSs recommend that individuals wear their **thermal** uniforms if they are traveling in uncontrolled environments. Persons who have had bad backs and are in **traction** use their CIPSs to determine the exact amount they need.

Certain **technicians**, who have special **technical** ability, are responsible for the care and upkeep of everyone's CIPS. Only they have the **technique** to fix a malfunctioning CIPS. Any unauthorized person who attempts to **abstract** information about the operation of a CIPS can be arrested. In the new age of technology everyone has his or her own job to do based on his or her ability, and is expected to do it. There are people who care for the external environment and those who care for the internal environment. (Everyone lives inside a huge **sphere**.) There are people who control the water supply and care for the **hydrants** and people who grow and care for the food supply.

People who do not fulfill their contracts have their individual CIPSs **retracted**. Without CIPS, a person can **dehydrate** and eventually die. Also, life in the new age of **technology** depends on a person's **fortitude** and ability to **fortify** himself or herself against attacks from outside forces. CIPS makes a person's home into a **fortress**. The more **affluent** people usually have more than one CIPS, but everyone must have at least one in order to survive.

People carry their personal CIPSs with them wherever they go. Of course, CIPS is small enough to fit into a person's pocket so that it does not **detract** from what the person is doing or saying.

## Step IV. Practice

**A. Directions:**   A number of sentences with missing words follow. Choose the word that *best* fits the sentence. Put the word in the blank. Notice that two words are presented twice because they are used twice.

**Word List**

| | | |
|---|---|---|
| abstract | fortify | technical |
| abstract | fortitude | technician |
| affluent | fortress | technique |
| atmosphere | hemisphere | technology |
| contract | hydrant | thermal |
| contract | influence | thermometer |
| dehydrate | retract | thermostat |
| detract | sphere | traction |
| fluid | | |

1. When the three men in trench coats walked into the diner, the

    _____ seemed to change.

2. The coach said that the only thing I need to _____
    me against my opponent is the knowledge that I am better than he and that I will win the match.

3. The _____ woman donated a large amount of money to charity.

4. The governor used his _____ to help the poor family who had been treated so badly.

5. Herbert was afraid that Jane's outlandish costume would _____
    from what she had to say.

6. When the speaker realized that he had made an error, he said that he wanted to

    _____ his former statement.

7. The author said that she was in a state of ecstasy when she signed her first

    _____ to write a book.

8. The victims of the fire said that they didn't think that they had the

    _____ to continue after their house and all their belongings were burned to ashes, but they did.

9. We knew that we were in serious trouble when the concrete for the foundation of

    our house began to _____ from the cold.

10. When the _____ read 104 degrees, we thought it was broken, but the doctor said that the reading was correct and that our friend had pneumonia.

11. The athlete was in terrible pain from a pulled muscle, so the doctor put him in

    _____.

12. In what _____ is Canada?

13. The students protested that the _____ was set too
    low in the dormitory and that they were freezing.

14. Many people sleep with a(n) _____ blanket in the
    winter to keep warm.

15. That is too _____ for me; I need something more
    concrete.

16. The report is too _____ for me to understand; put
    it in plain language.

17. Her _____ for making jam earned her a fortune.

18. My brother is a(n) _____ in an electronics plant.

19. The twenty-first century will be known for even more _____
    than the twentieth century.

20. The doctor was concerned that his patient with the very high fever would

    _____ unless he was put into the hospital and
    given special care.

21. Jennifer couldn't _____ the information she needed
    from the various journals.

22. When it is very hot, the city usually allows one _____
    in each area to be opened so that the children can run in the water and cool off.

23. The situation is a very _____ one, so let's wait
    and see what happens.

24. The police said that the gangster's home was a(n) _____
    that was filled with machine guns and other weapons.

25. The architect designed a house that looked like a(n) _____.

---

**STOP.** Check answers at the end of this chapter (p. 300).

**B. Directions:**   Match each word with the *best* definition.

_____ 1. abstract

_____ 2. abstract

_____ 3. contract

_____ 4. contract

_____ 5. technical

_____ 6. technique

_____ 7. fortify

_____ 8. hydrant

_____ 9. sphere

_____ 10. thermostat

_____ 11. atmosphere

_____ 12. technology

_____ 13. hemisphere

_____ 14. detract

_____ 15. dehydrate

_____ 16. retract

_____ 17. fortitude

_____ 18. traction

_____ 19. thermometer

_____ 20. thermal

_____ 21. technician

_____ 22. fortress

_____ 23. fluid

_____ 24. influence

_____ 25. affluent

a.  to sway

b.  an upright pipe for drawing water from a water main

c.  any place of security

d.  a specialist in the details of a skill

e.  to remove water from

f.  strength of mind that enables persons to bear pain

g.  having to do with an art, science, discipline, or profession

h.  the air that surrounds the earth

i.  causing heat

j.  the manner in which a complex task is accomplished

k.  an automatic device for regulating temperature

l.  to strengthen against attack

m.  the act of drawing

n.  likely to change; a liquid

o.  to take away secretly

p.  rich

q.  half the earth's surface

r.  a binding agreement

s.  a short statement giving the main points of an article

t.  an instrument for measuring temperature

u.  to take away a part, as from quality

v.  to take back

w.  applied science

x.  to draw together

y.  a globe

**STOP.**   Check answers at the end of this chapter (p. 300).

**C. Directions:** Write the words from this exercise that go with the meanings.

| Meanings | Words |
|---|---|
| 1. To strengthen against attack | _____ |
| 2. The act of drawing | _____ |
| 3. Having to do with an art or profession | _____ |
| 4. To draw back | _____ |
| 5. To divert | _____ |
| 6. An instrument for measuring temperature | _____ |
| 7. A globe | _____ |
| 8. Half the earth's surface | _____ |
| 9. The air that surrounds the earth | _____ |
| 10. To take away secretly | _____ |
| 11. A binding agreement between two or more persons | _____ |
| 12. A short statement giving the main points of an article | _____ |
| 13. Causing heat | _____ |
| 14. The manner in which a complex task is accomplished | _____ |
| 15. An automatic device for regulating temperature | _____ |
| 16. To draw together | _____ |
| 17. Applied science | _____ |
| 18. Strength of mind that enables persons to bear pain | _____ |
| 19. To remove water from | _____ |
| 20. Any place of security | _____ |
| 21. An upright pipe for drawing water | _____ |
| 22. A specialist in the details of a skill | _____ |
| 23. A substance such as a liquid or gas | _____ |
| 24. To sway | _____ |
| 25. Wealthy | _____ |

**STOP.** Check answers at the end of this chapter (p. 300).

# *EXTRA WORD POWER*

**fy.** Make; cause to be; change into; become. *Fy* is found at the end of a number of verbs. For example: *fortify*—to make strong; *simplify*—to make easier; *beautify*—to make beautiful; *modify*—to change slightly or make minor changes in character, form, and so on, to change or alter; *verify*—to affirm.

**an, ian.** Native of; belonging to. *An* or *ian* is found at the end of words that express some kind of connection with a place, person, doctrine, and so on. For example: *American*—a native of America; *Asian*—a native of Asia; *Mohammedan*—believing in the principles of Mohammed; *Christian*—believing in Christ (the Christian religion).

## Additional Words Derived from Combining Forms

From your knowledge of combining forms, can you define the following words?

1. **thermophilic** (ther·mo·phil·ic) (ther·mō·fil′ik) *adj.* *The scientists were studying the* **thermophilic** *organisms to try to determine why they flourish in heat.*

   _____

2. **thermography** (ther·mog·ra·phy) (ther·mog′ra·fē) *n.* *Doctors are using* **thermography** *to detect certain diseases or abnormalities in the body.*

   _____

3. **technocracy** (tech·noc·ra·cy) (tek·nok′ra·sē) *n.* *In the science fiction film the government, which was a* **technocracy**, *was run by the technical experts and anything that did not have a useful function was not supported by the government.*

   _____

4. **hydraulics** (hy·drau·lics) (hī·drau′liks) *n.* *My brother is studying* **hydraulics** *in engineering because he is interested in the practical uses of water and other liquids.*

   _____

5. **hydrotherapy** (hy·dro·ther·a·py) (hī·drō·ther′a·pē) *n.* *Many doctors use* **hydrotherapy** *to treat their patients who have certain diseases.*

   _____

6. **forte** (forté) *n.* *After listening to her speech, we knew that public speaking was not her* **forte**.

   _____

7. **forte** (for·te) (for′tā) *adj., adv.* *The musician played the passage* **forte**.

   _____

8. **tractable** (trac·ta·ble) (trak′ta·bul) *adj.*    *The dangerous animal was so **tractable**, it had to have been tranquilized.*

_____

9. **protract** (pro·tract) (prō·trakt′) *v.*    *The lawyers tried to **protract** the case so that they would have more time to prepare an adequate defense.*

_____

10. **fluent** (flū′ent) *adj.*    *He is **fluent** in three languages, so he works at the United Nations as an interpreter.*

_____

11. **fluctuate** (fluc·tu·ate) (fluk′chū·āte) *v.*    *Gary seems to **fluctuate** from feeling good to feeling bad all the time.*

---

**STOP.**   Check answers at the end of this chapter (p. 300).

---

## Practice for Additional Words Derived from Combining Forms

***Directions:***   Match each word with the *best* definition.

_____ 1. thermophilic

_____ 2. thermography

_____ 3. technocracy

_____ 4. hydraulics

_____ 5. hydrotherapy

_____ 6. forte

_____ 7. forte (for′tā)

_____ 8. tractable

_____ 9. protract

_____ 10. fluctuate

_____ 11. fluent

a. ready in the use of words

b. in a loud and forceful manner

c. to prolong in time

d. to shift back and forth

e. a technique for measuring variations of heat in the body to detect disease

f. the use of water to treat disease

g. a branch of science dealing with the practical uses of liquid in motion

h. government ruled by technical experts

i. growing at a high temperature

j. easily controlled

k. one's strong point

---

**STOP.**   Check answers at the end of this chapter (p. 300).

---

# CHAPTER WORDS IN SENTENCES

**Directions:** Use the given words to write a sentence that makes sense. Also, try to illustrate the meaning of the words without actually defining the words.

*Example* (traction; technical) When the doctors explained why I needed *traction* for my slipped disk, they used such *technical* language that I did not understand a word they said.

1. (patriotic; philanthropist)

_____

2. (divorce; divide)

_____

3. (juror; dilemma)

_____

4. (affluent; interrogate)

_____

5. (influence; hemisphere)

_____

# CHAPTER WORDS IN A PARAGRAPH

Here is a list of words from this chapter. Write a paragraph using at least 8 of these words. The paragraph must make sense and be logically developed.

**Word List**

| | | |
|---|---|---|
| adverse | interrogate | psychology |
| advertise | juror | psychotic |
| affluent | justice | reversible |
| arrogant | justification | seclusion |
| controversy | maternal | segregate |
| derogatory | matrimony | similar |
| divide | paternal | sphere |
| divorce | patriotic | technical |
| eulogy | patron | technician |
| gregarious | philanthropist | versatile |
| hemisphere | psychiatrist | |

# ANALOGIES 6

**Directions:** Find the word from the following list that *best* completes each analogy. There are more words in the list than you need.

## Word List

| | | |
|---|---|---|
| abstract | flock | philanthrope |
| adversity | fort | phobia |
| arrogant | forte | protect |
| atmosphere | gregarious | psychiatrist |
| attract | half | psychic |
| body | hemisphere | psychology |
| claustrophobia | hide | psychotic |
| contract | hydrophobia | ruler |
| dehydrated | impediment | separate |
| divert | injustice | shorten |
| dollar | isolate | sphere |
| error | limbs | technical |
| fairness | mother | technique |
| fleet | murder | thermal |

1. Paternal : father : : maternal : _____.

2. Foot : podiatrist : : mind : _____.

3. Sophisticated : naive : : concrete : _____.

4. Height : acrophobia : : water : _____.

5. Tense : calm : : congregate : _____.

6. Attitude : posture : : medium : _____.

7. Uniform : same : : justice : _____.

8. Full : satiated : : dry : _____.

9. Dime : nickel : : sphere : _____.

10. Deportment: behavior : : detract : _____.

11. Life : biology : : mind : _____.

12. Healthy : well : : insane : _____.

13. Marriage : unite : : divorce : _____.

14. Retract : withdraw : : contract : _____.

15. Plump : corpulent : : proud : _____.

16. Shy : introverted : : outgoing : _____.

17. Siren : warn : : fortress : _____.

18. Lucid : ambiguous : : misanthrope : _____.

19. Following : subsequent : : misfortune : _____.

20. Heart: defect : : speech : _____.

**STOP.** Check answers at the end of this chapter (p. 301).

# MULTIPLE CHOICE
# VOCABULARY TEST 6

**Directions:**   This is a test on words in Exercises 16–18. Words are presented according to exercises. *Do all exercises before checking answers.* Underline the meaning that *best* fits the word.

## Exercise 16

1. paternal
   a.  a father
   b.  loving a father
   c.  fatherhood
   d.  related on the father's side

2. paternity
   a.  fatherly
   b.  fatherhood
   c.  a father
   d.  ruling like a father

3. paternalism
   a.  fatherly
   b.  managing a company
   c.  fatherhood
   d.  the practice of managing a country as a father

4. patricide
   a.  hatred of a father
   b.  murder of one's father
   c.  murder of a father
   d.  a horrible murder

5. patriotic
   a.  loyal to one's country
   b.  marching in parades
   c.  fighting in a war
   d.  a soldier

6. patron
   a.  a frequent moviegoer
   b.  a regular customer
   c.  a person who goes to lots of different places
   d.  an irregular customer

7. philanthropist
   a.  a lover of mankind
   b.  a helper
   c.  a person who shows love of mankind by practical helpfulness
   d.  a person who participates in public life

8. psychology
   a.  a healing science
   b.  a helping science
   c.  science of life
   d.  science of the mind

9. psychiatrist
   a. a specialist
   b. a doctor who specializes in the treatment of mental disorders
   c. a doctor
   d. a doctor who specializes in the treatment of nerves

10. psychotic
    a. ill
    b. confined to a mental institution
    c. mentally ill
    d. a murderer

11. gregarious
    a. a follower of others
    b. marked by a fondness of noise
    c. marked by a fondness for company
    d. an animal lover

12. congregate
    a. a fondness for company
    b. to join
    c. to bring
    d. to collect in a particular place

13. aggregate
    a. to separate
    b. to collect into a whole
    c. to collect
    d. to form

14. segregate
    a. to collect together
    b. to separate
    c. to divide
    d. to total

15. seclusion
    a. isolation
    b. the act of storing
    c. the act of hiding something illegal
    d. a hard place to find

16. seduce
    a. to deceive
    b. to lie
    c. to entice into wrongdoing
    d. to bring charges against

17. sedition
    a. an illegal act
    b. an insult leveled at the government
    c. a crime
    d. an act seeking to incite persons to overthrow the government

18. eulogy
    a. an insult
    b. a good speaker
    c. feeling well
    d. speaking well of someone

Exercise 17

19. maternal
    a. motherhood
    b. like a mother
    c. loving a mother
    d. a mother

20. maternity
    a. giving birth
    b. a home for mothers
    c. referring to a special place
    d. motherhood

21. matrimony
    a. the act of being married
    b. motherhood
    c. a marriage proposal
    d. the marriage ceremony

22. justice
    a. the court system
    b. the act of making a judgment
    c. the judge and jury
    d. fairness

23. justification
    a. good reason
    b. the act of justice
    c. the act of reasoning
    d. something done according to law

24. juror
    a. a person
    b. a person sworn to deliver a verdict
    c. a person appointed by the judge
    d. a person sworn to be a witness

25. divorce
    a. a separation
    b. a decision to separate
    c. a legal ending of a marriage
    d. a court decision

26. dilemma
    a. something confusing
    b. a choice
    c. an argument that is difficult to settle
    d. a choice between two equally difficult alternatives

27. divide
    a. to separate into two parts
    b. to separate into many parts
    c. to isolate
    d. to separate into parts

28. divert
    a. to separate
    b. to turn from a course
    c. to turn toward a course
    d. to turn around

29. versatile
    a. a changeable person
    b. able to do a few things well
    c. many-sided
    d. able to act

30. converse
    a. opposite
    b. to turn toward
    c. to turn away
    d. to turn back

31. reversible
    a. able to be the same
    b. something equally good
    c. able to be opposite to a previous position
    d. able to be removed

32. adverse
    a. turned toward
    b. turned away
    c. unfavorable
    d. turned in

33. controversy
    a. minor quarrel
    b. an argument that is never settled
    c. a lengthy dispute
    d. a difficult decision

34. advertise
    a. to call attention to
    b. to discuss
    c. to make judgments about
    d. to please

35. interrogate
    a. to spy
    b. to informally question
    c. to speak to
    d. to formally question

36. arrogant
    a. questioning
    b. important
    c. overbearing
    d. distrustful

37. derogatory
    a. questioning in a rude manner
    b. prying
    c. coarse
    d. belittling

38. similar
    a. descriptive phrase
    b. alike in essentials
    c. certain
    d. exactly alike in everything

39. simile
    a. a comparison of two unlike things using *like* or *as*
    b. a comparison of two like things using *like* or *as*
    c. a comparison without the use of *like* or *as*
    d. a comparison

## Exercise 18

40. sphere
    a. something found in the sky
    b. something without air
    c. a globe
    d. a special planet

41. hemisphere
    a. North America
    b. a half globe
    c. the earth
    d. two bodies that are round

42. atmosphere
    a. outer space
    b. gases
    c. the air that surrounds the earth
    d. the vacuum that exists when there is no air

43. thermometer
    a. an instrument designed to measure air pressure
    b. an instrument designed to measure fever of a person
    c. a measuring instrument
    d. an instrument to measure the temperature of a body or of space

44. thermostat
    a. a measuring device
    b. an automatic device for regulating temperature
    c. a heat regulator
    d. a device for controlling the temperature of gases

45. thermal
    a. refers to underwear
    b. causing control of heat
    c. causing heat
    d. causing fever

46. fluid
    a. a gas
    b. a liquid
    c. a substance that flows
    d. a drink of water

47. influence
    a. to hold back
    b. to frighten
    c. to command
    d. to sway

48. affluent
    a. hardworking
    b. wealthy
    c. proud
    d. faulty

49. technical
    a. meaningful to laypersons
    b. marked by common knowledge
    c. marked by specialization
    d. marked by common interpretation

50. technique
    a. the manner in which a task is accomplished
    b. hard work
    c. proper manner to accomplish a difficult task
    d. a technician's work

51. technician
    a. a specialist
    b. a specialist in a certain field
    c. a worker
    d. a specialist in the details of a skill

52. technology
    a. a technical skill
    b. the production of goods
    c. the providing of comfort
    d. applied science

53. hydrant
    a. a water main
    b. a street fixture with a valve for drawing water
    c. a water faucet
    d. an upright cylinder

54. dehydrate
    a. to take water from
    b. to squeeze
    c. to give water to
    d. to squeeze thoroughly

55. fortress
    a. a large place
    b. a hideout
    c. any place of security
    d. a place of seclusion

56. fortify
    a. to surround
    b. to help
    c. to strengthen against attack
    d. to surround a town

57. fortitude
    a. help against pain
    b. strength of mind
    c. help against danger
    d. any place of security

58. contract
    a. to draw apart
    b. to draw back
    c. to shrink
    d. to make something

59. detract
    a. to draw to
    b. to take in
    c. to draw away
    d. to shorten

60. retract
    a. to draw out
    b. to withdraw
    c. to draw
    d. to use friction to draw away something

61. traction
    a. the act of drawing
    b. the act of drawing back
    c. the act of staying still
    d. the act of drawing away

62. abstract
    a. concrete
    b. difficult to understand
    c. confusing story
    d. associated with a particular instance

# TRUE/FALSE TEST 6

**Directions:** This is a true/false test on Exercise 16–18. Read each sentence carefully. Decide whether it is true or false. Put a *T* for *true* or an *F* for *false* in the blank. If the answer is false, change a word or part of the sentence to make it true. The number after the sentence tells you if the word is from Exercise 16, 17, or 18.

_____ 1. Psychology is only concerned with animal behavior. 16

_____ 2. Patricide is the killing of a father only by a son. 16

_____ 3. A patron does not regularly buy at the same place. 16

_____ 4. Something technical is usually easily understood by anyone. 18

_____ 5. When something contracts, it gets smaller. 18

_____ 6. *Divorce* and *divert* are synonyms. 17

_____ 7. An introvert would not be gregarious. 17, 16

_____ 8. Something easily understood would not be abstract. 18

_____ 9. When someone has an aversion to something, he or she likes it. 17

_____ 10. All patriotic persons are heroes. 16

_____ 11. A psychiatrist is a specialist who treats mentally healthy persons. 16

_____ 12. A philanderer is prone to propose matrimony. 16, 17

_____ 13. A fortress is a stronghold. 18

_____ 14. A matriarch is never the ruler of a country. 17

_____ 15. A prune is a dehydrated fruit. 18

_____ 16. Thermophilic organisms thrive in the heat. 18

_____ 17. *Divert* and *detract* are synonyms. 17, 18

_____ 18. An expatriate lives in his or her native land. 16

_____ 19. A psychic is a mentally ill person. 16

_____ 20. When you have something in the aggregate, you have the whole amount. 16

---

| **STOP.** Check answers for both tests at the end of this chapter (p. 301). |

# SCORING OF TESTS

| **MULTIPLE-CHOICE VOCABULARY TEST** | | **TRUE/FALSE TEST*** | |
|---|---|---|---|
| Number Wrong | Score | Number Wrong | Score |
| 0–3 | Excellent | 0–1 | Excellent |
| 4–6 | Good | 2–3 | Good |
| 7–9 | Weak | 4–5 | Weak |
| Above 9 | Poor | Above 5 | Poor |
| Score _____ | | Score _____ | |

1. If you scored in the excellent or good range on *both tests*, you are doing well. You have now completed the work in this text.

2. If you scored in the weak or poor range on either test, look at the next page and follow directions for Additional Practice. Note that the words on the tests are arranged so that you can tell in which exercise to find them. This will help you if you need additional practice.

*When the answer is false, you must get both parts of the true/false question correct in order to receive credit for it.

# ADDITIONAL PRACTICE SETS

**A. Directions:** Write the words you missed on the tests from the three exercises in the space provided. Note that the tests are presented so that you can tell to which exercises the words belong.

Exercise 16 Words Missed

1. _____    6. _____
2. _____    7. _____
3. _____    8. _____
4. _____    9. _____
5. _____    10. _____

Exercise 17 Words Missed

1. _____    6. _____
2. _____    7. _____
3. _____    8. _____
4. _____    9. _____
5. _____    10. _____

Exercise 18 Words Missed

1. _____    6. _____
2. _____    7. _____
3. _____    8. _____
4. _____    9. _____
5. _____    10. _____

**B. Directions:** Restudy the missed words from the three exercises. Study the combining forms from which those words are derived. Do Step I and Step II for those you missed. Note that Step I and Step II of the combining forms and vocabulary derived from those combining forms are on the following pages:

Exercise 16 — pp. 253–256.

Exercise 17 — pp. 262–265.

Exercise 18 — pp. 273–276.

**C. Directions:** Do Additional Practice 1 on p. 294 if you missed words from Exercise 16. Do Additional Practice 2 on p. 295 if you missed words from Exercise 17. Do Additional Practice 3 on pp. 296–297 if you missed words from Exercise 18.

## Additional Practice 1 for Exercise 16

**A. Directions:**   The combining forms presented in Exercise 16 follow. Match each combining form with its meaning.

_____ 1. pater, patr

_____ 2. phil, phile, philo

_____ 3. greg

_____ 4. se

_____ 5. psych, psyche, psycho

_____ 6. eu

a.  flock; herd; crowd; mob

b.  spirit; mind; soul

c.  well

d.  love

e.  apart

f.  father

---

**STOP.**   Check answers at the end of this chapter (p. 302).

---

**B. Directions:**   The words presented in Exercise 16 follow. Match each word with its meaning.

_____ 1. paternal

_____ 2. paternity

_____ 3. paternalism

_____ 4. patricide

_____ 5. patriotic

_____ 6. patron

_____ 7. philanthropist

_____ 8. psychology

_____ 9. psychiatrist

_____ 10. psychotic

_____ 11. gregarious

_____ 12. congregate

_____ 13. aggregate

_____ 14. segregate

_____ 15. seclusion

_____ 16. seduce

_____ 17. sedition

_____ 18. eulogy

a.  an influential supporter of an artist

b.  one who shows goodwill by helping others

c.  the speaking well of someone

d.  the science of the mind

e.  marked by a fondness for being with others

f.  incitement to rebellion

g.  to come together in a group

h.  fatherhood

i.  loving one's country

j.  fatherly

k.  the murder of one's father

l.  to tempt to wrongdoing

m.  the act of isolating oneself

n.  the practice of managing a business as a father

o.  a doctor who specializes in treatment of the mentally ill

p.  total

q.  to separate

r.  insane

---

**STOP.**   Check answers at the end of this chapter (p. 302).

---

# Additional Practice 2 for Exercise 17

**A. Directions:** The combining forms presented in Exercise 17 follow. Match each combining form with its meaning.

| | |
|---|---|
| 1. matr, matri, matro | a. turn |
| 2. juris, jus | b. ask; beg |
| 3. di | c. like; resembling |
| 4. vers, vert | d. law |
| 5. rog | e. two |
| 6. simil, simul | f. mother |

---

**STOP.**  Check answers at the end of this chapter (p. 302).

---

**B. Directions:** The words presented in Exercise 17 follow. Match each word with its meaning.

| | |
|---|---|
| _____ 1. maternal | a. good reason |
| _____ 2. maternity | b. to end a marriage legally |
| _____ 3. matrimony | c. a comparison of two unlike things using *like* or *as* |
| _____ 4. justice | d. to turn from a path |
| _____ 5. justification | e. a person sworn to deliver a verdict |
| _____ 6. juror | f. motherly |
| _____ 7. divorce | g. alike in essentials |
| _____ 8. dilemma | h. having two usable sides |
| _____ 9. divide | i. rightfulness |
| _____ 10. divert | j. many-sided |
| _____ 11. versatile | k. haughty |
| _____ 12. converse | l. to ask questions formally |
| _____ 13. reversible | m. motherhood |
| _____ 14. adverse | n. the state of being married |
| _____ 15. controversy | o. to separate into parts |
| _____ 16. advertise | p. an argument that presents two equally unfavorable alternatives |
| _____ 17. interrogate | q. a statement that is turned around |
| _____ 18. arrogant | r. a dispute |
| _____ 19. derogatory | s. to praise the good qualities of a product |
| _____ 20. similar | t. belittling |
| _____ 21. simile | u. hostile |

---

**STOP.**  Check answers at the end of this chapter (p. 302).

---

# Additional Practice 3 for Exercise 18

**A. Directions:**   The combining forms presented in Exercise 18 follow. Match each combining form with its meaning.

| | |
|---|---|
| _____ 1. sphere | a. strong |
| _____ 2. therm, thermo | b. water |
| _____ 3. techni, techno | c. draw; pull |
| _____ 4. hydr, hydra, hydro | d. flowing |
| _____ 5. fort | e. heat |
| _____ 6. tract | f. arts and crafts (especially industrial arts); method; system; skill |
| _____ 7. flu, fluc | g. ball |

---

**STOP.**   Check answers at the end of this chapter (p. 302).

---

**B. Directions:**   The words presented in Exercise 18 follow. Match each word with its meaning.

| | |
|---|---|
| _____ 1. sphere | a. a substance such as a liquid or gas that flows |
| _____ 2. hemisphere | b. the act of drawing |
| _____ 3. atmosphere | c. to divert |
| _____ 4. thermometer | d. to make smaller |
| _____ 5. thermostat | e. to strengthen against attack |
| _____ 6. thermal | f. a half globe |
| _____ 7. technical | g. a street fixture for drawing water from a water main |
| _____ 8. technique | h. the air that surrounds the earth |
| _____ 9. technician | i. theoretical |
| _____ 10. technology | j. an instrument for measuring temperature |
| _____ 11. hydrant | k. the degree of skill shown in a performance |
| _____ 12. dehydrate | l. having to do with applied science |
| _____ 13. fortress | m. strength of mind |
| _____ 14. fortify | n. an automatic device for regulating temperature |
| _____ 15. fortitude | o. to sway |
| _____ 16. contract | p. a specialist in the details of a skill |
| _____ 17. detract | |
| _____ 18. retract | |
| _____ 19. traction | |

_____ 20. abstract

_____ 21. fluid

_____ 22. influence

_____ 23. affluent

q.  to remove water from

r.  a stronghold

s.  to withdraw

t.  applied science

u.  wealthy

v.  a ball

w.  causing heat

---

**STOP.**   Check answers at the end of this chapter (p. 302).

---

# ANSWERS: *Chapter Seven*

## Exercise 16 (pp. 253–262)

### Practice A

(1) related on the father's side, (2) the practice of managing the affairs of a company like a father, (3) the killing of a father by his son or daughter, (4) loving of one's country, (5) separated, (6) tempted into wrongdoing, (7) totaled, (8) isolation, (9) regular customer, (10) fatherhood, (11) person who shows goodwill toward his or her fellow human beings by practical kindness, (12) outgoing, (13) a doctor who specializes in mental disorders, (14) assemble, (15) the study of the mind, (16) insane, (17) incitement to rebellion, (18) speech praising the dead.

### Practice B

(1) g, (2) r, (3) k, (4) p, (5) f, (6) b, (7) a, (8) o, (9) n, (10) c, (11) h, (12) m, (13) i, (14) j, (15) q, (16) e, (17) l, (18) d.

### Practice C

(1) aggregate, (2) psychiatrist, (3) paternal, (4) psychology, (5) patron, (6) psychotic, (7) gregarious, (8) congregate, (9) segregate, (10) seclusion, (11) seduce, (12) paternity, (13) sedition, (14) Patricide, (15) paternalism, (16) eulogy, (17) patriotic, (18) philanthropist.

### Additional Words Derived from Combining Forms (pp. 260–261)

1. **expatriate.**   To banish; exile; to withdraw oneself from one's native country; to renounce one's citizenship; an exile; an expatriated person. (The term *expatriated* is an adjective.)

2. **bibliophile.**   A lover of books; a book collector.

3. **philanthrope.**   A lover of mankind; a philanthropist; a humanitarian.

4. **philanderer.** A person who makes love without serious intentions; a person who flirts; a person who has many love affairs; a person who has many love affairs without intentions of marriage.

5. **psychosis.** Any severe form of mental disturbance or disease that has far-reaching and deep disorders of behavior; mental derangement by defective or lost contact with reality.

6. **psychopath.** A person suffering from mental disease.

7. **psychic.** A person sensitive to nonphysical forces; a medium (a person thought to have powers of communicating with the spirits of the dead); lying outside the sphere of physical science or knowledge; immaterial or spiritual in origin or force; marked by extraordinary or mysterious sensitivity, perception, or understanding.

8. **egregious.** Remarkably bad; conspicuously bad; outrageous; flagrant.

9. **euphemism.** The substitution of a word or phrase that is less direct, milder, or vaguer for one thought to be harsh, offensive, or blunt; a word or phrase considered less distasteful or less offensive than another, for example, *plump* for *fat*.

10. **euphoria.** A feeling of well-being.

11. **euphonious.** Pleasing to the ear; harmonious.

12. **euthanasia.** Mercy killing; the act of killing someone who is hopelessly ill.

### Practice for Additional Words Derived from Combining Forms (p. 262)

(1) g, (2) l, (3) h, (4) f, (5) b, (6) i, (7) e, (8) k, (9) j, (10) c, (11) a, (12) d.

## Exercise 17 (pp. 262–272)

### Practice A

(1) justification, (2) juror, (3) maternity, (4) justice, (5) interrogate, (6) derogatory, (7) divorce, (8) arrogant, (9) matrimony, (10) reversible, (11) divert, (12) dilemma, (13) converse, (14) controversy, (15) adverse, (16) advertise, (17) maternal, (18) divide, (19) versatile, (20) similar, (21) simile.

### Practice B

(1) divorce, (2) matrimony, (3) maternal, (4) maternal, (5) divorce, (6) justification, (7) justice, (8) arrogant, (9) derogatory, (10) interrogated, (11) juror, (12) juror, (13) justice, (14) justice, (15) controversy, (16) controversy, (17) justification, (18) juror, (19) divert, (20) dilemma, (21) matrimony, (22) maternity, (23) advertise, (24) arrogant, (25) converse, (26) adverse, (27) maternity, (28) versatile, (29) divorce, (30) divorce, (31) divide, (32) similar, (33) simile.

### Practice C

(1) the state of marriage, (2) the legal ending of a marriage, (3) motherly, (4) explanation, (5) a situation that necessitates a choice between two equally unfavorable alternatives, (6) having two usable sides, (7) belittling, (8) formally question, (9) haughty, (10) unfavorable, (11) relating to a pregnant woman, (12) draw,

(13) separate, (14) able to do many things well, (15) dispute, (16) opposite, (17) call attention to, (18) member of a jury, (19) assignment of deserved rewards and punishments, (20) alike in essentials (21) a comparison of two unlike things using *like* or *as*.

## Additional Words Derived from Combining Forms (pp. 270–272)

1. **matriarch.** A mother who is the ruler of a family or tribe; a woman who is ruler of a family, group, or state.

2. **matricide.** The murder of a mother by her son or daughter.

3. **jurisdiction.** The right or power of administering justice or law; authority; power; control; the extent of authority; the territory over which such authority extends; the limits in which authority may be exercised.

4. **jurisprudence.** A system or body of law; the course of court decisions; the science or philosophy of law; a branch of law.

5. **dichotomy.** Division into two parts, especially mutually exclusive or contradictory parts; division into two parts, kinds, and so on; a schism.

6. **adversity.** A condition marked by unhappiness, misfortune, or distress; a stroke of misfortune; an unfavorable or harmful event; a hardship.

7. **pervert.** To lead astray; to turn or lead from the right way; to corrupt; a person who has been led astray; a person who practices sexual perversion, that is, one who deviates from the normal in sexual habits.

8. **aversion.** A strong dislike; a fixed dislike; a feeling of distaste toward something with a desire to avoid it or turn from it.

9. **subversion.** A systematic attempt to overthrow or undermine a government or political system by persons working secretly within the country involved; anything that tends to overthrow.

10. **introvert.** A person who directs his or her thoughts inward; a person who is more interested in his or her own thoughts and feelings than in what is going on around him or her.

11. **abrogate.** To abolish a law, custom, and so on, by an authoritative act; to repeal; to do away with; to invalidate.

12. **prerogative.** The right or privilege that no one else has; special superiority or privilege that one may get from an official position, office, and so on.

13. **surrogate.** A substitute; a deputy; a person appointed to act in the place of another; something that serves as a substitute.

14. **simultaneously.** At the same time; occurring concurrently.

15. **assimilate.** To take in; to absorb; to make similar.

16. **simulation.** An imitative representation of a process or system.

## Practice for Additional Words Derived from Combining Forms (p. 272)

(1) f, (2) d, (3) h, (4) l, (5) j, (6) m, (7) n, (8) o, (9) e, (10) k, (11) g, (12) p, (13) b, (14) c, (15) i, (16) a.

# Exercise 18 (pp. 273–282)

## Practice A

(1) atmosphere, (2) fortify, (3) affluent, (4) influence, (5) detract, (6) retract, (7) contract, (8) fortitude, (9) contract, (10) thermometer, (11) traction, (12) hemisphere, (13) thermostat, (14) thermal, (15) abstract, (16) technical, (17) technique, (18) technician, (19) technology, (20) dehydrate, (21) abstract, (22) hydrant, (23) fluid, (24) fortress, (25) sphere.

## Practice B

(1) o, s, (2) o, s, (3) x, r, (4) x, r, (5) g, (6) j, (7) l, (8 b, (9) y, (10) k, (11) h, (12) w, (13) q, (14) u, (15) e, (16) v, (17) f, (18) m, (19) t, (20) i, (21) d, (22) c, (23) n, (24) a, (25) p.

## Practice C

(1) fortify, (2) traction, (3) technical, (4) retract, (5) detract, (6) thermometer, (7) sphere, (8) hemisphere, (9) atmosphere, (10) abstract, (11) contract, (12) abstract, (13) thermal, (14) technique, (15) thermostat, (16) contract, (17) technology, (18) fortitude, (19) dehydrate, (20) fortress, (21) hydrant, (22) technician, (23) fluid, (24) influence, (25) affluent.

## Additional Words Derived from Combining Forms (pp. 281–282)

1. **thermophilic.**   Growing at a high temperature; requiring high temperature for development.

2. **thermography.**   A process of writing or printing involving the use of heat; a technique for detecting and measuring variations of heat emitted by various regions of the body and transforming them into signals that can be recorded photographically—used to diagnose abnormal or diseased underlying conditions.

3. **technocracy.**   Government by technical experts.

4. **hydraulics.**   The science dealing with water and other liquids in motion, their uses in engineering, the laws of their actions, and so on.

5. **hydrotherapy.**   The treatment of disease by the use of water.

6. **forte.**   Something a person does very well; a strong point.

7. **forte (for′tā).**   Loud; strong; in a loud and forceful manner; loudly; strongly.

8. **tractable.**   Easily managed or controlled; easy to deal with; obedient.

9. **protract.**   To draw out; lengthen in time; to extend forward or outward; to prolong in time.

10. **fluent.**   Ready in the use of words.

11. **fluctuate.**   To shift back and forth uncertainly.

## Practice for Additional Words Derived from Combining Forms (p. 282)

(1) i, (2) e, (3) h, (4) g, (5) f, (6) k, (7) b, (8) j, (9) c, (10) d, (11) a.

## Chapter Words in Sentences (p. 283)

Sentences will vary.

## Chapter Words in a Paragraph (p. 283)

Paragraphs will vary.

## Analogies 6 (p. 284)

(1) mother, (2) psychiatrist, (3) abstract, (4) hydrophobia, (5) isolate, (6) psychic, (7) fairness, (8) dehydrated, (9) hemisphere, (10) divert, (11) psychology, (12) psychotic, (13) separate, (14) shorten, (15) arrogant, (16) gregarious, (17) protect, (18) philanthrope, (19) adversity, (20) impediment.

## Multiple-Choice Test 6 (pp. 285–291)

Exercise 16

(1) d, (2) b, (3) d, (4) b,[1] (5) a, (6) b, (7) c, (8) d, (9) b, (10) c, (11) c, (12) d, (13) b, (14) b, (15) a, (16) c, (17) d, (18) d.

Exercise 17

(19) b, (20) d, (21) a, (22) d, (23) a, (24) b, (25) c, (26) d, (27) d, (28) b, (29) c, (30) a, (31) c, (32) c, (33) c, (34) a, (35) d, (36) c, (37) d, (38) b, (39) a.

Exercise 18

(40) c, (41) b, (42) c, (43) d,[2] (44) b, (45) c, (46) c, (47) d, (48) b, (49) c, (50) a, (51) d, (52) d, (53) b, (54) a, (55) c, (56) c, (57) b, (58) c, (59) c, (60) b, (61) a, (62) b.

## True/False Test 6 (pp. 291–292)

(1) F, is only to is not only; (2) F, only by a son to by a son or daughter; (3) F, does not to does; (4) F, is to is not; (5) T; (6) F, are to are not or divert to disunite; (7) T; (8) T; (9) F, likes to hates or likes to does not like; (10) F, are to are not; (11) F, healthy to ill; (12) F, propose to not propose; (13) T; (14) F, is never to may be; (15) T; (16) T; (17) T; (18) F, lives to does not live; (19) F, is to is not or a mentally ill person to a medium or psychic to psychopath; (20) T.

> **STOP.**  Turn to page 292 for the scoring of the tests.

[1]The answer *b* is better than *c* because the *murder of a father* could refer to the murder of any person who is a father, not necessarily one's own father.

[2]The answer *d* is better than *b* because *d* is a more complete answer.

## Additional Practice Sets (pp. 293–297)

### Additional Practice 1

A.  (1) f, (2) d, (3) a, (4) e, (5) b, (6) c.
B.  (1) j, (2) h, (3) n, (4) k, (5) i, (6) a, (7) b, (8) d, (9) o, (10) r, (11) e, (12) g, (13) p, (14) q, (15) m, (16) l, (17) f, (18) c.

### Additional Practice 2

A.  (1) f, (2) d, (3) e, (4) a, (5) b, (6) c.
B.  (1) f, (2) m, (3) n, (4) i, (5) a, (6) e, (7) b, (8) p, (9) o, (10) d, (11) j, (12) q, (13) h, (14) u, (15) r, (16) s, (17) l, (18) k, (19) t, (20) g, (21) c.

### Additional Practice 3

A.  (1) g, (2) e, (3) f, (4) b, (5) a, (6) c, (7) d.
B.  (1) v, (2) f, (3) h, (4) j, (5) n, (6) w, (7) l, (8) k, (9) p, (10) t, (11) g, (12) q, (13) r, (14) e, (15) m, (16) d, (17) c, (18) s, (19) b, (20) i, (21) a, (22) o, (23) u.

# APPENDIX: THE DICTIONARY

The dictionary, which is an important reference book for all people, is filled with information about individual words, as well as other useful information. Even though the dictionary is a necessary tool, with which all students should be familiar, it should not be used as a crutch; that is, every time you meet a word whose meaning is unknown to you, you should first try to use your knowledge of combining forms and context clues to unlock the meaning. If these techniques do not help, and the word is essential for understanding the passage, then you should look up the meaning.

To use the dictionary effectively, you should know that the purpose of dictionaries is not to prescribe or make rules about word meanings and pronunciations, but only to describe. Lexicographers use various methods to compile the words in the dictionary. One important method is based on citations of usage and research consulting older dictionaries. Another method involves choosing a group of people and recording the ways in which these subjects pronounce and use words. These then are recorded as the accepted standard spellings, definitions, and word usage.

Difficulties exist concerning pronunciation because persons in different parts of the country often pronounce words differently. Pronunciation in the East is often different from that in the South or Midwest. As a result, pronunciation of a word as given in the dictionary may not be in accord with your region's pronunciation of it.

Also, to compound this problem, different dictionaries may use different pronunciation keys. The pronunciation key is composed of words with diacritical marks. To know how to pronounce a word in a particular dictionary, you must familiarize yourself with the pronunciation key in that dictionary. For example, look at the way that five different dictionaries present a few similar words.

| Word | Webster's New Twentieth Century Dictionary | Webster's Third New International Dictionary | Random House Dictionary of the English Language | The American Heritage Dictionary of the English Language | Funk & Wagnalls Standard College Dictionary |
|------|------|------|------|------|------|
| 1. coupon | cöu'pon | 'k(y)ü,pän | ko͞o'pon | ko͞o'pŏn | ko͞o'pon |
| 2. courage | cŏur'aġe | 'kər·ij | kûr'ij | kûr'ĭj | kûr'ij |
| 3. covet | cŏv'et | 'kəvət | kuv'it | kŭv'ĭt | kuv'it |

If you had no knowledge of the pronunciation key of the specific dictionary, you would have difficulty in pronouncing the word. (See p. 305 for the Pronunciation Key in *The Random House Dictionary of the English Language*.) Pronunciation guides are generally found at the beginning of dictionaries. Many dictionaries also have a concise pronunciation key at the bottom of every page.

Because this text will be used in various parts of the country, it uses a simplified pronunciation key, which is presented in Chapter One.

Before reading any further, list in the space on p. 304 all the uses that you can think of for the dictionary.

# USES OF THE DICTIONARY

_____

_____

_____

_____

_____

_____

_____

_____

_____

Now compare your list with the following:

I.  *Uses of the Dictionary*
    A.  *Information Concerning a Word*
        1.  Spelling.
        2.  Definitions.
        3.  Correct usage.
        4.  Pronunciation.
        5.  Syllabication.
        6.  Antonyms.
        7.  Synonyms.
        8.  Parts of speech.
        9.  Idiomatic phrases.
        10. Etymology–the history of the word.
        11. Semantics–the analysis of the word's meanings.
    B.  *Other Useful Information*
        1.  Biographical entries.
        2.  Lists of foreign countries, provinces, and cities with their population figures.
        3.  Charts of other geographical data.
        4.  Air distances between principal cities.
        5.  Listing of foreign words and phrases.
        6.  Complete listing of abbreviations in common use.
        7.  Tables of weights and measures.
        8.  Signs and symbols.
        9.  Forms of address.

Most people do not realize what an abundance of information can be gained from the dictionary. (The kind of information presented varies according to the dictionary.)

Using your dictionary, answer the following questions:

1. In what countries do centaurs live? _____

2. Where is Mount Everest? _____

3. Was Prometheus the goddess of fire? _____

4. Is a songstress a man who writes songs? _____

5. Is Miss. an abbreviation for Missus? _____

# PRONUNCIATION KEY

**Stress.** The symbol (′), as in **mother** (muth′ər), and **red′ wine′**, marks primary stress; any syllable immediately followed by (′) is pronounced with greater emphasis than syllables not marked(′). The symbol (′), as used following the second syllables of **grandmother** (grand′muth′ər), and **ice′ wa′ter**, marks secondary stress; a syllable marked for secondary stress is pronounced with less emphasis than one marked (′) but with more than those bearing no stress mark.

| | | | | | | | | |
|---|---|---|---|---|---|---|---|---|
| a | act, bat, marry | **ēr** | ear, mere | j | just, tragic, fudge | ô | order, ball, raw | cented syllables to indicate the sound of the reduced vowel in |
| ā | age, paid, say | | | | | oi | oil, joint, joy | |
| â(r) | air, dare, Mary | f | fit, differ, puff | k | keep, token, make | ōō | book, tour | |
| ä | ah, part, balm | | | | | ōō | ooze, fool, too | |
| | | g | give, trigger, beg | l | low, mellow, all, bottle (bot′l) | ou | out, loud, cow | alone |
| b | back, cabin, cab | | | | | | | system |
| | | h | hit, behave, hear | | | p | pot, supper, stop | easily |
| ch | child, teacher, beach | | | m | my, summer, him | | | gallop |
| | | hw | which, nowhere | | | r | read, hurry, near | circus |
| d | do, madder, bed | | | n | now, sinner, on, button (but′n) | s | see, passing, miss | ′ occurs between **i** and **r** and between |
| | | i | if, big, mirror, furniture | ng | sing, Washington | sh | shoe, fashion, push | **ou** and **r** to show |
| e | edge, set, merry | | | | | t | ten, matter, bit | triphthongal quality, as in **fire** (fīªr), |
| ē | equal, seat, bee, mighty | ī | ice, bite, pirate, deny | o | ox, bomb, wasp | th | thin, ether, path | **hour** (ouªr) |
| | | | | ō | over, boat, no | | | |

| | | | | | |
|---|---|---|---|---|---|
| **th** | that, either, smooth | | u | up, sun | |
| | | | û(r) | urge, burn, cur | |
| | | | v | voice, river, live | |
| | | | w | witch, away | |
| | | | y | yes, onion | |
| | | | z | zoo, lazy, those | |
| | | | zh | treasure, mirage | |
| | | | ə | occurs in unac- | |

Reproduced by permission from *The Random House Dictionary of the English Language*, Second Edition, Unabridged, Copyright © 1987 by Random House, Inc.

6. Is haiku a Hawaiian mountain? _____

7. Did Andrew Jackson fight in the Civil War? _____

8. Is a statute a work of art? _____

9. Is a quadruped an extinct animal? _____

10. Is a centipede a unit of measurement in the metric system _____

Using the given dictionary page (see p. 306), see how well you can answer the following questions. Answers are on page 307.

1. Would the word *felon* be found on this page? _____

2. Would the word *fence* be found on this page? _____

3. Between what two words would you find *feisty*? _____

4. How many definitions are give for *felt*? _____

5. What parts of speech can *felt* be? _____

6. Where is a *felucca* used? _____

7. To what family do *felines* belong? _____

8. Is a *felony* a worse crime than a misdemeanor? _____

9. How many chromosomes does a *female* have? _____

10. How many syllables does *felonious* have? _____

11. Which syllable is accentuated in *fellow*? _____

12. When is a *felony* murder committed? _____

# Sample Dictionary Page



**feir·ie** (fēr′ē), *adj. Scot.* healthy; strong. [1375–1425; late ME (Scots) *fery*, equiv. to *fer* (OE *fēre* able-bodied, fit, deriv. of *fōr* journey; see FARE) + -Y[1]]

**Fei·sal I** (fī′səl). See **Faisal I.** Also, **Feisul I.**

**Feisal II.** See **Faisal II.** Also, **Feisul II.**

**feist** (fīst), *n.* **1.** *Chiefly South Midland and Southern U.S.* a small mongrel dog, esp. one that is ill-tempered; cur, mutt. —*v.i.* **2.** *South Midland U.S.* to prance or strut about: *Look at him feist around in his new clothes.* Also, **fice, fist.** [1760–70; cf. (from 16th cent.) *fisting hound, fisting cur,* as contemptuous epithets for any kind of dog (prp. of *fist* to break wind, late ME; cf OE *fisting* breaking wind, MLG *vist*, G *Fist* fart); (def. 2) perh. back formation from FEISTY]

**feist·y** (fī′stē), *adj.,* **feist·i·er, feist·i·est.** **1.** full of animation, energy, or courage; spirited; spunky; plucky: *The champion is faced with a feisty challenger.* **2.** ill-tempered; pugnacious. **3.** troublesome; difficult: *feisty legal problems.* [1895–1900, *Amer.*; FEIST + -Y[1]] —**feist′i·ly,** *adv.* —**feist′i·ness,** *n.*

**fe·la·fel** (fə lä′fəl), *n.* falafel.

**Fel·dene** (fel′dēn), *Pharm., Trademark.* a brand of piroxicam.

**feld·spar** (feld′spär′, fel′-), *n.* any of a group of minerals, principally aluminosilicates of potassium, sodium, and calcium, characterized by two cleavages at nearly right angles: one of the most important constituents of igneous rocks. Also, **felspar.** [1750–60; *feld-* (< G: field) + SPAR[3]; r. *feldspath* < G (*Feld* field + *Spath* spar)]

**feld·spath·ic** (feld spath′ik, fel-, feld′spath-, fel′-), *adj. Mineral.* of, pertaining to, or containing feldspar. Also, **felspathic, feld′spath·ose′, felspathose.** [1825–35; < G *Feldspath* (see FELDSPAR) + -IC]

**feld·spath·oid** (feld′spa thoid′, fel′-), *Mineral.* —*adj.* **1.** Also, **feld′spath·oi′dal.** of or pertaining to a group of minerals similar in chemical composition to certain feldspars except for a lower silica content. —*n.* **2.** a mineral of this group, as nepheline. [1895–1900; < G *Feldspath* (see FELDSPAR) + -OID]

**Fe·lice** (fə lēs′), *n.* a female given name, form of **Felicia.**

**Fe·li·cia** (fə lish′ə, -lish′ē ə, -lē′shə, -lis′ē ə), *n.* a female given name: from a Latin word meaning "happy."

**fe·li·cif·ic** (fē′lə sif′ik), *adj.* causing or tending to cause happiness. [1860–65; < L *fēlīci-* (s. of *fēlīx*) happy + -FIC]

**fe·lic·i·tate** (fi lis′i tāt′), *v.,* **-tat·ed, -tat·ing,** *adj.* —*v.t.* **1.** to compliment upon a happy event; congratulate. **2.** *Archaic.* to make happy. —*adj.* **3.** *Obs.* made happy. [1595–1605; < LL *fēlīcitātus* made happy (ptp. of *fēlīcitāre*). See FELICITY, -ATE[1]] —**fe·lic′i·ta′tor,** *n.*

**fe·lic·i·ta·tion** (fi lis′i tā′shən), *n.* an expression of good wishes; congratulation. [1700–10; FELICITATE + -ION]

**fe·lic·i·tous** (fi lis′i təs), *adj.* **1.** well-suited for the occasion, as an action, manner, or expression; apt; appropriate: *The chairman's felicitous anecdote set everyone at ease.* **2.** having a special ability for suitable manner or expression, as a person. [1725–35; FELICIT(Y) + -OUS] —**fe·lic′i·tous·ly,** *adv.* —**fe·lic′i·tous·ness,** *n.*

**fe·lic·i·ty** (fi lis′i tē), *n., pl.* **-ties.** **1.** the state of being happy, esp. in a high degree; bliss: *marital felicity.* **2.** an instance of this. **3.** a source of happiness. **4.** a skillful faculty: *felicity of expression.* **5.** an instance or display of this: *the many felicities of the poem.* **6.** *Archaic.* good fortune. [1350–1400; ME *felicite* (< AF) < L *fēlīcitās*, equiv. to *fēlīci-* (s. of *fēlīx*) happy + *-tās* -TY[2]]
—**Syn.** **1.** See **happiness.**

**Fe·lic·i·ty** (fi lis′i tē), *n.* a female given name, form of **Felicia.** Also, **Fe·lic·i·ta** (fi lis′i tə).

**fe·lid** (fē′lid), *n.* any animal of the family Felidae, comprising the cats. [1890–95; < NL *Felidae*; see FELIS, -ID[2]]

**fe·line** (fē′līn), *adj.* **1.** belonging or pertaining to the cat family, Felidae. **2.** catlike; characteristic of animals of the cat family: *a feline tread.* **3.** sly, stealthy, or treacherous. —*n.* **4.** an animal of the cat family. [1675–85; < L *fēl(ēs)* (see FELIS) + -INE[1]; cf. LL *fēlīneus* of a wild cat] —**fe′line·ly,** *adv.* —**fe′line·ness, fe·lin·i·ty** (fi lin′i tē), *n.*

**fe′line distem′per,** distemper[1] (def. 1c). Also called **fe′line agranulocyto′sis, fe′line infec′tious enteri′tis, fe′line panleukope′nia.** [1940–45]

**fe′line leuke′mia vi′rus,** a retrovirus, mainly affecting cats, that depresses the immune system and leads to opportunistic infections, lymphosarcoma, and other disorders. *Abbr.:* FeLV, FLV [1975–80]

**Fe·li·pe** (fe lē′pe), *n.* **Le·ón (Ca·mi·no)** (le ôn′ kä mē′nō), 1884–1968, Spanish poet, in South America after 1939.

***Fe·lis*** (fē′lis), *n.* a genus of mostly small cats including the domestic cat, margay, puma, and ocelot, sharing with certain cats of related genera an inability to roar due to ossification of the hyoid bone in the larynx. Cf. ***Panthera.*** [< NL (Linnaeus); L *fēlis, fēlēs* any of several small carnivores, including the wild cat]

**Fe·lix** (fē′liks), *n.* a male given name: from a Latin word meaning "happy, lucky."

**Felix I, Saint,** died A.D. 274, pope 269–274.

**Felix III, Saint,** died A.D. 492, pope 483–492.

**Felix IV, Saint,** died A.D. 530, pope 526–530.

**fell[1]** (fel), *v.* pt. of **fall.**

**fell[2]** (fel), *v.t.* **1.** to knock, strike, shoot, or cut down; cause to fall: *to fell a moose; to fell a tree.* **2.** *Sewing.* to finish (a seam) by sewing the edge down flat. —*n.* **3.** *Lumbering.* the amount of timber cut down in one season. **4.** *Sewing.* a seam finished by felling. [bef. 900; ME *fellen*, OE *fellan*, causative of *feallan* to FALL; c. Goth *falljan* to cause to fall]

**fell[3]** (fel), *adj.* **1.** fierce; cruel; dreadful; savage. **2.** destructive; deadly: *fell poison; fell disease.* **3. at** or **in one fell swoop.** See **swoop** (def. 5). [1250–1300; ME *fel* < OF, nom. of *felon* wicked. See FELON] —**fell′ness,** *n.*

**fell[4]** (fel), *n.* the skin or hide of an animal; pelt. [bef. 900; ME, OE; c. D *vel*, G *Fell*, ON *-fjall* (in *berfjall* bearskin), Goth *-fill* (in *thrutsfill* scab-skin, leprosy); akin to L *pellis* skin, hide]

**fell[5]** (fel), *n. Scot. and North Eng.* an upland pasture, moor, or thicket; a highland plateau. [1300–50; ME < ON *fell, fjall* hill, mountain, akin to G *Felsen* rock, cliff]

**fel·la** (fel′ə), *n. Informal.* fellow. [cf. FELLER[1]]

**fell·a·ble** (fel′ə bəl), *adj.* capable of being or fit to be felled. [1575–85; FELL[2] + -ABLE]

**fel·lah** (fel′ə), *n., pl.* **fel·lahs,** *Arab.* **fel·la·hin, fel·la·heen** (fel′ə hēn′). a native peasant or laborer in Egypt, Syria, etc. [1735–45; < Ar *fallāḥ* peasant]

**fel·late** (fə lāt′), *v.,* **-lat·ed, -lat·ing.** —*v.t.* **1.** to perform fellatio on. —*v.i.* **2.** to engage in fellatio. [1965–70; by back formation from FELLATIO] —**fel·la′tor,** *n.*

**fel·la·ti·o** (fə lā′shē ō′, -lä′tē ō′, fe-), *n.* oral stimulation of the penis, esp. to orgasm. Also, **fel·la·tion** (fə lā′shən, fe-). [1885–90; < NL *fellātiō*, equiv. to L *fel(l)ā-t(us)* (ptp. of *fel(l)āre* to suck) + *-iō* -ION]

**fell·er[1]** (fel′ər), *n. Informal.* fellow. [1815–25; orig. dial.; by reduction of (ō) to (ə) and merger with words ending in *-er*]

**fell·er[2]** (fel′ər), *n.* **1.** a person or thing that fells. **2.** *Sewing.* a person or thing that fells a seam. [1350–1400; ME *fellere*. See FELL[2], -ER[1]]

**Fel·ler** (fel′ər), *n.* **Robert William Andrew** (*Bob*), born 1918, U.S. baseball player.

**Fel·li·ni** (fə lē′nē; *It.* fel lē′nē), *n.* **Fe·de·ri·co** (*It.* fe′de rē′kô), born 1920, Italian film director and writer.

**fell·mon·ger** (fel′mung′gər, -mong′-), *n. Chiefly Brit.* a preparer of skins or hides of animals, esp. sheepskins, prior to leather making. [1520–30; FELL[4] + MONGER] —**fell′mon′ger·ing, fell′mon′ger·y,** *n.*

**fel·loe** (fel′ō), *n.* the circular rim, or a part of the rim of a wheel, into which the outer ends of the spokes are inserted. Also, **felly.** [bef. 900; ME *felwe*, OE *felg(e)*; c. G *Felge*]

**fel·low** (fel′ō), *n.* **1.** a man or boy: *a fine old fellow; a nice little fellow.* **2.** *Informal.* beau; suitor: *Mary had her fellow over to meet her folks.* **3.** *Informal.* person; one: *They don't treat a fellow very well here.* **4.** a person of small worth or no esteem. **5.** a companion; comrade; associate. *They have been fellows since childhood.* **6.** a person belonging to the same rank or class; equal; peer: *The doctor conferred with his fellows.* **7.** one of a pair; mate; match: *a shoe without its fellow.* **8.** *Educ.* **a.** a graduate student of a university or college to whom an allowance is granted for special study. **b.** *Brit.* an incorporated member of a college, entitled to certain privileges. **c.** a member of the corporation or board of trustees of certain universities or colleges. **9.** a member of any of certain learned societies: *a fellow of the British Academy.* **10.** *Obs.* a partner. —*v.t.* **11.** to make or represent as equal with another. **12.** *Archaic.* to produce a fellow to; match. —*adj.* **13.** belonging to the same class or group; united by the same occupation, interests, etc.; being in the same condition: *fellow students; fellow sufferers.* [bef. 1050; ME *felowe, felawe*, late OE *fēolaga* < ON *fēlagi* partner in a joint undertaking, equiv. to *fé* money, property (c. OE *feoh*, G *Vieh*) + *-lagi* bedfellow, comrade; akin to LAIR[1], LIE[2]]

**fel′low crea′ture,** a kindred creature, esp. a fellow human being. [1640–50]

**fel′low feel′ing,** **1.** sympathetic feeling; sympathy: *to have fellow feeling for the unfortunate.* **2.** a sense of joint interest: *to act out of fellow feeling to support one's country.* [1605–15]

**fel·low·ly** (fel′ō lē), *adj.* **1.** sociable or friendly. —*adv.* **2.** in a sociable or friendly manner. [1175–1225; ME *feolahlich, felawely*; see FELLOW, -LY]

**fel·low·man** (fel′ō man′), *n., pl.* **-men.** another member of the human race, esp. a kindred human being: *Don't deny full recognition to your fellowmen.* Also, **fel′low man′.** [1750–60]

**fel′low serv′ant,** (under the fellow-servant rule) an employee working with another employee for the same employer. [1525–35]

**fel′low-serv′ant rule′** (fel′ō sûr′vənt), the common-law rule that the employer is not liable to an employee for injuries resulting from the negligence of a fellow employee.

**fel·low·ship** (fel′ō ship′), *n., v.,* **-shipped** or **-shiped, -ship·ping** or **-ship·ing.** —*n.* **1.** the condition or relation of being a fellow: *the fellowship of humankind.* **2.** friendly relationship; companionship: *the fellowship of father and son.* **3.** community of interest, feeling, etc. **4.** communion, as between members of the same church. **5.** friendliness. **6.** an association of persons having similar tastes, interests, etc. **7.** a company, guild, or corporation. **8.** *Educ.* **a.** the body of fellows in a college or university. **b.** the position or emoluments of a fellow of a college or university, or the sum of money he or she receives. **c.** a foundation for the maintenance of a fellow in a college or university. —*v.t.* **9.** to admit to fellowship, esp. religious fellowship. —*v.i.* **10.** to join in fellowship, esp. religious fellowship. [1150–1200; ME *felaweshipe*. See FELLOW, -SHIP]
—**Syn.** **2.** comradeship, camaraderie, friendship, society, intimacy.

**fel′low trav′eler,** **1.** a person who supports or sympathizes with a political party, esp. the Communist party, but is not an enrolled member. **2.** anyone who, although not a member, supports or sympathizes with some organization, movement, or the like. —**fel·low-trav·el·ing** (fel′ō trav′ə ling, -trav′ling), *adj.* [1605–15, for literal sense]

**fel·ly[1]** (fel′ē), *n., pl.* **-lies.** felloe. [ME *felien* (pl.), var. of *felwe* FELLOE]

**fel·ly[2]** (fel′ē), *adv.* in a fell manner; fiercely; ruthlessly. [1250–1300; ME *felliche*. See FELL[3], -LY]

**fe·lo-de-se** (fel′ō di sē′, -sā′), *n., pl.* **fe·lo·nes-de-se** (fel′ə nēz′di sē′, -sā′, fə lō′nēz-), **fe·los-de-se** (fel′ōz di sē′, -sā′). **1.** a person who commits suicide or commits an unlawful malicious act resulting in his or her own death. **2.** the act of suicide. [1645–55; < AL, equiv. to *felō* a felon + *dē* in respect to, of + *sē* oneself]

**fel·on[1]** (fel′ən), *n.* **1.** *Law.* a person who has committed a felony. **2.** *Archaic.* a wicked person. —*adj.* **3.** *Archaic.* wicked; malicious; treacherous. [1250–1300; ME *fel(o)un* wicked < AF; OF *fel* (nom.), *felun* (obl.) wicked person, traitor, perh. < Old Low Franconian **fillo*, n. corresponding to OS *fillian* to ill-treat, whip, MD *villen* to flay, OHG *fillen* to beat, whip; cf. FELL[3]]

**fel·on[2]** (fel′ən), *n.* an acute and painful inflammation of the deeper tissues of a finger or toe, usually near the nail: a form of whitlow. [1375–1425; late ME *felo(u)n* < ML *fellōn-* (s. of *fellō*) scrofulous tumor, of uncert. orig.]

**fe·lo·ni·ous** (fə lō′nē əs), *adj.* **1.** *Law.* pertaining to, of the nature of, or involving a felony: *felonious homicide; felonious intent.* **2.** wicked; base; villainous. [1375–1425; FELONY + -OUS; r. late ME *felonous* < AF, OF] —**fe·lo′ni·ous·ly,** *adv.* —**fe·lo′ni·ous·ness,** *n.*

**fel·on·ry** (fel′ən rē), *n.* **1.** the whole body or class of felons. **2.** the convict population of a penal colony. [1830–40; FELON + -RY]

**fel·o·ny** (fel′ə nē), *n., pl.* **-nies.** *Law.* **1.** an offense, as murder or burglary, of graver character than those called misdemeanors, esp. those commonly punished in the U.S. by imprisonment for more than a year. **2.** *Early Eng. Law.* any crime punishable by death or mutilation and forfeiture of lands and goods. [1250–1300; ME *felonie* < AF, OF: villainy, a felony. See FELON[1], -Y[3]]

**fel′ony mur′der,** a killing treated as a murder because, though unintended, it occurred during the commission or attempted commission of a felony, as robbery.

**fel·sic** (fel′sik), *adj. Geol.* (of rocks) consisting chiefly of feldspars, feldspathoids, quartz, and other light-colored minerals. Cf. **mafic.** [1910–15; FEL(DSPAR) + S(ILICA) + -IC]

**fel·site** (fel′sīt), *n.* a dense, fine-grained, igneous rock consisting typically of feldspar and quartz, both of which may appear as phenocrysts. [1785–95; FELS(PAR) + -ITE[1]] —**fel·sit·ic** (fel sit′ik), *adj.*

**fel·spar** (fel′spär′), *n.* feldspar. [< G *Fels* rock + SPAR[3], by false etymological analysis]

**fel·spath·ic** (fel spath′ik), *adj.* feldspathic. Also, **fel′·spath·ose′.**

**felt[1]** (felt), *v.* pt. and pp. of **feel.**

**felt[2]** (felt), *n.* **1.** a nonwoven fabric of wool, fur, or hair, matted together by heat, moisture, and great pressure. **2.** any article made of this material, as a hat. **3.** any matted fabric or material, as a mat of asbestos fibers, rags, or old paper, used for insulation and in construction. —*adj.* **4.** pertaining to or made of felt. —*v.t.* **5.** to make into felt; mat or press together. **6.** to cover with or as with felt. —*v.i.* **7.** to become matted together. [bef. 1000; ME, OE; c. G *Filz*; see FILTER]

**felt·ing** (fel′ting), *n.* **1.** felted material, either woven or felt fabric. **2.** the act or process of making felt. **3.** the materials of which felt is made. [1680–90; FELT[2] + -ING[1]]

**felt′ mark′er,** a felt pen with a wide nib for making identifying marks, as on clothing.

**felt′ side′,** the top side of a sheet of paper, the side against the felt rollers during manufacture, normally preferred for printing. Cf. **wire side.** [1955–60]

**felt′-tip pen′** (felt′tip′), a pen that holds quick-drying ink conveyed to a writing surface by means of a felt nib. Also called **felt′ pen′.** [1955–60]

**fe·luc·ca** (fə luk′ə, -lo͞o′kə), *n.* **1.** a sailing vessel, lateen-rigged on two masts, used in the Mediterranean Sea and along the Spanish and Portuguese coasts. **2.** a small fishing boat formerly used in the San Francisco Bay area. [1620–30; earlier *falluca* < Sp *faluca*, earlier var. of *falua*, perh. < Catalan *faluga* < Ar *falūwah* small cargo ship]

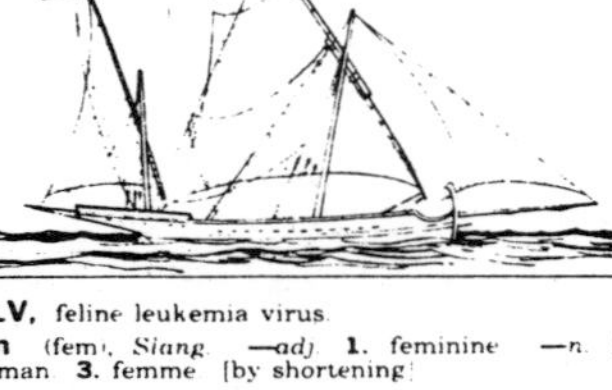

**felucca** (def. 1)

**FeLV,** feline leukemia virus.

**fem** (fem), *Slang.* —*adj.* **1.** feminine. —*n.* **2.** a woman. **3.** femme. [by shortening]

**fem.,** **1.** female. **2.** feminine.

**FEMA,** Federal Emergency Management Agency.

**fe·male** (fē′māl), *n.* **1.** a person bearing two X chromosomes in the cell nuclei and normally having a

CONCISE PRONUNCIATION KEY: act, cāpe, dâre, pärt; set, ēqual; if, īce; ox, ōver, ôrder, oil, bo͝ok, bo͞ot, out; up, ûrge; child; sing; shoe; thin, that; zh as in *treasure*. ə = a as in *alone*, e as in *system*, i as in *easily*, o as in *gallop*, u as in *circus*; ᵊ as in *fire* (fīᵊr), *hour* (ouᵊr). l and n can serve as syllabic consonants, as in *cradle* (krād′l), and *button* (but′n). See the full key inside the front cover.

Reproduced by permission from *The Random House Dictionary of the English Language,* Second Edition, Unabridged, Copyright © 1987 by Random House, Inc.

# ANSWERS: Appendix

1. yes

2. No, *female* is the last word on this page.

3. *feist* and *felafel*

4. seven

5. noun, verb, and adjective

6. in the Mediterranean and along Spanish and Portuguese coasts

7. cat family

8. yes

9. two

10. four

11. first

12. during the commission of a felony such as a robbery

# GLOSSARY/INDEX

## Combining Forms Presented in *Vocabulary Expansion*

The number after the meaning refers to the page on which the combining form is first presented; it is the main entry for the combining form.

**A.** Without. 60
**Able.** Can do; able. 53
**Agog.** Leading; directing; inciting. 55
**Agogue.** Leading; directing; inciting. 55
**Al.** Relating to. 207
**Ali.** Other. 55
**Ambi.** both. 199
**An.** Native of; belonging to. 281
**Ance.** Act of; state of; quality of. 207
**Anima.** Spirit; mind; soul. 219
**Animus.** Spirit; mind; soul. 219
**Anni.** Year. 5
**Annu.** Year. 5
**Anthrop.** Mankind; man; human. 62
**Anthropo.** Mankind; man; human. 62
**Anti.** Against. 119
**Aqua.** Water. 89
**Aqui.** Water. 89
**Ar.** One who; that which. 10
**Arch.** Rule; chief. 55
**Archae.** Ancient. 165
**Archaeo.** Ancient. 165
**Astro.** Star. 89
**Aud.** Hear. 111
**Audi.** Hear. 111
**Aut.** Self. 5
**Auto.** Self. 5

**Belli.** War. 199
**Bello.** War. 199
**Bene.** Good. 111
**Bi.** Two. 5
**Biblio.** Book. 145
**Bio.** Life. 5
**Brevi.** Short; brief. 165

**Cap.** Take; receive. 154
**Capit.** Head. 99
**Cata.** Down. 145

**Cede.** Go; give in; yield. 165
**Ceed.** Go; give in; yield. 165
**Cent.** Hundred; hundredth part. 47
**Centi.** Hundred; hundredth part. 47
**Cep.** Take; receive. 154
**Chron.** Time. 165
**Chrono.** Time. 165
**Cide.** Murder; kill. 99
**Civ.** Citizen. 199
**Civis.** Citizen. 199
**Co.** With. 97
**Col.** With. 97
**Com.** With. 97
**Con.** With. 97
**Contra.** Against; opposite. 21
**Cor.** With. 97
**Corp.** Body. 99
**Corpor.** Body. 99
**Cred.** Believe. 47
**Crypt.** Secret; hidden. 165
**Crypto.** Secret; hidden. 165
**Cura.** Care. 111
**Cycl.** Circle; wheel. 165
**Cyclo.** Circle; wheel. 165

**De.** Away; from; off; completely. 163
**Dec.** Ten. 47
**Deca.** Ten. 47
**Deci.** Tenth part. 49
**Dem.** People. 55
**Demo.** People. 55
**Derm.** Skin. 154
**Dermo.** Skin. 154
**Di.** Two. 262
**Dia.** Through. 145
**Dic.** Say; speak. 21
**Dict.** Say; speak. 21
**Dis.** Away from; apart; not. 174

**Dorm.** Sleep. 210
**Duc.** Lead. 165

**E.** Out of; from; lacking. 163
**Ego.** I; me; the self. 210
**Em.** In; into. 99
**En.** In; into. 99
**Ence.** Act of; state of; quality of. 207
**Enni.** Year. 5
**Epi.** Upon; beside; among. 145
**Equi.** Equal. 219
**Er.** One who; that which. 10
**Err.** Wander. 210
**Eu.** Well; good; pleasant. 253
**Ex.** Out of; from; lacking; former. 163

**Fac.** Make; do. 111
**Fect.** Make; do. 111
**Feder.** Trust; faith. 219
**Fer.** Bring; bear; yield. 145
**Fic.** Make; do. 111
**Fid.** Trust; faith. 219
**Fide.** Trust; faith. 219
**Fin.** End. 145
**Flu.** Flowing. 273
**Fluc.** Flowing. 273
**Fort.** Strong. 273
**Frater.** Brother. 99
**Fratr.** Brother. 99
**Fy.** Make; cause to be; change into; become. 281

**Gamy.** Marriage. 62
**Gen.** Kind; race; descent. 62
**Geno.** Kind; race; descent. 62
**Geo.** Earth. 13
**Gnosi.** Knowledge. 154
**Gnosis.** Knowledge. 154
**Gram.** Something written or drawn; a record. 21
**Graph.** Something written; machine. 5
**Greg.** Flock, herd; crowd; mob. 253
**Gyn.** Woman. 154
**Gyno.** Woman. 154

**Hect.** Hundred. 49
**Hecto.** Hundred. 49
**Hom.** Same; man; human. 62
**Homo.** Same; man; human. 62
**Hydr.** Water. 273
**Hydra.** Water. 273
**Hydro.** Water. 273
**Hyper.** Over; above; excessive. 210
**Hypn.** Sleep. 219
**Hypno.** Sleep 219

**Hypo.** Under. 154

**Ian.** Native of; belonging to. 281
**Ible.** Can do; able. 53
**Il.** Not. 152
**Im.** Into; not. 152
**In.** Into; not. 152
**Inter.** Between; among. 217
**Intra.** Within; inside of. 217
**Ion.** State of; act of; result of. 27
**Ir.** Not. 152
**Ist.** One who. 67
**Ize.** To cause to be or become; to be like; to be formed into. 260

**Juris.** Law. 262
**Jus.** Law. 262

**Kilo.** Thousand. 49

**Leg.** Law. 62
**Legis.** Law. 62
**Less.** Without. 97
**Lex.** Law. 62
**Loc.** Place. 111
**Loco.** Place. 111
**Log.** Speech; word. 145
**Logo.** Speech; word. 145
**Luc.** Light; clear. 210
**Lum.** Light; clear. 210

**Magna.** Great; large. 219
**Mal.** Bad; ill; evil; wrong; not perfect. 228
**Man.** Hand. 111
**Manu.** Hand. 111
**Matr.** Mother. 262
**Matri.** Mother. 262
**Matro.** Mother. 262
**Mega.** Very large. 199
**Meter.** Measure. 13
**Micro.** Very small. 13
**Milli.** Thousand; thousandth part. 47
**Mis.** Wrong; hate. 62
**Miso.** Wrong; hate. 62
**Miss.** Send. 219
**Mitt.** Send. 219
**Mon.** One. 55
**Mono.** One. 55
**Mors.** Death. 99
**Mort.** Death. 99

**Nasc.** Born. 219
**Nat.** Born. 219
**Naut.** Sailor. 89

**Ness.** Quality of; state of. 270
**Nomin.** Name. 111
**Non.** Not. 119
**Nov.** New. 210

**Ology.** Study of; science of. 5
**Omni.** All. 89
**Onym.** Name. 111
**Or.** One who; that which. 10
**Ous.** Full of; having. 260

**Pac.** Peace. 199
**Pater.** Father. 253
**Pathy.** Feeling; suffering. 99
**Patri.** Father. 253
**Pax.** Peace. 199
**Ped.** Foot; child. 5, 154
**Pedo.** Child. 154
**Peri.** Around. 210
**Phil.** Love. 253
**Phile.** Love. 253
**Philo.** Love. 253
**Phob.** Fear. 21
**Phobo.** Fear. 21
**Phon.** Sound. 13
**Phono.** Sound. 13
**Pod.** Foot. 5
**Polis.** City. 199
**Poly.** Many. 62
**Pon.** Place; set. 219
**Pop.** People. 219
**Port.** Carry. 47
**Pos.** Place; set. 219
**Post.** After. 199
**Poten.** Powerful. 89
**Pre.** Before. 108
**Pro.** Before; forward. 145
**Pseudo.** False. 111
**Psych.** Spirit; mind; soul. 253
**Psyche.** Spirit; mind; soul. 253
**Psycho.** Spirit; mind; soul. 253

**Re.** Again; back. 18
**Ri.** Laughter. 154
**Ridi.** Laughter. 154
**Risi.** Laughter. 154
**Rog.** Ask; beg. 262

**Sci.** Know. 89
**Scio.** Know. 89
**Scope.** A means for seeing; watching or viewing. 13
**Scrib.** Write. 13
**Scrip.** Write. 13

**Se.** Apart. 253
**Semi.** Half; not fully; partly; occurring twice in a period. 228
**Sequi.** Follow. 165
**Simil.** Like; resembling. 262
**Simul.** Like; resembling. 262
**Sion.** State of; act of; result of. 27
**Sist.** Stand. 210
**Soph.** Wise. 210
**Spect.** See; view; observe. 21
**Sphere.** Ball. 273
**Sta.** Stand. 210
**Sub.** Under; beneath; below; lower in rank. 174
**Syl.** Same; with; together; along with. 99
**Sym.** Same; with; together; along with. 99
**Syn.** Same; with; together; along with. 99

**Tain.** Hold. 165
**Techni.** Arts and crafts (especially industrial arts); method; system; skill. 273
**Techno.** Arts and crafts (especially industrial arts); method; system; skill. 273
**Tele.** From a distance. 13
**Temp.** Time. 154
**Tempo.** Time. 154
**Tempor.** Time. 154
**Ten.** Hold. 165
**Tend.** Stretch; strain. 199
**Tens.** Stretch; strain. 199
**Tent.** Hold; stretch; strain. 165, 199
**Theo.** God. 55
**Therm.** Heat. 273
**Thermo.** Heat. 273
**Tion.** Act of; state of; result of. 27
**Tox.** Poison. 154
**Toxo.** Poison. 154
**Tract.** Draw; pull. 273
**Trans.** Across; beyond; through; on the other side of; over. 152
**Tude.** Condition of; state of. 270

**Un.** Not. 108
**Uni.** One. 21

**Ven.** Come. 89
**Veni.** Come. 89
**Vent.** Come. 89
**Vers.** Turn. 262
**Vert.** Turn. 262
**Vid.** See. 89
**Vis.** See. 89
**Voc.** Voice; call. 199
**Vox.** Voice; call. 199

# Vocabulary Words Presented in
## *Vocabulary Expansion*[1]

The number after the meaning refers to the page on which the vocabulary word is presented; it is the main entry for the word. If there is more than one number, it means the word has also appeared in "Extra Word Power."

**Abbreviation.**  A shortened form of a word or phrase.  167

**Abstract.**[2]  Thought of apart from any specific object; disassociated from any particular instance; difficult to understand; theoretical; not concrete; a short statement giving the main points of a book, article, or research paper.  275

**Abstract.**[2]  To take away or remove; to withdraw; to take away secretly; slyly, or dishonestly; to divert; to make an abstraction.  275

**Admission.**  Act of allowing to enter; entrance fee; a price charged or paid to be admitted; acknowledgment; a confession, as to a crime.  220

**Adverse.**  Hostile; contrary to one's interest or welfare; unfavorable.  264

**Advertise.**  To give public notice of in newspapers, radio, television, and so on; to praise the good qualities of a product, service, and so on; to call attention to; to notify, inform.  264

**Affect.**  To act upon or to cause something; to influence; to produce an effect or change in.  113

**Affluent.**  Wealthy, rich; having a generous supply of material possessions.  275

**Aggregate.**  A mass of separate things joined together; the whole sum or amount; formed by the collection of units or particles into a body, mass, or amount; total; to amount to; to come to; to total; to come together in a mass or group; to collect; to unite; accumulate.  255

**Agoraphobia.**  Fear of being in open spaces or fear of leaving one's house.  23

**Ailurophobia.**  Fear of cats.  23

**Alias.**  Another name taken by a person, often a criminal.  56

**Alien.**  A foreigner; a person from another country; foreign.  57

**Alienate.**  To make others unfriendly to one; to estrange (to remove or keep at a distance).  57

**Allocate.**  To set apart for a special purpose; to divide up something; to divide and distribute something.  114

**Ambiguous.**  Having two or more meanings.  201

**American.**  A native of America.  281

**Americanize.**  To become an American.  260

**Amoral.**  Without morals; without a sense of right or wrong.  60

**Anarchist.**  One who believes that there should be no government.  67

**Anarchy.**  The absence of government; no rule; a state of disorder; chaos.  56, 60

**Animosity.**  Hatred; resentment.  220

**Anniversary.**  Yearly return of a date marking an event or an occurrence of some importance; returning or recurring each year.  6

**Annual.**  Every year.  6, 207

**Anonymous.**  Lacking a name; of unknown authorship.  114

**Antacid.**  Something that acts against acid.  119

**Anthropologist.**  One who is in the field of anthropology.  67

**Anthropology.**  Study of mankind; study of the cultures and customs of people.  63

**Antigambling.**  Against gambling.  119

**Antilabor.**  Against labor.  119

**Antimachine.**  Against machines.  119

[1]Additional Words are presented separately; see p. 326.

[2]*Abstract* and *abstract* are presented separately because they are pronounced differently.

**Antimen.** Against men. 119

**Antiwar.** Against war. 119

**Antiwomen.** Against women. 119

**Antonym.** A word opposite in meaning to some other word. 114, 119

**Apathy.** Lack of feeling; indifference. 100

**Apodal.** Relating to being without feet. 207

**Aquanaut.** One who travels undersea; a person trained to work in an underwater chamber. 91

**Aquarium.** A pond, a glass bowl, a tank, or the like, in which aquatic animals and/or plants are kept; a place in which aquatic collections are shown. 91

**Aquatic.** Living or growing in or near water; performed on or in water. 91

**Arachniphobia.** Fear of spiders. 23

**Archaeology.** The study of the life and culture of ancient people, as by the digging up of old settlements, ruins from the past, and old man-made or other objects. 166

**Archaic.** Belonging to an earlier period; ancient; old-fashioned; no longer used. 166

**Arrogant.** Full of pride and self-importance; overbearing; haughty. 264

**Asian.** A native of Asia. 281

**Assist.** To give help to; an act of helping. 211

**Assistance.** Act of helping. 207

**Astrapophobia.** Fear of lightning. 23

**Astrology.** The art or practice that claims to tell the future and interpret the influence of the heavenly bodies on the fate of people; a reading of the stars. 91

**Astronaut.** One who travels in space; a person trained to travel in outer space. 91

**Astronomy.** The science that deals with stars, planets, and space. 91

**Atheist.** One who does not believe in the existence of God. 56, 60

**Atmosphere.** The air that surrounds the earth; the mass of gases that surrounds the earth and is held to it by the force of gravity; the air in any given place; a mental or moral environment; surrounding influence; the feeling or coloring that surrounds a work of art. 274

**Attention.** Mental concentration; care, a position of readiness: acts of courtesy. 200

**Audible.** Capable of being heard. 113

**Audience.** An assembly of listeners or spectators at a concert, play, speech, and so on. 113

**Audiovisual.** Of, pertaining to, involving, or directed at both hearing and sight. 113

**Audit.** To examine or check such things as accounts; to attend class as a listener; an examination of accounts to report the financial state of a business. 113

**Audition.** A trial hearing, as of an actor or singer; the act of hearing; to try out for a part in an audition. 113

**Auditorium.** A building or hall for speeches, concerts, public meetings, and so on; the room in a building occupied by an audience. 113

**Author.** OIne who writes. 10

**Autobiography.** Life story written by oneself. 6

**Autocracy.** A form of government in which one person rules absolutely. 56

**Autocrat.** A ruler who has absolute control of a country. 56

**Autograph.** Signature; written by a person's own hand: an *autograph* letter; containing autographs: an *autograph* album; to write one's name on or in. 6

**Beautify.** To make beautiful. 281

**Beggar.** One who begs. 10

**Belligerent.** Warlike; any nation, person, or group engaged in fighting war. 200

**Benefactor.** One who gives help or confers a benefit; a patron. 113

**Beneficiary.** One who receives benefits or advantages; the one to whom an insurance policy is payable. 113

**Benefit.** That which is helpful; advantage; a payment; a performance given to raise funds for a worthy cause; to aid. 113

**Biannual.** Twice a year; (loosely) occuring every two years.  6

**Bibliography.** A listing of books on a subject by an author (the description includes author's name, title, publisher, date of publication, and so on).  147

**Bicentennial.** Pertaining to or in honor of a two-hundredth anniversary; consisting of or lasting two hundred years; occurring once in two hundred years; a two-hundredth anniversary.  48

**Biennial.** Once every two years; lasting for two years.  6

**Bigamist.** One who is married to two spouses at the same time.  67

**Bigamy.** Marriage to two spouses at the same time.  62

**Bimonthly.** Every two months; twice a month.  6

**Biographer.** A person who writes biographies.  10

**Biography.** Person's life story.  6

**Biologist.** One who is in the field of biology.  67

**Biology.** Science of life.  6

**Biped.** Two-footed animal.  6

**Biweekly.** Every two weeks; twice a week.  6

**Blameless.** Without blame; without fault.  97

**Capable.** Able to be affected; able to understand; having ability; having qualities that are able to be developed.  155

**Capital.** City or town that is the official seat of government; money or wealth; first letter of a word at the beginning of a sentence; excellent.  101

**Capitalism.** The economic system in which all or most of the means of production such as land, factories, and railroads, are privately owned and operated for profit.  101

**Capital punishment.** The death penalty.  100

**Capitol.** The building in which a legislative body meets.  102

**Capsule.** A small container made of gelatin (or other material that melts) that holds a dose of medicine; a special removable part of an airplane or rocket.  155

**Captive.** One who is taken prisoner; one who is dominated.  155

**Captor.** One who holds someone a prisoner.  10

**Catalog.** A listing of names, titles, and so on in some order; a book containing such a list; to make a catalog.  146

**Centennial.** Pertaining to a period of one hundred years; lasting one hundred years; a one-hundredth anniversary.  48

**Century.** Period of one hundred years.  48

**Christian.** Believing in Christ (the Christian religion).  281

**Chronic.** Continuing for a long time; prolonged; recurring.  166

**Chronological.** Arranged in time order (earlier things or events precede later ones).  166

**Circumference.** The distance around a circle; a boundary line of any rounded area.  147

**Circumstance.** Something connected with an act, event, or condition; (often pl.) the conditions, influences, and so on surrounding and influencing persons or actions; formal display, as in *pomp and circumstance*.  211

**Civics.** (Used in the singular.) The part of political science dealing with the study of civic affairs and the rights and responsibilities of citizenship.  200

**Civil.** Of a citizen or citizens; relating to citizens and their government; relating to ordinary community life as distinguished from military or church affairs; polite.  201

**Civilian.** One who is not in the military; of civilians; nonmilitary.  200

**Civilization.** A state of human society that has a high level of intellectual, social, and cultural development; the cultural development of a specific people, country, or region.  201

**Collect.** To gather together.  97

**Combine.** To join together; unite.  97

**Concede.** To give in; surrender, yield; grant; admit.  167

**Conceive.** To become pregnant with; to form in the mind; to understand; to think; to believe; to imagine; to develop mentally.  155

**Conductor.** One who guides or leads; a guide or director; one who has charge of a railroad train; the director of an orchestra or a chorus; any substance that conducts electricity, heat, and so on.  167

**Conference.** A discussion or meeting on some important matter.  147, 207

**Confide.** To tell in trust; to tell secrets trustingly.  221

**Congregate.** To come together into a group, crowd, or assembly; to come together or collect in a particular place or locality.  255

**Consequence.** That which follows from any act; a result; an effect.  166

**Consist.** To be made up of.  211

**Contemporary.** Belonging to the same age; living or occurring at the same time; current; one living in the same period as another or others; a person or thing of about the same age or date of origin.  157

**Content.**[3] Satisfied; not complaining; not desiring something else.  166

**Content.**[3] What something holds (usually plural in this sense); subject matter; the material that something is made up of; the main substance or meaning.  166

**Contract.**[4] A binding agreement between two or more parties; a covenant.  275

**Contract.**[4] To draw together; to make smaller; shrink; shorten; to shorten a word by omitting one or more sounds or letters; to bring on oneself as an obligation or debt; to get.  275

**Contradiction.** Something (such as a statement) consisting of opposing parts.  22

**Contrary.** Opposite.  22

**Contrast.** Difference between things; use of opposites for a certain result.  22

**Controversy.** A dispute, especially a lengthy and public one, between sides holding opposing views; a quarrel; debate; argument.  264

**Convene.** To come together; to assemble.  91, 97

**Convenient.** Well suited to one's purpose, personal comfort, or ease.  92

**Convention.** A formal meeting of members for political or professional purposes; accepted custom, rule, or opinion.  92, 97

**Converse.** A thing, especially a statement, that is turned around, usually producing a different idea or meaning; something that is opposite or contrary.  264

**Corporal punishment.** Bodily punishment; a beating.  101

**Corporation.** A group of people who get a charter granting them as a body certain of the powers, rights, privileges, and liabilities (legal responsibilities) of an individual, separate from those of the individuals making up the group.  101

**Corpse.** Dead body.  101

**Correspond.** To be equivalent; to write letters to one another.  97

**Co-worker.** Someone working with you.  97

**Credential.** Something that entitles one to credit or confidence; something that makes others believe in a person; (pl.) testimonials entitling a person to credit or to exercise official power.  48

**Credible.** Believable.  48, 53

**Credit.** Belief in something; trust; faith; good name; in an account, the balance in one's favor; a unit of academic study; to supply something on credit to.  48

**Crypt.** An underground vault.  168

**Cryptic.** Having a hidden or secret meaning; mysterious.  168

**Cycle.** A period that keeps coming back, in which certain events take place and complete themselves in some definite order; a round of years or ages; a pattern of regularly occurring events; a series that repeats itself.  166

**Cyclone.** A system of violent and destructive whirlwinds.  166

**Cynophobia.** Fear of dogs.  23

---

[3]*Content* and *content* are presented separately because they are pronounced differently.

[4]*Contract* and *contract* are presented separately because they are pronounced differently.

**Decade.** Period of ten years. 48

**Decapitate.** To take off the head; to kill. 163

**Deceive.** To mislead by lying; to lead into error. 155

**Decode.** To change from code to simple language. 163

**Decolor.** To take color away. 163

**Deduction.** The act of drawing a conclusion by reasoning or reasoning that goes from the general to the particular; the taking away or subtraction of something; an inference or a conclusion. 168

**Deflea.** To take off fleas. 163

**Dehydrate.** To remove water from; to lose water or moisture; dry. 274

**Delouse.** To free from lice. 163

**Demagogue.** A person who stirs up the emotions of people in order to become a leader and achieve selfish ends. 56

**Democracy.** a form of government in which there is rule by the people either directly or through elected representatives. 56

**Denude.** To strip the covering from completely. 163

**Dependence.** Act of trusting; act of relying on someone for support. 207

**Deport.** To send someone away. 163

**Deprive.** To take something away from. 163

**Dermatologist.** A doctor who deals with skin disorders. 157

**Derogatory.** Tending to make less well regarded; tending to belittle someone or something; disparaging; belittling. 264

**Description.** An account that gives a picture of something in words. 14, 27

**Detoxify.** To take away poison; to destroy the poison. 163

**Detract.** To draw away or divert; to take away a part, as from quality, value, or reputation. 275

**Diagnose.** To determine what is wrong with someone after an examination. 156

**Diagram.** An outline figure that shows the relationship between parts or places; a graph or chart. 146

**Dialogue.** A conversation in which two or more take part; the conversation in a play. 146

**Diameter.** A straight line passing through the center of a circle. 146

**Dictation.** The act of speaking or reading aloud to someone who takes down the words. 22, 27

**Dictator.** A ruler who has absolute power; one who dictates. 22

**Diction.** Manner of speaking; choice of words. 22, 27

**Dictionary.** A book for alphabetically listed words in a language, giving information about their meanings, pronunciations, and so forth. 22

**Dilemma.** Any situation that necessitates a choice between equally unfavorable or equally unpleasant alternatives; an argument that presents two equally unfavorable alternatives. 263

**Disable.** To make an object or someone not able to do something. 174

**Disapprove.** Not to approve of; not to regard as worthy. 174

**Disband.** To break up (a group). 174

**Dishonest.** Not honest; not to be trusted. 174

**Disloyal.** Not loyal. 174

**Dismiss.** To tell or allow to go; to discharge, as from a job; to get rid of; to have done with quickly; to reject. 220

**Disrobe.** To take off clothes. 174

**Distant.** Separated or apart by space and/or time; away from; far apart; not closely related. 211

**Divert.** To turn aside or from a path or course; to draw off to a different course, purpose, and so on. 264

**Divide.** To separate into parts. 264

**Divorce.** A legal dissolvement of a marriage relation usually by a court or other body having the authority; the legal ending of a marriage; to legally end a marriage; separate; disunite.  263

**Dormant.**  Asleep or as if asleep; not active.  212

**Dormitory.**  A large room in which many people sleep; a building providing sleeping and living quarters, especially at a school, college, or resort.  212


**Effect.**  Something brought about by some cause; the result; consequence.  113

**Effective.**  Producing or having the power to bring about an intended result; producing results with the least amount of wasted effort.  113

**Egocentric.**  Self-centered; relating everything to oneself.  212

**Empathy.**  The imaginative putting of oneself into another person's personality or skin; ability to understand how another feels because one has experienced it first-hand or otherwise.  100

**Enjoyable.**  Able to be enjoyed; able to take pleasure in.  53

**Epilogue.**  A short section added at the end to a book, poem, and so on; a short speech added to a play and given at the end.  146

**Equivalent.**  Equal in value, meaning, force, and so on.  221

**Error.**  A mistake; something done, said, or believed incorrectly; a wandering from what is correct.  211

**Eulogy.**  The speaking well of someone; usually a formal speech of high praise for the dead.  255

**Evidence.**  That which serves to prove or disprove something.  91

**Evident.**  Obvious; clearly seen; plain.  91

**Exactitude.**  The state of being exact.  270

**Exception.**  The act of taking out; something that is taken out or left out; an objection.  155

**Exclude.**  To keep from.  163

**Excuse.**  To forgive.  163

**Exhale.**  To breathe out.  163

**Exit.**  To go out of.  163

**Expect.**  To look out for.  163

**Export.**  To carry away; to carry or send some product to some other country or place; something that is exported.  49

**Ex-president.**  Former president.  163

**Ex-wife.**  Former wife.  163


**Factory.**  A building or buildings in which things are manufactured.  112

**Fatherless.**  Without a father.  97

**Federal.**  Of or formed by a compact; relating to or formed by an agreement between two or more states, groups, and so on; relating to a union of states, groups, and so on, in which central authority in common affairs is established by consent of its members.  221

**Fertile.**  Able to produce a large crop; able to produce; capable of bearing offspring, seeds, fruit, and so on; productive in mental achievements; inventive; having abundant resources.  147

**Fertilization.**  The act of making something able to produce; in biology, the union of a male and female germ cell; impregnation.  147

**Final.**  Last; coming at the end; conclusive.  147

**Finite.**  Having a limit or end; able to be measured.  147

**Fluid.**  A substance such as liquid or gas that flows; employing a smooth easy style; easily convertible into cash; likely to change.  275

**Fortify.**  To strengthen against attack; to surround with defenses; to strengthen and secure (as a town) by forts; to give physical strength and courage to; to add mental and moral strength to.  275, 281

**Fortitude.** Strength of mind that enables persons to bear pain or encounter danger with courage. 275

**Fortress.** A large place strengthened against attack; a fort or group of forts, often including a town; any place of security; a stronghold. 274

**Fraternity.** A group of men joined together by common interests for fellowship; a brotherhood; a Greek letter college organization. 100

**General.** Referring to all; in the U.S. Army and Air Force, an officer of the same rank as an admiral in the U.S. Navy. 63

**Generic.** Referring to all in a group or class. 63

**Genocide.** The systematic and deliberate killing of a whole group or a group of people bound together by customs, language, politics, and so on. 100

**Geography.** Study of the earth's surface and life. 14

**Geologist.** One who is in the field of geology. 63

**Geology.** Study of earth's physical history and makeup. 14

**Geometry.** Branch of mathematics dealing with the measurement of points, lines, planes, and so on. 14

**Germicide.** An agent that destroys germs. 102

**Goodness.** The state of being good. 270

**Gratitude.** The state of being grateful. 270

**Gregarious.** Tending to live in a flock, herd, or community rather than alone; marked by a fondness to be with others than alone; outgoing; sociable. 255

**Gynecologist.** A doctor dealing with women's diseases, especially in reference to reproductive organs. 157

**Happiness.** The state of being happy. 270

**Harmless.** Without harm; without hurting. 97

**Hemisphere.** A half sphere or globe; half the earth's surface (either the northern or southern half of the earth as divided by the equator or the eastern or western half as divided by a meridian). 273

**Herbicide.** An agent that destroys or holds in check plant growth. 102

**Homicide.** Any killing of one human being by another. 100

**Homogeneous.** Being the same throughout; being uniform. 63

**Homograph.** A word spelled the same way as another but having a different meaning. 63

**Homonym.** A word that agrees in pronunciation with some other word but differs in spelling and meaning. 114

**Homosexual.** Referring to the same sex or to sexual desire for those of the same sex; a homosexual individual. 63

**Hydrant.** An upright pipe or street fixture with a valve for drawing water directly from a water main; fireplug. 274

**Hyperactive.** Overactive. 212

**Hyperproductive.** Overproductive. 212

**Hypersensitive.** Oversensitive. 212

**Hypertension.** High blood pressure. 212

**Hypnosis.** A sleeplike trance that is artificially brought about. 221

**Hypodermic.** Referring to the area under the skin; used for injecting under the skin; a hypodermic injection; a hypodermic syringe or needle. 157

**Hypothesis.** An unproved scientific conclusion drawn from known facts; something assumed as a basis for argument; a possible answer to a problem that requires further investigation. 157

**Illegal.** Not legal; not lawful. 152

**Immoral.** Not moral; knows difference between right and wrong but chooses to do wrong. 60

**Immortal.** Referring to a being who never dies; undying; one who never dies. 101

**Imperfect.** Not perfect; having a fault. 152

**Import.** To carry in; bring in goods from another country; something that is imported. 49

**Important.** Deserving of notice; of great value. 152

**Impotent.** Without power to act; physically weak; incapable of sexual intercourse (said of males). 92

**Incorporate.** To unite; combine. 101

**Incredible.** Not believable. 49

**Ineffectual.** Not being able to bring about results. 152

**Infinite.** Having no limit or end; not able to be measured. 147, 152

**Influence.** The power to produce an effect without the exertion of physical force or authority; to affect by indirect means; to sway. 275

**Innate.** Inborn; born with; not acquired from the environment; belonging to the fundamental nature of something. 221.

**Innovation.** Something newly introduced; a new method, something new. 211

**Insecticide.** An agent that destroys insects. 102

**Inspection.** The act of looking into something. 152

**Intense.** Having great or extreme force; very strong; existing or occurring to a high or extreme degree. 200

**Intention.** Aim; goal; purpose. 200

**Intercollegiate.** Between colleges. 217

**Interdepartmental.** Between departments. 217

**Interdependent.** Dependent upon one another. 217

**Intermission.** Time between events; recess. 220

**Interrogate.** To ask questions of formally; to examine by questioning. 264

**Interstate.** Between states. 217

**Intracollegiate.** Within the college. 217

**Intradepartmental.** Within the department. 217

**Intramural.** Within a school or an institution. 217

**Invisible.** Not able to be seen. 90

**Irregular.** Not uniform; not the same. 152

**Joyous.** Full of joy. 260

**Juror.** One of a group of persons sworn to deliver a verdict in a case submitted to them; member of a jury. 263

**Justice.** The maintenance of what is reasonable and well founded; the assignment of deserved rewards or punishments; the quality or characteristic of being fair and impartial; rightfulness; fairness; correctness. 263

**Justification.** A reason, circumstance, explanation, or fact that justifies or defends; good reason. 263

**Killer.** One who kills. 10

**Laughable.** Able to be laughed at. 53

**Legal.** Referring to law; lawful. 63, 207

**Legislature.** Body of persons responsible for lawmaking. 63

**Liquidize.** To become liquid. 260

**Local.** Referring to a relatively small area, region, or neighborhood; limited. 113

**Location.** A place or site; exact position or place occupied; a place used for filming a motion picture or a television program. 114

**Logical.** Relating to the science concerned with correct reasoning. 146

**Lucid.** Clear; easily understood; bright; shining. 210

**Magnanimous.** Forgiving of insults or injuries; high-minded; great of soul. 221

**Magnificient.** Splendid; beautiful; superb. 221

**Magnify.** To increase the size of; to make larger.   221

**Maintain.** To carry on or continue; to keep up; to keep in good condition.   166, 207

**Maintenance.** The act of keeping up.   207

**Malformed.** Abnormally formed.   228

**Malfunction.** To function badly.   228

**Malnourished.** Badly nourished.   228

**Maltreated.** Treated badly.   228

**Manageable.** Able to be managed.   53

**Manicure.** Care of the hands and fingernails; to care for the hands; to cut evenly.   111

**Manual.** Referring to the hand; made, done, or used by the hands; a handy book used as a guide or source of information.   111, 207

**Manufacture.** To make goods or articles by hand or by machinery; to make something from raw materials by hand or machinery; the act of manufacturing.   112

**Manuscript.** Written by hand or typed; not printed; a document written by hand; a book written by hand and usually sent in for publication; style of penmanship in which letters are not joined together.   112

**Maternal.** Motherly; having to do with a mother; inherited or derived from a mother; related on the mother's side of the family.   263

**Maternity.** The state of being a mother; motherhood; a hospital or a section of a hospital designated for the care of women immediately before and during childbirth and for the care of newborn babies.   263

**Matrimony.** The act or state of being married; the union of man and woman as husband and wife; marriage.   263

**Megabit.** 1,000,000 bits.   202

**Megabucks.** 1,000,000 dollars   202

**Megaphone.** A device used to increase sound.   201

**Metropolitan.** Referring to a major city center and its surrounding area; a person who inhabits a metropolis or one who has the manners and tastes associated with a metropolis.   201

**Microscope.** Instrument used to make very small objects appear larger so that they can be seen.   14

**Millennium.** Period of one thousand years; a one-thousandth anniversary; a period of great happiness (the millennium).   48

**Million.** A thousand thousands (1,000,000); a very large or indefinitely large number; being one million in number.   48

**Misanthrope.** Hater of mankind.   63

**Misnomer.** A name wrongly applied to someone or something; an error in the naming of a person or place in a legal document.   114

**Mission.** Group or team of persons sent somewhere to perform some work; the task, business, or responsibility that a person is assigned; the place where missionaries carry out their work; a place where poor people may go for assistance.   219

**Modify.** To change slightly or make minor changes in character, form, and so on; to change or alter.   281

**Mohammedan.** Believing in the principles of Mohammed.   281

**Monarchy.** A government or state headed by a king, a queen, or an emperor; called absolute (or despotic) when there is no limitation on the monarch's power and constitutional (or limited) when there is such limitation.   56

**Monogamist.** One who believes in or practices monogamy.   67

**Monogamous.** Having to do with monogamy.   260

**Monogamy.** Marriage to one spouse at a time.   62

**Morgue.** Place where dead bodies (corpses) of accident victims and unknown persons found dead are kept; for reporters, it refers to the reference library of old newspaper articles, pictures, and so on.   101

**Mortal.** Referring to a being who must eventually die; causing death; ending in death; a human being.   101

**Mortality.** The state of having to die eventually; proportion of deaths to the population of the region; death rate; death on a large scale, as from disease or war. 101

**Mortgage.** The pledging of property to a creditor (one to whom a sum of money is owed) as security for payment; to pledge. 101

**Mortician.** A funeral director; undertaker. 101

**Motherless.** Without a mother. 97

**Nature.** The necessary quality or qualities of something; sort; kind; wild state of existence; uncivilized way of life; overall pattern or system; basic characteristic of a person; inborn quality; the sum total of all creation. 221

**Nautical.** Relating to sailing. (See Additional Words Glossary.) 207

**Non-Arab.** Not an Arab. 119

**Nonbeliever.** Not a believer. 119

**Noncapitalist.** One who is not a capitalist. 119

**Non-Catholic.** Not a Catholic. 119

**Non-Communist.** One who is not a Communist. 119

**Noncriminal.** Not criminal. 119

**Nonefficient.** Not efficient. 119

**Non-English.** Not English. 119

**Novel.** A work of fiction of some length; new; strange; unusual. 211

**Obstacle.** Something that stands in the way or opposes; an obstruction. 211

**Omnipresent.** Being present everywhere at all times. 92

**Pacify.** To bring peace to; to calm; to quiet. 201

**Paternal.** Of or like a father; fatherly; related on the father's side of the family; inherited or received from the father. 254

**Paternalism.** The principle or practice of managing the affairs of a country or group of employees as a father manages the affairs of children. 254

**Paternity.** Fatherhood; state of being a father; origin or descent from a father; provides for citizenship of the child born out of wedlock if fatherhood is established. 254

**Patricide.** The murder of one's own father. 254

**Patriotic.** Characteristic of a person who loves his or her country; loving one's country; showing support and loyalty of one's country. 254

**Patron.** A person who buys regularly at a given store or who goes regularly to a given restaurant, resort, and so on; a regular customer; a wealthy or influential supporter of an artist or writer; one who gives one's wealth or influence to aid an institution, an individual, or a cause; a guardian saint or god. 254

**Pedestrian.** One who goes on foot. 6

**Pediatrician.** A doctor who specializes in children's diseases. 156

**Perception.** The act of becoming aware of something through the senses of seeing, hearing, feeling, tasting, and/or smelling. 155

**Period.** A portion of time; a portion of time into which something is divided; a punctuation mark that signals a full stop at the end of a sentence; used after abbreviations. 212

**Periodical.** Referring to publications, such as magazines, that appear at fixed time intervals; a periodical publication. 212

**Permission.** Act of allowing the doing of something; a consent. 220

**Persist.** To continue in some course or action even though it is difficult. 211

**Philanthropist.** A person who shows love toward one's fellow human beings by active efforts to promote their welfare; one who shows goodwill toward others by practical kindness and helpfulness. 254

**Philosophy.** The study of human knowledge; the love of wisdom and the search for the general laws that give a reasonable explanation of something. 211

**Phobia.** Extreme fear. 22

**Player.** One who plays. 10

**Politician.** A person engaged in politics; a person involved in the science or art of government; a person who seeks advancement or power within an organization by dubious (doubtful) means. 201

**Politics.** (Although plural, it is usually looked upon as singular.) The science or art of government or of the direction and management of public or state affairs. 201

**Polygamist.** One who is married to more than one spouse at the same time; one who is married to many spouses at the same time. 67

**Polygamy.** Marriage to more than one spouse at the same time; marriage to many spouses at the same time. 62

**Popular.** Approved of; admired; liked by most people; referring to the common people or the general public. 221

**Population.** Total number of people living in a country, city, or any area. 221

**Port.** Place to or from which ships carry things; place where ships may wait. 49

**Portable.** Can be carried; easily or conveniently transported. 49, 53

**Porter.** A person who carries things; one who is employed to carry baggage at a hotel or transportation terminal. 49

**Position.** An act of placing or arranging; the manner in which a thing is placed; the way the body is placed; the place occupied by a person or thing; the proper or appropriate place; job; a feeling or stand; social standing. 220

**Positive.** Being directly found to be so or true; real; actual; sure of something; definitely set; confident. 220

**Post.** A position or employment, usually in government service; an assigned beat; a piece of wood or other material to be used as a support; a place occupied by troops; to inform; to put up (as on a wall); to mail (as a letter). 220

**Postnatal.** Occurring after birth. 221

**Postpone.** To put off to a future time; to delay. 220

**Postscript.** Something added to a letter after the writer's signature; something added to written or printed legal papers. 201

**Posture.** The placing or carriage of the body or parts of the body; a mental position or frame of mind. 220

**Potent.** Physically powerful; having great authority; able to influence; strong in chemical effects. 92

**Potential.** The possible ability or power one may have; having force or power to develop. 92

**Precede.** To go or come before. 167

**Pre-Christian.** Referring to the time before there were Christians. 108

**Predict.** To say before; to foretell; to forecast; to tell what will happen. 108

**Preference.** The choosing of one person or thing over another; the valuing of one over another; a liking better. 147

**Preheat.** To heat before. 108

**Prehistoric.** Referring to the time before history was recorded. 108

**Prejudge.** To judge or decide before. 108

**Prejudice.** An opinion or judgment made beforehand. 108

**Premature.** Ripened before. 108

**Prenatal.** Being or taking place before birth. 221

**Preparedness.** The state of being prepared or ready. 270

**Prerevolutionary.** Referring to time before a revolution. 108

**Preset.** To set before. 108

**Preunite.** To join together before. 108

**Prisoner.** One who is kept in prison. 10

**Proceed.** To go on; to go forward; to carry on an action. 167

**Prognosis.** A prediction or conclusion regarding the course of a disease and the chances of recovery; a prediction. 156

**Prologue.** An introduction, often in verse (poetry), spoken or sung before a play or opera; any introductory or preceding event; a preface.  146

**Proposal.** An offer put forth to be accepted or adopted; an offer of marriage; a plan.  220

**Provision.** The act of being prepared beforehand; something made ready in advance; a part of an agreement referring to a specific thing.  91

**Pseudonym.** False name, used by an author to conceal his or her identity; pen name; false name.  114

**Psychiatrist.** A doctor who specializes in the treatment of persons with mental, emotional, or behavioral disorders.  255

**Psychology.** The science of the mind; the science that studies the behavior of humans and other animals; the mental or behavioral characteristics of a person or persons.  255

**Psychotic.** Having to do with or caused by serious mental disease; insane.  255

**Question.** The act of asking.  27

**Reception.** The act of receiving or being received; a formal social entertainment; the manner of receiving someone.  155

**Recomb.** To comb again.  18

**Redo.** To do again.  18

**Reference.** A referring or being referred; the giving of a problem to a person, committee, or authority for settlement; a note in a book that sends the reader for information to another book; the name of another person who can offer information or recommendation; the mark, or sign, as a number or letter, directing the reader to a footnote and so on; a written statement of character, qualification, or ability; testimonial.  147

**Repay.** To pay back.  18

**Reporter.** A person who gathers information and writes reports for newspapers, magazines, and so on.  49

**Rerun.** To run again.  18

**Retract.** To draw back; to take back; to withdraw.  275

**Return.** To go back  18

**Reversible.** Capable of being opposite or contrary to a previous position; having two finished or usable sides (of a fabric, and so on).  264

**Rework.** To work again.  18

**Rewrite.** To write again.  18

**Ridicule.** Language or actions that make a person the object of mockery or cause one to be laughed at or scorned; to mock or view someone in a scornful way; to hold someone up as a laughingstock; to make fun of.  155

**Ridiculous.** Unworthy of consideration; absurd (senseless); preposterous.  155

**Science.** Any area of knowledge in which the facts have been investigated and presented in an orderly manner.  91

**Scotophobia.** Fear of darkness.  23

**Script.** Writing that is cursive, printed, or engraved; a piece of writing; a prepared copy of a play for the use of actors.  14

**Scripture.** Books of the Old and New Testaments; a text or passage from the Bible; the sacred writings of a religion.  14

**Seclusion.** The act of keeping apart from others; the act of confining in a place hard to find; the act of segregating or hiding; the act of isolating oneself; isolation.  255

**Sedition.** Conduct consisting of speaking, writing, or acting against an established government or seeking to overthrow it by unlawful means; incitement to rebellion or discontent.  255

**Seduce.** To tempt to wrongdoing; to persuade into disobedience; to persuade or entice (lead on by exciting desire) into partnership in sexual intercourse. 255

**Segregate.** To set apart from others; to separate. 255

**Semiannual.** Twice in a year; every half year. 228

**Semiblind.** Partly blind. 228

**Semicircle.** Half circle. 228

**Semistarved.** Partly starved. 228

**Semiwild.** Partly wild. 228

**Sequence.** The following of one thing after another; order; a continuous or related series, with one thing following another. 166, 207

**Similar.** Alike in essentials; having characteristics in common. 264

**Simile.** A figure of speech comparing two unlike things using *like* or *as*. 265

**Simplify.** To make easier. 281

**Solitude.** The state of being alone. 270

**Sophisticated.** Not in a simple, natural, or pure state; worldly-wise, not naive; cultured; highly complicated; complex, experienced. 211

**Sophomore.** A second-year student in American high schools or colleges; an immature person; one who thinks he or she knows more than he or she does. 211

**Spectacle.** Something showy that is seen by many (the public); an unwelcome or sad sight. 22

**Spectacles.** Eyeglasses. 23

**Spectacular.** Relating to something unusual, impressive, exciting, or unexpected. 22

**Spectator.** An onlooker; one who views something. 22

**Sphere.** A round geometrical body whose surface is equally distant at all points from the center; any rounded body; a globe; a ball. 273

**Subcommittee.** A committee under the original committee. 174

**Subfloor.** Floor beneath. 174

**Submarine.** Ship that sails under the sea. 174

**Submit.** To give in to another; to surrender; to concede; to present for consideration or approval; to present as one's opinion. 220

**Subsequent.** Following soon after; following in time, place, or order; resulting. 166

**Subset.** Something that is under the larger set. 174

**Substitute.** To put in place of another person or thing; one who takes the place of another person; something that is put in place of something else or is available for use instead of something else. 211

**Subtraction.** The act of taking something away. 174

**Succeed.** To accomplish what is attempted; to come next in order; to come next after or replace another in an office or position. 167

**Suffer.** To feel pain or distress. 147

**Suicide.** Killing of oneself. 100

**Sympathy.** Sameness of feeling with another; ability to feel pity for another. 100

**Synonym.** A word having the same or nearly the same meaning as some other word. 114

**Technical.** Having to do with an art, science, discipline, or profession; having to do with industrial arts, applied sciences, mechanical trades, or crafts; marked by specialization; meaningful or of interest to persons of specialized knowledge rather than to laypersons; marked by a strict legal interpretation. 274

**Technician.** A specialist in the details of a subject or skill, especially a mechanical one; any artist, musician, and so on with skilled technique. 274

**Technique.** The manner in which a scientific or complex task is accomplished; the degree of skill or command of fundamentals shown in any performance. 274

**Technology.** Applied science; a technical method of achieving a practical purpose; the totality of the means employed to provide objects necessary for human existence and comfort. 274

**Telegram.**  Message sent from a distance.  21

**Telegraph.**  Instrument for sending a message in code at a distance; to send a message from a distance.  13

**Telephone.**  Instrument that sends and receives sound, such as the spoken word, over distance; to send a message by telephone.  13

**Telescope.**  Instrument used to view distant objects.  14

**Television.**  An electronic system for the transmission of visual images from a distance; a television receiving set.  91

**Temporary.**  Lasting for a short period of time.  157

**Tenant.**  A person who holds property; one who lives on property belonging to another; one who rents or leases from a landlord; one who lives in a place.  165

**Tension.**  The act of stretching or the condition of being stretched tight; mental strain.  200

**Theocracy.**  A form of government in which there is rule by a religious group.  56

**Theologist.**  One who is in the field of theology.  67

**Theology.**  The study of religion.  56

**Thermal.**  Pertaining to, using, or causing heat.  274

**Thermometer.**  An instrument for measuring the temperature of a body or of space, especially one consisting of a graduated glass tube with a bulb, usually mercury, that expands and rises in the tube as the temperature increases.  274

**Thermostat.**  An automatic device for regulating temperature; any device that automatically responds to temperature changes and activates switches controlling equipment such as furnaces, refrigerators, and air conditioners.  274

**Toxic.**  Relating to poison.  157

**Traction.**  The act of drawing; the state of being drawn; the force exerted in drawing; friction; in medicine, a pulling or drawing of a muscle, organ, and so on for healing a fracture, dislocation, and so on.  275

**Transatlantic.**  Across the Atlantic Ocean.  152

**Transfer.**  To carry or send from one person or place to another; to cause to pass from one person or place to another; an act of transferring or being transferred.  147, 152

**Transhuman.**  Beyond human limits.  152

**Translucent.**  Permitting light to go through but not permitting a clear view of any object.  210

**Transmit.**  To send from one place to another; to pass on by heredity; to transfer; to pass or communicate news, information, and so on.  220

**Transparent.**  Able to be seen through.  152

**Transport.**  To carry from one place to another.  152

**Triskadekaphobia.**  Fear of the number thirteen.  23

**Unable.**  Not able.  108

**Unaided.**  Not helped.  108

**Uncarpeted.**  Not carpeted.  108

**Uncaught.**  Not caught.  108

**Unclaimed.**  Not claimed.  108

**Uncooked.**  Not cooked.  108

**Uniform.**  Being always the same; a special form of clothing.  21

**Union.**  A joining; a putting together.  21

**Unionize.**  To form into a union.  260

**Unique.**  Being the only one of its kind.  21

**Unison.**  A harmonious agreement; a saying of something together.  22

**Universal.**  Applying to all.  22

**Universe.**  Everything that exists.  22

**Unloved.**  Not loved.  108

**Unwed.**  Not married.  108

**Verify.** To affirm. 281
**Versatile.** Capable of turning from one subject, task, or occupation to another; able to do many things well; many-sided; changeable; variable. 264
**Visible.** Able to be seen; evident; apparent; on hand. 90
**Vision.** The sense of sight. 90
**Vocabulary.** A list of words and phrases, usually arranged alphabetically, that are defined or translated from another language; a stock of words possessed by an individual or group. 201
**Vocal.** Referring to the voice; having voice; oral; freely expressing oneself in speech, usually with force; speaking out. 201, 207
**Vocation.** A calling; a person's work or profession. 201

**Wondrous.** Full of wonder; amazed admiration. 260

# ADDITIONAL WORDS PRESENTED IN
# Vocabulary Expansion

The number after the meaning refers to the page on which the vocabulary word is first presented; it is the main entry for the word.

**Abrogate.** To abolish a law, custom, and so on by an authoritative act; to repeal; to do away with; to invalidate. 271
**Accreditation.** Act of bringing into favor; a vouching for; a giving authority to. 54
**Acrophobia.** An abnormal fear of high places. 28
**Adversity.** A condition marked by unhappiness, misfortune, or distress; a stroke of misfortune; an unfavorable or harmful event; a hardship. 271
**Affinity.** Close relationship; attraction to another. 153
**Agnostic.** Professing uncertainty; one who is not for or against; one who doubts that the ultimate cause (God) and the essential nature of things are knowable. 163
**Ambidextrous.** Able to use both hands equally well. 208
**Amortize.** The gradual extinction of a debt such as a mortgage or a bond issue by payment of a part of the principal at the time of each periodic interest payment. 109
**Anachronism.** Something out of time order; an error in chronology in which a person, an object, or an event is assigned an incorrect date or period. 174
**Animate.** To make alive; to move to action. 230
**Annuity.** An investment yielding a fixed sum of money, payable yearly. 11
**Anthropoid.** A person resembling an ape either in stature, walk, or intellect; resembling man, used especially of apes such as the gorilla, chimpanzee, and orangutan; resembling an ape. 67
**Anthropomorphic.** Giving human shape or characteristics to gods, objects, animals, and so on. 67
**Antipathy.** A dislike for someone. 119
**Antitoxin.** Something used against bacterial poison; a substance formed in the body that counteracts a specific toxin; the antibody formed in immunization with a given toxin, used in treating certain infectious diseases or in immunizing against them. 163
**Apodal.** Having no feet. 60
**Archetype.** The original pattern or model of a work from which something is made or developed. 60
**Assimilate.** To take in; to absorb; to make similar. 271
**Audiology.** The study of hearing. 119
**Audiometer.** An instrument used to measure hearing. 119
**Automatic.** Moving by itself; performed without thinking about it. 11

**Automaton.** A person or animal acting in an automatic or mechanical way.   11

**Autonomous.** Self-governing; functioning independently of other parts.   12

**Aversion.** A strong dislike; a fixed dislike; a feeling of distaste toward something with a desire to avoid it or turn from it.   271

**Avocation.** Something a person does in addition to his or her regular work, usually for enjoyment; a hobby.   209

**Benediction.** A blessing; the expression of good wishes.   119

**Bibliophile.** A lover of books; a book collector.   260

**Bifocals.** Pair of glasses with two-part lenses.   11

**Bilateral.** Involving two sides.   11

**Bilingual.** Able to use two languages equally well; a bilingual person.   11

**Binary.** Made up of two parts; twofold; relating to base two.   11

**Biopsy.** In medicine, the cutting out of a piece of living tissue for examination.   11

**Bisexual.** Of both sexes; having both male and female organs, as is true of some plants and animals; a person who is sexually attracted by both sexes.   67

**Capitulate.** To give up; surrender.   109

**Caption.** The heading of a chapter, section, or page in a book; the title or subtitle of a picture.   109

**Centimeter.** In the metric system, a unit of measure equal to 1/100 meter (.3937 inch).   54

**Centipede.** Wormlike animal with many legs.   54

**Chronometer.** A very accurate clock or watch; an instrument used to measure time.   174

**Claustrophobia.** An abnormal fear of being confined, as in a room or a small place.   28

**Concession.** An act of giving in; a right granted by the government or other authority for a specific purpose.   175

**Convocation.** A group of people called together; an assembly.   208

**Corpulent.** Fat; fleshy; obese.   108

**Creditor.** One to whom a sum of money or other thing is due.   54

**Creed.** A statement of religious belief; a statement of belief; principles.   54

**Curator.** Head of a museum or of a department of a museum; one in charge.   120

**Decameter.** In the metric system, a measure of length containing 10 meters, equal to 393.70 inches or 32.81 feet.   54

**Decimal.** Numbered by tens; based on ten; pertaining to tenths or the number 10; a decimal fraction.   53

**Decimate.** To take or destroy a tenth part of; to destroy but not completely; to destroy a great number or proportion of.   53

**Decimeter.** In the metric system, a unit of length equal to 1/10 meter.   54

**Defer.** To leave to another's opinion or judgment; to delay; to postpone.   153

**Deference.** Respect; a giving in to another's opinion or judgment.   153

**Definitive.** Conclusive; final; most nearly complete or accurate.   152

**Demography.** The statistical study of human populations, including births, deaths, marriages, population movements, and so on.   60

**Deportment.** Manner of conducting or carrying oneself; behavior; conduct.   54

**Depose.** To remove from a throne or other high position; to let fall.   230

**Derisive.** Mocking; jeering.   163

**Detain.** To stop; to hold; to keep from proceeding; to delay.   175

**Deténte.** Easing of strained relations, especially between nations.   209

**Detention.** A keeping or holding back; confinement.   209

**Dialect.** A variety of speech; a regional form of a standard language.   152

**Dichotomy.** Division into two parts, especially mutually exclusive or contradictory parts; division into two parts, kinds, and so on; a schism.   270

**Dictaphone.** A machine for recording and reproducing words spoken into its mouthpiece (differs from a tape recorder because it has controls that fit it to use in transcription). 27

**Dictum.** An authoritative statement; a saying. 28

**Disposition.** One's usual frame of mind or one's usual way of reacting; a natural tendency. 230

**Egotistic.** Conceited; very concerned with oneself; selfish; vain. 217

**Egregious.** Remarkably bad; conspicuously bad; outrageous; flagrant. 261

**Emancipate.** To set free from servitude or slavery; to set free. 119

**Emissary.** A person or agent sent on a specific mission. 229

**Envision.** To imagine something; to picture in the mind. 98

**Epidermis.** Outermost layer of skin. 163

**Equivocate.** To use ambiguous language on purpose. 229

**Erratic.** Wandering; not regular; not stable. 218

**Euphemism.** The substitution of a word or phrase that is less direct, milder, or vaguer for one thought to be harsh, offensive, or blunt; a word or phrase considered less distasteful or less offensive than another. 261

**Euphonious.** Pleasing to the ear; harmonious. 261

**Euphoria.** A feeling of well-being. 261

**Euthanasia.** Mercy killing; the act of killing someone who is hopelessly ill. 261

**Expatriate.** To banish; exile; to withdraw oneself from one's native country; to renounce one's citizenship; (as a noun) an exile; (as an adjective) an expatriated person. 260

**Expound.** To state in detail; to set forth; to explain. 230

**Extemporaneous.** Done or spoken with little or no special preparation; impromptu; makeshift; done or spoken as if without special preparation. 164

**Facsimile.** An exact copy; to make an exact copy of. 120

**Faction.** A number of persons in an organization, group, government, party, and so on, having a common goal, often self-seeking. 120

**Finale.** The last part; end; the concluding movement of a musical composition; the last scene of an entertainment. 153

**Fluctuate.** To shift back and forth uncertainly. 282

**Fluent.** Ready in the use of words. 282

**Forte.**[1] Something a person does very well; a strong point. 281

**Forte.**[1] (for'tā). Loud; strong; in a loud and forceful manner; loudly; strongly. 281

**Fratricide.** Killing of a brother; may also refer to the killing of a sister. 108

**Genealogy.** The science or study of one's descent; a tracing of one's ancestors. 68

**Generate.** To produce; to cause to be; to bring into existence. 68

**Genus.** A class, kind, or group marked by shared characteristics or by one shared characteristic. 68

**Geocentric.** Relating to the earth as the center. 19

**Grammar.** That part of the study of language that deals with the construction of words and word parts (morphology) and the way in which words are arranged relative to each other in utterances (syntax); the study or description of the way language is used. 28

**Graphic.** Marked by realistic and vivid detail; related to pictorial arts. 10

**Graphology.** The study of handwriting. 10

**Hydraulics.** The science dealing with water and other liquids in motion, their uses in engineering, the laws of their actions, and so on. 281

---

[1]*Forte* and *forte* are presented separately because they are pronounced differently.

**Hydrophobia.** An abnormal fear of water; rabies, a viral infectious disease of the central nervous system whose symptoms include an inability to swallow. (Because of the association of water with the act of swallowing, the term hydrophobia is used for rabies.)  28

**Hydrotherapy.** The treatment of disease by the use of water.  281

**Hyperbole.** Great exaggeration; an overstatement.  217

**Illuminate.** To give light to; make clear.  217

**Indictment.** A charge; an accusation.  28

**Inference.** Something derived by reasoning; something that is not directly stated but suggested in the statement; a logical conclusion that is drawn from statements; deduction.  152

**Infidelity.** Breach of trust; lack of faith in a religion; unfaithfulness of a marriage partner; adultery.  230

**Infinitesimal.** Too small to be measured; very minute.  153

**Inscription.** Something written or engraved on a surface; a brief or informal dedication in a book to a friend.  19

**Intercede.** To come between; to come between as an influencing force; to intervene.  229

**Intercept.** To stop or interrupt the course of.  164

**Intermittent.** Starting or stopping again at intervals; not continuous; coming and going at intervals.  229

**Intervene.** To come between; to act as an influencing force; to intercede.  229

**Introvert.** A person who directs his or her thoughts inward; a person who is more interested in his or her own thoughts than what is going on around him or her.  271

**Irrevocable.** Not to be recalled, withdrawn, or annulled; irreversible; not able to be changed.  209

**Jurisdiction.** The right or power of administering justice or law; authority; power; control; the extent of authority; the territory over which such authority extends; the limits in which authority may be exercised.  270

**Jurisprudence.** A system or body of law; the course of court decisions; the science or philosophy of law; a branch of law.  270

**Kilometer.** In the metric system, a unit of length equal to one thousand meters.  54

**Magnate.** A very important or influential person.  230

**Malediction.** A speaking badly of someone; slander; a curse.  230

**Malefactor.** Someone who does something bad; a criminal.  230

**Manipulation.** The act of handling or operating; the act of managing or controlling skillfully or by shrewd use of influence; the act of changing or falsification for one's own purposes or profit.  120

**Matriarch.** A mother who is the ruler of a family or of a tribe; a woman who is ruler of a family, group, or state.  270

**Matricide.** The murder of a mother by her son or daughter.  270

**Megalopolis.** One very large city made up of a number of cities; a vast, populous, continuously urban area.  208

**Meter.** In the metric system, a unit of length equal to approximately 39.37 inches; an instrument for measuring the amount of something (as water, gas, electricity); an instrument for measuring distance, time, weight, speed, and so forth; a measure of verse.  18

**Microbe.** A very small living thing; a microorganism.  18

**Microfilm.** Film on which documents are photographed in a reduced size for storage convenience.  19

**Micrometer.**[2] An instrument used to measure accurately very small distances, angles, and diameters. 18

**Micrometer.**[2] A unit of length equal to one millionth of a meter, also called *micron*. 18

**Microorganism.** An organism so small that it can be seen only under a microscope. 18

**Microphone.** A device that magnifies weak sounds (nontechnical definition used as shorthand for the entire sound amplification system); a device to convert sound waves to electrical waves (technical definition). 19

**Millimeter.** In the metric system, a unit of length equal to 1/1,000 meter (.03937 inch). 54

**Misogamist.** Hater of marriage. 67

**Misogynist.** Hater of women. 163

**Missile.** An object, especially a weapon, intended to be thrown or discharged, as a bullet, arrow, stone, and so on. 229

**Monoglot.** Person who knows, speaks, or writes only one language; speaking and writing only one language. 61

**Monologue.** A long speech by one person; a dramatic sketch performed by one actor. 152

**Monophobia.** Abnormal fear of being alone. 60

**Monopoly.** Exclusive control of a commodity or service in a given market; control that makes possible the fixing of prices and the elimination of free competition. 61

**Monorail.** A single rail serving as a track for trucks or cars suspended from it or balanced on it. 60

**Monosyllable.** A word consisting of one syllable. 109

**Monotone.** Speech not having any change in pitch; to speak in an unvaried tone. 60

**Monotonous.** Changeless; dull; uniform; having no variety. 60

**Mortify.** To cause to feel shame; to punish (one's body) or control (one's physical desires or passions) by self-denial, fasting, and the like, as a means of religious or ascetic (severe) discipline. 108

**Nautical.** Pertaining to sailors, ships, or navigation. 98

**Novice.** Someone new at something; a rookie; a beginner. 217

**Obstinate.** Stubborn; tenacious. 218

**Oligarchy.** A form of government in which there is rule by a few (usually a privileged few). 61

**Omnibus.** A large bus; an *omnibus* bill is a legislative bill that carries a mixture of provisions. 97

**Omnipotent.** All-powerful. 97

**Omniscient.** All-knowing. 97

**Orthography.** The part of language study that deals with correct spelling. 11

**Pacifist.** One who is against war. 208

**Pedagogue.** A teacher. 163

**Pedestal.** A base or bottom support. 11

**Pedicure.** Care of the feet, toes, and toe nails. 120

**Perceptive.** Being aware; having insight, understanding, or intuition, as a *perceptive* analysis of the problems involved. 164

**Perfidious.** Violating good trust; treacherous; deceitful; deliberately faithless. 230

**Perimeter.** A measure of the outer part or boundary of a closed plane figure; boundary line of a closed plane figure. 217

**Periodic.** Taking place, occurring, or appearing at regular intervals. 218

[2]*Micrometer* and *micrometer* are presented separately because they are pronounced differently.

**Periphery.** The outer part or boundary of something.  217

**Periscope.** An instrument used by a submarine to see all around.  217

**Personification.** A figure of speech in which a nonliving thing or idea is made to appear as having the qualities of a person.  120

**Pervert.** To lead astray; to turn or lead from the right way; to corrupt; a person who has been led astray; a person who practices sexual perversion, that is, one who deviates from the normal in sexual habits.  271

**Philanderer.** A person who makes love without serious intentions; a person who flirts; a person who has many love affairs; a person who has many love affairs without intentions of marriage.  260

**Philanthrope.** A lover of mankind; a philanthropist; a humanitarian.  260

**Phonetics.** A study dealing with speech sounds and their production.  19

**Phonics.** Study of the relationship between letter symbols of a written language and the sounds they represent; a method used in teaching word recognition in reading.  19

**Podiatrist.** Foot doctor.  67

**Podium.** A raised platform for the conductor of an orchestra; a dais.  11

**Polyglot.** A person who knows, speaks, or writes several languages; speaking or writing many languages.  67

**Polygon.** A closed plane figure with several angles and sides.  67

**Posterior.** In the rear; later; following after; coming after in order; succeeding; located behind; the buttocks.  208

**Posterity.** Future generations; all of one's descendants (offspring).  208

**Posthumously.** After death.  208

**Postmortem.** Happening or performed after death; referring to an examination of a human body after death; autopsy.  208

**Potentate.** A person possessing great power: a ruler; a monarch.  98

**Prerogative.** The right or privilege that no one else has; special superiority or privilege that one may get from an official position, office, and so on.  271

**Prescription.** A doctor's written directions for the preparation and use of medicine; an order; direction; rule.  19

**Procession.** A parade, as a funeral *procession*; any continuous course.  175

**Proficient.** Knowing something very well; able to do something very well.  152

**Proposition.** A plan or something put forth for consideration or acceptance.  229

**Protract.** To draw out; to lengthen in time; to extend forward or outward; to prolong in time.  282

**Provoke.** To stir up anger or resentment; to irritate.  208

**Pseudopodium.** False foot.  119

**Pseudoscience.** A false science.  120

**Psychic.** A person sensitive to nonphysical forces; a medium; lying outside the sphere of physical science or knowledge; immaterial or spiritual in origin or force; marked by extraordinary or mysterious sensitivity, perception, or understanding.  261

**Psychopath.** A person suffering from mental disease.  261

**Pyschosis.** Any severe form of mental disturbance or disease, which has far-reaching and deep disorders of behavior; mental derangement by defective or lost contact with reality.  261


**Recession.** The act of going back; in economics, the decline of business activity.  175

**Remission.** A temporary stopping or lessening of a disease; a pardon.  229

**Retentive.** Having the ability to retain or keep in things; tenacious, as a *retentive* memory; having a good memory.  175


**Scribe.** A writer, author; a public writer or secretary; in Scripture and Jewish history, a man of learning.  19

**Secede.** To withdraw from.  175

**Simulation.** An imitative representation of a process or system. 272

**Simultaneously.** At the same time; occurring concurrently. 271

**Sophistry.** Faulty reasoning; unsound or misleading but clever and plausible (appearing real) argument or reasoning. 218

**Speculate.** To think about something by viewing it from all sides; to take part in a risky business venture. 28

**Stamina.** Staying power; resistance to fatigue, illness, and the like. 217

**Stethoscope.** A hearing instrument used in examining the heart, lungs, and so on. 19

**Subscription.** An agreement; a promise in writing to pay some money; an agreement to receive something and pay for it. 175

**Subversion.** A systematic attempt to overthrow or undermine a government or political system by persons working secretly within the country involved; anything that tends to overthrow. 271

**Surrogate.** A substitute; a deputy; a person appointed to act in the place of another; something that serves as a substitute. 271

**Susceptible.** Easily influenced by or affected with; especially liable to. 164

**Syllable.** A vowel or a group of letters with one vowel sound. 109

**Symbol.** Something that stands for or represents another thing; an object used to represent something abstract. 109

**Symmetry.** Balanced form or arrangement; balance on both sides. 110

**Symphony.** Harmony of sound; harmony of any kind. 110

**Symptom.** In medicine, a condition that results from a disease and serves as an aid in diagnosis; a sign or token that indicates the existence of something else. 110

**Synchronize.** To cause to agree in rate or speed; to occur at the same time. 174

**Synthesis.** A putting together of two or more things to form a whole. 110

**Technocracy.** Government by technical experts. 281

**Telemeter.** An instrument that measures distance; instrument that sends information to a distant point. 18

**Tempo.** The rate of speed at which a musical composition is supposed to be played; rate of activity. 164

**Tenacious.** Stubborn; tough; holding or tending to hold strongly to one's views, opinions, rights, and so on; retentive, as a *tenacious* memory. 175

**Thermography.** A proces of writing or printing involving the use of heat; a technique for detecting and measuring variations of heat emitted by various regions of the body and transforming them into signals that can be recorded photographically—used to diagnose abnormal or diseased underlying conditions. 281

**Thermophilic.** Growing at a high temperature; requiring high temperature for development. 281

**Toxicologist.** One who specializes in the study of poisons. 163

**Tractable.** Easily managed or controlled; easy to deal with; obedient. 282

**Transcript.** A written or typewritten copy of an original; a copy or reproduction of any kind. 19

**Unify.** To make or form into one. 28

**Unilateral.** Occurring on one side only; done by one only; one-sided. 28

**Untenable.** Not able to be held or defended. 175

**Venture.** A risky or dangerous undertaking. 98

**Visa.** Something stamped or written on a passport that grants an individual entry to a country. 98

**Visage.** The face; the appearance of the face or its expression. 97

**Visionary.** A person who sees visions. 98

**Visor.** The projecting front brim of a cap for shading the eyes. 97

**Vociferous.** Of forceful, aggressive, and loud speech; clamorous. 208